STEP
and *Connoisseur* magazines, now manages his book and magazine editorial service in New York City.

STEVEN K. AMSTERDAM has been a resident of New York City for over 20 years and has written extensively about Central Park. Formerly editor of Chicago's *Grey City Journal*, he is currently a travel editor in New York City.

ELEANOR BERMAN is a widely published travel writer. Her *Away for the Weekend: New York* guide has been a regional best seller since 1982. She has contributed to all the major metropolitan daily newspapers as well as to such national magazines as *Harper's Bazaar, Savvy, Modern Bride,* and *Diversion*.

DAVID BERREBY is a member of the Outer Critics Circle. His work has appeared in the *Village Voice, The New York Times, V, Diversion,* and *New York Newsday*. He reviews theater for *The New York Law Journal*.

ANDY BIRSH has edited New York's *The Restaurant Reporter* since 1978. He is also a contributing editor to *Gourmet*, for which he writes a monthly column on New York dining.

STEPHEN R. ETTLINGER is a free-lance picture editor and photography consultant, and an independent book producer. He was formerly associate picture editor at *GEO* magazine, and is currently an editor of *Photo Opportunity*. His most recent book project is *Vietnam: The Land We Never Knew, Recent Images by Geoffrey Clifford*.

SUSAN FAREWELL, formerly associate travel editor of Condé Nast's *Bride's* magazine, is a free-lance writer and a longtime resident of Manhattan. Most recently, she has contributed to *Travel and Leisure, Diversion,* and *Caribbean Travel and Life* magazines.

DAVID FRANKEL, who was formerly an editor of *New York* magazine, has written on music for *New York* and *Rolling Stone*. He is an editor of *Artforum*.

DWIGHT V. GAST has written about the city for numerous publications. He has studied New York formally as an undergraduate and graduate student at the city's New School for Social Research, and has been observing it informally for over two decades. He lives in downtown Manhattan.

MATTHEW GUREWITSCH is a senior editor at *Connoisseur* magazine, where he concentrates on the performing arts. He has written about music and dance for *Opus, The New York Times, Vogue, Opera News, The Wall Street Journal,* and other publications.

ELEANOR HEARTNEY is a writer and critic specializing in contemporary art. She is a regular contributor to *Artnews, Art in America, Contemporania,* and *The New Art Examiner*.

HEIDI KRIZ, a resident of the Upper West Side, is a graduate of Columbia University—as well as its famous bartending course. She has written about the people, places, and bars of New York City for such publications as the *Village Voice* and *7 Days*.

BARRY LEWIS, an architectural historian, has created tour programs and produced lecture series for New York's 92nd Street Y. He has also written articles on the city's architectural history for various publications, and was a contributer to the Municipal Art Society's *Juror's Guide to Lower Manhattan*.

INGRID NELSON, formerly an editor of *GEO* magazine, is currently a free-lance writer living on Manhattan's Upper West Side.

JOANNA NEY is a free-lance writer specializing in dance. She was formerly dance critic for *East Side Express* and *Other Stages*. She has contributed to *The New York Times, Cosmopolitan, Cue,* and *V*. Currently she reviews dance for WBAI radio.

DEAN J. SEAL was formerly associate editor of the *U.S. Food Journal,* a trend monitor of the American food industry. He is now the Associate Publisher of the *Manhattan Catalog,* and a frequent contributor to food-related magazines.

RANDALL SHORT is a cultural journalist who writes on books and theater for *The New York Times, New York Newsday,* and *Spy* magazine.

LYNN YAEGER is the author of a biweekly column in the *Village Voice* on antiques and collectibles, and was also a contributor to *The Village Voice Guide to Manhattan's Shopping Neighborhoods.* A resident of New York for over 15 years, she has written on fashion for *Cosmopolitan, Australian Woman,* and other publications.

# THE PENGUIN TRAVEL GUIDES

AUSTRALIA
CANADA
THE CARIBBEAN
ENGLAND & WALES
FRANCE
IRELAND
ITALY
NEW YORK CITY

# THE PENGUIN GUIDE TO NEW YORK CITY 1989

ALAN TUCKER
*General Editor*

PENGUIN BOOKS

Penguin Books

Published by the Penguin Group
Viking Penguin Inc., 40 West 23rd Street,
New York, New York 10010, U.S.A.
Penguin Books Ltd, 27 Wrights Lane,
London W8 5TZ, England
Penguin Books Australia Ltd, Ringwood,
Victoria, Australia
Penguin Books Canada Ltd, 2801 John Street,
Markham, Ontario, Canada L3R 1B4
Penguin Books (N.Z.) Ltd, 182–190 Wairau Road,
Auckland 10, New Zealand

Penguin Books Ltd, Registered Offices:
Harmondsworth, Middlesex, England

First published in Penguin Books 1989
Published simultaneously in Canada

1  3  5  7  9  10  8  6  4  2

Copyright © Viking Penguin Inc., 1989
All rights reserved

ISBN 0 14 019.907 1
ISSN 0898-8072

Printed in the United States of America

Set in ITC Garamond Light
Designed by Beth Tondreau Design
Maps by Mark Stein Studios
Illustrations by Bill Russell
Editorial Services by Stephen Brewer Associates

Except in the United States of America, this
book is sold subject to the condition that it
shall not, by way of trade or otherwise, be lent,
re-sold, hired out, or otherwise circulated without
the publisher's prior consent in any form of binding
or cover other than that in which it is published and
without a similar condition including this condition
being imposed on the subsequent purchaser.

# THIS GUIDEBOOK

The Penguin Travel Guides are designed for people who are experienced travellers in search of *exceptional* information to help them sharpen and deepen their enjoyment of the trips they take.

*The Penguin Guide to New York City 1989* highlights the more rewarding parts of the city so that you can quickly and efficiently home in on the right hotel and the best way for you to get the most out of the city.

Of course, the guide does far more than just help you choose a hotel and plan your visit. *The Penguin Guide to New York City 1989* is designed for use *in* the city. Our Penguin New York City writers (each of whom is an experienced travel writer who lives in New York and specializes in the subject he or she covers for us) tell you what you really need to know, what you can't find out so easily on your own. They identify and describe the truly out-of-the-ordinary restaurants, shops, night spots, activities, and sights, and guide you toward the best way to "do" the city.

Our writers are highly selective. They avoid the common clutter of choices in order to enhance the items of special appeal in New York City. For exhaustive detailed coverage of the city's various museums and historical sites street by street we suggest that you also use a supplementary reference-type guidebook, such as the Michelin Green Guide, along with the Penguin Guide.

*The Penguin Guide to New York City 1989* is full of reliable and timely information, revised each year. We would like to know if you think we've left out some very special place.

ALAN TUCKER
*General Editor*
*Penguin Travel Guides*

40 West 23rd Street
New York, New York 10010
or
27 Wrights Lane
London   W8 5TZ

# CONTENTS

| | |
|---|---|
| *This Guidebook* | vii |
| *Overview* | 5 |
| *Useful Facts* | 12 |
| *Bibliography* | 22 |
| *Accommodations* | 33 |
| | |
| **Neighborhoods** | **49** |
| *Lower Manhattan and the Harbor* | 49 |
| *Chinatown to the Villages* | 73 |
| *Midtown* | 106 |
| *The Upper West Side* | 131 |
| *Central Park* | 148 |
| *The Upper East Side* | 153 |
| *Brooklyn* | 164 |
| *Queens* | 174 |
| **Day Trips from Manhattan** | **186** |
| *Bronx Zoo* | 187 |
| *New York Botanical Garden* | 190 |
| *Wave Hill* | 191 |
| *Historic Hudson Valley* | 192 |
| *Hyde Park* | 194 |
| *West Point Military Academy* | 195 |
| *Yale University* | 197 |
| *Litchfield, Connecticut* | 198 |
| *The Hamptons* | 200 |
| *Princeton University* | 202 |
| **The City's Specialties** | **205** |
| *Art* | 205 |
| *Antiques, Antiquities, and Collectibles* | 216 |
| *Architecture* | 226 |
| *Fashion* | 246 |

ix

## x CONTENTS

| | |
|---|---:|
| *Photography and Filmmaking* | 266 |
| *Classical Music* | 275 |
| *Dance* | 284 |
| *The Theater* | 289 |
| *Literary New York* | 297 |
| *Other Shopping* | 308 |
| *Food* | 315 |
| **After Hours** | **325** |
| *Dining* | 325 |
| *Bars and Cafés* | 379 |
| *Popular Music and Nightlife* | 401 |
| *Index* | **423** |

## MAPS

| | |
|---|---:|
| New York City's Five Boroughs | 2 |
| Manhattan Neighborhoods | 7 |
| Manhattan Address Locator | 20 |
| Manhattan | 48 |
| New York Harbor | 56 |
| Wall Street | 60 |
| Chinatown to the Villages | 74 |
| TriBeCa | 77 |
| Chinatown and Little Italy | 80 |
| The Lower East Side and East Village | 86 |
| SoHo and Greenwich Village | 92 |
| Midtown | 108 |
| Gramercy Park and Chelsea | 111 |
| The Upper West Side | 132 |
| Central Park | 149 |
| The Upper East Side | 154 |
| Brooklyn | 166 |
| Queens | 176 |
| Metropolitan Region | 188 |

# THE PENGUIN GUIDE TO NEW YORK CITY 1989

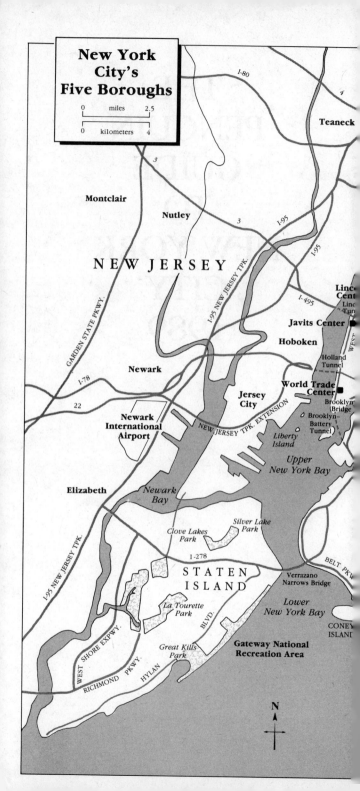

# OVERVIEW

*By Alan Tucker*

*Alan Tucker came to Manhattan under cover of darkness in 1964 and has lived on the Upper West Side for all but two of his years here. He is general editor of the Penguin Travel Guides and a member of the Society of American Travel Writers and the New York Travel Writers Association.*

Yes, yes, we know: New York City is the cultural and creative cynosure of the entire world, and still the foremost national and international financial center—the place where the big deals are made in the film industry, the broadcasting industry, in the art and theatrical businesses, in publishing and advertising, in banking and fashion and export-import.

Trends may start elsewhere, but they're not official until they're acknowledged here.

The people who live and work here create the strikingly high level of ambient human energy that fuels all this activity and is also drawn forth by it (the chicken and the egg). Talented folks from all over the country (and the world) choose to live here not just because they want to survive, but because they have something they want to *do*—and they figure this is the place to do it.

As for you, the visitor, you might want to come to see the totalitarian architecture of the World Trade Center, the robber barons' booty in the Metropolitan Museum of Art, the latest Broadway musical extravaganza, and the like. These "major attractions" are interesting, or at the very least, diverting. But Niagara Falls is interesting, too, and yet it's not quite parallel to the real lure of New York City.

We think you will probably get the most out of visiting

the city if you also look for the less obvious benefits that New Yorkers enjoy—while of course at the same time sidestepping the well-known day-to-day nuisances that living here brings (such as the privilege of paying half your salary in rent, being accosted every day of the year by dozens of beggars, not having your own back yard for growing tomatoes, and leaving the office at 8:30 every night).

What benefits? For example, the restaurants; the neighborhoods; the variety of people (What an understatement! More on that later) and their conversation; the easy, casual access to jazz, classical music, and other performing arts even outside the Sacred Palaces of Culture; the mania for graphic art and arresting design (everywhere); the shops and artisans and galleries (you name it, and it's on sale here—probably cheaper than it is in Hong Kong, too).

These are the things we want to tell you about in our guidebook. We have to mention Lincoln Center, the Museum of Modern Art, Macy's, and such (it may be a state law), but our hearts really lie in talking about downtown performance lofts, where to have brunch while you read your Sunday *New York Times,* where to buy private-label opera recordings, and how to take an afternoon's stroll in New York City from China to Italy to Bohemia.

To get to the goodies that you want to hear about we have had to cover the city in two dimensions.

One is in terms of *neighborhoods*. The other is by way of the city's *specialties,* such as antiques, dance, food, the literary world, fashion shopping, and so on.

## The Neighborhoods

Even Midtown, the business center where most visitors huddle and where the great department stores are concentrated, is really a collection of neighborhoods (gamy Clinton, residential Murray Hill and Gramercy Park, the area around the United Nations, the Garment District around Seventh Avenue in the 30s, etc.). But there's more variety—and more of those special New York experiences we've been talking about—in some of the city's other neighborhoods.

- The **Wall Street area** is full of the history of early New York, as well as offering the South Street

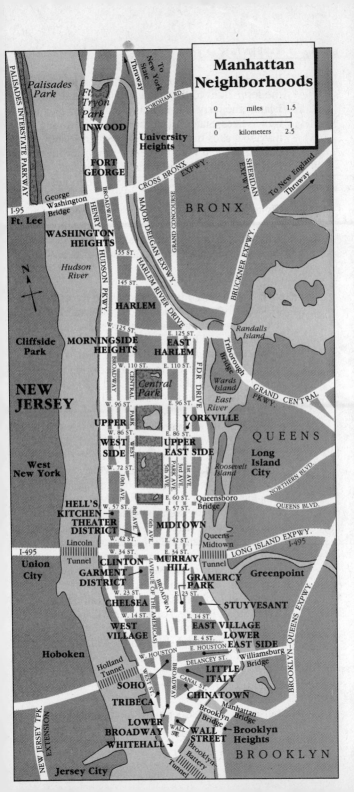

Seaport historical/shopping/dining district and the ferry rides to the Statue of Liberty and Staten Island (the ferry ride itself is the wonderful experience here; Staten Island has a few interesting historical sites but is best left to Staten Islanders). And you'll want to see the New York Stock Exchange and the World Trade Center (have a civilized drink and get the view at the top of the north tower, number 1).

- **Chinatown** is one of the largest such enclaves in the world—and it's no living museum, either.
- **TriBeCa** is an area of artists' and arty lawyers' lofts, and unusual bars, restaurants, cafés, and clubs.
- **Little Italy** is for eating.
- **SoHo** was once an inexpensive place for artists seeking large work space, and is now an expensive but interesting area of galleries, boutiques, restaurants, and bars.
- **Lower Broadway** has trendy shops, punk barbershops, Tower Records, roomy if undistinguished restaurants, the Public Theater, and Cooper Union arts and sciences school—all between Canal and 8th streets. It is a sort of Luxembourg, with Little Italy, Chinatown, and the Lower East Side (or "East Village") on one side and SoHo and Greenwich Village on the other.
- The **Lower East Side** and the **East Village** are perhaps the last remaining bastions of youthful avant-garde artistic and literary activity on Manhattan Island, with attendant clubs and cafés—and lots of street crime and drug sales amid the remnants of an earlier Eastern European immigrant culture.
- **Greenwich Village** has New York University at its heart and is populated by comfortable mid- to upper-level professionals as well as (along Christopher Street in the so-called West Village) a concentrated gay community. There are lots of good bars, restaurants, and shops in the Village, but its bohemian days have given over to a sort of *New York Review of Books* gentility—ironically, the Village proper no longer even has a really good bookstore.
- **Chelsea**, its main street being along Eighth Avenue above 14th Street, has lots of rough edges,

but it does have some of the bohemian elements that the Village has lost. Chelsea also has more than its share of nifty restaurants and clubs and a few leading-edge modern-dance venues, as well as punk rockers, the last especially along West 23rd Street (its northern border) near the famous Chelsea Hotel.

- The **Lower Fifth Avenue** area, also known variously as the Flatiron District, "SoFi" (*So*uth of the *Flati*ron Building), the Ladies' Mile, and the Madison Square area, has trendy restaurants and photographers' lofts on the side streets in the high teens and the 20s up to 23rd Street.

- The **Upper West Side**, north of Midtown and west of **Central Park**, is anchored at the south by Lincoln Center and at the north by Columbia University. Its Columbus Avenue shop and restaurant strip is for those so-called bridge-and-tunnel people (Manhattan's neighbors on all sides must use one or the other to get onto the island) with more money than they should have. Amsterdam Avenue and Broadway are for the Upper West Side's own residents—who are much tighter with their money (they generally have less) and much more inclined toward the shabby genteel than their East Side compatriots. Look here for casual jazz clubs and pretty good Chinese restaurants—and some good bookstores. Many West Siders (the authentic ones, not the parvenu yuppies) look as if they've only recently stopped planning the overthrow of something or other. The ones who aren't carrying musical instruments or coming from dance or play rehearsals, that is. Finally, way up at the northern tip of Manhattan is The Cloisters, the Metropolitan Museum's bastion of Medieval art.

- The **Upper East Side** (east of the park), on the other hand, is the embodiment of everything that might *be* overthrown: Bankers, brokers, doctors, and lawyers live in apartments along Fifth and Park avenues that cost as much as the Latin American nations owe Chase Manhattan Bank; private schools occupy just about every side street; every other shop on Madison Avenue sells museum-quality art or antiques; and on Third, Second, and First avenues young corporate fodder prowl bars and restaurants with names like Tooties and J. J. Monkerton. In **Yorkville** along East 86th Street and a little down Second Avenue there are also vestiges of the earlier German and Middle European working-class presence. The Metropolitan and other museums lie along Fifth Avenue from the 70s to the 90s and even higher, and the Whitney Museum of American Art is over on Madison Avenue.

- **Brooklyn** is a sort of residential alternative to Manhattan for increasing numbers of professionals, but it is the residence of choice for genuine Brooklynites, those of "youse" and "whaddaya dune" and "geddadayear" renown from places such as Bensonhoist (as pronounced) and Bay Ridge (both heavily Italian-American), Canarsie, and Red Hook. Visitors go to Brooklyn for the adventurous Brooklyn Academy of Music (BAM) and the Brooklyn Museum (Egypt!), as well as for great Middle Eastern food on Atlantic Avenue.
- Largely residential **Queens** has its ethnic areas as well: Greeks in Astoria, Koreans and Chinese in Flushing, and more. But most Manhattanites only go to Queens to get a flight at LaGuardia or JFK airports; more's the pity.
- And then there are interesting day-trip destinations from New York City: **The Hamptons** at the eastern end of Long Island, an area that was once an artists' colony (Winslow Homer, then Jackson Pollock and Willem de Kooning) and is now a toney summer resort for rich or highly leveraged Manhattanites; Franklin Delano Roosevelt's home at **Hyde Park** up on the Hudson; the United States Military Academy at historic **West Point** not far from there; early American farms, homes, and estates in the still-beautiful **Hudson River valley**; and **Princeton** and **Yale** universities, the former being more attractive in a movie-set sort of way.

In all these places, particularly in Manhattan neighborhoods, however, what you are primarily looking for, as a visitor in search of the New York Experience, are the *people* and their colorful turns of phrase, as in the "She can't do relationships" or "He gives good phone" or "What am I, chopped liver?" genre of fast talk and one-liners. Although occasionally you'll hear talk of Poincaré or William Blake, most conversations will be on a higher plane: job complaints, money, and the price of cooperative apartments (currently about $250,000 for a one-bedroom apartment even on the not-most-desirable Upper West Side). We've taken considerable care to place you in restaurants, bars, and other venues where you'll hear more of the citizens' patter than you may in the end want to. And places where *you* can try *your* hand at it, too; forget the nonsense about New Yorkers being inaccessible.

We've also conspired to get you into as many different neighborhoods as possible. And different each is, with its own distinct subspecies. What subspecies they are, too! Practitioners of thuggee, with orange spiked hair and chrome studs on their tongues (next year, anyway). Wild-eyed messengers looking like a cross between Don Johnson and Donald Pleasance. Female models with no ankles or muscles. Female models with 18-inch biceps. Overweight cabdrivers from Baffin Island who speak no known language. A couple wearing jellabas and dancing on stilts. A goon with no neck reading Trollope in the subway. You can stand on any street corner here—at any time of day or night—and see "types" that even the most coke-addled Hollywood director hasn't had the imagination to hallucinate for his stylish made-for-TV melodrama of discontinuity, crime, and urban decay.

These same subspecies, from our civic leaders on down (or up), will amaze and mystify you with their adaptability as well. After all, earlier New Yorkers didn't exactly earn a place in the annals of indomitable patriotic resistance when the British were comfortably ensconced here during the American Revolution. New Yorkers can figure out a way around anything. Now, we do indeed have clear principles; we're just prepared to change them as circumstances dictate.

## The City's Specialties

Besides by neighborhood, the other way to come to terms with how to "do" the city is by what special interests you yourself have. Here again we've been selective, opting for the most brilliant aspects as against the more mundane. Surely no one will contest that the city's best efforts show in the areas of:

- Art
- Marketing antiques and antiquities
- Architecture
- Fashion, and shopping for clothes and accessories
- Photography and filmmaking
- Classical music
- Popular music
- Dance
- Theater
- The literary world and bookstores
- Shopping (especially for unusual things)
- Food

Another kind of specialty—and one on which we lavish quite a bit of space—is what we call "After Hours," meaning after the day's nine-to-five activities are accomplished:

- Dining
- Bars and cafés
- Nightlife and entertainment

We've tried to weed out the humdrum in order to put you *in position* to have a satisfying visit to New York City. We consider our guidebook to be a sort of starter kit. It's up to you to take it from here and begin developing your own New York for yourself. It may take a number of visits, and it will be a different town every time.

## USEFUL FACTS

### When to Go
A popular postcard depicts the four seasons in New York, showing the same shot of a gray, treeless street four times. However, New York actually has four distinct seasons: a hot, humid summer; crisp autumn; cold, sloppy winter; and gentle spring. Unless you enjoy extremes, April, May, September, and October are the best months for a visit, and the weeks between Thanksgiving and New Year's can be almost embarrassingly cheerful. You can expect thunderstorms in the summer, snow and rain in the winter, and showers at other times.

### What to Wear
New Yorkers dress well. You will feel out of place wearing shorts at the theater and concerts, in many restaurants, and even on the streets of Midtown during business

hours. On the other hand, you will rarely feel overdressed in this city where it is not unusual to find yourself seated next to someone in full evening dress. Women should pack skirts, dresses, or fashionable slacks; men, slacks, sports coats and/or suits, and ties (you may be able to get by with just a jacket in many places). Do not wear expensive-looking jewelry on the street and public transportation; otherwise, you may be a target for thieves.

To equip yourself for the weather, bring: *in winter,* wool clothing, gloves, scarf, raincoat with liner or overcoat, boots or galoshes, umbrella; *in summer,* lightweight cotton clothing; *other seasons,* a sweater and raincoat; *all seasons,* good, sensible walking shoes.

## *Getting In*

The United States requires passports and visitor's or longterm visas of all visitors other than Canadians who are not United States citizens. Check with the United States Embassy or consulate nearest you before you depart. Lines for customs clearance at Kennedy and Newark airports tend to be long; non–United States citizens can expect to wait an hour and often longer at peak arrival times (between 4:00 and 6:00 P.M. for those coming from Europe).

## *Arrival by Air*

New York is served by three major airports: La Guardia, in Queens, for shorter domestic flights (does not handle 747s); Kennedy ("JFK"), also in Queens, for domestic and international flights; and Newark, outside Newark, New Jersey, for domestic and some international flights.

Excellent public transportation links the three airports to Manhattan.

*By taxi:* The half-hour cab ride from La Guardia to Midtown costs about $20; the 45-minute ride from Kennedy about $30; the 45-minute trip from Newark about $40. At all airports cabs leave from well-marked stands, manned by dispatchers, outside flight arrival areas. It is illegal for cabs to pick up passengers ouside of these areas. Do not be intimidated by the long lines; they move quickly. To partake of the New York custom of "cutting on line" is a sure way of starting a row.

*By bus from La Guardia:* Carey buses (Tel: 718-632-0500) run every 20 minutes between 6:00 A.M. and midnight; they leave from posted areas at curbside outside air terminal arrival areas and go to Grand Central Station at

42nd Street and Park Avenue in Midtown; $6; allow 30 to 40 minutes.

*By bus from Kennedy:* Carey buses run every 20 minutes between 6:00 A.M. and midnight from posted areas at curbside outside terminal arrival areas to Grand Central Station in Midtown; $8; allow 45 minutes to one hour.

*By bus from Newark:* Olympia Trails (Tel: 212-964-6233) buses run every 15 minutes between 6:00 A.M. and midnight from posted areas outside terminal arrival areas to the World Trade Center (West Street next to the Vista Hotel in the Wall Street area downtown); $7; allow 25 minutes. Olympia Trails buses also run every 15 minutes between 6:00 A.M. and midnight from Newark to Grand Central Station at 42nd Street and Park Avenue in Midtown; $7; allow 35 to 45 minutes. New Jersey Transit (Tel: 201-460-8444) buses run every 15 minutes 24 hours a day from Newark to Port Authority Bus Terminal at 42nd Street and Eighth Avenue near Times Square; $7; allow 20 minutes to half an hour.

*By boat from La Guardia:* Passengers arriving at the Marine Air Terminal on Pan Am shuttle flights from Washington and Boston may take the Water Shuttle (Tel: 212-687-2600) to Pier 11 on the East River at the foot of Wall Street; $20; allow half an hour. Sailings at 7:45 A.M., 8:45 A.M., 9:45 A.M., 2:45 P.M., 3:45 P.M., and 4:45 P.M.. Vans meet the boats and take passengers to points in the Wall Street area, free of charge.

*By subway from Kennedy:* A bus-and-subway service, the JFK Express, a.k.a. the Train-to-the-Plane (Tel: 718-330-1234), connects Kennedy with subway stops in Brooklyn and Manhattan, including several along Sixth Avenue in Midtown; $6.75; buses stop at posted areas outside Kennedy arrival areas; allow at least an hour.

*By helicopter from Kennedy:* New York Helicopter (Tel: 800-645-3494) flies from major JFK terminals to the East Side Heliport, 34th Street at the East River in Midtown, every half hour between 1:30 P.M. and 7:30 P.M.; $58; the trip takes just ten minutes.

### *Arrival by Train*
Most Amtrak trains, including those travelling the busy Washington–New York–Boston corridor, arrive at Pennsylvania ("Penn") Station, at 34th Street and Seventh Avenue (Tel: 212-560-7374). Some trains, including many from Canada, arrive at Grand Central Station at 42nd Street and Park Avenue (Tel: 212-560-7360). Amtrak ser-

vice to Grand Central is being phased out and as of 1990 all Amtrak trains will service only Penn Station. For Amtrak information, call (212) 736-4545. Both stations are well served by buses and subways. As both stations are also terminals for commuter railroads, taxis are difficult to procure at rush hours; be patient and steadfast in your efforts. A tip: At Grand Central, cabs are easiest to come by at the Lexington Avenue exits.

*Arrival by Sea*
The only transatlantic liner that still regularly serves New York is the Cunard Line's *Queen Elizabeth II*. She and the many cruise ships that dock in New York tie up at the Hudson River piers off 12th Avenue in the West 50s. A fleet of taxis meets all ships.

*Arrival by Car*
If you do insist on bringing a car into already overcrowded Manhattan, you'll soon discover it really is an island, connected to the rest of the United States by a dozen or so bridges and four tunnels. It usually takes longer to traverse any of these crossings than it does to fly from New York to Paris on the Concorde. Most tolls are $3, and at most bridges and tunnels are imposed only on cars entering Manhattan. Once here, park in a garage (costly and hard to find) and walk or take public transportation. If you do park on the street, remember that New York enforces an alternate-side-of-the-street-parking law—you may not leave your car in a space for more than one night. (And *never* leave anything in your car unguarded, unless you want to lose it and one window.)

*Sightseeing*
Some of the many tours that will help you see New York at its best are:
  **Backstage on Broadway.** 228 West 47th Street; Tel: (212) 575-8065. Actors and directors show you their behind-the-scenes domain.
  **Circle Line Cruise.** Leaves from West 42nd Street and Hudson River; Tel: (212) 563-3200. A three-hour boat cruise around the Manhattan shoreline, all 31 miles of it.
  **Gray Line of New York.** 900 Eighth Avenue; Tel: (212) 397-2600. Well-narrated bus tours give you a choice of lower Manhattan, upper Manhattan, or both.

# 16   USEFUL FACTS

**Greenwich Village Walking Tours.** Tel: (212) 675-3213. An insightful look at Village landmarks.

**Island Helicopter.** East River at 34th Street; Tel: (212) 683-4575. Unforgettable aerial tours, from $30 to $140.

**NBC Studio Tour.** 30 Rockefeller Plaza; Tel: (212) 664-4444. A look at New York as television and radio capital.

**New York Stock Exchange.** 20 Broad Street; Tel: (212) 656-5168. A bird's-eye view of the trading floor.

**Petrel.** A boat tour that leaves from Battery Park at the southern tip of Manhattan; Tel: (212) 825-1976. Sails across New York Harbor on a 70-foot yawl; April through October only.

**Staten Island Ferry.** Leaves from Battery Park ferry terminal; Tel: (212) 806-6941. Still the world's best short ocean voyage—across New York Harbor, past the Statue of Liberty—and only 25¢ for a round-trip passage.

**United Nations.** First Avenue and 46th Street; Tel: (212) 963-7713. Tours include the General Assembly and Secretariat.

## *Local Time*

New York observes Eastern Standard Time from November through April and Eastern Daylight Time from May through October. The city is three hours ahead of the West Coast, five hours behind London, six hours behind Paris, and 15 hours behind Sydney.

## *Electric Current*

Despite its dissimilarity to the rest of America, New York uses standard North American current: 110 volts, 60 cycles. Many of the better hotels have installed special wiring to accommodate European appliances.

## *Currency*

Major foreign money exchanges in New York include: American Express, Tel: (212) 640-4357; Citicorp Foreign Currency Exchange, Tel: (718) 632-2500; and Deak International, Tel: (212) 757-6915. All have outlets throughout the city; call for locations nearest you.

Foreigners using this guidebook will probably find a branch of their major national bank in Manhattan. To name but a few: Barclays, at 9 West 57th Street and other locations, Tel: (212) 644-0850; Bank of Ireland, 640 Fifth Avenue, Tel: (212) 397-1700; Canadian Imperial Bank, 245 Park Avenue, Tel: (212) 557-5300; Australian and New

Zealand Bank, 535 Madison Avenue, Tel: (212) 308-1015. Check the Manhattan telephone directory for others.

Most larger shops and restaurants accept credit cards, especially VISA, MasterCard, and American Express. Traveller's checks are also widely accepted, although a surprising number of establishments are reluctant to do so. To report lost or stolen traveller's checks, contact: American Express, Tel: (212) 221-7282; Bank America, Tel: (800) 227-3460; or VISA, Tel: (800) 227-6811. Bankcard holders who subscribe to the Cirrus Network (instant cash) will find outlets throughout Manhattan; Tel: (212) 424-7787.

## Telephoning

New York is divided into two area codes: 212 for Manhattan and the Bronx, 718 for Brooklyn, Queens, and Staten Island. This is a distinction born of volume: Subterranean New York is crisscrossed by 20 million miles of telephone wire, and there are almost 6 million telephones in the city. (The most used set is a public phone at Penn Station on the Long Island Railroad concourse; it is used 230 times a day.) There are other public telephones on almost every corner in Manhattan, although when you try to use one you will observe a peculiarly New York phenomenon: They are almost always in use.

When calling long distance in the United States, you must dial "1" before dialing the area code.

## Tipping

As a rule of thumb, tip 15 percent in restaurants (a handy way to determine the tip is to double the 8¼ percent sales tax amount shown on the bill); tip cabdrivers 20 percent of the fare; give $1 to doormen who help you carry packages or procure a cab for you; tip delivery people $1 or $2, more for heavy bundles; leave $1 or $2 a day for helpful chambermaids; give a helpful maître d' $5 or so. Don't tip anyone who is rude or decidedly unhelpful.

### Business Hours and Holidays

Many shops in New York do not open until 10:00 or 10:30 A.M. and close at 6:00 or 6:30 P.M. There are a great number of exceptions. In neighborhoods outside of Midtown, many businesses open at noon and don't close until 8:00 or 9:00 P.M., so they can cater to residents on their way home from work. (Numerous New Yorkers don't report to their jobs until 9:30 or 10:00 A.M., often even later, and work until 6:00 or 7:00 P.M., often even later; a nine-to-fiver is the exception here.) Most major department stores are open in addition to regular daytime hours on Monday, Thursday, and Friday evenings and on Sunday afternoons. Many Jewish businesses close on Saturday for the Sabbath and open on Sunday.

Most museums are open Sunday but closed Monday; a notable exception is the Museum of Modern Art, which is open Monday but closed Wednesday.

Restaurants tend to serve lunch from noon to 2:30 or 3:00 P.M. (1:00 is the most popular time for a lunch date) and dinner from 6:30 or 7:00 to 10:30 and later (Manhattanites eat late, often at 9:00 or later). In the theater district, many restaurants offer special before- and after-theater menus.

Most bars and clubs stay open until 2:00 A.M. and many as late as 4:00, the latest they are allowed to serve liquor. A New York Sunday brunch, a popular meal in the city, rarely begins before noon, as establishments are not allowed to serve liquor until then.

Many New York businesses are always open, even on such traditional holidays as Christmas and New Year's Day. However, holidays that are commonly observed in New York include: New Year's Day; Martin Luther King's Birthday, January 15, observed the third Monday of the month; Lincoln's Birthday, February 12; Washington's Birthday, February 22, observed on the closest Monday; St. Patrick's Day, March 17, noted by the presence of a million-some inebriated suburban teenagers who descend upon the city to watch the parade on Fifth Avenue and vomit on city sidewalks; Easter Sunday; the first day of Passover; Memorial Day, May 30, observed on the closest Monday; Fourth of July; Labor Day, September 2, observed on the first Monday of September; the first day of Rosh Hashanah; Yom Kippur; Columbus Day; Veterans Day, November 11; Thanksgiving Day, the fourth Thursday of November; the first day of Hanukkah; Christmas Day.

## *Street Fairs and Festivals*

New York graces its concrete canyons with an inordinate number of parades and street fairs, where you can expect to find booths selling exotic foods and goods. Some of the major ones are: Chinese New Year, Chinatown, January or February (an explosive event); St. Patrick's Day Parade, Fifth Avenue, March 17; Greek Independence Day

Parade, Park Avenue, late March; Easter Parade (not an official parade; rather, New Yorkers parade up and down Fifth Avenue in finery and costumes), Easter Sunday, Fifth Avenue.

Ninth Avenue International Festival (meaning *food*), mid-May, Ninth Avenue from 35th to 57th streets; Amsterdam Avenue Festival, late May, Amsterdam from 77th to 90th streets; Memorial Day Parade, Memorial Day, very late May, 72nd and Broadway to Soldiers and Sailors Monument at 89th Street and Riverside Drive; Feast of St. Anthony, ten days in early June, Sullivan Street, Greenwich Village (a most nonholy mix of games of chance and carnival attractions); Second Avenue Festival, early June, 68th to 96th streets; 52nd Street Fair, mid-June, Park Avenue to Sixth Avenue; Lexington Avenue Festival, late June, Lexington from 23rd to 34th streets.

Fourth of July, Macy's Fireworks, East River; Third Avenue Summerfest, mid-August, Third from 42nd to 57th streets; Third Avenue Fair, mid-September, Third from 14th to 34th streets; Columbus Avenue Festival, mid-September, Columbus from 66th to 86th streets; Feast of San Gennaro, Mulberry Street in Little Italy, ten days in mid-September (like the feast of St. Anthony, but bigger).

Columbus Day Parade, on or around October 12, Fifth Avenue; Halloween Parade, October 31, Greenwich Village (very strange costumes); Veterans Day Parade, November 11, Fifth Avenue; Macy's Thanksgiving Day Parade, Thanksgiving Day, fourth Thursday in November, Central Park West from 77th to Columbus Circle, Broadway from Columbus Circle to Herald Square.

## *Getting Around*

A few basic rules to keep in mind when moving around Manhattan:

Avenues run north–south and streets run east–west. Avenues increase in number from east to west—First Avenue is on the East Side and Tenth Avenue is on the West Side. Streets increase in number from south to north, with 4th Street being downtown and 74th being uptown.

Fifth Avenue is the dividing line between East and West; 1 East 50th Street would be just east of Fifth, 1 West 50th just west of Fifth.

Most streets are one way, with traffic on even-numbered streets travelling east, traffic on odd-numbered streets travelling west. Traffic flows both ways on major crosstown

# Manhattan Address Locator

To find an avenue address, cancel the last figure in the address number, divide by 2, and add (+) or subtract (−) the key number below. The result is the nearest numbered cross street. Cross-street addresses increase east or west from Fifth Avenue, which runs north to south (see examples on 57th Street below). The cross streets west of Central Park (see West 72nd Street), which increase from Central Park West, are the exception.

| Avenue | Key |
|---|---|
| Ave. A, B, C, D | +3 |
| 1st, 2nd Ave. | +3 |
| 3rd Ave. | +10 |
| 4th Ave. | +8 |
| 5th Ave. | |
| Up to 200 | +13 |
| Up to 400 | +16 |
| Up to 600 | +18 |
| Up to 775 | +20 |
| 775 to 1286 | Cancel last figure and −18 |
| To 1500 | +45 |
| Above 2000 | +24 |
| 6th Ave. (Ave. of the Americas) | −12 |
| 7th Ave. | +12 |
| 8th Ave. | +10 |
| 9th Ave. | +13 |
| 10th Ave. | +14 |
| Amsterdam Ave. | +60 |
| Broadway (23-192 Sts.) | −30 |
| Columbus Ave. | +60 |
| Central Park West | Divide house no. by 10 and +60 |
| Lexington Ave. | +22 |
| Madison Ave. | +26 |
| Park Ave. | +35 |
| Riverside Dr. | Divide house no. by 10 and add 72 (up to 165th St.) |
| St. Nicholas Ave. | +110 |
| West End Ave. | +60 |
| York Ave. | +4 |

streets, including Canal, Houston, 14th, 23rd, 34th, 42nd, 57th, 72nd, 79th, 86th, and 96th (the last three are routes across Central Park).

Addresses on north–south streets are not consistently numbered, so 500 Fifth Avenue is actually many blocks north of 500 Second Avenue. Always get a cross street when you ask for an address.

*By subway and bus:* The $1 subway and bus fare is payable with tokens (available at subway stations) or, on buses only, with exact change, no bills. Subway lines frequently used by visitors include the IRT 1, which makes frequent stops on the West Side (mostly along Broadway), and the IRT 6, which makes frequent stops on the East Side (mostly along Lexington Avenue). Buses run uptown on Tenth, Eighth, Sixth, Madison, Third, and First avenues and downtown on Ninth, Seventh, Fifth, and Second avenues. Some of the major east–west bus routes are 14th, 23rd, 34th, 42nd, 57th, 65th/66th, 79th, 86th, and 96th streets (the last four are the only crosstown streets that traverse Central Park).

Bus and subway maps are available at subway stations and at the office of the New York Convention and Visitors Bureau on Columbus Circle and in Times Square.

*By taxi:* Cabs licensed by the New York City Taxi and Limousine Commission are equipped with lighted signs on their roofs. When the sign is lit, the cab is available to pick up passengers. When the sign is not lit, the cab is occupied. When the sign reads "Off Duty" the driver is supposedly not picking up passengers. Cabs charge $1.15 for the first one-eighth of a mile and $.15 for each one-eighth of a mile thereafter. Most impose a $.50 surcharge after 8:00 P.M. A 20 percent tip is customary.

*By car:* A word of advice: Don't. Parking runs $20 a day. Streets are full of potholes. New York drivers are criminally insane or are in some stage of becoming so. What's the point of driving to, say, Macy's, when there's no place to park once you get there? (See also "Arrival by Car," above.)

### Renting a Car

Most major rental car agencies have outlets in Manhattan. Like many other goods and services, rental cars cost more in Manhattan than they do elsewhere, and you are likely to get a better rate if you pick a car up at one of the airports. Check with your airline for fly-drive packages. Also remember that many New Yorkers do not own cars,

## Other Sources of Information

The New York Convention and Visitors Bureau distributes a wealth of information about New York from its offices at Columbus Circle and on 42nd Street in Times Square; Tel: (212) 397-8222.

For up-to-date information on shows, exhibitions, and other events, consult weekly editions of *The New Yorker, New York* magazine, the *Village Voice,* or *7 Days* as well as daily newspapers, especially the entertainment section of the Friday *New York Times.*

## Getting Outside the City

New York is surrounded by beautiful countryside (see our Day Trips section) and you don't have to rent a car to see it. The city is served by an extensive network of public transportation. Some numbers of note: Amtrak, Tel: (212) 736-4545; Hudson, Harlem, and New Haven rail lines (Connecticut and other points north of the city), Tel: (212) 532-4900; Metro-North rail (Westchester County and other points north of the city), Tel: (212) 340-2615; New Jersey Transit (buses and trains), Tel: (201) 460-8444; Long Island Railroad, Tel: (718) 739-4200; Hampton Jitney (buses to Eastern Long Island), Tel: (212) 936-0440; Greyhound (bus), Tel: (212) 635-0800.

—*Stephen Brewer*

# BIBLIOGRAPHY

## History and Biography

Biographies are listed alphabetically by subject; other works are arranged alphabetically by author.

PATRICIA BOSWORTH. *Diane Arbus* (1984). An insightful look at the life and times of this native New Yorker best known for her stark photographs of freaks.

STEPHEN BIRMINGHAM. *Life at the Dakota, New York's Most Unusual Address* (1979). A highly readable blend of a hundred years' worth of architecture, social history, and gossip.

JEAN STEIN. *Edie, An American Biography* (1982). Blue-blooded actress-model Warhol groupie Edie Sedgwick caught up in the social whirl of 1960s New York.

STEPHEN GARMEY. *Gramercy Park* (1984). An illustrated history of a New York neighborhood, from Peter Stuyvesant to the present.

JOHN STEELE GORDON. *The Scarlet Woman of Wall Street* (1988). Good storytelling about mid-19th-century New York and the Erie Railway wars.

HELEN HAYES AND ANITA LOOS. *Twice Over Lightly* (1972). A thoroughly charming and sprightly account of how the "first lady of the American stage" and the author of *Gentlemen Prefer Blondes* spent a summer exploring unlikely aspects of New York City.

IRVING HOWE. *World of Our Fathers: The Journey of the East European Jews to America and the Life They Found and Made* (1976). Fascinating chronicle of arrival and assimilation; lavishly illustrated.

ELIA KAZAN. *A Life* (1988). An encyclopedic account of a long career, much of it spent on the New York stage.

ALFRED KAZIN. *New York Jew* (1978). Coming of age in the political and literary circles of mid-century New York.

JOHN A. KOUWENHOVEN. *The Columbia Historical Portrait of New York* (1972). A social and physical history of New York; richly illustrated and fact filled.

MABEL DODGE LUHAN. *Movers and Shakers* (1936). An eyewitness account of Greenwich Village before World War I.

DAVID MCCULLOUGH. *The Great Bridge* (1972). A thorough and lively account of the construction of the Brooklyn Bridge.

ARTHUR MILLER. *Timebends* (1988). An autobiographical journey from Harlem to Brooklyn to the New York stage.

JAN MORRIS. *The Great Port: A Passage through New York* (1969). A chronicle of New York as a hub of transportation.

ROBERT A. CARO. *The Power Broker: Robert Moses and the Fall of New York* (1975). The highly acclaimed biography of the man who built much of the city we see today.

JERRY E. PATTERSON. *The City of New York: A History Illustrated from the Collections of The Museum of the City of New York* (1978). History at its most entertaining and attractive.

A. SCOTT BERG. *Max Perkins, Editor of Genius* (1978) and *Editor to Author: The Letters of Maxwell E. Perkins* (1987). A superb biography and selected letters document the career of New York's most famous editor, the man who published Hemingway, Fitzgerald, Wolfe, and most of the other great American writers of the 20th century.

ANDREW PORTER. *A Musical Season: Music of Three Seasons: 1974–1977; Music of Three More Seasons: 1977–1980; Musical Events, A Chronicle: 1980–1983*. These collected reviews and essays by the music critic of *The New Yorker* give a magnificent overview of the city's recent musical history.

JACOB RIIS. *How the Other Half Lives: Studies among the Tenements of New York* (1971). These sociological studies of poverty in turn-of-the-century New York instigated massive reforms in housing and social programs.

NED ROREM. *The Paris & New York Diaries* (1983). A composer's journal of his New York experiences during the 1950s and 1960s.

RON ROSENBAUM. *Manhattan Passions: True Tales of Power, Wealth, and Excess* (1987). Fascinating portraits of the rich and famous: Malcolm Forbes, Governor Mario Cuomo, gossip columnist Liz Smith, et al.

JOSEPH C. GOULDEN. *Fit to Print: A. M. Rosenthal and His Times* (1988). How the executive director of *The New York Times* rose to power; based on 317 interviews.

STEVEN RUTTENBAUM. *Mansions in the Clouds* (1986). The life of architect Emery Roth (1871–1948) and the evolution of the New York skyscraper apartment house.

JAMES ATLAS. *Delmore Schwartz: The Life of an American Poet* (1977). A superb portrait of one of the century's finest poets and the New York world in which he lived.

ARNOLD SHAW. *Fifty Second Street: The Street of Jazz* (1977). Fifty-second Street during its mid-century heyday as a jazz center.

KATE SIMON. *Fifth Avenue: A Very Special History* (1979). A very readable history of the city's poshest avenue. *Bronx*

*Primitive* (1983) chronicles the writer's beginnings in a less glamorous part of town.

EILEEN SIMPSON. *Poets in Their Youth* (1982). Sympathetic portraits of John Berryman, Robert Lowell, Delmore Schwartz, and their like, poets who lived and worked in New York in the 1940s.

GAY TALESE. *The Kingdom and the Power* (1986). A foray into the workings of *The New York Times*.

JAMES THURBER. *The Years with Ross* (1959). A memoir of Harold Ross, founding editor of *The New Yorker,* to which Thurber contributed volumes-worth of his sardonic essays and short stories.

JAMES TRAGER. *West of Fifth: The Rise and Fall of Manhattan's West Side* (1984). Social and architectural history of a New York neighborhood.

JEROME TUCCILLE. *Trump* (1985). All you ever wanted to know about New York's biggest ego.

FLORENCE TURNER. *At the Chelsea* (1987). An affectionate history of the shabby but famous 23rd Street hotel, a favorite among New York's literati.

ELLIOT WILLENSKY. *When Brooklyn Was the World: 1920–1957* (1986). Text and photographs evoke Brooklyn in its golden days.

### Literature

WOODY ALLEN. *Without Feathers* (1976), *Getting Even* (1977), *Side Effects* (1980). Humor that exposes New York as the hotbed of neurosis and anxiety it really is.

JAMES BALDWIN. *Go Tell It on the Mountain* (1953) and *Just Above My Head* (1979). Both novels are set in the author's native Harlem.

TRUMAN CAPOTE. *Breakfast at Tiffany's* (1958). The Manhattan adventures of stylish, free-spirited Holly Golightly. *Answered Prayers* (unfinished at the author's death in 1984, published posthumously in 1987) is populated by thinly disguised versions of real-life, upper-crust New Yorkers (who aren't at all happy with their portrayals).

BARBARA COHEN, SEYMOUR CHWAST, AND STEVEN HELLER. *New York Observed: Artists and Writers Look at the City* (1987). Selections from 96 writers and 51 artists.

STEPHEN CRANE. *Maggie: A Girl of the Streets* (1893). Realist fiction about life in the slums of lower Manhattan at the end of the last century.

E. L. DOCTOROW. *Ragtime* (1975). New York in the first half of this century, as experienced by a Jewish immigrant, a suburbanite WASP, and a black. *World's Fair* (1986) revolves around a middle-class Jewish family in 1930s Queens.

JOHN DOS PASSOS. *Manhattan Transfer* (1925). Hundreds of sketches of characters and events in New York between the two world wars.

JACK FINNEY. *Time and Again* (1970). A man shuttles back and forth between the New York of today and of the 1880s, providing an exceptionally detailed and vivid account of the city in the late 19th century.

F. SCOTT FITZGERALD. *The Great Gatsby* (1925). New York before the Great Depression.

WASHINGTON IRVING. *History of New York from the Beginning of the World to the End of the Dutch Dynasty* (1809). Satirical, fact-filled account of Dutch New York, as presented by the fictional Diedrich Knickerbocker.

HENRY JAMES. *Washington Square* (1881). Greenwich Village in the middle of the last century.

TAMA JANOWITZ. *Slaves of New York* (1986). These slick tales of offbeat New Yorkers do provide a glimpse into contemporary New York—but prove just how vapid contemporary writing about New York can be.

BEL KAUFMAN. *Up the Down Staircase* (1965). Trials and triumphs of a Manhattan schoolteacher.

FRAN LIEBOWITZ. *Metropolitan Life* (1978). Humorous essays on life in the country's largest metropolis.

FEDERICO GARCIA LORCA. *Poet in New York* (1955). Early alienation poetry from the Spanish surrealist poet and dramatist.

MARY MCCARTHY. *The Group* (1963). Vassar graduates descend on New York in the 1950s.

JAY MCINERNEY. *Bright Lights, Big City* (1984). Glib, empty novel about glib, empty young New Yorkers, yet it does picture a certain New York. More of the same surfaces in *The Story of My Life* (1988).

BERNARD MALAMUD. *The Tenants* (1971). Anguish of a lonely immigrant in an abandoned New York tenement.

MIKE MARQUESEE AND BILL HARRIS. *New York, An Anthology* (1985). In poetry and prose, how writers feel about New York.

HOWARD MOSS, EDITOR. *New York Poems* (1980). Poets inspired by a common subject.

CLIFFORD ODETS. *Awake and Sing* (1935). One of the first plays by the master playwright who shaped the New York stage chronicles the life of a Jewish family in the Bronx.

CONRAD OSBORNE. *O Paradiso* (1988). An outrageous novel of New York's opera crazies.

GRACE PALEY. *Enormous Changes at the Last Minute* (1975). Short stories, many of them set in Greenwich Village.

DOROTHY PARKER. *The Portable Dorothy Parker* (1944). Poems, stories, and reviews by this renowned denizen of the Algonquin Round Table.

JOHN RECHY. *City of Night* (1952). Fictionalized account of New York's homosexual underworld.

HENRY ROTH. *Call It Sleep* (1964). A novel centered on the family life of Jewish immigrants.

DAMON RUNYON. *The Bloodhounds of Broadway and Other Stories* (1981). The author of *Guys and Dolls* explores the Broadway underworld.

J. D. SALINGER. *Catcher in the Rye* (1945). A modern classic in which Holden Caulfield, upper-middle-class son of New York, comes of age.

HUBERT SELBY, JR. *Last Exit to Brooklyn* (1964). A seething portrait of low life in a Brooklyn neighborhood.

BETTY SMITH. *A Tree Grows in Brooklyn* (1943). A sentimental novel about an Irish girl growing up in Brooklyn.

WILLIAM STYRON. *Sophie's Choice* (1976). An evocative tale of a Holocaust survivor in Brooklyn after the war.

CHUCK WACHTEL. *Joe the Engineer* (1983). A novel of working-class life in Queens.

EDWARD LEWIS WALLANT. *The Pawnbroker* (1961). Tribulations of a concentration camp survivor in Harlem.

NATHANAEL WEST. *Miss Lonelyhearts* (1933). Economic and emotional depression as it affects an advice-to-the-lovelorn columnist in 1930s New York.

EDITH WHARTON. *The Age of Innocence* (1920). Pulitzer Prize–winning novel of upper-class life in late 19th-century New York.

E. B. WHITE. *Essays of E. B. White* (1977). A superb collection of works by this contributor to *The New Yorker*, including "Here Is New York" (1949), perhaps the best lines ever written about the city.

THOMAS WOLFE. *Of Time and the River: A Legend of Man's Hunger in His Youth* (1935). Despairing novel of New York during the Great Depression; sequel to *Look Homeward, Angel*.

TOM WOLFE. *Bonfire of the Vanities* (1987). This highly stylized novel draws on the tumultuous social realities of New York in the 1980s.

HERMAN WOUK. *Marjorie Morningstar* (1955). Social aspirations of a middle-class Jewish family on the Upper West Side.

## *Architecture and Photography*

BERENICE ABBOTT. *New York in the Thirties* (1939). Photographs by this master who made it her business to chronicle the entire city.

MARY BLACK. *Old New York in Early Photographs: 196 Prints, 1853–1901, from the Collection of The New-York Historical Society* (1973). The best from the society's collection.

CHRISTIAN BLANCHET AND BERTRAND DARD. *Statue of Liberty: The First Hundred Years* (1985). A rich text (translated from the French) and a treasure trove of historic illustrations, many from European collections; the best book ever on the much-publicized Lady of the Harbor.

BENJAMIN BLOM. *New York: Photographs, 1850–1950* (1982). A fine collection on New York people and buildings.

JOSEPH BYRON. *Photographs of New York Interiors at the Turn of the Century* (1976) and *New York Life at the Turn of the Century in Photographs* (1985). Exquisite photographs from the Byron Collection of the Museum of the City of New York.

BARBARALEE DIAMONSTEIN. *The Landmarks of New York* (1988). Thorough documentation of historic New York, by one of the city's most visible socialites.

LORRAINE B. DIEHL. *The Late, Great Pennsylvania Station* (1985). The construction, decay, and tragic demolition in 1963 of New York's greatest landmark, one of the "few buildings vast enough to hold the sound of time" (Thomas Wolfe).

CARIN DRECHSLER-MARX AND RICHARD F. SHEPARD. *Broadway* (1988). The 293 blocks from the Battery to the Bronx along this famous street are discussed in terms of people, culture, and history.

ANDREAS FEININGER. *New York in the Forties* (1983). One of the greatest photographers of his age takes on a willing subject.

MARGOT GAYLE AND EDMUND V. GILLON. *Cast Iron Architecture in New York* (1974). A photographic record of the style that flourished in New York at the end of the last century.

PAUL GOLDBERGER. *The City Observed* (1979). The architecture critic of *The New York Times* comments on the major buildings of Manhattan.

ADA LOUISE HUXTABLE. *Classic New York: Georgian Gentility to Greek Elegance* (1964). Remarkable observations from the former architecture critic of *The New York Times*.

CHARLES LOCKWOOD. *Bricks and Brownstones* (1972). A thorough history of the New York row house.

DONALD MARTIN REYNOLDS. *The Architecture of New York City* (1984). History and commentary on 80 major buildings and monuments.

REBECCA REED SHANOR. *The City That Never Was: Two Hundred Years of Fantastic and Fascinating Plans That Might Have Changed the Face of New York City* (1988). A landing strip in Central Park and other schemes that never made it off the drawing board; well written and illustrated.

NATHAN SILVER. *Lost New York* (1967). A heavily illustrated account of New York's lost architectural landscape.

ROBERT A. M. STERN, GREGORY GILMARTIN, AND THOMAS MELLINS. *New York 1900* (1983). Overview of the city's Beaux Arts architecture. This book was followed by *New York 1930* (1987), focusing on architecture between the wars.

J. C. SUARES. *Manhattan* (1981). This expensive and arty photo collection is the best of our time.

JOHN TAURANAC. *Essential New York* (1979). Short, incisive write-ups on Manhattan's major buildings, parks, and bridges.

JOHN TAURANAC AND CHRISTOPHER LITTLE. *Elegant New York: The Builders and the Buildings, 1895–1915* (1985). Ninety great residential and corporate palaces.

EDWARD B. WATSON AND EDMUND V. GILLON, JR. *New York Then and Now* (1976). Old and new photographs of the same sites show how the city has and hasn't changed.

NORVAL WHITE AND ELLIOT WILLENSKY. *AIA Guide to New York City* (1967). An authoritative, building-by-building guide to New York, sanctioned by the American Institute of Architects.

NORVAL WHITE AND ELLIOT WILLENSKY. *New York: A Physical History* (1988). A unique cultural, economic, and technical account of man-made New York.

### Unusual Guidebooks

RICHARD ALLEMAN. *The Movie Lover's Guide to New York: The Ultimate Guide to Movie New York* (1988). Movie stars' homes, film locations, and the like; exhaustive.

JEROME CHARYN. *Metropolis: New York as Myth, Marketplace, and Magical Land* (1986). A tour of Manhattan people, places, and legends.

JUDI CULBERTSON AND TOM RANDALL. *Permanent New Yorkers: A Biographical Guide to the Cemeteries of New York* (1987). New York cemeteries as museums.

SUSAN EDMISTON AND LINDA D. CIRINO. *Literary New York: A History and Guide* (1976). This geographic tour tells who wrote what where.

MARGOT GAYLE AND MICHELE COHEN. *The Art Commission and the Municipal Art Society Guide to Manhattan's Outdoor Sculpture* (1988). Expert commentary.

JOYCE GOLD. *From Windmills to the World Trade Center: A Walking Guide to Lower Manhattan History* (1988). Personal and anecdotal guide to lower Manhattan.

HARMON GOLDSTONE AND MARTHA DALRYMPLE. *History Preserved: A Guide to New York City Landmarks and Historic Districts* (1974). Well-guided tours for history buffs.

JOSEPH LEDERER AND ARLEY BONDARIN. *All Around the Town: A Walking Guide to Outdoor Sculpture in New York City* (1975). Comprehensive and fun.

JAMES D. MCCABE, JR. *New York by Gaslight* (1882). A southern journalist's guide to the city; now in a reprint.

HENRY MOSCOW. *The Book of New York Firsts: Unusual, Arcane, and Fascinating Facts in the Life of New York City* (1982). The first balloon ascent over Manhattan and other interesting New York facts. Moscow's *The Street Book: An Encyclopedia of Manhattan's Street Names and Their Origins* (1978) provides more fun New York history.

*New York City Guide* (Reprint, 1982). The original, 1939 WPA guide to New York. Insightful though dated.

*The New York Times World of New York: An Uncommon Guide to the City of Fantasies* (1985). Essays by Vincent Canby, Nora Ephron, David Frost, and their famous like; often so clever they miss the point but good reading all the same.

LYNN SCHNURNBERGER. *Kids Love New York!: The A–Z Resource Book* (1984). Some 800 suggestions on how to keep the little ones happy in the Big Apple.

KATE SIMON. *New York: Places and Pleasures* (1971). The eloquent travel writer directs her innate charm to her home city.

### Movies
New York has been a favorite film location since the movie camera was invented. *The Movie Lover's Guide to New York* by Richard Alleman (see "Unusual Guidebooks," above) is your best guide to the Big Apple as movieland. The following films are only a few of the best in which New York steals the show.

*Breakfast at Tiffany's* (1961). A sophisticated movie version of Truman Capote's classic, with Audrey Hepburn as Holly Golightly.

*East Side, West Side* (1949). Typical New Yorkers—chic, savvy, neurotic, selfish—portrayed by Barbara Stanwyck, James Mason, Ava Gardner, Nancy Davis (Reagan), others.

*Easter Parade* (1948). Fred Astaire and Judy Garland show how to partake of this annual Fifth Avenue tradition in high style.

*Forty-Second Street* (1933). Backstage drama with onstage extravaganzas by Busby Berkeley; you can also see it live on Broadway.

*Guys and Dolls* (1955). A snappy film version of the Broadway musical, inhabited by those amusing Damon Runyon characters.

*Hester Street* (1975). A nice Jewish girl from the Old Country (Carol Kane) doesn't like turn-of-the-century New York one bit.

*King Kong* (1933). The big hairy ape goes to the top of the Empire State Building and he doesn't even use the elevator. (He does a repeat performance at the World Trade Center in a campy 1976 remake.)

*Miracle on 34th Street* (1947). A highly convincing and charming argument for the validity of the Santa Claus myth.

*My Sister Eileen* (1955 musical version, based on the 1938 novel by Ruth McKenney). Two Ohio girls come to Greenwich Village with songs in their hearts. (The real-life Eileen married novelist Nathanael West; the couple was killed in an automobile accident in 1940.)

*Next Stop, Greenwich Village* (1976). Brooklyn boy explores 1950s bohemia.

*On the Town* (1949). Gene Kelly and Frank Sinatra dance their way up and down Manhattan.

*On the Waterfront* (1954). Marlon Brando sweats, scowls, and scrapes on the New York area docks.

*Prisoner of Second Avenue* (1975). The city begins to get to Anne Bancroft and Jack Lemmon.

*An Unmarried Woman* (1978). Upper East Side housewife loses her husband, takes up with a SoHo artist, and moves into an Upper West Side brownstone: What could be more typically New York?

*Where's Poppa?* (1970). Ruth Gordon at her best as a batty Upper West Side Jewish mamma.

*The World of Henry Orient* (1964). New York as experienced by two wacky adolescents.

Finally, the films of Woody Allen, most of which are really just manifestations of the director's love affair with his native city. Of special note for their indulgence of New York: *Annie Hall* (1977), *Manhattan* (1979), *Broadway Danny Rose* (1984), *Hannah and Her Sisters* (1986), and *Radio Days* (1987).

—*Stephen Brewer*

# ACCOMMODATIONS

New York's hotel roster is enlarging by the day, as a recent surge in building and renovation adds new luxury and variety for visitors. Exorbitant city real-estate values, however, mean high prices. Moderate rates are $135 to $200 a night; luxury hotels start at $210 and go way up. So many midtown hotels have crossed the $200 boundary that it pays now to compare rates, as it is often possible to stay in a small exclusive property for almost the same tab as the large commercial hotels. The few budget choices available run from $85 to $125, and range from pleasant to dreary.

The selection here is divided into geographic areas and is listed *from most to least expensive in each group*. The Upper East Side north of 59th Street, with its art galleries, boutiques, and museums, is home to many of the city's most prestigious hotels. The West Side from 42nd to 61st streets gives access to Lincoln Center, Broadway theaters, and Carnegie Hall—an important advantage because cabs are hard to find just before and after performances. Midtown east is convenient for shoppers and business travellers, while the Murray Hill neighborhood, a quieter residential district in the east 30s, offers some of the most appealing accommodations in the moderate range. A final potpourri offers a rundown on the city's growing number of all-suite properties, a listing of the big convention hotels, and a selection of hotels and bed-and-breakfast options for travellers on a genuine budget.

All hotels have better rates on weekends; ask for the weekend package, then the regular rates. An 8¼ percent sales tax is added to all hotel bills.

The telephone area code for Manhattan is 212.

### *Upper East Side*

**The Pierre**, a longtime favorite of the rich and powerful, has the air of a luxurious and exclusive private club and provides crackerjack service and welcome privacy for business barons and diplomats from around the world. Half the rooms are leased on a permanent basis. Chippendale and Chinoiserie are the styles, and the lobby gleams with Old World elegance. High tea in front of the grand staircase in **The Rotunda** is a daily ritual, and many a business deal has been consummated here over breakfast croissants.

2 East 61st Street (at Fifth Avenue), New York, NY 10021. Tel: 838-8000.

**The Stanhope** has been transformed by a recent $30-million renovation into an ornate showplace filled with Louis XVI furnishings and Baccarat chandeliers. Rooms are decorated to the last tiny corner with reproduction 18th-century armoires, displays of antique porcelain, and a mini-library of antique books. The choicest of the 23 rooms and 94 suites overlook the Metropolitan Museum across the street and Central Park beyond. Staff outnumber guests here two to one, and the hotel provides convenient limousine transportation to Midtown. The sidewalk café outside is one of New York's most popular oases.

995 Fifth Avenue (at 81st Street), New York, NY 10028. Tel: 288-5800.

**The Carlyle**'s understated elegance and impeccable service have kept it at the top of the New York list for decades, the choice of CEOs, society, and two United States presidents. There's a hushed quality to the dimmed lobby with its antiques and tapestries. The spacious rooms are done in fresh florals accented with antiques and greenery—nothing ostentatious, just pleasantness and quiet good taste. Rooms provide all the amenities of one of the world's best hotels, including serving pantries. Things are surprisingly lively in the evening, when top pianists play under the colorful murals at **Bemelmans Bar**—and Bobby Short holds court at the **Café Carlyle**.

35 East 76th Street (at Madison Avenue), New York, NY 10021. Tel: 744-1600.

The **Plaza Athénée**, instead of trying to match the grandeur of its Parisian sister, has been made into a pampering, intimate sanctuary. In the small formal lobby, softened by a blue-green pastoral tapestry and pale rugs, guests are seated at an 18th-century desk for check-in, then personally escorted by a manager to their well-appointed rooms. Duplicates of the trademark gilt clocks of the original hotel await in every room, along with traditional furnishings, fresh flowers, and such niceties as trouser pressers, tie racks, shoe trees, safes, pantries, Porthault bathrobes—even humidifiers to combat dry room heat in winter. **La Regence** serves top-caliber French food amid hand-painted panels, cloud ceilings, and chandeliers.

37 East 64th Street (between Madison and Park avenues), New York, NY 10021. Tel: 734-9100.

The **Mayfair Regent** reflects the personal warmth of manager Dario Mariotti, once of the Grand Hotel and the Gritti Palace, who sets a cosmopolitan tone for his small and charming hotel, which attracts a loyal clientele from royalty to Italian fashion designers to Greek shipping magnates. The spacious quarters are a pretty and tasteful world of soft colors and thoughtful comforts, such as the umbrella hanging in the closet, just in case. Coffered ceilings, wing chairs, and a fireplace make the lobby a place for lingering, and the columned and mirrored lounge has become a favorite setting in the city for business breakfasts and afternoon teas. Guests also have charging privileges at the little restaurant off the lobby—the four-star **Le Cirque**.

610 Park Avenue (at 65th Street), New York, NY 10021. Tel: 288-0800.

The lobby is understated at the **Westbury** and the rooms are agreeably fussy, with stripes, flowery chintz, oriental rugs, and ruffles and plants all around, a combination that seems to appeal to the many well-dressed European travellers who keep the hotel well booked. The **Polo Lounge**, with its dark mahogany bar and paisley seats, is popular with the toney neighborhood crowd as well as with guests.

840 Madison Avenue (at 69th Street), New York, NY 10021. Tel: 535-2000.

There's a bit of show-biz glitz to the **Regency**, the grand hotel in the Loews chain where biggies from Prince

Rainier to Hollywood studio execs like to stay. The decor, just redone to the tune of plenty of millions, is elaborate Regency style with lots of marble, brocade, and mirrors. The lower lobby holds a fitness center where guests can stay in shape.

540 Park Avenue (between 60th and 61st streets), New York, NY 10021. Tel: 759-4100.

**The Mark**, until recently known as the Madison Avenue, has been acquired by a group headed by a former Regent executive, and is being turned into a first-class entry with an Art Deco look and rooms featuring contemporary colors and lacquer accent pieces. Eighty-five of the 185 rooms are suites. Open but not quite finished at press time, the hotel looks promising—and prices are below those of most of its East Side neighbors.

25 East 77th Street (off Madison), New York, NY 10021. Tel: 744-4300.

**The Barbizon**, once a residence hotel where well-bred young ladies like Grace Kelly and Lauren Bacall were properly chaperoned when they arrived in New York, has been stylishly renovated, and the pastel contemporary rooms, while small, are a good value in the neighborhood. The tower suites with terraces and city views appeal to many celebrities; ABC puts up its top "Good Morning America" guests here. Steve Rubell and Ian Schrager, who did such a smashing job renovating the Royalton and Morgans (see below) have recently taken over the Barbizon and intend to redo it as a spa—the results have yet to be seen.

140 East 63rd Street (at Lexington Avenue), New York, NY 10021. Tel: 838-5700.

## Midtown West

The New York **Peninsula** was once the 1905 Beaux Arts landmark Gotham Hotel. It reopened in 1988 as Maxim's, with an opulent Art Nouveau theme, but in short order the hotel was acquired by the noted Peninsula group and it remains to be seen what will be added or subtracted. Meanwhile, the Parisian touch prevails. A sweeping double staircase leads to marble arches, antiques, and huge floral bouquets. Guest rooms have custom cherry furnishings, three telephones, a writing desk with leather blotters, and Art Nouveau accessories. Some baths have six-foot whirlpool tubs and bidets. Fifth Avenue views from higher floors are striking, but the best will be from the tri-level fitness center and rooftop pool soon to open overlooking Manhattan.

700 Fifth Avenue (at 55th Street), New York, NY 10019. Tel: 247-2200.

The first true luxury hotel to be established near the theater district, the sophisticated **Grand Bay** is a hit just off Broadway. The two-story lobby, with pink marble, sculpted pedestals, paintings of the four seasons, and a giant chandelier, is wonderfully removed from the bustle of the neighborhood. No look-alike rooms here: With decor from French Provincial to Art Deco to black-and-white modern, there should be something to please everyone. There's dining on the balcony over the lobby; tea and cocktails in the lobby café; and one of the city's hottest restaurants, Harry Cipriani's **Bellini**, adjoins just outside. Among the many amenities are beepers available at the front desk so VIPs needn't miss important calls during the theater.

152 West 51st Street (at Seventh Avenue), New York, NY 10019. Tel: 765-1900.

The **Ritz Carlton** is a clubby enclave with the spirit of an English country house. Rooms were done by noted decorator Sister Parish at a reported $100,000 per room, with mahogany furniture from Henredon and fine print fabrics from Brunschwig & Fils. The rooms aren't large compared to others in this price category, but the understated English look has its appeal—judging from a reported guest list that includes Nancy Reagan, Sophia Loren, Elizabeth Taylor, and Donald Sutherland. Most in demand are the front rooms with breathtaking Central Park views; settle for a quiet back room and the rates go down considerably. The **Jockey Club** restaurant, a meld of antique pine and leather, offers a library to keep you occupied while you wait for your cronies in the bar.

112 Central Park South, New York, NY 10019. Tel: 757-1900.

**The Plaza**, New York's true grande dame, has the best location in town, at the foot of Central Park on the most European of the city's plazas. The big busy hotel is an official national historic monument; the soaring **Palm Court** is a local landmark for luncheon and tea; and many a business tycoon has quaffed a cocktail at the **Oak Bar**. The future of these quintessential New York settings is unknown, since the Plaza has been acquired by Donald Trump, who plans renovations he declares will make it the country's best hotel.

786 Fifth Avenue (at 59th Street), New York, NY 10019. Tel: 759-3000.

The look of the **Royalton** is somewhere between a

21st-century luxury liner and the Orient Express. The playful new hotel incorporates the favorite travel experiences of owners Steve Rubell and Ian Schrager, formerly of the famous—or infamous—disco, Studio 54. Designer Phillippe Starck's tapered columns, curved lines, and sweeps of mahogany and granite make for a stunning modern lobby with trendy features such as a 24-hour high-tech lunch counter, a skylit billiard table, and a tiny round bar that seats exactly 15 people. Walking the narrow dark-blue corridors is like making your way toward a slick train compartment, made efficient with built-in seating and storage and a big bed tucked in like a captain's bunk. Love it or hate it, there's nothing else like it.

44 West 44th Street (between Fifth and Sixth avenues), New York, NY 10036. Tel: 869-4400.

For **Le Parker Meridien**, the French chain has chosen showy elegance rather than Gallic charm, with a pink-columned, two-story entry arcade setting the tone. Modern light woods, French prints, and marble baths make for attractive if not distinctive guest rooms. A memorable bonus, however, is the glass-enclosed 42nd-floor pool and the outside sun deck and running track with soaring city views. For indoor exercise, the basement health club has a weight room, squash and racquetball courts, whirlpool, sauna, and aerobics classes. Fitness buffs and business travellers particularly enjoy the facilities, which allow them to work off the calories acquired at **Maurice**, the hotel's esteemed French restaurant.

118 West 57th Street (between Sixth and Seventh avenues), New York, NY 10019. Tel: 245-5000.

**The Dorset** gives off a dignified, quiet, Old English air in its gracious paneled lobby and muraled dining room. Rooms are large and attractive with modern furnishings, Picasso prints on the walls, and convenient serving pantries. Prices fall between the moderate and luxury categories because the bathrooms have not been modernized, making the hotel a relatively good buy.

30 West 54th Street (between Fifth and Sixth avenues), New York, NY 10019. Tel: 247-7300.

The **Mayflower**, a genteel dowager on Central Park and an aria away from Lincoln Center, has an Old World look in the lobby corridor lined with paintings. Rooms, however, while comfortable, are beginning to show their age. Of course, with a park view you may never notice, and there's often interesting artistic company in the **Conservatory Café**. Recent residents were the Bolshoi Ballet troupe.

15 Central Park West (at 61st Street), New York, NY 10023. Tel: 265-0060.

The **Warwick** is a safe if uninspired choice with a fine location and good-sized rooms that should be more appealing after the renovation scheduled for early 1989. The lobby is also slated for a needed face-lift. There are a restaurant and bar on the premises.

65 West 54th Street (at Sixth Avenue), New York, NY 10010. Tel: 247-2700.

Dorothy Parker, Alexander Woollcott, and their fabled Round Table of the 1920s are gone from the **Algonquin**, but conversation still hums in the **Rose Room** and the paneled lobby sitting room–cum–cocktail lounge, a haven where authors, publishers, actors, producers, and people watchers gather, summoning the waiter with a traditional brass bell. Here is where *The New Yorker* magazine was born (and is still found in every room), where Lerner and Loewe wrote *My Fair Lady,* where Angela Lansbury lived when she starred in *Mame,* and where guests still include names like Mordecai Richler, Eudora Welty, and Maya Angelou. What the moderately priced, determinedly old-fashioned rooms lack in modern amenities they make up for in coziness, warmth, and the palpable feeling of tradition.

59 West 44th Street (between Fifth and Sixth avenues), New York, NY 10036. Tel: 840-6800.

The **Wyndham** has no brochures or rate sheets—they don't need them. The spacious, pretty, old-fashioned rooms upstairs are among New York's best buys, personally decorated by resident owners of taste who put their money into paintings and charm rather than room service or fancy new plumbing. (Everything works—it just isn't state of the art.) The deep red lobby–sitting room is as cozy as a home parlor, and you ring the bell for admittance as in a home. The hotel is a favorite of visiting performers; Jessica Tandy and Hume Cronyn keep a permanent apartment here. Reserve well in advance to join them.

42 West 58th Street (between Fifth and Sixth avenues), New York, NY 10019. Tel: 753-3500.

### *Midtown East*

In brochures and advertisements, Leona Helmsley proclaims herself the queen of the **Helmsley Palace**, a hotel whose distinction lies in incorporating the opulent public rooms of the restored 1881 Villard Houses. Afternoon tea in the Gold Room is a perfect way to see the treasures, including the sweeping staircase, grand ballroom, exquisite carving, and Stanford White interiors inspired by the Palazzo della Cancelleria in Rome. The pale, oversized rooms of the 55-story hotel beyond presumably reflect Mrs. Helmsley's own Baroque tastes, which seem to appeal to many monied guests—but seldom to the truly sophisticated traveller.

455 Madison Avenue (at 50th Street), New York, NY 10022. Tel: 888-7000.

Architect Kevin Roche won a prize for the superb, soaring, contemporary **United Nations Plaza Hotel**, where luxurious guest rooms begin on the 28th floor and big windows provide the best East River views in town, particularly from the 27th-floor pool and health club (there's also a tennis court on the 39th floor). Marble, chrome, and mirrors reflecting Japanese floral arrangements mark the lobby, where a harpist offers soothing music in the afternoon. When the UN is in session, ambassadors, diplomats, and people like the secretary of state may be in residence. The hotel provides a quick Continental breakfast for busy guests in the Wickery, a bower off the lobby, and limousine service to Wall Street.

One United Nations Plaza (44th Street and First Avenue), New York, NY 10017. Tel: 355-3400.

The **Inter-Continental New York** has been revived by the distinguished international chain, retaining the brass birdcage and Tiffany ceiling in the lobby and the air of genteel refinement from the old Barclay. Rooms have been redecorated, are traditionally furnished, spacious, and in good taste.

111 East 48th Street (at Lexington Avenue), New York, NY 10017. Tel: 755-5900.

**The Waldorf-Astoria**, the first bastion of New York elegance, is now a busy Hilton property, but there is still cachet to the handsome Art Deco lobby. The giant clock executed for the Chicago World's Fair of 1893 is a carryover from the original hotel (which gave way to the Empire State Building). Rooms are big and very nicely done in French Provincial style. Tucked away from the crowd with its own entrance, the **Waldorf Towers** is as toney as ever. The flower-adorned piano played nightly in the hotel cocktail lounge belonged to Cole Porter when he was a Towers resident. For those who like the variety of restaurants and services of a large hotel, this one remains special.

301 Park Avenue (between 49th and 50th streets), New York, NY 10022. Tel: 355-3000.

A contemporary hideaway in the heart of Midtown, the **Manhattan Viscount** has just one hundred rooms, three or four on each of 36 floors, all done in tailored modern with plaid carpeting, lacquer furniture, and bold colors. Amenities include dressing rooms, trouser pressers, shoe racks, and bidets in many baths. Some rooms also have terraces. The lobby is divided by tall arches into a sitting area and the glass-paneled Zodiac Bar, where a complimentary Continental breakfast is served in the morning. The spiffy pinstripe-clad young ladies at the desk seem eager to please, and the Viscount itself should please those who want a slick, small, reasonable hotel.

127 East 55th Street (between Lexington and Park avenues), New York, NY 10022. Tel: 826-1100.

"Quirky" best describes the **Elysée**, a small moderately priced Midtown hotel with personality. Rooms have names rather than numbers—the Taupe Room, Le Cordon Bleu, the Italian Room, the Lanai Room—and each has a totally different look, from iron and brass headboards to chintz to shoji screens. Some are charming, some are tacky, none is boring. Off the intimate lobby, Pisces Restaurant invites with a colorful room-size mural of the Côte d'Azur; L'Atelier Simbari, an art gallery, offers work by an Italian graphics artist; and the **Monkey Bar** serves up singers and piano entertainment amid whimsical murals.

60 East 54th Street (between Madison and Park avenues), New York, NY 10022. Tel: 753-1066.

The family-owned **Beverly** is the best value in the lineup of commercial hotels across from the Waldorf on Lexington Avenue. There are quiet, comfortable, good-sized rooms here, as well as suites with kitchens that are good buys for families. The lobby is warm and unpretentious, and there are a restaurant, cocktail lounge, and coffee shop on the premises.

125 East 50th Street (at Lexington Avenue), New York, NY 10022. Tel: 753-2700.

If it weren't for the tour groups that clog the lobby, the **Doral Inn** would be the top choice for a reasonably priced Midtown hotel with modern, well-decorated rooms. For those willing to put up with possible waits at the desk, however, there are rewards, such as a fitness center on the fourth floor with saunas and three squash courts, a 24-hour coffee shop as well as a bar and restaurant, and a convenient, money-saving, do-it-yourself laundry room.

541 Lexington Avenue (at 50th Street), New York, NY 10022. Tel: 755-1200.

The **Roosevelt** offers no glamor, but it fills the bill for those who want a clean, well-located Midtown business hotel with decent rooms, all the standard services, and moderate rates. **Crawdaddy Restaurant** serves up New Orleans–style fare; commuters headed for nearby Grand Central Station favor the Crowing Cock Bar.

45 East 45th Street (at Madison Avenue), New York, NY 10017. Tel: 661-9600.

## *Murray Hill*

An old brick façade and flower boxes filled with geraniums and trailing vines make it clear that the **Sheraton Park Avenue** is not the usual chain hotel. The paneled lobby with needlepoint upholstery and a library of leatherbound books is English country. The rooms upstairs have Chippendale-style furniture, with soft florals, long drapes, and old New York prints on the walls. Many have fireplaces (nonworking). Bookshelves and banquettes make the bar a cozy place for a fast lunch or to hear jazz at night. Guests are also welcome at the monthly lunch meeting of the Park Avenue Literary Club, which features authors as speakers.

45 Park Avenue (at 37th Street), New York, NY 10016. Tel: 685-7676.

Even the tieless doorman looks like a rock star at **Morgans**, the first high-tech hot property of Steve Rubell and Ian Schrager (see the Royalton). Among the celebrity guests so far have been Giorgio Armani, Bianca Jagger, Cher, Margaux Hemingway, Brooke Shields, and Boy George. No hotel clichés here—not even a sign out front. French designer Andree Putnam's black-and-white minimalist world is clean, uncluttered modern, from the optical-illusion cube carpeting in the lobby to the gray-and-white pinstripes on the beds and the stainless steel sinks in the bath. Furniture in the smallish rooms is functional—padded window seats lift to make room for suitcases and clutter, coffee tables have casters to roll where they are wanted—and all rooms come with both a refrigerator and a stereo. Prices are not as high as you might expect for a celebrity spot.

237 Madison Avenue (at 38th Street), New York, NY 10016. Tel: 686-0300.

The chic **Doral Park Avenue**, a small hotel with big-time ways and very fair rates, is treasured by those who discover it. The round entryway sets the mood, with chandeliers, marble, and brass. The newly decorated rooms are light, modern, and appealing; many have sweeping views of Park Avenue. Willing room-service people here will provide anything from breakfast in bed to a VCR to an exercise bicycle on request. Energetic guests are welcome at the health club at the more expensive Doral Tuscany around the corner. The Park Avenue Grill, with leather paneling and equestrian prints, has a cozy feel, and the sidewalk café out front is a Continental touch.

70 Park Avenue (at 38th Street), New York, NY 10016. Tel: 687-7050.

**Doral Court**, one of three sister properties in leafy Murray Hill, has just emerged from remodeling as the best value of the lot. The good-sized rooms are fresh and pretty, with entry foyers, king-size beds, and 25-inch television. Each bath has a dressing alcove with a vanity and a refrigerator. Four choice digs on the 15th floor have terraces with views of the Chrysler Building and the New York skyline. And the **Courtyard Café** downstairs provides a greenhouse setting and a hidden garden with a gurgling waterfall.

130 East 39th Street (at Lexington Avenue), New York, NY 10016. Tel: 685-1100.

The most interesting feature of the Japanese-owned **Kitano** is its two tatami suites with bamboo rugs, floor seating, and shoji screens at the window. Otherwise, rooms are motelish modern, and some could use redecorating. But rates are moderate and the hotel does offer a different mood, with a Japanese tearoom and a serene restaurant with an indoor Oriental garden.

66 Park Avenue (at 38th Street), New York, NY 10016. Tel: 685-0022.

## *All-Suite Hotels*

With double the space of a hotel room plus cooking facilities, each of these is a good value in its price category.

**The Lowell**, one of the city's smallest and most unusual lodgings, offers just 61 luxurious suites with fireplaces, libraries, full kitchens, marble baths, and a sophisticated mix of French, Art Deco, and Oriental decor. Breakfast, lunch, and tea are served in the lacy Pembroke Room, which seats just 35 and might have been lifted from a fine European hotel. The staff here outnumbers the guests, who range from California movie moguls to knowing Europeans who want both luxury and seclusion.

28 East 63rd Street (between Fifth and Madison avenues), New York, NY 10021. Tel: 838-1400.

**The Kimberly** was built as a condominium, but when the apartments didn't sell management turned it into an all-suite hotel with all the comforts of home, including a terrace with most one-bedroom apartments. The furnishings have an impersonal feel, but there's plenty of space, even in the studio suites, and 24-hour concierge service in the very tasteful lobby.

145 East 50th Street (between Lexington and Third avenues), New York, NY 10022. Tel: 755-0400.

There's no sign outside to tell you that the **Lombardy** is not just another posh New York apartment building. In fact, the studios and apartments are privately owned, and are rented out hotel-style by absent owners. This means that furnishings vary according to owners' tastes, but all units are spacious, and the rates are tops for the neighborhood. Guests can also enjoy full hotel service—including room service from the excellent **Laurent** restaurant off the lobby.

111 East 56th Street (between Lexington and Park avenues), New York, NY 10022. Tel: 753-8600.

The **Beekman Tower** belongs to the Manhattan East Suite Hotels group, which has nine properties in the city, most offering roomy accommodations for less than the price of a luxury hotel room. This one has a convenient location, top views, and a lovely Old World lobby with a handsome Persian rug and brass chandelier. The furnishings are traditional and the service is caring. **La Petite Marmite** restaurant offers fine French fare, and the **Top of the Tower** cocktail lounge on the 26th floor is dazzling at night, with superb views of the East River and the Midtown Manhattan office towers.

Three Mitchell Place (off First Avenue at 49th Street), New York, NY 10017. Tel: 355-7300.

**The Shelburne–Murray Hill** is perhaps the most attractive of the Manhattan East Suite Hotels, with Persian rugs, chandeliers, and antiques in the lobby, and room furnishings a shade above some of the other properties. Once again, the space and facilities are exceptional for the price. Lunch and dinner are served downstairs in a restaurant that doubles as a piano bar.

303 Lexington Avenue (at East 37th Street), New York, NY 10016. Tel: 689-5200.

Other Manhattan East properties include:
- ▶ **The Surrey** (the priciest of the group), 20 East 76th Street, New York, NY 10021. Tel: 288-3700.
- ▶ **Dumont Plaza**, 150 East 34th Street, New York, NY 10016. Tel: 481-7600.
- ▶ **Eastgate Tower**, 222 East 39th Street, New York, NY 10016. Tel: 687-8000.
- ▶ **Lyden Gardens**, 215 East 64th Street, New York, NY 10021. Tel: 355-1230.
- ▶ **Lyden House**, 20 East 53rd Street, New York, NY 10011. Tel: 888-6070.
- ▶ **Plaza Fifty**, 155 East 50th Street, New York, NY 10022. Tel: 751-5710.
- ▶ **Southgate Tower**, 371 Seventh Avenue (at 31st Street), New York, NY 10001. Tel: 563-1800.

## *Convention Hotels*

New York's largest properties (800 to 1,800 rooms) are first-class hotels, and, while busy, can provide any needed amenity. The Vista's location near Wall Street may appeal to some travellers. Most rates are in the luxury category.
- ▶ **Grand Hyatt**, Park Avenue at Grand Central Terminal (42nd Street), New York, NY 10017. Tel: 883-1234.
- ▶ **Marriott Marquis**, 1535 Broadway (at 45th Street), New York, NY 10036. Tel: 398-1900.
- ▶ **New York Hilton**, 1335 Sixth Avenue (at 53rd Street), New York, NY 10019. Tel: 586-7000.
- ▶ **Penta**, 401 Seventh Avenue (at 33rd Street), New York, NY 10001. Tel: 736-5000.
- ▶ **Sheraton Centre**, 811 Seventh Avenue (at 53rd Street), New York, NY 10019. Tel: 581-1000.
- ▶ **Vista International**, 3 World Trade Center, New York, NY 10048. Tel: 938-9100.

## *Budget-priced Hotels*

The **Empire**, right across the street from Lincoln Center, is one of the better budget choices in the city, offering no frills but big, freshly redecorated, attractively furnished rooms that are a sound value. **O'Neal's Balloon** on the corner facing Lincoln Center is a favorite New York sidewalk café before and after the concert.

1889 Broadway (at 63rd Street), New York, NY 10023. Tel: 265-7400.

The **Salisbury**, located near Carnegie Hall, offers a good central location, a quiet and pleasant lobby, spacious if undistinguished rooms, and the convenient, affordable Terrace Café. Most rooms also include serving pantries, making this a good bet for families.

123 West 57th Street (between Sixth and Seventh avenues), New York, NY 10019. Tel: 246-1300.

The **Gorham**, a small, quiet hotel opposite the City Center performance hall, is another top value, particularly the rooms that have been redone in the stylish renovation underway, in a clean modern Italian design. Many of the new rooms even have whirlpool baths. All rooms and suites offer kitchenettes and ample room for families. People hear about the Gorham mostly through word of mouth, and at the moment the grapevine is bringing a number of South American guests.

136 West 55th Street (between Sixth and Seventh avenues), New York, NY 10019. Tel: 245-1800.

The façade of the **Chelsea**, a historic landmark and literary shrine, bears plaques in memory of the likes of Dylan Thomas, Thomas Wolfe, O. Henry, Arthur Miller, Brendan Behan, Mark Twain, and other assorted geniuses who lived and worked here. More recently the residents have included Virgil Thomson, Sid Vicious, and artists who hope someone will know their names someday, which may tell something about the condition of the place. Rooms are big, cheap, and reasonably clean; many have kitchens, but they are *desperately* in need of refurbishing. The lobby is filled with art both Op and odd, and an equally diverse assortment of arty people. The neighborhood is similarly funky—but interesting.

222 West 23rd Street (between Seventh and Eighth avenues), New York, NY 10011. Tel: 243-3700.

The name of the lobby restaurant in the **Tudor**, Back to Basics, tells the tale. This is an establishment where looking at rooms is well advised. Some are quite passable, like 1612, a big "junior suite" with a platform bed and a terrace. Others are shabby and dreary. There's nothing near the price in this neighborhood, however, so the hotel stays busy and has a wide international mix, partly because it is so convenient to the United Nations. And there's a certain nostalgic charm about the Art Deco lady cutouts on the mirrored lobby walls.

304 East 42nd Street (at Second Avenue), New York, NY 10017. Tel: 986-8800.

Just a bit out of the way in the pleasant Carnegie Hill residential area, the **Wales** has Beaux Arts architecture, marble fireplaces, and hand carving that bespeak better days. Presently, it's a run-down but acceptable bargain;

new owners promise to spruce it up but say they will maintain reasonable rates. Stay tuned.

1295 Madison Avenue (at 92nd Street), New York, NY 10128. Tel: 876-6000.

## *New York Bed and Breakfast*

The most encouraging development for travellers within limited budgets is the blooming of bed-and-breakfast lodgings in city apartments, many in some of New York's best neighborhoods, where resident hosts have decided to make use of extra space to help with the heady rent bills. Some of these rooms are short on privacy, but all are strong on friendliness. Rates are $50 to $90 nightly for a double, including breakfast, and are frequently less for longer stays. The following registries have a number of listings around the city:

▶ **City Lights Bed & Breakfast Ltd.** P.O. Box 20355, Cherokee Station, New York, NY 10028. Tel: 737-7049.

▶ **Urban Ventures, Inc.** P.O. Box 426, Planetarium Station, New York, NY 10024. Tel: 594-5650.

▶ **Bed & Breakfast (& Books).** (Specializes in hosts in the arts.) 35 West 92nd Street (Attn: Judith Goldberg), Apt. 2C, New York, NY 10025. Tel: 865-8740.

▶ **New World Bed and Breakfast Ltd.** 150 Fifth Avenue, Suite 711, New York, NY 10011. Tel: 675-5600.

▶ **Hosts & Guests, Inc.** P.O. Box 6798, FDR Station, New York, NY 10150. Tel: 874-4308.

—*Eleanor Berman*

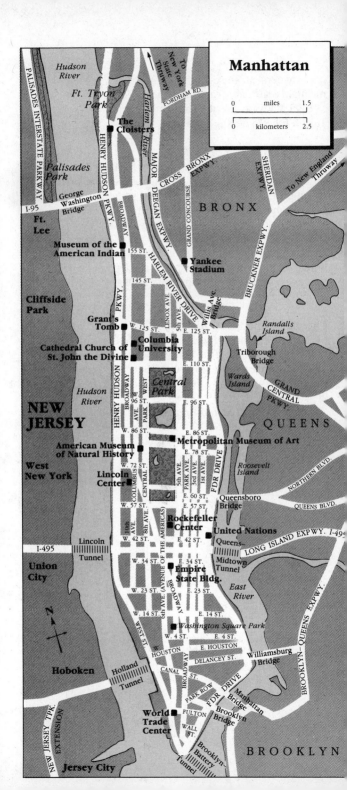

# NEIGHBOR-HOODS

## LOWER MANHATTAN AND THE HARBOR

*By Dwight V. Gast*

*Dwight V. Gast has written about New York City for numerous publications. He has studied the city formally as an undergraduate and graduate student at the city's New School for Social Research, and has been observing it informally for over two decades. He lives in downtown Manhattan.*

New York City's history starts with the settlement of Lower Manhattan. From its very beginning—long before Washington Irving's satirical *History of New York ... by Diedrich Knickerbocker* of 1809—the city's story has been an often amusing amalgamation of fact, fiction, and hype.

More than once it has involved vociferous confrontations between the numerous ethnic groups that have long characterized the city. The city's largest river, the Hudson, was named after English explorer Henry Hudson, who sailed into Upper New York Bay in 1609 on the Dutch East India Company's *Half Moon*. Another navigator, however, had already been there almost a century before. "We found a very agreeable situation located within two prominent hills," he wrote of the bay in 1524, "in the midst of which flowed a very great river." That explorer was the Florentine Giovanni da Verrazano, sailing under the French flag. When the tercentenary of Hudson's voyage was celebrated in 1909, Charles Barsotti, the editor of the Italian-American newspaper *Il Progresso,* took advantage of the occasion to dedicate a monument to Verrazano at the mouth of the Hudson in Battery Park.

Around the same time as Verrazano, Portuguese explorer Esteban Gómez entered the bay on a mission for the Spanish, but only the Dutch eventually settled the island. A permanent Dutch community called Nieuw Amsterdam was established on Manhattan in 1625. The following year Peter Minuit of the Dutch West India Company purchased Manhattan from the Indians ("Mannahatta," the "aboriginal name" described by Walt Whitman in the poem of the same name, is an Indian word meaning "island of hills") for the legendary $24 worth of trinkets, even though the Canarsee tribe who negotiated the deal only occupied the southern tip of the island.

Most of the original settlers were not Dutch, but refugees who had been living in Holland. Protestants, Walloons, French, and other groups so filled the settlement that by 1643 a French Jesuit visitor would write, "there may well be four or five hundred men of different sects and nations ... there are men of eighteen different languages." Ten years later, Nieuw Amsterdam received its charter as a town, and Director General Peter Stuyvesant had a protective wall built at its northern edge, on the site of what is now Wall Street. In 1654 the first of many Jewish refugees arrived when the former Dutch colony of Recife in Brazil was recaptured by the Portuguese. Though initially in Dutch with Stuyvesant for not adhering to the beliefs of the Dutch Reform church, they were allowed to remain, and soon another visitor would note that "the people seem not concerned what religion their neighbor is of, or whether he hath any or none."

In 1664 the English took command of Nieuw Amsterdam and renamed it New York. In 1673 its name changed again, when the Dutch briefly regained control and called it New Orange. (Ralph Waldo Emerson was later to call it "a sucked orange," well before it came to be known as the Big Apple.) In 1674 the town passed permanently into the hands of the British, who held it through the American Revolution until 1783. The following year it became the capital of the nation and the state. It held the former title until 1790, the latter until 1797.

After suffering from a British blockade during the War of 1812, the port of New York gained unprecedented prosperity with the opening of the Erie Canal linking the

Great Lakes with the Hudson, in 1825. By 1870 it was the wealthiest city in the nation, and the waves of German and Irish immigration through the port that began in the middle of the century were followed by others from Eastern and Southern Europe. In 1898 the five boroughs of Manhattan, Brooklyn, the Bronx, Queens, and Staten Island were combined to create Greater New York, then the world's largest city with a population of over three million.

The early years of this century saw great feats of engineering in the city. In 1903 the Williamsburg Bridge joined its neighbor, the 1883 Brooklyn Bridge, over the East River, followed by the Queensboro and Manhattan bridges in 1909; the IRT subway opened in 1904; tunnels opened from Manhattan to Brooklyn and New Jersey in 1908; the late Pennsylvania Station opened in 1910, followed by the present Grand Central Terminal in 1913; and skyscrapers shot up in lower Manhattan.

In 1924 a law was passed to limit immigration (and only recently has it begun to increase again, with groups coming from Asia, Latin America, and the Caribbean). The city's rapid growth and ethnic variety reached an unprecedented summit around 1930. The peak years of ethnic dysfunction were perhaps best personified by a Russian immigrant named Benjamin Sonnenberg, who in the 1930s invented for himself the lifestyle of an English lord in Gramercy Park—complete with an Edwardian wardrobe, a home filled with European antiques, and never fewer than six servants. He found the means to do so by single-handedly inventing the profession of public relations. With such local precedents as P. T. Barnum and F. Scott Fitzgerald's fictional Great Gatsby, Sonnenberg—and PR—could only have happened in New York, and are as much a part of the historical spirit of the city as anyone or anything else. "I'm the builder of bridges into posterity," he often said of himself, "building large plinths for little men to stand on."

Much else has been built since Sonnenberg's day—the city's great airports, the United Nations, Lincoln Center, commercial skyscrapers in Midtown and Lower Manhattan—but more than ever New York remains a city of bridges into posterity.

# LOWER MANHATTAN

The southern end of Manhattan is where the city began, expanded, and its economic power is still concentrated. It is one of the few places in New York where you can get a feeling for the city as a port: The expansive Upper New York Bay and the bustling South Street Seaport, with their modern and historical oceangoing vessels, are both located there. So is the outgrowth of their commercial activity: the economic center of the capitalist world, known as the Financial District and exemplified by the surprisingly narrow thoroughfare called Wall Street. To keep it all running smoothly—or merely running—the city has also placed its administrative buildings near at hand: Civic Center stretches from City Hall to Chinatown.

People ebb and flow in Lower Manhattan along with its waterfront tides. If you like crowds, you'll find good company all day long. On weekends, most of the activity takes place at the South Street Seaport and Battery Park, adding a sense of discovery to a walk in the Financial District and Civic Center; at night the entire area is always fairly deserted except for the seaport.

**MAJOR INTEREST**

The Statue of Liberty
Harbor views from Battery Park
The Staten Island Ferry
The Financial District
200-mile panorama from the top of the World Trade Center
The World Financial Center
South Street Seaport
Civic Center
City Hall
The Brooklyn Bridge

## The Battery

"The Bronx is up and the Battery's down," is how New York's geography was succinctly described in the Comden-Green-Bernstein musical, *On the Town*. At the tip of downtown Manhattan, the Battery is as far down as you can go. It takes its name from the battery of cannon that protected Manhattan at what was once the island's tip, coinciding with the current Battery Place. They were aimed directly at the area now occupied by Battery Park, which has been built up over the centuries with landfill. If the cannon were still there they might help to stem the tide of white-collar workers from the nearby Financial District who bring their lunch to the park on weekdays, and the hordes of pastel-clad tourists from more distant parts who traipse through it on their way to the Statue of Liberty during the warmer months. In lieu of cannon, the best defense against the crowds in Battery Park is to arrive outside the lunch hour on a weekday, when the area becomes a relatively snug harbor for the visitor. New York and foreign accents are then replaced by the cries of seagulls, the sounds of ships' horns at sea and ships' bells in the clock tower at the park's Pier A, and the lapping of waves at the ramparts. The smell of salt air stirred by bracing sea breezes and the panorama of Upper New York Bay can make Battery Park especially refreshing—and appetite-stimulating, but be forewarned that there are few amenable eating and drinking establishments in the area.

At the park's entrance on Battery Place, the Netherlands Memorial Monument briefly recounts the history of the settlement of Manhattan, in English and Dutch. A long mall then leads to **Castle Clinton National Monument**. Besides being further evidence of the defense of Manhattan (it was begun in 1807 as West Battery to provide protection against the British), the circular sandstone fort is best seen as a monument to New York entrepreneurship. In 1824 it reopened as Castle Garden, where in 1850 P. T. Barnum made a fortune staging a concert by Jenny Lind, a singer who he promoted as "the Swedish Nightingale." He drummed up even more publicity (and ticket sales) by planting anonymous letters in the papers claiming she was vastly overrated, selling out the house of 6,000 at the then-exorbitant fee of three dollars for the cheapest seat. The facilities were subsequently used as the Immigrant Landing Depot (1855–1890), and remodeled by the architectural firm of McKim, Mead & White as the New York Aquarium (1896–1941). Restored to its original incarnation as a fort, Castle Clinton hasn't forgotten its penchant for box office: It now sells tickets to the Statue of Liberty out on Liberty Island.

## The Statue of Liberty

Just beyond Castle Clinton, facing the Statue of Liberty, is a plaque commemorating Emma Lazarus, author of the poem "The New Colossus" that is engraved on the base of the statue across the water. "Give me your tired, your poor..." it reads, "I lift my lamp beside the golden door!" The lamp itself is now newly golden, owing to an elaborate restoration of the statue and its support structure undertaken to celebrate its centennial in 1986.

Since its inception, *Liberty Enlightening the World* (as French sculptor Frédéric Auguste Bartholdi entitled his statue) has been considered more a symbol than a sculpture. The French, who paid for the statue, supported it partially as an implicit criticism of the French government. (Literally, it is supported by an iron skeleton designed by Alexandre Gustave Eiffel.) The Americans, who paid for its pedestal (designed by architect Richard Morris Hunt), have used it over the past century to invoke concepts of liberty ranging from idealistic to mawkish. Writers, artists, and filmmakers have even made use of its powerful symbolism in various ways: Franz Kafka (who had never been in the United States) describes the classic immigrant's first view of it in the opening paragraph of *Amerika*, Alfred Hitchcock uses it for the climactic scene in *Saboteur*—it also provides the dramatic close to the film *Planet of the Apes*—and sculptor Claes Oldenburg once proposed replacing it with a monumental electric fan.

The Statue of Liberty's force as a symbol is matched by the sheer magnitude of its physical presence. The Lady in the Harbor stands 151 feet tall, and has a 3-foot mouth and a 35-foot waist; her pedestal lifts her up another 89 feet. The statistics take on real meaning as the ferry leaves the Battery for Liberty Island, Manhattan receding magnificently in the distance and the massive statue looming larger. Once on the island, you can visit its **American Museum of Immigration** to learn more about the huddled masses, many of whom seem to be in line for the elevator that takes visitors to an observation deck on the base of the statue after an often considerable wait in summer and on weekends. For the fit, the additional 162 steps that lead to the crown are worth the effort for views of Manhattan and the harbor.

**Ellis Island,** the primary point of entry for immigrants

to the United States from 1892 to 1925, is currently closed to the public, but its main building, the Ellis Island Immigration Station, is being converted to a museum of immigration, scheduled to open in late 1989.

## Back in Manhattan

East of the Statue of Liberty ferry landing in Battery Park, **Admiral George Dewey Promenade** offers an even more spectacular view of the city and the harbor. Facing out toward the bay you can see Brooklyn Heights to the left, Governors Island (the former Nut Island, the first island inhabited by the Dutch, and now occupied by the United States Coast Guard, which opens its surprising small-town-America community to the public each May during Armed Forces Weekend), the working-class borough of Staten Island, Liberty Island, and Ellis Island. Inside Battery Park are two noteworthy monuments. Just inside from the Statue of Liberty ferry landing is the 1909 monument to Giovanni da Verrazano by Ettore Ximenes, mysteriously vandalized in 1951 and reassembled in the two pieces of its present arrangement. Farther south is the East Coast War Memorial, in which a giant bronze American eagle by Albino Manca is surrounded by eight granite slabs rising sharply like the lower Manhattan skyline behind them.

The **Staten Island Ferry** leaves from a terminal near the end of the Battery. Primarily used by commuters from Staten Island, at 25¢ for a round-trip fare the ferry also provides a one-and-a-half-hour pauper's boat tour of Upper New York Bay, passing near Governors Island and Liberty Island and offering spectacular views of lower Manhattan and its bridges. An especially giddy tourist was Edna St. Vincent Millay, who wrote about one such trip in her poem "Recuerdo":

> We were very tired, we were very merry,
> We had gone back and forth all night on the ferry.
> We hailed "Good morrow, mother!" to a shawl-covered head,
> And bought a morning paper, which neither of us read;
> And she wept, "God bless you!" for the apples and pears,
> And we gave her all our money but our subway fares.

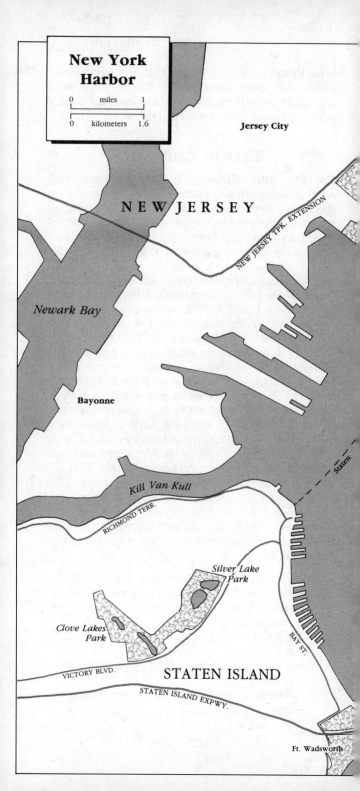

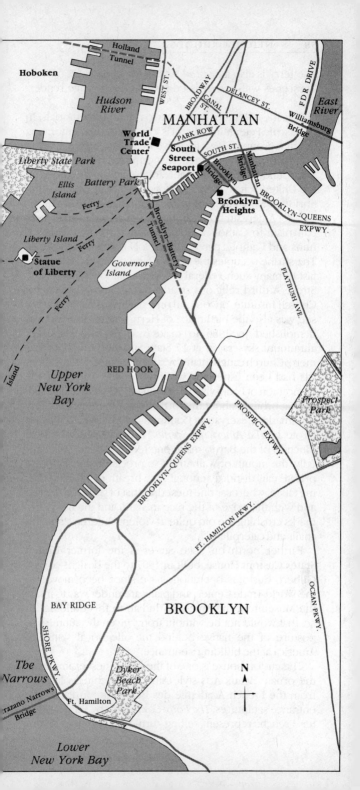

The ferry is also a favored setting for filmmakers, usually for scenes with star-crossed lovers or espionage rendezvous.

Outside of Battery Park are two religious memorials. In minuscule Peter Minuit Plaza is a flagpole commemorating the first group of Jews to arrive in this country, a Spanish and Portuguese contingent that came from Brazil in 1654 and founded Shearith Israel Congregation, the oldest in the United States. Farther uptown, at 7 State Street, is the Shrine of Saint Mother Elizabeth Ann Seton (1774–1821), the first American-born saint, who converted from Episcopalianism to Catholicism and founded the first order of nuns and Catholic parochial schools in the United States. The shrine occupies the former James Watson House, the last of many such Federal mansions that once lined State Street. A third religious structure, the beloved Seamen's Church Institute, once stood on a site just to the north (the site was also the birthplace of Herman Melville) and was demolished in 1986 to make way for the glass-and-aluminum skyscraper at 17 State Street. The loss of Seamen's Church caught many by surprise, since preservationists had been especially watchful in New York after the demolition of Pennsylvania Station in 1963, an act of brutality that brought about the formation of the New York City Landmarks Preservation Commission. But as Henry James wrote in *The American Scene:* "If it had been the final function of the Bay to make one feel one's age, so, assuredly, the mouth of Wall Street so proclaimed it, for one's private ear, distinctly enough; the breath of existence being taken, wherever one turned, as that of youth on the run and with the prize of the race in sight, and the new landmarks crushing the old quite as violent children stamp on snails and caterpillars."

Farther north on State Street is the former **United States Custom House**, built in 1907 to the designs of Cass Gilbert. Customs operations have since been moved to the World Trade Center, and plans are under way to move the Museum of the American Indian to this building, an act that would not be without irony, given the submissive posture of the native behind the allegorical statue of America at the building's entrance.

The customhouse is one of the city's finest examples of the ornate Beaux Arts style American architects learned from the French Académie des Beaux-Arts in Paris. The entrance sculptures, *The Four Continents* by Daniel Chester French, represent telling turn-of-the-century American attitudes to more than Indians. *Asia* and *Africa* sit at the most removed extremes (*Africa* is actually asleep), *Europe* is surrounded by icons of education, and *America* looks progressively forward with her own torch of liberty and enlightenment, accompanied by Labor turning the wheel of progress. On the cornice are 12 statues representing commercial powers from history, past and present (*Germany* was renamed *Belgium* during World War I). A more recent vision of commerce is provided by the Reginald Marsh murals of nautical themes in the oval rotunda indoors on the second floor.

Across from the customhouse is **Bowling Green**, the city's first park. Originally part of the Dutch cattle market, it became a green for the sport of bowling and later contained a statue of King George III, which was melted down for bullets after the Declaration of Independence was read publicly on July 9, 1776. The exuberant patriots also tore off the crowns that once topped the iron fence erected around the park in 1771, but the rest remains and was recently restored to its pre-Revolutionary glory. While there, have a look at the Bowling Green subway station. Clean, spacious, and bright with glazed orange tile, it is the most pleasant station you'll see in New York's heavily criticized system.

Two nearby buildings recall the area's former importance as the center of the city's shipping industry. The immense Renaissance-style structure at 25 Broadway was designed by Benjamin Wistar Morris and built in 1921 for the Cunard line. Its lavish lobby is now occupied by the United States Postal Service, which has preserved the ornate interior with its intricate (if badly illuminated) ceilings and frescoes. (Number 26 Broadway across the street, the former headquarters of the Standard Oil Company, has another fine lobby.) At 1 Broadway is the United States Lines–Panama Pacific Lines Building. It recalls more than shipping because it occupies a site that was once the tip of Manhattan, where the original Dutch Fort Amsterdam, the headquarters of George Washington and, later, Richard Howe, once stood.

# *THE FINANCIAL DISTRICT*

Some of the most expensive land in the world lies in this area of lower Manhattan, and only a privileged few can afford to occupy it. In fact, except for the residents of

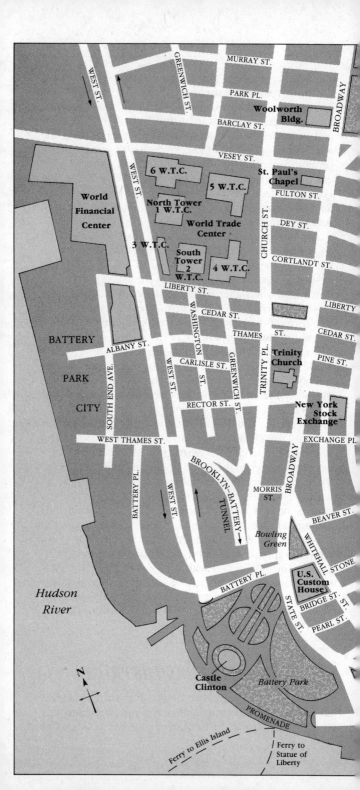

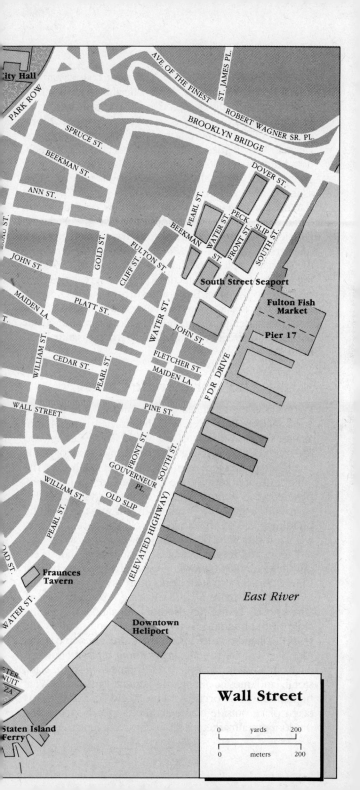

Battery Park City (and their permanent counterparts in Trinity Church cemetery), the Financial District, like London's City, is hardly occupied at all. The vast majority of its population consists of dayworkers for large corporations. In his 1853 short story, "Bartleby, the Scrivener," Herman Melville described a Wall Street "which of weekdays hums with industry and life, at nightfall echoes with sheer vacancy, and all through Sunday is forlorn." That aspect of the area has not changed.

What *has* changed are the buildings owned by the banking and other institutions that give the Financial District its name. Many corporations have built their headquarters in the area—the World Financial Center being the latest example—and the corporate emphasis on edifying edifices makes architecture one of the great pleasures of a visit to the area. But don't worry about neck strain: Down-to-earth attractions such as some of the finest outdoor public sculpture this side of Chicago and the salt air of the South Street Seaport will keep you pleasantly levelheaded.

## The World Trade Center

Dominating the Financial District (and most of the New York metropolitan area, for that matter) are Minoru Yamasaki's twin towers of the World Trade Center, two 110-story buildings rising like the prongs of a colossally unaligned tuning fork from the depths of Manhattan. The scale and monotony of the buildings are, in fact, completely out of tune with the romantic skyscrapers that surround it. If record-breaking height was the goal, the buildings lose on that scale as well, since their altitude was soon surpassed by the Sears Tower in Chicago.

Though there are attempts to humanize the seven-building complex (sprawling westward from the base of Church Street) with such works of art as a tapestry by Joan Miró and sculpture by Fritz Koenig, Masayuki Nagare, James Rosati, Louise Nevelson, and Alexander Calder, the scale of the buildings is too overpowering to allow the works to stand on their own. (For more accessible sculpture, see Ned Smyth's *The Upper Room,* a playful outdoor environment made of concrete embedded with glass, stone, and mosaic in nearby Battery Park City.) What humanization has occurred at the World Trade Center has taken place outside of the architects' plans, such as the outdoor greenmarket held Tuesdays from June to December and Thursdays year-round. Some of the more spectacular human activities that have occurred there have been appearances by tightrope artist Phillip Petit, who gave new meaning to the term "high wire" when he walked on one stretched between the towers, and mountain climber George Willig, who scaled the towers. There was even a spectacular animal feat at the Trade Center when King Kong, in the 1976 film, also climbed to the top.

The more conventional means of ascent are the high-speed elevators, which whisk visitors to the observation decks on the 107th and 110th floors of the south tower (number 2) and the bars and restaurants of the north tower (number 1). **Windows on the World** is a popular brunch spot among New Yorkers hosting out-of-town guests (with a waiting list as long as the building is high, so reserve well in advance; Tel: 212-938-1111), but the **City Lights Bar** will give you much of the same 100-mile view, in this case over Brooklyn and Long Island. The height, the narrow-paned glass windows, and a few glasses of wine from the bars' and restaurants' wide selection can truly give the impression of flying.

If you are interested in the theater, note the **TKTS booth** on the mezzanine level of 2 World Trade Center (south tower) before leaving. It sells half-price tickets for shows on the day of performance, and there is usually a shorter line than at its counterpart in Times Square.

A recent aesthetic and commercial challenge to the World Trade Center has been the **World Financial Center** in the heart of Battery Park City (just west of the World Trade Center). Designed by Cesar Pelli and Associates, the complex consists of four 34- to 51-story towers clad in granite and reflective glass and topped with geometrically shaped copper roofs, visible along the entire length of Sixth Avenue. It comprises some of the most exciting new public spaces to open in New York in years. Outdoors is the city's first plaza on the Hudson River, and indoors is the Courtyard—a glass-covered European-style plaza—as well as the Winter Garden, a 120-foot-high vaulted glass-and-steel structure graced by palm trees, where free concerts are often held during the lunch hour and after work; call (212) 945-2600 for information. Dozens of shops, restaurants, and cafés cater to the upscale crowd working at the center, world headquarters for such firms as American Express, Merrill Lynch, and Dow Jones. As modern as the facilities are, a stroll through this *dernier cri* in New

York's public spaces somehow recalls the promenades depicted in Currier & Ives prints of old New York, in a much more genuine way than in the city's more obvious tourist attractions.

## Lower Broadway

Vesey Street leads east out of the World Financial Center's northern edge. After one block you'll encounter 140 West Street, the entrance to the New York Telephone Building, a 1926 skyscraper by Voorhees, Gmelin & Walker, complete with Art Deco detailing on the façade and in the lobby. Its Vesey Street side has a sheltered arcade. At 20 Vesey Street is the former New York Post Building, a soaring Art Nouveau structure topped with statues by John Gutzon Borglum, the sculptor of Mount Rushmore. Take Church Street to Cortlandt Street, which crosses Broadway to become Maiden Lane, named for the young girls who did the family washing in a brook that once flowed along the site. On the northeast corner of Broadway and Maiden Lane you can check the hour at an unusual glass-covered clock set in the sidewalk. At 33 Maiden Lane is the entrance to Federal Plaza, where on the lower level is the newly reopened downtown branch of the **Whitney Museum of American Art**. It houses space for temporary exhibitions put together by the museum's younger curators, so the shows vary from just-on-the-edge to just-out-of-the-classroom.

Maiden Lane leads to William Street, where in a small park called **Louise Nevelson Plaza** there are seven black constructions by the sculptor. Around the corner, at 33 Liberty Street is the **Federal Reserve Bank of New York**, a rusticated stone building inspired by various Florentine Renaissance palazzi. The building stores one-quarter of the official monetary gold of 80 countries—more than Fort Knox. These billions of dollars of gold bars are available for public viewing during free one-hour tours (Tel: 212-720-6130 at least one week in advance; tickets will be mailed to you). Nearby is another fanciful edifice, the Beaux Arts New York Chamber of Commerce Building at 65 Liberty Street.

Returning to Broadway, you'll pass through Chase Manhattan Plaza, the first in a series of open spaces that eventually leads to the World Trade Center. Decorated with a sunken garden by Isamu Noguchi and the *Group of Four Trees* sculpture by Jean Dubuffet, the plaza is dominated by the glass-and-aluminum Chase Manhattan Bank building by the architectural firm of Skidmore, Owings & Merrill. The same team was responsible for the Marine Midland Bank, just ahead of it at 140 Broadway, which has a dark matte-black-steel-and-glass façade that plays nicely off the ornamentation of the nearby buildings reflected in it. The spacious plaza in front of the building, with its huge sculpture *The Red Cube* by Isamu Noguchi, is the most welcoming of the series of spaces. It is certainly more inviting than 1 Liberty Plaza across Broadway, another Skidmore, Owings & Merrill creation, this one a cynical concession to the newest zoning law, which requires public open space in exchange for more floor space. Even J. Seward Johnson, Jr.'s sculpture *Double Check,* a banker immortalized in bronze in the plaza, seems oblivious to his surroundings.

The Equitable Building at 120 Broadway was what brought such zoning laws into existence. Its massive bulk caused such a commotion when it was built in 1915 that the following year the nation's first law was passed requiring that buildings be stepped back at certain levels in order to admit light to the street, thus forming the "zoning envelope," or legal limit to building proportions, that has since shaped so many of the city's skyscrapers. Farther downtown, at 100 Broadway, is the Bank of Tokyo, an 1895 Beaux Arts building restored and adapted for use as a modern bank in 1975. The contrast of old and new extends to the building's art: outdoors are Greek-inspired statues above Ionic columns, indoors an aluminum sculpture by Noguchi.

Farther down Broadway, at the head of Wall Street, is the 1846 **Trinity Church**, the third such Episcopal church on the site. Its Gothic Revival complex with its well-maintained cemetery is an architectural oasis in this part of Manhattan. It has also long been a spiritual oasis. "And in this yard stenogs, bundle boys, scrubwomen, sit on the tombstones, and walk on the grass of graves," wrote Carl Sandburg in his poem "Trinity Peace," "speaking of war and weather, of babies, wages and love." People still go to the churchyard there to visit the graves of Alexander Hamilton and Robert Fulton, as well as to hear the concerts held during the lunch hour. The cast-iron lamppost in front of the church adds another old-fashioned touch to the scene. Dating from 1896, it is one of some 30 such "bishop's crooks" that remain on the city streets.

**Wall Street** gets its name from the wall Dutch Governor

Peter Stuyvesant built on the site in 1653 to protect New Amsterdam from the Indians. Today it is better known as the location of the **New York Stock Exchange**, that bastion of capitalism founded in 1792 when 24 brokers met beneath a buttonwood tree at the corner of Wall and William streets. The entrance to the building is around the corner of Wall, at 8 Broad Street; above its Corinthian columns is a pediment depicting *Integrity Protecting the Works of Man*. For a look at the trading floor, go to the visitors' center through the 20 Broad Street entrance weekdays between 9:20 A.M. and 4:00 P.M.; displays and recorded narration explain the chaotic activity.

Across from the stock exchange on Wall Street is another Greek-inspired building, **Federal Hall National Memorial**, a Doric temple built of Westchester marble. It stands on the site of the first English City Hall, later Federal Hall, where George Washington took his oath of office in 1789 (a bronze statue by John Quincy Adams Ward commemorates the event). The present building dates from 1842 and houses exhibits related to George Washington and other aspects of American history.

Farther down, Broadway leads to two other noteworthy buildings. The Morgan Guaranty Trust Company at 23 Wall was built by financier J. Pierpont Morgan in 1913 as an understated symbol of his wealth. The symbolism was not lost on anarchists, who in 1920 exploded a bomb in front of the bank, killing 33 people and leaving marks in the building that are still visible. At 55 Wall Street is Citibank, a blend of Ionic and Corinthian elements housing an impressively classical interior space.

At its intersection with Pearl Street (the original East River shoreline) you get the definitive view of Wall Street as the canyon of Manhattan, with the steeple of Trinity Church, once the tallest structure in the city, rising at the end. Pearl leads south to Hanover Square, where the Italian palazzo–style India House stands at number 1. Originally built as the Hanover Bank in 1851, it is made of the same brownstone so associated with the later town houses on Manhattan's Upper West Side, and, though the square is commercial, the mellow stone and the innocuous monumental statue in the middle of the square make it easy to imagine the area's former days as a residential district. The building also houses **Harry's at Hanover Square**, a meat-and-potatoes restaurant that gets such a serious drinking crowd from Wall Street that it might as well be called "Harry's at Hangover Square."

At 54 Pearl Street is **Frauncis Tavern**, a 1927 reconstruction of a tavern where George Washington bade farewell to his troops. Inside are displays of memorabilia from the Revolution and a restaurant serving food that some claim dates from the same period, but having a drink here is a harmless way of paying homage to history. More recent American history is commemorated nearby at the New York Veterans' Memorial in Vietnam Veterans Plaza (55 Water Street), a translucent wall of glass block engraved with letters from Vietnam soldiers and other writings. It is especially effective at dusk, when interior lights give the memorial an eerie glow. At the 55 Water Street building to the north there is another plaza, accessible by escalator, with fine views across the East River.

## South Street Seaport

Water Street passes many interesting sights on its way uptown. At the corner of Old Slip is the Postmodern Engine Company No. 10, and just down Old Slip is the Renaissance palazzo–style First Precinct Police Station. There are more plazas at 77 Water Street and at the I. M. Pei–designed building at 88 Pine Street, where a sculpture by Yu Yu Yang reflects passersby in a mirrored disk. The delightful public space at 127 John Street is full of brightly colored metal tubes and canvas canopies, and in case you miss the point, a lobby plaque announces with characteristic Gotham candor, "This building was designed to create an atmosphere of pleasure, humor and excitement for people." At the corner of Water and Fulton streets is a lighthouse that marks the entrance to South Street Seaport.

New York's busiest port district during the 19th century, the area fell into disuse over the intervening years, except for the ever-thriving Fulton Fish Market and a few pleasantly seedy seafood restaurants. Over the past couple of decades the area has been undergoing renovation as a pedestrian mall by the Rouse Company, which was responsible for similar projects at Faneuil Hall in Boston and Harbor Place in Baltimore. The old salt of the area has been substituted with a somewhat salt-free version of New York history, attracting everyone from tourists to beer-guzzling traders from the Financial District, with such attractions as a multimedia show called "The Seaport Experience" and a plethora of bars and restaurants with contrived names. For a more singular seaport experience, avoid the area on Friday evenings and weekends.

Despite the theme-park atmosphere, there is much history to be found amid the histrionics here. The old **Fulton Fish Market** itself, most of which is now located in a new brick building also housing suburban-style shops, supplies the most authentic energy at South Street Seaport—and is a perfect place for insomniacs, since the boisterous transactions are in full swing by 4 A.M. (Tours given later, at 6 A.M., may be reserved by calling 212-669-9400.) **Schermerhorn Row**, which runs from 2 to 18 Fulton Street, is an original group of warehouses dating from 1811 built by Peter Schermerhorn on landfill some 600 feet from the original shoreline; it gives an idea of what much of the area was like until just a few decades ago. Water Street houses the "museum block," where at number 211 there is an operating 18th-century print shop, and at 215 the **Seaport Gallery** with nautical exhibits. Historic ships are moored in the East River at Piers 15 and 16, from which harbor cruises on the *Andrew Fletcher* and the *Pioneer* also depart during the warmer months. Pier 17 is topped by a pavilion with magnificent views over the East River. Many of the above sights may be seen on the guided tours leaving from the visitors' center at 207 Water Street.

Present-day attractions at the South Street Seaport include various concert series held throughout the year, its own greenmarket (on Front Street) Wednesdays and Saturdays from June to December, and the well-known comedy club **Caroline's**. For an amusing preview of the Brooklyn Bridge, walk north on Fulton to 41 Peck Slip, where the real thing looms over a painted version of it in a mural by trompe l'oeil artist Richard Haas.

## *CIVIC CENTER*

Fulton Street leads from South Street Seaport a few blocks west to Nassau Street, another pedestrian mall, this time catering to the food and clothing needs of white-collar workers from the Financial District. Fortunately, not all the shops and streets in the area are so lacking in character. One of the oldest bookstores in the city, the **Isaac Mendoza Book Company**, is located around the corner at 15 Ann Street, a little street memorialized in a little song of the same name by Charles Ives.

At the north end of Nassau is Park Row, known as Newspaper Row at the turn of the century because of the newspaper offices that once lined the street, a fact commemorated by a statue of printer Benjamin Franklin at the intersection. (In keeping with the times, Park Row is now lined with discount electronics stores.) The street veers toward the left to **St. Paul's Chapel** of Trinity Parish on the other side of Broadway. Modeled on St. Martin's-in-the-Fields in London, it was designed by Thomas McBean in 1766. George Washington worshiped in the elegant Georgian interior, which contains a starburst (over the high altar) designed by Pierre L'Enfant, who laid out Washington, D.C. St. Paul's is the oldest surviving building in New York—a fact to contemplate while gazing at its steeple rising before the towers of the World Trade Center in the background.

On the northwest corner of Broadway and Barclay Street is everyone's favorite skyscraper, the **Woolworth Building**. Designed with heavy Gothic detailing (it was nicknamed "The Cathedral of Commerce" when it opened) by Cass Gilbert, the building was completed in 1913 and remained the world's tallest until the Chrysler Building went up in 1930. Frank Woolworth of the discount store chain paid for his building entirely in cash, an act depicted along with other amusing scenes in bas-reliefs in the ornate three-story lobby.

Across from the Woolworth Building is **City Hall Park**, the southern end of the few blocks where the city's civic buildings are scattered. Decorated with statues of patriot Nathan Hale and newspaper mogul Horace Greeley, the park's real centerpiece is palatial **City Hall**, a surprisingly small and genteel building for such a large and noisy metropolis. When it was built between 1802 and 1811 it was faced in marble on the south side and cheaper brownstone on the north side, the side then facing away from the city. Though the city is pinching pennies as tightly as ever, in 1959 it loosened up enough to replace the entire façade with limestone, and later converted the second-floor Governor's Room into a museum and portrait gallery.

## The Brooklyn Bridge

Opposite the east side of City Hall Park is the Manhattan pedestrian entrance to the Brooklyn Bridge. Immortalized in poetry by Walt Whitman, Hart Crane, and Vladimir Vladimirovich Mayakovski, painted by John Marin and Joseph Stella, and gloriously illuminated by the Grucci family's fireworks during its centennial celebration in 1983, the bridge's practical significance was perhaps best described by architecture historian James Marston Fitch: "The nineteenth century saw three great developments in structural theory: the enclosure of great areas in the Crystal Palace, the spanning of great voids in the Brooklyn Bridge, and the reaching of great heights in the Eiffel Tower."

A series of tragedies befell its designers John A. and Washington Roebling. Father John died of gangrene following a crushed foot he incurred while taking measurements for the bridge, and his son Washington developed the bends from taking pressurized caissons underwater to work on the foundations. After the loss of many men, the bridge was completed in 1883. It is composed of two Gothic-style granite towers, from which the world's first steel span is suspended from four huge cables and a vast network of wires. One of the best ways of seeing it is to accept poet Elizabeth Bishop's "Invitation to Miss Marianne Moore":

> From Brooklyn, over the Brooklyn Bridge, on this
>   fine morning,
> please come flying.
> In a cloud of fiery pale chemicals,
> please come flying,
> to the rapid rolling of thousands of small blue
>   drums
> descending out of the mackerel sky
> over the glittering grandstand of harbor-water,
> please come flying.

You can also, of course, cross over to Brooklyn from Manhattan on the bridge's center walkway. A fine evening at sunset is another nice time to do so.

## *NORTH OF CITY HALL*

On the Chambers Street (that is, north) side of City Hall Park is the old **New York City Courthouse**, a Victorian building now familiarly called Tweed Courthouse after William Marcy "Boss" Tweed, the corrupt New York City official who made off with $10 million of the $14 million budgeted for the construction of the building. You can see present-day politicos in action at lunchtime in two of their favorite restaurants nearby, **Ellen's Café** at 270 Broadway and **Roeblings** at 11 Fulton Street.

Across the street, on the northeast corner of Broadway and Chambers, is the last remnant of the area's past as a center for newspaper publishing—the outdoor clock that marks the building that once housed the offices of the *New York Sun*. (The Italian palazzo–style building, originally built for the A. T. Stewart Department Store, began a trend for Italianate commercial buildings in the city.) There are also two lobbies worth looking into on Chambers Street: Number 51 is the Emigrant Savings Bank Building, with its stately banking facilities on the first floor; number 31 is the Surrogate's Court or Hall of Records, an ornately façaded Beaux Arts building (the sculpture, by Philip Martiny, represents *New York in Its Infancy* and *New York in Revolutionary Times*) with a theatrical foyer to match.

Rising across Centre Street, which runs north of Chambers, is the **Municipal Building**, another Beaux Arts skyscraper, designed by McKim, Mead & White. Built in 1914 to house city offices, it, too, has become too small for the job, but many of the city's functions remain there—including the Marriage License Bureau. Many a couple can be seen ceremoniously leaving the building beneath its central arch, through which Chambers Street once flowed. In typical Beaux Arts fashion, the building is adorned with statuary. Adolph Alexander Weinman's *Civic Fame,* the tallest statue in the city (25 feet), graces the top of the building.

Through the arch, a pedestrian mall leads to three-acre Police Plaza, Manhattan's largest public space, dominated by an aptly arresting Cor-Ten steel sculpture by Bernard Rosenthal, *Five in One*. The Police Headquarters building is the large red brick structure toward the river. Like many of the nearby modern buildings, it was designed by Gruzen & Partners in the 1970s as part of a redevelopment program for this part of the city. The Neo-Georgian church in the plaza is St. Andrew's, which adds a comforting touch to its large-scale surroundings, as do the food vendors' booths set up during the warmer months.

Cross Foley Square, a low-lying area that was once the site of the Collect Pond, the city's reservoir during its early years. In the square in front of 26 Federal Plaza is Richard Serra's *Tilted Arc,* a rusting Cor-Ten steel arc that bisects the space, a strong artistic statement that has generated a deluge of equally strong statements that it obstructs the square. After much legal bantering, the arc still flounders in its place, though its fate is uncertain.

At 60 Lafayette is the Family Court Building, a black granite mass that seems somewhat alien to its function. A steel sculpture by Ray Gussow, *Three Forms,* stands in front of the building. Farther up the street is the side entrance to the Civil and Municipal Court Building, a plain façade enlivened by Joseph Kiselewski's bas-relief, *Justice.* (William Zorach's *Law* bas-relief is at the main entrance at 111 Centre Street.) Across White Street at 87 Lafayette is a fanciful building housing a community center for nearby Chinatown. Though it looks like a French château, it may be even more surprising to learn that it was originally a fire station.

Returning downtown on Centre Street: At number 100 is the notorious towering Art Deco prison known as **The Tombs**. The name was originally given to an Egyptian-style prison that once stood across Centre Street, though the menacing appearance of the present structure has equally deadly connotations: Architecture critic Paul Goldberger has described its front door as "one of the most brilliantly contrived, if evil, stage sets in the City of New York." Officially called the New York Criminal Courts Building, it hosts courtroom procedures in a system so overloaded that some take place at its special night court, a fascinating and free spectacle—especially if it's not compulsory.

Somewhat appropriately, the site of the intersection of Baxter, Park, and Worth streets a block south of The Tombs was the most dangerous slum in the city in the mid-19th century. Known as Five Points, it was the center for such street gangs as the Dead Rabbits, the Shirt Tails, and the Plug Uglies. People in the area lived in the kind of squalor recounted by Jacob Riis in *How the Other Half Lives:* "The family's condition was most deplorable. The man, his wife, and three small children shivering in one room through the roof of which the pitiless winds of winter whistled. The room was almost barren of furniture; the parents slept on the floor, the elder children in boxes, and the baby swung in an old shawl attached to the rafters by cords by way of a hammock. The father, a seaman, had been obliged to give up that calling because he was in consumption, and was unable to provide either bread or fire for his little ones."

Riis's documentation changed public attitudes toward

social injustice, and the construction of the Foley Square courthouse complex transformed the slum dwellers' former domain into a display of the justice system. Its strongest architectural statements are the templelike New York County Courthouse designed by Guy Lowell and the United States Courthouse by Cass Gilbert and his son, Cass, Jr. Both court buildings are replete with allegorical sculpture to the point that you begin to feel overwhelmed by the spirit of Justice. Lest you get carried away, venture into the New York County Courthouse and take a look at the fantastic zodiac depicted in its rotunda pavement.

Right behind The Tombs lies the southwest corner of Chinatown. But before venturing into Manhattan's corner of the Orient, let's go west into TriBeCa.

# CHINATOWN TO THE VILLAGES

*By Dwight V. Gast*

The generous section of Manhattan extending south of 14th Street roughly to City Hall is generally referred to as downtown. Its residents are fiercely proud of the entire area, often claiming to suffer nosebleeds if they venture above 14th Street. To be able to say "I live downtown" implies, at least to them, a character and creativity they find lacking in other parts of the city.

They have much to be proud of. Downtown Manhattan has the history, ethnic variety, and free spirit that for many is the essence of life in New York City. Those qualities, combined for the most part with a human-scale architecture missing elsewhere in Manhattan, make the extensive area a particularly pleasant place for the outsider as well. From its shops and art galleries by day to its restaurants and clubs by night, downtown Manhattan is perhaps the most exciting part of New York City.

**MAJOR INTEREST**

Avant-garde art in TriBeCa
Chinatown

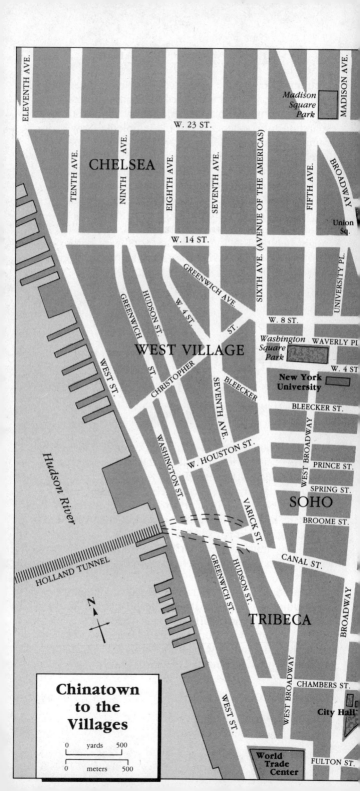

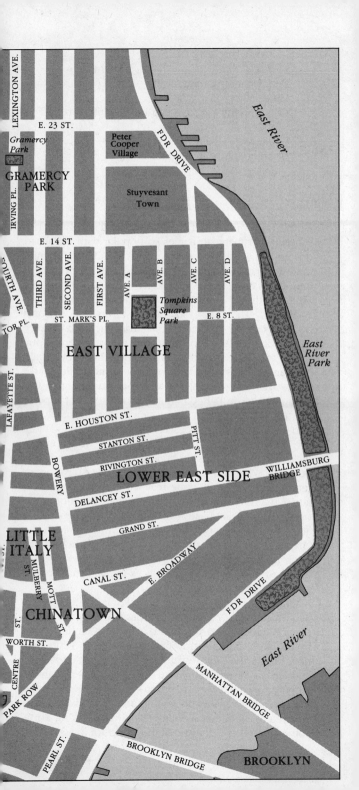

Remnants of immigrant life on the Lower East Side
Little Italy
Contemporary art and cast-iron architecture in SoHo
Greenwich Village
Counterculture in the East Village

## *TRIBECA*

Farthest downtown in the downtown area is TriBeCa, one of many portmanteau names so popular with real-estate developers in this part of town. It stands for *Tri*angle *Be*low *Ca*nal, referring to the West Side area roughly defined by three streets: Canal Street, Broadway, and West Street, with Hudson and West Broadway its main thoroughfares. The area's stalwart cast-iron and masonry buildings, many of them dating from the 19th century, were originally used for industrial and commercial purposes, and indeed many still are (therefore they usually have ample loft space). Following the gentrification of the SoHo area to the north, however, artists began to find cheaper space in TriBeCa, which became a sort of appendage to SoHo. Though development has inevitably occurred (the area provides convenient accommodations for Wall Street lawyers and other types who consider living in a loft "a lifestyle option" rather than a practical necessity), TriBeCa is still somewhat of a vestigial organ. Its art galleries never quite reached the blue-chip status attained above Canal, nor have trendy boutiques yet opened in the area—though there are some good bars and restaurants. It is that rough, experimental edge that characterizes the area today; mixed in with honest and often anonymous architecture, it makes TriBeCa one of the most visually rewarding places in Manhattan for the adventurous boulevardier.

One of the oldest of TriBeCa's cultural institutions is at 346 Broadway, the former New York Life Insurance Company. Its clock tower was added at the turn of the century by the architectural firm of McKim, Mead & White, and now houses the Clocktower gallery of the Institute for Art and Urban Resources, whose art exhibitions are always worth a look (see the Art section). So is the view from its terrace, where giant eagle sculptures stand watch over TriBeCa as its unofficial culture vultures. Looking north, you can also get a glimpse of the stretch of lower Broad-

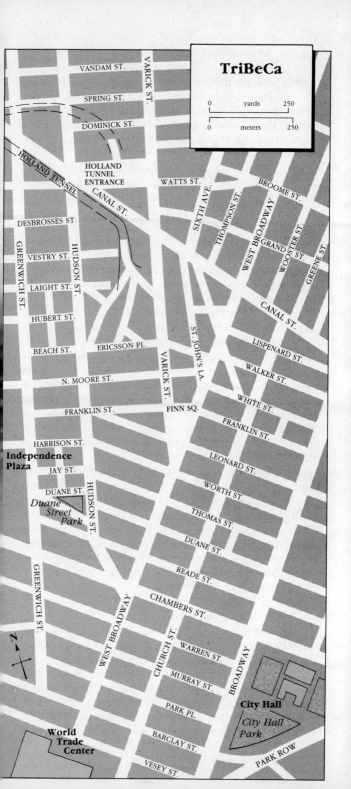

way (amusingly dubbed LoBro), which extends as far as the bend at the spire of Grace Church at East 10th Street and is lined with discount clothing and home furnishings stores. The church complex, by the way, is James Renwick, Jr.'s, architectural masterpiece and is worth a visit in its own right.

A block south, at Broadway and Worth Street, is the monolith called the AT & T Long Lines Building, actually a giant piece of electronic equipment clad in pink granite. At 8 Thomas, the next street, there is a Victorian building mixing brick, sandstone, granite, and cast iron as well as a number of architectural styles. Its ground floor houses the **Thomas Street Inn**, one of the area's most established restaurants. If you're interested in more contemporary art, walk two blocks farther south at this point, where at 22 Reade Street is an outdoor mural, *Sens Dessus Dessous,* by French artist François Morellet. Follow Reade across Church Street, another main thoroughfare for serious discount shopping, though the mural there by Jerry Johnson, *Oceana by the Sea,* adds a touch of whimsy. Between Reade and Chambers streets on the west side of Church is the **Cary Building**, which dates from 1856, making it one of the oldest cast-iron buildings in existence. The next block west is West Broadway (which continues north across Canal Street to become SoHo's main drag), where a block north Hudson Street leads to Duane Park (the once-trendy TriBeCa restaurant, **The Odeon**, is at 145 West Broadway). The park is a pleasant urban oasis, formerly lined with Federal houses and until recently the center of the Washington Market, New York City's food market, before the area was slated for redevelopment. There are still a few butter and egg wholesalers in the vicinity, and if you're there on a Wednesday or a Saturday during the warmer months you can pay homage to the past by doing some marketing at nearby Independence Plaza, which hosts a greenmarket then. Otherwise there are a number of alternatives for sustenance near Duane Park: Tommy Tang's, a Thai restaurant around the corner at 323 Greenwich Street; Puffy's Tavern at 81 Hudson; and the Sporting Club, at 99 Hudson, where jocks served by waitresses dressed as cheerleaders watch sports TV on a giant screen.

If you'd rather feast your eyes, there are other architectural sights around Duane Park. The Art Deco Western Union Building at 60 Hudson is clad in some 19 different shades of brick; the Mercantile Exchange at 6 Harrison Street is an admirable pile of stone and brick; farther down Harrison are six examples of Federal town houses transplanted from the Washington Market.

Head up West Broadway for further cultural pursuits. **Artists Space** at number 223 sponsors exhibitions by emerging artists; half a block east at 112 Franklin Street is the equally innovative **Franklin Furnace** exhibition center; a block north at 17 White is the **Alternative Museum**. Finally, to read about the art and artists you've been seeing (and more), browse through the **Printed Matter Bookshop** at 7 Lispenard. You can digest your reading matter, if not the food, at **Exterminator Chili**, a comfortable and inexpensive chili parlor at 305 Church, or pause at the roomy bar and restaurant Smoke Stacks Lightning at 380 Canal, on the southeast corner of West Broadway.

North across Canal is SoHo, but we will move east instead now, into Chinatown.

# *CHINATOWN*

Go east on the "Ca" of TriBeCa—**Canal Street**, named for the 40-foot-wide canal dug on the site in 1805 to drain the waters of the Collect Pond (then New York's reservoir) into the Hudson River—to Chinatown, New York's most ethnically distinctive neighborhood, where the signs are predominantly Chinese and many structures (including phone booths) are topped with pagodas. The area becomes especially animated during the Chinese New Year festival held in January or February (depending on the lunar calendar), when a giant dragon puppet snakes through the streets, martial arts demonstrations take place, banqueters fill the restaurants, and firecrackers explode nonstop. Gone are the opium dens that made the expression "going to Chinatown to kick the gong around" synonymous with getting high during the Jazz Age, but Chinese street gangs such as the Ghost Shadows still make drug trafficking of other types one of Chinatown's problems, which also include dense overcrowding from an influx of immigrants from a soon-to-become-Communist Hong Kong. Add to it the enormous hordes of tourists who flock to its famous restaurants each weekend, and you have the fascinating bazaar that is Chinatown.

Canal Street East provides a good introduction to the raw ingredients of Chinese food. Fish, meat, exotic vegetables, and fruits are sold in shops and stalls along its south side between Centre and Mulberry streets, and **Kam Man**

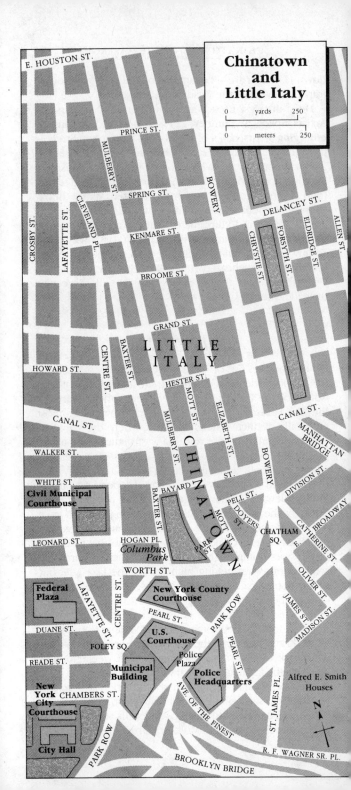

# CHINATOWN TO THE VILLAGES

at 200 Canal between Mott and Mulberry offers the area's widest selection of Chinese food, cooking utensils, and unusual pharmaceuticals.

**Mott Street** is Chinatown's main drag, where the dragon and other revelers parade during New Year's (for a noiseless taste of the scene off-season, have a look at the mural *Wall of Respect for the Working People of Chinatown* on the Bowery at Hester Street). This is the place to wander freely, to stop in at practically any of its restaurants for an inexpensive and excellent meal (tradition dictates ordering several dishes per table and sharing); coffee shops for such snacks as pork buns and custard tarts with tea or coffee routinely served with real cream; Chinese bookstores (**Hong Kong Bookstore** at number 72 and **Chinatown Books** at 70A have good selections); a Buddhist Temple (number 64); curio shops (try Tai Heng Lee at number 60); and the bizarre **Chinatown Fair Amusement Arcade and Chinese Museum** (number 8), a sideshow-type emporium where amusements include a live chicken that answers questions, wax displays of Chinese food, and the dragon that winds through the streets during the New Year's festivities. Don't neglect the side streets for further diversions: Especially rich is the arcade between Elizabeth and Bowery, which contains, among other things, the ever-popular **Phoenix Garden Restaurant**.

At the end of Mott Street is Chatham Square, surrounded by architecturally distinguished modern apartment buildings such as Chatham Towers (170 Park Row) and Chatham Green (85 Park Row) as well as the towering red-brick curve of Confucius Plaza, with its bronze statue of the sage by Tiu Shih. The Chatham Square area's architectural distinction is over a hundred years old, however. The Chatham Square Branch of the New York Public Library at 33 East Broadway was designed by McKim, Mead & White in 1903; the Mariners' Temple and Baptist Meeting House at 12 Oliver Street was built in 1842; St. James Roman Catholic Church at 32 St. James Place in 1837; the Chinatown Mission at 48 Henry in 1830; the William Clark House at 51 Market Street in 1824; the Sea and Land Church at 61 Henry Street in 1817; 6 Bowery (the site of the former Olliffe's Apothecary, the oldest drug store in America) in 1803; and a Federal-style house at 18 Bowery in 1785. On the south side of the square is the area's—in fact, Manhattan's—earliest extant artifact. It is the First Shearith Cemetery, the original burying ground for the city's Spanish and Portuguese Jewish community, dating from 1683.

## *LITTLE ITALY*

Though the Chinese now own the majority of the real estate in Little Italy, and the area's Italian residents have been systematically moving to Brooklyn and suburban areas, Little Italy retains much of its Italian character. It is most pronounced—almost theatrically so—along **Mulberry Street** north of Canal, where Italian community leaders have quietly asked the Chinese to post their signs in Roman letters only, a request they haven't refused. The street is lined with Italian restaurants, shops selling Italian food and other goods, and black limousines parked in front of brick-faced "social clubs" solemnly guarded by elegantly coiffed young men in tight clothing. Occasionally, *Godfather*-style gun wars break out, as occurred in 1972 when a member of the Colombo crime family allegedly shot rival Joey Gallo at Umberto's Clam House (there are bullet holes in the window to prove it), but the everyday street scene the tourist is likely to encounter is lower key, more akin to the infighting among street toughs in Martin Scorsese's film, *Mean Streets*.

The **Feast of San Gennaro** is the best or worst time to visit Little Italy, depending on your point of view. The street fair is named after the patron saint of Naples, reflecting the neighborhood's original residents' southern Italian origins. During the ten days around September 19 on which it takes place, amid the Baroque swirls of arches made of light bulbs and the batteries of Port-a-Potties set up especially for the occasion, thousands of people descend upon Mulberry Street determined to have a good time. Young Italian-Americans from outside the neighborhood prowl the streets along with busloads of tourists. The saint, whom old-time residents recall used to be celebrated by dancing in the street to the strains of a small orchestra, is currently commemorated by drinking beer, eating greasy versions of Italian (and, increasingly, Latin American and Asian) food on sale in stands along Mulberry, and playing games of skill or chance in other booths. Some come for what they sincerely believe is a taste of Italy; others are drawn to its decidedly grotesque carnival atmosphere. San Gennaro himself smiles on it all, his image decorated with dollar bills and paraded around the streets on September 19, then displayed through the end of the feast in a special grandstand constructed for the purpose.

The rest of the year, Little Italy is a quiet and peaceful place. Mulberry Street, as it leads north from Canal, is lined with restaurants and cafés ranging from the old-fashioned style of **Paolucci's Restaurant** (at number 149) in the former Stephen Van Rensselaer Federal-style house dating from 1816, to the high-tech elegance of **Caffè Biondo** (at number 141), designed by Antonio Morello and Donato Savoie, who have given a much-needed modern touch to many of Little Italy's establishments. (Conversely, another artist, Richard Haas, gave the area a retro touch by painting one of his trompe l'oeil murals of old storefronts on a wall space along the east side of Mulberry Street between Hester and Grand.) The modernity doesn't necessarily extend to Little Italy's restaurants, which tend to serve a heavier cuisine mutated from southern Italian immigrant cooking and virtually nonexistent in the mother country.

The intersection of Mulberry and Grand streets is the heart of Little Italy, where you'll find a variety of restaurants, cafés, and excellent neighborhood food stores (Italian Food Center at 186 Grand, Alleva Dairy at 188 Grand, and Piemonte at 190 Grand). If they were located in any other part of town, the food stores would be called gourmet shops, but here they are part of the remaining Italian residents' daily marketing routine. **Ferrara Café** (195 Grand) gets a particularly large crowd for dessert after dinner in Little Italy and Chinatown; **Caffè Roma** (385 Broome) a little farther north on Mulberry is more intimate. While in the area, don't miss one of the most delightful examples of the Chinese influx: **Pearl River** department store at 200 Grand, which carries a huge selection of Chinese merchandise of all sorts.

The copper dome you see looming to the west above Little Italy is the top of the former New York City Police Headquarters (the entrance is at 240 Centre Street), a Renaissance-style palazzo topped with a Baroque-type cupola—not altogether inappropriate given the area's historical ethnic affinity. After years of debate about what to do with it after its abandonment, the building has now been converted to luxury condominiums.

A block east of Mulberry, Mott Street (with its marvelous views of the Empire State Building neatly framed by the street's tenements) is becoming increasingly Chinese, but still has some of the most typically Italian institutions in the area. At 116 Mott is Fretta Bros. butcher shop, which sells a variety of domestic and foreign Italian sausages, as does DiPalo's at 206 Grand Street (on the corner of Mott), along with homemade and imported Italian cheeses. Farther uptown, Caruso's Fruit Market at 152 Mott Street is a remnant of the pushcart days (and one of the few places to get fresh basil in the neighborhood), and **Parisi Bakery** at 198 Mott sells loaves of fresh bread or makes them into sandwiches for you.

Finally, the pride of Little Italy is **Old St. Patrick's Cathedral** at 260–264 Mott Street. The site of the original 1815 Roman Catholic cathedral of New York, the present church was gutted by a fire and restored in 1868, only to have the archdiocese move to the uptown St. Patrick's in 1879. The church and its adjacent walled cemetery are well maintained and add a dignified air to the neighborhood.

## *THE LOWER EAST SIDE*

A large segment of New York's Jewish history is alive and well in the area to the northeast of Chinatown, called the Lower East Side. Though the city has had a Spanish and Portuguese Jewish community from its very beginning, in the 19th century Jewish refugees came from Eastern Europe as well. Most of them settled on the Lower East Side with the other immigrant populations, and remained there well into this century. Two films by Joan Micklin Silver, *Hester Street* and *Crossing Delancey,* offer historical and contemporary glimpses, respectively, into the area's Jewish community.

The Jewish population that occupied the area during much of the 19th and 20th centuries has since dispersed throughout the city, giving the New York metropolitan area a larger Jewish population than all of Israel. The Lower East Side is still about 25 percent Jewish (the rest is largely Hispanic and Chinese, with an increasing minority of artists attracted by cheap rents—an early sign of gentrification in an area that still has a long way to go to become another SoHo). Remnants of Jewish culture— most of them admittedly run-down—include synagogues, delicatessens, restaurants, and discount clothing stores, all of which attract Jewish and Gentile visitors alike. One note before going: Because the Jewish Sabbath runs from sundown Friday to sundown Saturday, most of the area's nonreligious sights are closed on Saturday.

Of the area's numerous synagogues, the first built for use as such (and still the most impressive) is **Congrega-**

tion **K'Hal Adath Jeshurun** at 14 Eldridge Street between Canal and Forsyth streets. An eclectic blend of Moorish, Gothic, and Romanesque architectural elements, it contrasts greatly with the surrounding tenements. Though it, too, is in a sad state of repair, it is slowly being restored to its former glory. (In better shape is the Bialystoker Synagogue at 7 Willett Street, between Grand and Broome, originally a Methodist Episcopal church built in 1826.)

Jewish history continues toward the east, where at 175 East Broadway is the building where the *Forward*, the Jewish newspaper, was originally published. Down the street, at 197 East Broadway, is the Educational Alliance, an organization founded by wealthy uptown Jews in 1883 to assist recent Jewish immigrants. Across the street, at 192 East Broadway, is the Seward Park Branch of the New York Public Library, where Leon Trotsky studied when he was in town. A block south and two blocks east is the Henry Street Settlement, a still-functioning community service organization that served as the prototype for such programs around the country.

For a vivid dose of the history of the area's Jews and other early immigrant groups, go to one of the city's newest museums, the **Lower East Side Tenement Museum** at 97 Orchard Street, near Delancey. Here domestic scenes from the past are reenacted in an authentic 19th-century tenement building as actors dressed as German, black, Irish, Chinese, Italian, and Jewish immigrants dramatize the events of their era.

Outside, the drama of contemporary life on **Orchard Street** continues with the passionate pursuit of shopping for discount clothing by famous designers from around the world (see Fashion), while the Essex Street area is the principal thoroughfare for more specifically Lower East Side institutions. One of its most distinguished contributions to American gastronomy—pickles—may be purchased fresh at Guss's Pickle Stand (42 Hester Street), Pickleman (27 Essex Street), or Hollander Kosher Pickle Stop (35 Essex Street), which pickles many other vegetables as well. Baked goods of all kinds can be sampled at Gertel's Kosher Bakery at 53 Hester Street. If you're still hungry you can try the **Grand Dairy Restaurant** (341 Grand Street) or **Ratner's** (138 Delancey Street), both of which are as famous for their meatless cuisine (Jewish law proscribes the eating of dairy products with meat products) as they are for their rude waiters. Crossing Delancey Street (that's the Williamsburg Bridge at its east

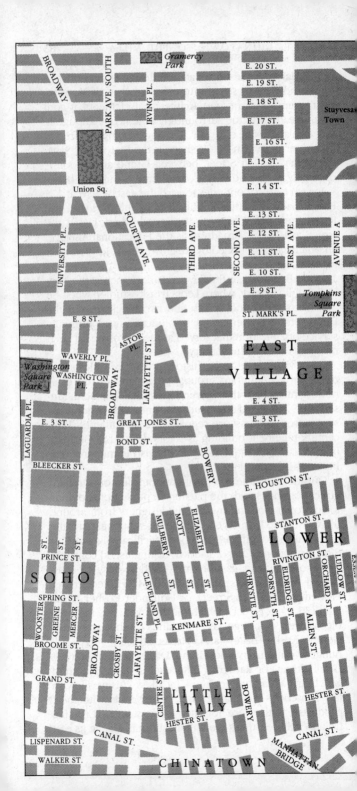

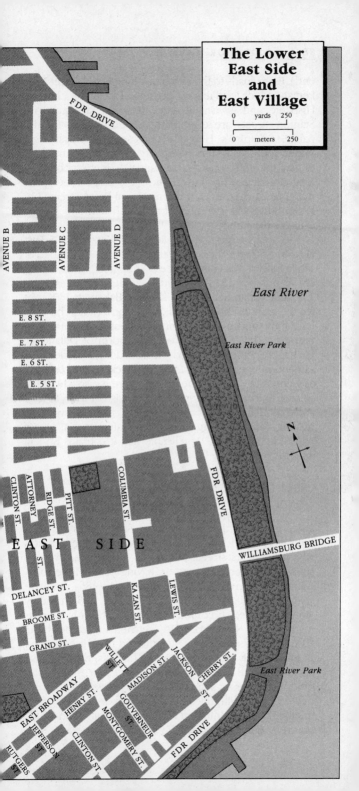

end), Essex leads to the two-block-long **Essex Street Market**, an indoor food market catering to the area's Chinese, Hispanic, and Jewish clientele. Between Rivington and Stanton streets are even more exotic delights for the palate: Schapiro's House of Kosher and Sacramental Wines, the only winery in the city (tours and samples of the syrupy stuff are given on Sundays), is at number 126 Rivington Street; Economy Candy (131 Essex Street) sells marzipan and halvah; and **Bernstein-on-Essex Street** (135 Essex Street) is a combination Jewish deli and kosher Chinese restaurant.

The area's largest deli restaurant is **Katz's** at 205 East Houston Street. The same street also has a number of other food shops (Ben's Cheese Shop and Moishe's Bakery at number 181, Russ and Daughters delicatessen at 179, and Yonah Schimmel's Knishes Bakery at 137), but for the grandest bouffe of all, have a meal (it may be your last) at the not-so-cheap **Sammy's Famous Rumanian Restaurant** at 157 Chrystie Street (just north of Delancey). Each table comes equipped with, in addition to the usual salt and pepper, a jar of rendered chicken fat (*schmaltz*) as a cholesterol-laden condiment; there is also a bottle of seltzer water (the owners call it "Jewish Perrier 1936"), and a container of milk and a bottle of chocolate syrup for making your own egg cream, the quintessential Lower East Side comestible. You'll note that it contains no egg and no cream.

# *THE BOWERY*

Once the road that led to Peter Stuyvesant's farm, or *bouwerie,* the Bowery today is famous for the derelicts who live on its streets and in its flophouses. Even its squalor is historical, however, having been where songwriter Stephen Foster died destitute in 1864, and the setting for *Maggie: A Girl of the Streets,* the 1893 novel by Stephen Crane, who called the Bowery "the only interesting street in New York." He sketched the scene there: "Long streamers of garments fluttered from fire escapes. In all unhandy places there were buckets, brooms, rags and bottles. In the street infants played or fought with other infants or sat stupidly in the way of vehicles. Formidable women, with uncombed hair and disordered dress, gossiped while leaning on railings, or screamed in frantic quarrels. Withered persons, in curious postures of submission to something, sat smoking pipes in obscure corners. A thousand odors of cooking food came forth to the street. The building quivered and creaked from the weight of humanity stamping about in its bowels."

The Bowery had been New York's theater and music-hall district in the mid-19th century and achieved renewed vitality after Crane's day when the Third Avenue elevated train brought people to its popular entertainments: John Sloan and other early-20th-century artists depicted the era in numerous prints and drawings. The theaters are gone, but the area retains a certain amount of architectural fantasy in the palatial Bowery Savings Bank (130 Bowery) by McKim, Mead & White, dating from 1894, and the 1909 Beaux Arts approach to the Manhattan Bridge (at the intersection of Canal Street at the edge of Chinatown), with its monumental sculpture representing *The Spirit of Commerce, The Spirit of Industry,* and, of all things, *Buffalo Hunt.* Today most people only see the Bowery through their windshields (often aided by an unexpected cleaning from one of the area's squeegee-brandishing derelicts) on their way to and from the Manhattan Bridge or Chinatown, or to shop in the restaurant-supply and lighting-equipment stores that line the wide street.

## *SOHO*

From Little Italy west of the Bowery, you can reach SoHo—*So*uth of *Ho*uston Street (pronounced Houseton)—by taking Prince west across Lafayette Street. First take a detour past the huge store selling castoffs of office buildings and their furnishings, **Urban Archaeology** at 285 Lafayette, to look at the **Puck Building** at 295 Lafayette, on the corner of Houston Street. It is the former headquarters of the satirical magazine *Puck*—hence the two statues of the Shakespearean imp above the entrance and at the building's northeast corner—and continues the tradition by housing the offices of *Spy,* a contemporary satirical magazine. Then follow Prince to LoBro, or Lower Broadway, where SoHo begins.

There is nothing lowbrow about SoHo, though. Such is its enduring trendiness that hip directors such as Woody Allen (*Hannah and Her Sisters*), Paul Mazursky (*An Unmarried Woman*), and Martin Scorsese (*After Hours*) have all set films there in recent years. Before that, however—in the 1960s—the area was "discovered" by two distinct groups: preservationists and artists. Preservationists liked the outsides of the 19th-century buildings in the area, the largest and most important concentration of cast-iron structures in the world. Artists liked the buildings' insides, former industrial space that gave them large studio space at low rent. "Oh, to be young and come to New York and move into your first loft," wrote Thomas Wolfe in *In Our Time,* "and look at the world with eyes that light up even the rotting fire-escape railings, even the buckling pressed-tin squares on the ceiling, even the sheet-metal shower stall with its belly dents and rusting seams...."

Our times have changed. In just a few years, the area's lofts have become luxuriously appointed, and most artists can no longer afford either to live in SoHo or show in its galleries. SoHo has become the most important center in the world for contemporary art, and its boundaries have spread every which way from West Broadway, still its main drag. Art-world figures engage in a regular ritual of looking at the new shows on Saturdays (the serious SoHo galleries are closed on Sundays and Mondays) during the art season, which extends roughly from Labor Day through Memorial Day. Gallery hopping has become a social event as well, so Saturday is also a good time to see the latest fashions being worn in the galleries, on the streets, or in such wateringholes as the **Cupping Room** (359 West Broadway near Broome) for coffee or tea, the **SoHo Wine Bar** (461 West Broadway between Houston and Prince) for a wide selection of vintages, and the **Manhattan Brewing Company** (40 Thompson Street) for beer.

## Galleries and Shops

Saturdays are when SoHo is most crowded and active, but if for some reason you'd prefer to avoid the scene, the galleries are open Tuesdays through Fridays as well, and the cast-iron architecture is always there. Now that SoHo has become full of trendy boutiques and other shops, bear in mind that most of them don't open until noon.

In the past few years, Broadway has given serious competition to West Broadway (note that the latter is a separate street four blocks west of Broadway) for the area's largest concentration of institutions—only appropriate since this area was New York's main shopping thoroughfare in the mid-19th century. The gourmet shop

Dean & DeLuca recently opened a huge new store at 560 Broadway (at Prince Street), which quickly filled with croissant- and cappuccino-consuming regulars. The building is also occupied by such prestigious galleries as Salvatore Ala and Max Protetch. This stretch of Broadway also has some of the area's most important buildings. Across the street, at 561 Broadway, is one façade of the L-shaped Singer Building (the other façade is on Prince) by Ernest Flagg. Toward the south is the Haughwout Building at 488 Broadway—a pleasant Palladian pastiche best known for its Otis elevator, which was the first in the world when it was installed in 1857. At 478 Broadway is another important cast-iron building, the Roosevelt Building, designed by Richard Morris Hunt in 1874.

SoHo's largest proliferation of galleries is currently at 568 Broadway, where you may want to stop into the John Gibson and Curt Marcus galleries to see what the art world is looking at. For a complete and current listing of the city's gallery shows, pick up a copy of *Art Now Gallery Guide,* available free of charge at most dealers' front desks.

At 583 Broadway is the **New Museum of Contemporary Art**, a noncommercial institution that mounts exhibitions from around the world, often worth looking at if only to be reminded that the art world can occasionally extend beyond SoHo. A closer example is the 1894 McKim, Mead & White–designed Cable Building at 611 Broadway, technically not in SoHo because it is north of Houston Street. On the fourth floor is the Vrej Baghoomian gallery, one of the most promising newcomers in the area (and from its windows you can get a close glimpse of the Forrest Myers wall sculpture on the north wall of 599 Broadway across the street). While in this part of "NoHo" (or LoBro), cross Broadway to 65 Bleecker Street for a look at the 1898 Bayard/Condict Building, the lone example of Louis Sullivan's architecture in New York.

Back at the corner of Prince and Mercer streets is **Fanelli**, which has existed since SoHo was known as the Eighth Ward, serving truck drivers from the nearby warehouses. It is still the only serious bar in SoHo, though its ownership has changed and the stains on its clientele's clothing are less likely to be from motor oil than from extra virgin Italian olive oil. Take a side trip to 163 Mercer to look into the Tony Shafrazi gallery.

Continuing on Prince: **Jerry's Restaurant** at number 101 has become the most popular hangout in SoHo even

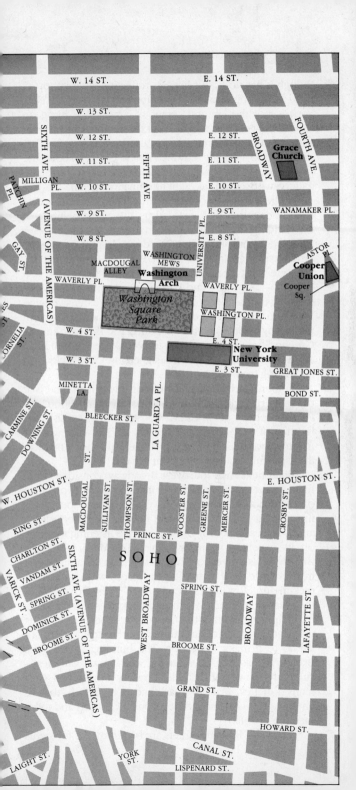

though it has no liquor license, reflecting another sort of dead seriousness in the contemporary art world. ("New York is not the cultural center of America," Chicagoan Saul Bellow once remarked, "but the business and administrative center of American culture.") Next door, at 103 Prince, stop into the Edward Thorp Gallery above the post office. It has one of the nicest spaces of any SoHo gallery, with a lovely skylight illuminating the art.

On the southwest corner of Prince and Greene streets is another mural by Richard Haas, this one a painting of the building's cast-iron façade on the brick wall of its east side and incorporating real windows. Important Greene Street galleries include Metro Pictures (number 150), Sperone Westwater, John Weber, and a branch of Leo Castelli—all at 142—and Barbara Gladstone at 99. While there, you might want a sample from the extensive wine list of the **SoHo Kitchen** (at number 103), perhaps accompanied by an inexpensive hamburger at the bar. Among Greene Street's cast-iron masterpieces are the buildings at 72–76 and 28–30, both designed by J. F. Duckworth and dating from 1872.

Another nearby option for reasonably priced food is at the cafeteria-style restaurant of the same name, **Food**, 127 Prince, corner of Wooster. Wooster Street is also the location of the Paula Cooper gallery at 155, which was the first to move to SoHo in the 1960s and still shows many of the same minimalist artists from that era.

Prince next runs into West Broadway, considered the main street of SoHo. Toward the north are two Italian oases: **Rizzoli Bookstore** (454 West Broadway) specializes in international art books and international periodicals and is a great place for browsing while listening to music on its excellent sound system; **I Tre Merli** (463 West Broadway) is a cavernous high-tech Italian restaurant serving palatable food or sparkling *prosecco* wine for a quick pick-me-up. Toward the south, at 417 West Broadway, is the Mary Boone gallery, whose high prices and patronizing help have made it the Gucci of the contemporary art world, though it's often a direct conduit from an artist's studio to a major collection. The building at 420 West Broadway has housed so many well-known galleries—currently Leo Castelli, Charles Cowles, 49th Parallel, Germans Van Eck, Marilyn Pearl, and Sonnabend—that its entrance has become a rendezvous for friends and tours meeting in SoHo.

Spring and Broome streets are better known for sights

other than art galleries. Among them, **Spring Street Books** at 169 and **Jaap Rietman**'s art bookstore at 134 draw a lively crowd, as does the **Spring Street Bar and Restaurant** (162 Spring). The outstanding piece of architecture on the street is the 1870 cast-iron building by Nicholas Whyte at number 101, which has a façade pierced with ample expanses of glass. On Broome Street, the **Broome Street Bar** (363 West Broadway) is a good place for an inexpensive hamburger in preparation for an architectural field day: number 484 is an 1890 Romanesque brick building by Alfred Zucker; numbers 478 (1885), 475 (1873), 461 (1871), and 455 (1873) are all cast-iron buildings by Griffith Thomas.

Before leaving the area you may want to locate some socio-cultural phenomena in SoHo that might bring you back to pursue special interests. On its southern fringes are the **Performing Garage**, a long-established experimental theater at 33 Wooster, and the **Museum of Holography** at 11 Mercer, where there are crowd-pleasing displays of three-dimensional laser photography. Toward the west are the **Film Forum**, at 57 Watts, which shows noncommercial films (the Thalia SoHo, at 15 Vandam Street, is a revival house); the **New York City Fire Museum** at 278 Spring, which has the most comprehensive collection of fire-fighting equipment in the country; **White Columns**, a sculpture gallery at 325 Spring; and the **Ear Inn**, a funky café-restaurant at 326 Spring. The latter contrasts greatly with the studied 1930s decor of the **Canal Bar** at 511 Greenwich Street around the corner—New York's latest celebrity hangout.

## The South Village

Perhaps the most relaxing part of what is now called SoHo is the long-standing residential area once known as the South Village at its west end, incorporating Thompson, Sullivan, and MacDougal streets south of Houston. Formerly predominantly Italian, the area retains that flavor in such quaint shops as the Vesuvio Bakery at 160 Prince, **Café Borgia II** at 161 Prince, Lanciani Pastry at 177 Prince, and the Melampo food store at 105 Sullivan. Over the past few years, however, its Portuguese population has quietly increased. Its parish church, dedicated to Saint Anthony of Padua (who, coincidentally, was born in Lisbon), holds an Italian street fair on Sullivan in June, but gives mass in Portuguese. The M & O Market at 124 Thompson is one of the few places in town where you can purchase Portuguese fish, cheese, sausages, olives, olive oil, and mineral water.

There is a pleasant Federal–Greek Revival house at 203 Prince and Federal houses on the detached residential streets of Charlton, King, and Vandam—now given landmark status—beyond Sixth Avenue, but a simple stroll in the area with no preconceived notions about compulsive sight-seeing adds a nice down-to-earth, real-people touch after spending a day among lofty trend setters. You can fortify yourself with provisions from the aforementioned Italian or Portuguese food shops, or perhaps some *charcuterie* from **Raoul's Butcher Shop** at 179 Prince (no pretense here either—they really are French); if you'd prefer sitting down, dinner at either **Raoul's** at 180 Prince (the steak and *pommes frites* at the bar is a less-expensive option here) or **Provence** at 38 MacDougal will end the day's ramblings on a mellow, Continental note.

## *GREENWICH VILLAGE*

If you ask people in SoHo how to get to Greenwich Village, their answer might require some translating. "The Village?" they'll say, meaning Greenwich Village, "Take Sixth Avenue" (what all New Yorkers call Avenue of the Americas) "across House-ton uptown" (north). Indeed, at that point Avenue of the Americas really does live up to its good-neighborly name. Thanks to a 1976 restoration, it almost resembles a boulevard from some South American capital in its broadness and the use of pattern in its pavement, and provides a great entrance (and contrast) to the narrow, winding streets of the Village.

And wind they do, even though they lie within the area of the grid plan imposed on Manhattan beginning in 1808. (West 4th Street intersects with West 10th, 11th, and 12th streets in the Village, to the consternation of tourists and residents alike.) The reason is that the area had long been established, first as an Algonquin Indian settlement, then as a Dutch tobacco plantation, and finally as a small British town called Greenwich, which enjoyed such a pleasant climate it was used by residents of New York in the early 19th century as a refuge from smallpox and yellow-fever epidemics. Its reputation as a haven for artists and writers dates from the late 19th century, when John La Farge, Winslow Homer, Mark Twain, Henry

James, and others lived there. In this century John Sloan, Edward Hopper, Eugene O'Neill, Edna St. Vincent Millay, Edmund Wilson, and many others continued the tradition, which died out after the inevitable rising rents drove the Beat poets and beatniks away. Paul Mazursky's film *Next Stop, Greenwich Village* represents the swan song of that era.

Somehow, Greenwich Village maintains its mystique. As recently as 1971 John Lennon said, "I should have been born in the Village, that's where I belong." And today a bohemian feeling can still be sensed in its cafés, restaurants, and clubs, which are, admittedly, visited mostly by outsiders. Even among its residents, however—students and professors, gays and straights, ethnics and middle class—a tolerant and pleasant community spirit prevails. It can be experienced on a person-to-person basis during the area's numerous "block parties," fund-raising and social events held throughout the year by community groups; the ragtag Annual Village Halloween Parade also attracts a good-natured group of revelers and outrageously costumed marchers from inside and outside the area.

## The West Village

The area west of Sixth Avenue between Houston and 14th streets has the largest amount of the atmosphere and architecture associated with the Village, and you can get a preview of it by looking east up narrow Minetta Street near the intersection of Sixth Avenue and Bleecker. For a strong taste of Greenwich Village's Italian community, follow **Bleecker Street** north: The parish church of Our Lady of Pompeii (which holds a street festival each July) is at the intersection of Carmine Street; there are baked goods at Rocco's (number 243), Dellarovere and Musa (245), and Zito's (259); various foods are sold at Faicco's Pork Store (260), Zampognaro (262), Mario Bosco (263), and Ottomanelli & Sons (281).

Take Leroy Street (which has a nice array of residential architecture) across Bedford and Seventh Avenue South to St. Luke's Place, a stunning row of brownstone houses dating from the 1850s. Mayor Jimmy Walker lived at number 6, which accounts for the lanterns at the entrance, an old New York custom for indicating the mayor's residence. St. Luke's leads to Hudson Street, where just south of number 487 is the church of St. Luke-in-the-Fields, which stood on the river's edge when it was built in 1821, before the landfill that extended the island. Number 487, the first in a series of Federal houses, was once the residence of Bret Harte, whose tales of life in California mining camps earned him a literary reputation in the United States and Great Britain in the late 19th century.

A block north is **Christopher Street**, the center of New York's gay community. Gone are the days of the pre-AIDS 1970s so sensationalistically depicted in William Friedkin's film *Cruising,* but the street scene still gets quite active on Gay Pride Day each June, when participants in the parade down Fifth Avenue—including Rollerina, a drag queen who has achieved celebrity status by rollerskating in the streets in a flurry of chiffon waving her magic wand—congregate in and around Christopher Street afterward. There are a number of establishments in the area that cater to a homosexual clientele: On Christopher itself are two men's bars—Ty's at number 114 and Boots & Saddle at 76—as well as the **Oscar Wilde Memorial Bookshop** at number 15. The Grove Club (70 Grove Street) and The Cubbyhole (438 Hudson) are lesbian bars; **Marie's Crisis Café** (59 Grove Street) is where men gather to sing show tunes in Thomas Paine's former home (the name of the establishment is a reference to one of the patriot's publications); and The Monster (80 Grove) offers drag cabaret and video. Rougher bars are found, appropriately enough, closer to the waterfront at the west end of Christopher. The community is also tolerant of outsiders, who come for off-Broadway theater at the **Lucille Lortel** (121 Christopher), shopping at such specialty shops as Li-Lac Chocolates at 120 Christopher, McNulty's Tea & Coffee provisioners at 109 Christopher, and the Pleasure Chest at 156 Seventh Avenue South, which sells sexual equipment for all persuasions.

From Christopher, head south down Bedford Street for a leisurely stroll around the West Village's most characteristic residential streets, where many of the houses date from the early 1800s. The ramshackle structure at 102 Bedford has a characteristically Greenwich Village history: Originally a town house built in 1830, in 1926 it reopened in its elaborate present state as "Twin Peaks," a haven for artists, writers, and actors. Number 86 Bedford is the secret entrance to **Chumley's**, a quiet bar that was formerly a speakeasy with a back door leading to Barrow Street for hasty retreats; 75½ Bedford is the narrowest residence in the city (9½ feet wide), but once housed one of the Village's most expansive residents, the poet Edna St. Vincent Millay (given her middle name from another Village institution, St. Vincent's Hospital). If you are interested in historical residences, turn right on Commerce Street where Washington Irving lived at number 11 and Aaron Burr at number 17.

Nearby, 17 Barrow houses **One If By Land**, a restaurant serving excellent Continental cuisine, but there are a number of nearby options for traditional American cuisine well suited to the neighborhood's architecture: **Ye Waverly Inn** up at 16 Bank Street is famous for its chicken potpie; **The Coach House** at 110 Waverly Place east of Sixth Avenue serves southern food in a town-house setting; and the **Pink Teacup** at 42 Grove Street specializes in soul food. Traditional Village drinking establishments include the **White Horse Tavern** at 567 Hudson Street (where Dylan Thomas had his booze-laden last supper before being taken to St. Vincent's Hospital) and the bar at the **Lion's Head** at 59 Christopher east of Seventh, which still gets a literary crowd from the days when the *Village Voice* offices were nearby.

## Jefferson Market Area

Across Seventh Avenue South, Waverly Place leads to—characteristically—Waverly Place. The street intersects itself at the triangle-shaped Northern Dispensary, which once dispensed medicine to Edgar Allan Poe, and is known as the building with one side on two streets (the junction of Grove and Christopher) and two sides on one street (Waverly Place). Follow Waverly Place east to Gay Street, which, though it intersects Christopher, was so called as far back as 1827, long before the word got its present-day homosexual connotation. The original meaning of its frivolity is best recalled at number 14, where Ruth McKenney wrote *My Sister Eileen*, the definitive play (later made into a musical and two films) about the time-honored tradition of Midwesterners moving to New York City.

At the other end of Gay, follow Christopher east to Greenwich Avenue (Note: Greenwich *Street*, way to the west, is a different entity); turn left on Greenwich and right on West 10th Street to see two more narrow Village streets: **Patchin Place** to the left before Sixth Avenue (John Masefield, Theodore Dreiser, and E. E. Cummings all lived there), and Milligan Place to the left on Sixth.

Take Sixth Avenue a block north to 11th Street, where

on the northwest corner is one of many pizzerias in town that claims to be the original Ray's Pizza: The permanent line of loyal patrons is testimony that this is one of the best, if not the oldest. Across Sixth Avenue, at 76 West 11th Street, is the Second Shearith Israel Cemetery, a peaceful triangular plot (it was twice its present size until 11th Street was expanded in 1830), used by the congregation of the city's Spanish and Portuguese synagogue from 1805 to 1829. Across the street is an entrance to the main buildings of the **New School for Social Research**, founded in 1919 as an educational institution for adults, and referred to by Thomas Wolfe as the "School for Utility Cultures." Its graduate school at 65 Fifth Avenue enjoys a reputation for excellence in the academic world, particularly in the social sciences (Hannah Arendt and other exiled European intellectuals taught there), but its adult education division is better known among New Yorkers, who take courses for edification in an unusual variety of subjects (often merely as a pretext for meeting other adults, married and single) in its evening division. Walk through the school's pleasant sculpture garden in the main building to the 12th Street exit for a look at its 66 West 12th Street building, designed (as was its auditorium) by Joseph Urban in 1930. Room 712 in the building houses the recently restored 600-square-foot mural *The Coming Together of the Races,* painted by Mexican artist Jose Clemente Orozco in 1931.

Heading back down Sixth Avenue, take a look at the towering Victorian Gothic building at number 425. It was originally a courthouse, designed by Frederick Clarke Withers and Calvert Vaux (the architect of Central Park) in 1876. It is now the last remnant of a complex that included a women's jail, firehouse, and market on the adjacent property, now a bright spot of landscaping. Thanks to a 1967 conversion by Giorgio Cavaglieri, the building houses the **Jefferson Market** branch of the New York Public Library, though the neighborhood's most gentrified marketing takes place across the avenue at Balducci's, number 424. At 414 is C. O. **Bigelow Chemists**. Begun in 1838, it is New York's oldest continuously operating pharmacy. The famous counter that Truman Capote, Mel Brooks, and others once lunched at is gone; in its place, however, are more of the fine domestic and imported pharmaceuticals and grooming products for which the establishment is famous.

Head east on West 10th Street, which, like West 9th, 11th,

and 12th streets between Sixth Avenue and University Place, is a neatly combed version of the twisting streets found in the West Village, complete with trees, 18th-century architecture, and literary associations (Mark Twain lived briefly at number 14, as its plaque commemorates). On the northwest corner of Fifth Avenue and West 10th Street is the 1840 Church of the Ascension, which contains stained-glass windows and an altar mural by John La Farge and a marble altar relief by Augustus Saint-Gaudens. At 47 Fifth Avenue, between 11th and 12th streets, is the Salmagundi Club, the oldest artists' club in America. The club was founded in 1870 at its present site, an 1853 mansion (the avenue was once lined with such residences). Among its members were John La Farge, Louis Comfort Tiffany, and Stanford White, and it still sponsors exhibitions, worth attending more for a look at the building's Victorian interior than its members' art—the best places for that nearby are the **Forbes Magazine Galleries** at 60 Fifth Avenue, famous for their Fabergé eggs, and the **Grey Art Gallery** at 33 Washington Place, which mounts temporary exhibitions to suit all shades of fancy.

## Washington Square

Head south toward the arch of Washington Square—traditionally considered the heart of the Village—on this stretch of Fifth Avenue, one of the most pleasant few blocks for strolling in the city. At 1 Fifth Avenue is a towering apartment building with a popular bar-restaurant, **One Fifth**, on the ground floor; the building's south side flanks **Washington Mews**, originally stables behind the town houses along Washington Square North. (Its continuation, **MacDougal Alley**, lies behind the huge building at 2 Fifth Avenue and is entered from MacDougal Street.) The houses themselves are considered the finest examples of the Greek Revival style in America, and provided the setting for Henry James's novel *Washington Square,* though the actual house, number 18, where his grandmother lived was torn down in 1950 for the cumbersome 2 Fifth Avenue apartment building. Over the years, John Dos Passos, Edward Hopper, and others were all fortunate enough to have lived in the houses, known as The Row.

The **Washington Arch**, which marks the beginning of Fifth Avenue, was designed by Stanford White to commemorate the centenary of George Washington's 1789 inauguration, replacing a temporary wooden structure with marble in 1892. The statue of *Washington as President* on the west pier of the arch is by Alexander Stirling Calder; Herman MacNeil is responsible for the east-pier statue, *Washington as Commander-in-Chief*.

As if in homage to the staid Washington Square residents portrayed by Henry James, both statues have their backs turned on the lively scene in the square. A walk through it can often be an urban obstacle course—dodging joggers, frantic frisbee players, and skateboarders, and drug dealers offering what sounds like "Sex! Sex!" but is actually street parlance for a type of marijuana called sensimillia. The more Jamesian residents of the area may wish that the square return to its former function as a hanging gallows (executions took place from the giant elm tree—said to be the oldest in the city—in the northwest section of the park) and potter's field, but the scene is generally quite harmless, dominated by the youth of **New York University**, the institution that owns most of the real estate around Washington Square.

On the square's south side is the Judson Memorial Baptist Church, an 1892 Romanesque church by McKim, Mead & White that contains more stained glass by John La Farge and a relief by Herbert Adams done to the designs of Augustus Saint-Gaudens. In the 1960s and 1970s it housed the Judson Dance Theater, where such seminal figures in the dance world as Trisha Brown, Simone Forte, Yvonne Rainer, and Twyla Tharp gave performances early in their careers. At 70 Washington Square South is a prominent New York University building which the *AIA Guide to New York City* amusingly dubs one of The Redskins: the hulking red-granite Elmer Holmes Bobst Library designed by Philip Johnson. (The other two, from the same quarry, are the André and Bella Meyer Physics Hall at 707 Broadway and Tisch Hall at 40 West 4th Street.) Equally hulking buildings in the area are the I. M. Pei apartment blocks at 100–110 Bleecker Street and 505 La Guardia Place (a northern extension of SoHo's West Broadway), though the scale is somewhat softened by the Picasso sculpture, *Portrait of Sylvette,* in the building's central plaza. A far-from-amusing reminder of red is the plaque on the northwest corner of Washington Place and Greene Street commemorating the Triangle Shirtwaist Fire of 1911, in which 146 people perished in a blaze in a garment factory in the building because the fire exits had been locked by supervisors.

Before leaving the area, head south on **MacDougal Street** to one of the area's Italian cafés. Most evocative of Greenwich Village bohemia is **Caffè Reggio** at 119 MacDougal near 3rd Street, with its walls covered with paintings and discolored from decades of smoke and steam from its espresso machine. Farther down the street, at the corner of Bleecker, **Café Borgia** and **Le Figaro Café** sit opposite each other like funky Village versions of Café Flore and Les Deux Magots, while at 81 MacDougal is **Caffè Dante**, decorated with scenes of Florence. Any one of them makes a pleasant place for an afternoon of people watching, or to cap off a night at one of the nearby theaters such as the historic **Provincetown Playhouse** (133 MacDougal), where Village resident Eugene O'Neill had a number of plays produced, and the Sullivan Street Playhouse (181 Sullivan), where the charming production *The Fantasticks* has been running since 1960.

## THE EAST VILLAGE

In the 19th century, parts of the East Village were pleasant residential areas. Believe it or not, Tompkins Square once had the appearance, almost, of an English park; the Astor, Vanderbilt, and Delano families all had town houses on what was at the time the most fashionable address in New York—Lafayette Street, then Lafayette Place.

The area has now gone from high culture to counterculture. Its principal street, **St. Mark's Place** (the equivalent of 8th Street), is the main drag of the city's residual punk population, with the attendant fashion and music scenes, as typified by Susan Seidelman's film *Desperately Seeking Susan*. Some of the contemporary art world's most self-consciously outré galleries are located there (though the lively mosaics decorating the sidewalks and lamppost bases throughout the area are as retro as they are renegade, looking like a punked-out version of Antonio Gaudí); and the seeds of the 1960s grass-roots movement have sprouted somewhat scraggly results in the East Village, with the proliferation of social realist murals and public gardens along its eastern perimeter.

Though the eastern portion of the East Village (the area including Avenues A, B, C, and D—called Alphabet City) is a center of New York's heavy drug trade, there is much to see elsewhere in the vicinity. The best time to go is on a warm Sunday morning, when most of the usual crowd is sleeping off the previous night's excesses, for a punk-watching brunch at, say, **Kiev** (117 Second Avenue at 7th Street). Preceded by a visit to the **Astor Place** area and followed by a romp through the art galleries scattered throughout the area (there's not much to the architecture of the eastern part of the East Village beyond what long-time resident Allen Ginsberg described as "tenement streets' brick sagging cornices" in his poem "Waking in New York"), an afternoon in the East Village can still be a pleasant experience.

Bernard Tony Rosenthal's huge, rotating, black steel cube called *Alamo,* at Astor Place, is one of the principal rendezvous of the East Village. Its shape unconsciously echoes many of the hairdos created just down the street at Astor Place Hair Designers (2 Astor Place), where the line of punks and New York University students waiting to be cheaply shorn and shaped often extends around the block. Walk south down Lafayette Street to Colonnade Row at 428–434, a group of four of the original nine town houses called La Grange Terrace that once stood on the spot (number 430 houses **Indochine**, a popular and trendy Vietnamese restaurant). The houses date from 1833, but the Corinthian columns could almost be original, they are in such bad shape. Number 376 Lafayette is an 1888 warehouse building designed by Henry J. Hardenbergh, architect of the Plaza Hotel and the Dakota Apartments. Cross Lafayette Street and continue back uptown to the northeast corner of East 4th Street, where at 399 Lafayette there is another noteworthy warehouse, the De Vinne Press Building, designed by Babb, Cook & Willard in 1885. Down East 4th Street, at number 29, is another remnant of the area's fashionable days, the Old Merchant's House, a Greek Revival residence dating from 1832. Back up Lafayette, number 425 is the **Public Theater**. Originally the Astor Library, it was converted to theater spaces in 1966 by Giorgio Cavaglieri.

At the corner of Lafayette and Astor Place, step through the morass of vendors selling what seem to be articles lifted from poor people's refuse bins, and walk past the Cooper Union Foundation Building, the centerpiece of **Cooper Union for the Advancement of Science and Art**, an important art, architecture, and engineering school. Its 1859 brownstone exterior masks a total reconstruction, which gave the building a high-tech interior in 1975. On the south side of the building is an 1894 bronze statue of the school's industrialist founder Peter Cooper, by Augustus Saint-Gaudens, with a base by Stanford White.

Continue back to St. Mark's Place for a strong dose of street theater. (Real avant-garde theater can be still found at another area cultural landmark, the **La MaMa Experimental Theater** on 74 East 4th Street.) To get a taste of the variety of the neighborhood's activities, take a look at the bulletin board of the newly enlarged **St. Mark's Bookshop** at 12 St. Mark's Place. Boisterous punks, shops, and restaurants characterize St. Mark's, which has the appearance of unusual width because most of its buildings were built farther back from the sidewalk than on other streets in the city. Pause at **Gem Spa**, on the southwest corner of St. Mark's Place and Second Avenue, for an egg cream. The traditional Lower East Side refresher is now made here by East Indians, but they prepare the concoction well (though not as well, perhaps, as the Indian food served in the profusion of Indian restaurants on and around East 6th Street—**Gaylord's** at 87 First Avenue is one of the best).

Head up Second Avenue, where at number 140 is the Ukrainian National Home, the center for the area's sizable Ukrainian community: There is an excellent and inexpensive restaurant inside, and a museum of Ukrainian folk art at number 203. On the northwest corner of Second Avenue and 10th Street is the area's most historic building, the **Church of St. Mark's-in-the-Bowery**. Built on the site of Dutch Governor Peter Stuyvesant's original mansion (he is buried in the cemetery next to the church), it dates from 1799. Its Episcopalian congregation is far from stodgy, however, sponsoring an innovative program of poetry and performing arts.

Depending on your sense of adventure, you can either head east to the galleries (pick up a copy of *Art Now Gallery Guide* at the Gracie Mansion Gallery at 167 Avenue A for the latest show listings), or retreat west down Stuyvesant Street, a remaining tract of the former carriage lane that once extended from the Bowery to the governor's mansion (the Stuyvesant Fish House at number 21 dates from 1803). Refreshment may be taken locally at **The Cloister**, a relaxing indoor-outdoor café-restaurant at 238 East 9th Street, or **McSorley's Old Ale House** (15 East 7th Street). A pleasant, dingy dive taken over by Cooper Union and New York University students during the academic year, McSorley's dates from 1854 and claims to be the oldest bar in the city.

# MIDTOWN

*By Dwight V. Gast*

Midtown, the huge chunk of Manhattan between 14th Street and Central Park, is where most of the city's business is conducted. Fortunately for the visitor, much of the city's business is entertainment.

Midtown's boisterous street scene reflects its high-pressured essence. Besides the handfuls of Rolaids gulped down behind closed doors, there is much evidence of the relentless level of stress in this part of town. Construction workers hammer away with pneumatic drills as sidewalk superintendents voice their criticism of the new buildings shooting up throughout the area. Office clerks, coffee cups and food from a sidewalk vendor in hand, flock to feed in any space with a vaguely horizontal surface. Pedestrians crowd the sidewalks during the rush and lunch hours. Messengers whiz by on bicycles, often the fastest-moving vehicles in an impatient procession of honking trucks, taxis, buses, and cars on the rigid grid pattern of the streets.

But whether or not their business takes them there, New Yorkers and out-of-towners occasionally go to Midtown to have fun in spite of themselves. In addition to the charms of the older neighborhoods of its southern portion, Midtown is where you'll find major department stores and minor specialty shops, a strong concentration of bars and restaurants, Broadway and off-Broadway theaters, some of the most famous and glamorous buildings of the New York skyline, and—chances are—your hotel.

### MAJOR INTEREST

Union Square area
Gramercy Park area
Madison Square and the Ladies' Mile
The Empire State Building
Times Square
The New York Public Library
Grand Central Station
The United Nations
Rockefeller Center
The Museum of Modern Art

Major department stores
Broadway Theater District

## *UNION SQUARE*

Just north of the East Village, above 14th Street between Broadway and Third Avenue, is the Union Square–Gramercy Park area. Originally named Union Place after its role in uniting Bloomingdale Road (now Broadway) and Bowery Road (Fourth Avenue), Union Square was a residential square with its own private park in the mid-18th century, much as Gramercy Park is today. After a brief stint as New York's theater district in the 1850s, the square became the city's rallying point for radical political groups, a fact somewhat abstractly alluded to in the 1986 statue of Gandhi in its southeast pedestrian section. Until fairly recently the area flourished as a center for budget department stores. Of them, Mays is the last vestige: Klein's "On the Square" was recently replaced with considerable disunion by a towering apartment complex immodestly named after its developer and topped with pyramids. It blocks the classic view of the Consolidated Edison power company clock tower, which was somewhat of a symbol of the square—though, tellingly, it often gave the wrong time.

After a period of decline, during which most of its famous book dealers left the area (**The Strand** at Broadway and 12th Street is the last vestige of them) and it was primarily used by drug dealers, Union Square has made a complete turnaround. On Wednesdays, Fridays, and Saturdays, New York's largest greenmarket takes place there: New Yorkers, often pushing infants in strollers, come to finger the radicchio, sample the goat cheese, and generally exchange pleasantries instead of the usual business cards. Trendy American restaurants such as the **Union Square Café** (21 East 16th Street) and **America** (9 East 18th Street) have given the area the finishing touches of gentrification, leading to the opening of even more meteoric establishments throughout the general area (see also the Madison Square and Ladies' Mile sections below).

In addition to Gandhi, there is an unusual amount of statuary in the park. Henry Kirke Brown's 1853–1855 *George Washington* is the city's first monumental bronze; the same sculptor's 1868 *Lincoln* is also there; Frédéric Auguste Bartholdi, who created the Statue of Liberty, was

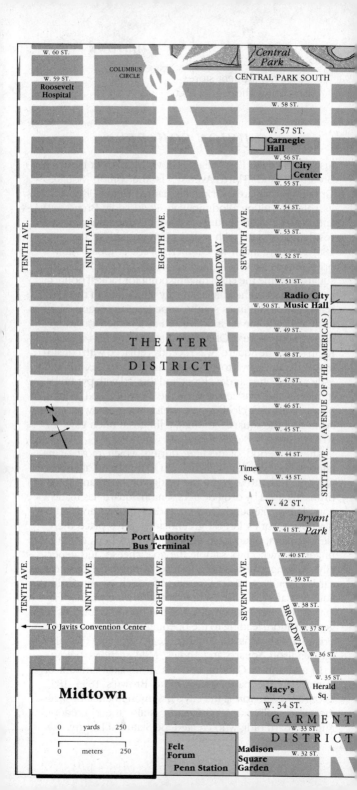

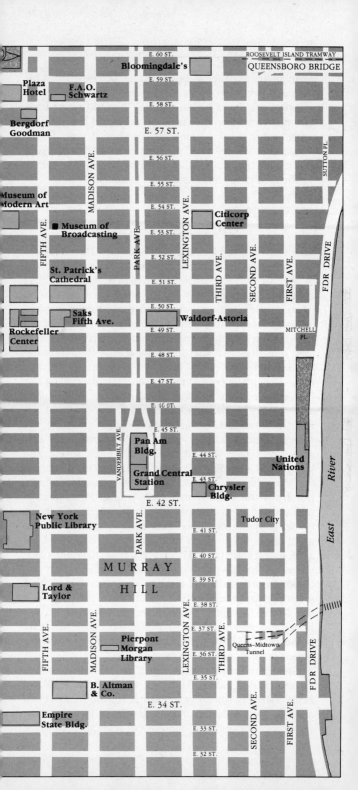

given another chance to honor his native France with his 1873 *Lafayette* (who once remarked, like one of the soapbox orators in Union Square, "I would never have drawn my sword in the cause of America if I could have conceived that I was founding a land of slavery."). Karl Adolf Donndorf designed the square's elaborate drinking fountain in 1881, and Anthony de Francisci did bas-reliefs for the base of the Independence Flagstaff in 1926.

## *GRAMERCY PARK*

Take 14th Street a block east to Irving Place. Have a look at the enormous mural above the entrance to the **Palladium** at 126 East 14th Street. The club was New York's trendiest disco a few seasons back, but has since been invaded by what Manhattanites call "the bridge-and-tunnel crowd," meaning those whose entry to the island is via one of the engineering structures specified in the expression, therefore, outsiders. (Another disparaging term for almost the same group of people is "BBQ," which stands for "Bronx, Brooklyn, and Queens.") The mural, by Hank Pressing and Jeff Green, contains an image of Pallas Athena pulling aside a curtain to reveal a rock concert. If not exactly social realism, it is at least one sort of social reality.

Irving Place leads uptown to **Pete's Tavern** at 129 East 18th Street. Like McSorley's Old Ale House in the East Village, it claims to be the oldest bar in the city, though its founding date of 1864 is a decade later than McSorley's. But from the look at the lively young crowd usually assembled there for simple food and drink, no one seems to be counting on more than a good time, let alone accuracy: Both Pete's and **Sal Anthony's**, a restaurant back at 55 Irving Place (near 17th Street), claim to be the place where O. Henry wrote *The Gift of the Magi*.

Head north on Irving Place to Gramercy Park, with a sidelong glance at East 19th Street between Irving Place and Third Avenue, a peaceful tree-lined street. To see how the peace is kept, head over to the **Police Academy Museum** at 235 East 20th Street, which has the world's largest collection of police memorabilia.

**Gramercy Park** begins at East 20th Street, there called Gramercy Park South. The park was built in 1831 and bears a striking similarity to squares in London, a fact that status-conscious New Yorkers often point to with pride. (Benjamin Sonnenberg, the Russian immigrant inventor

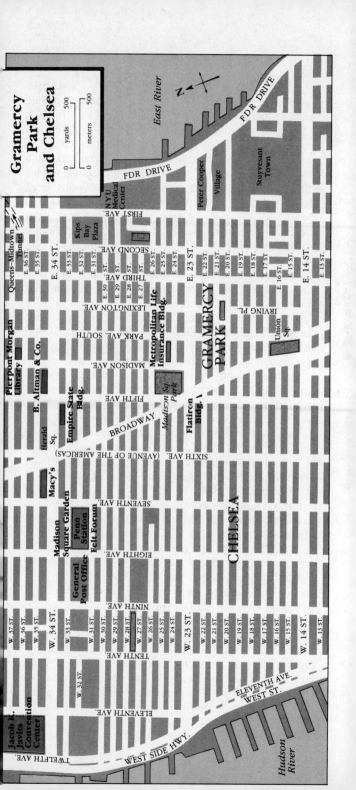

of public relations, lived his self-made Edwardian existence at 19 Gramercy Park South.) The park is private (area residents and guests of the Gramercy Park Hotel at 2 Lexington Avenue have their own keys to the stately iron gates), but if you peer through the iron fence you can catch some interesting statuary. Children especially enjoy a bronze in the southeast corner, Gregg Wyatt's 1983 *Fantasy Fountain,* with the water spouting from dancing giraffes. In the corner of the park is Edmond T. Quinn's 1917 statue of *Edwin Booth as Hamlet.* It faces the actor's former residence at 16 Gramercy Park South, which now houses The Players, a club founded by Booth, who commissioned Stanford White to remodel it. Besides Booth and White, Thomas Nast and Winston Churchill have counted themselves among the club's members. (Churchill's mother, Jennie Jerome, was born nearby, in a mansion that once stood on the site of the southeast corner of Madison Avenue and 26th Street.) The mansion at number 15 Gramercy Park South, remodeled by Calvert Vaux, is another club, the National Arts Club.

A stroll around Gramercy Park is enough to get a general sense of the square's charms: Specific points of interest include numbers 3 and 4 Gramercy Park West, with their fine cast-iron porches.

Walk west on 21st Street to Park Avenue South, where you'll see Gothic-style Calvary Church, designed in 1846 by James Renwick, Jr., who was also responsible for Grace Church and St. Patrick's Cathedral. Eleanor Roosevelt was baptized there in 1884.

If the Roosevelt family intrigues you, walk down to 28 East 20th Street, the birthplace and boyhood **home of Theodore Roosevelt**, now owned by the National Park Service. The home is actually a 1923 reconstruction, an architect and decorator's understated interpretation of "Speak softly and carry a big stick." From there, the most convenient place to end your visit to Gramercy Park would be **Positano** (250 Park Avenue South near 20th), a professional's wateringhole where the speaking is far from soft. If you prefer more meditative surroundings, it's a short walk back through Gramercy Park to 108 Lexington Avenue, between East 27th and East 28th streets, in an area increasingly becoming known as **Little India** because of its influx of East Indian businesses. There you'll find **Annapurna**, an Indian restaurant with a mural of a sunset over the swaying palms of an Indian beach. If you like what you eat, you can purchase some of the ingredients (along with other Indian products) at the Annapurna Indian store around the corner at 126 East 28th Street.

## THE MADISON SQUARE AREA

Located at the intersection of Broadway and Fifth Avenue, between East 23rd and East 26th streets, Madison Square is another version of Union Square, although rather than greengrocers filling its expanses, you're likely to find residents from the nearby hotels: Once the most glamorous in the city, the accommodations are now inhabited by welfare recipients. Madison Square has also been newly refurbished, has its own nearby clock tower (the Metropolitan Life Insurance Company headquarters), and boasts an abundance of statuary. One of its earliest monuments was the long arm of the Statue of Liberty, placed there as an early (and unsuccessful) ploy to raise funds for the statue's erection after it had been exhibited in the Philadelphia Centennial Exposition in 1876. The long arm of Chester Alan Arthur is also commemorated in Madison Square: Bronzes of the president and his associates William H. Seward, David Glasgow Farragut, and Roscoe Conkling adorn the park. Of these, the Admiral Farragut Monument on the north end of the park is the most interesting. Created by Augustus Saint-Gaudens in 1880, it is especially noteworthy for the relief sculptures of Loyalty and Courage adorning its base, which was designed by Stanford White.

White was responsible for the square's most famous architectural monument—the original Madison Square Garden, which stood on the northeast corner of East 26th Street and Madison Avenue. Demolished in 1925, the Garden was also the scene of White's demise: He was shot dead in 1906 in its Roof Garden Theater by Harry K. Thaw, the jealous husband of one of White's former mistresses, Evelyn Nesbit. Almost as architecturally dramatic is the 1900 Appellate Division of the New York State Supreme Court, a block south of the site, at the northeast corner of 25th Street and Madison Avenue. A small Palladian palace, it is a decorator's extravaganza, covered with idealized statuary depicting historical personages and lofty themes, and outfitted with an ornate interior. Among its noteworthy decorations is Daniel Chester French's *Justice,* the fourth statue from the left as you face the façade.

Today the most famous piece of architecture near Madison Square is the 1902 **Flatiron Building**, across 23rd Street from the square at the intersection of Broadway and Fifth Avenue. Immortalized in the photographs of Edward Steichen, the building is one of Chicago architect Daniel H. Burnham's masterpieces. Its triangular shape gave the building its name (it was originally called the Fuller Building), but to some it also suggests the prow of a ship and indeed does create a sense of movement. The shape also creates an unusual flurry of air currents, and in the building's first years men used to gather to watch the billowing skirts of 23rd Street's female shoppers blown about, giving rise to the expression "23 skiddoo!" which constables used in order to shoo gapers from the area. Real-estate developers are now trying to attract them, and the name of the area they've dubbed "SoFi" (*So*uth of the *F*lat*i*ron) has caught on at least with one local establishment, an elegant new restaurant called **Sofi** at 102 Fifth Avenue, between 15th and 16th streets.

Though the new development has attracted publishing companies and advertising agencies to the area, the photographers whose flashes brightened local lofts in recent years are now being driven farther west to less expensive studio space in Chelsea as many of the buildings are being converted to cooperative apartments and condominiums, the former being far more common in democratic Manhattan.

North of Madison Square are two churches of note. At 272 Fifth Avenue, on the northwest corner of West 28th Street, is the Marble Collegiate Reformed Church, an 1854 Gothic-style church by S. A. Warner. Dr. Norman Vincent Peale, author of *The Power of Positive Thinking,* was pastor here. Around the corner, at 1 East 29th Street, is the Gothic-style Church of the Transfiguration. Built from 1849 to 1856, in 1870 it was the site of the burial rites for an actor named George Holland, after a nearby church refused to perform them and referred the funeral party to a "little church around the corner." Since then it has been known as the Little Church around the Corner, and is a favorite spot for actors. It contains a stained glass window by John La Farge depicting Edwin Booth as Hamlet, and sponsors a small acting company. Around the corner from the Transfiguration, up at 120 Madison Avenue, is McKim, Mead & White's 1905 Colony Club, now home of the American Academy of Dramatic Arts.

# CHELSEA

Just west of the Flatiron District is Chelsea, which lies roughly between 14th and 30th streets from Sixth Avenue to the Hudson River. It was named for the estate of Captain Thomas Clarke, which covered most of the area when it was laid out in 1750. His scholarly grandson Clement Clarke Moore, the author of the *Compendious Lexicon of the Hebrew Language* but better remembered for the Christmas poem *A Visit from St. Nicholas* (" 'Twas the night before Christmas," etc.), grew up in the family mansion on the site of Eighth Avenue and West 23rd Street. Though Clement Clarke Moore donated a block of his land for the General Theological Seminary in the 1830s, much of Chelsea's later history is undistinguished. The Hudson River Railroad brought warehouses and tenements along 11th Avenue in the 1850s, and New York's first elevated railroad brought crowds to a flourishing theater district in the 1870s. Artists and writers moved in when the theaters moved to Times Square (the old theaters and warehouses were briefly recycled as movie studios), and creative residents—including rock musicians—still give the area a touch of character. Its predominant impression, however, comes from the large-scale apartment buildings scattered throughout the area and the palatial cast-iron buildings that once housed department stores along Sixth Avenue, which, despite efforts by developers, give the neighborhood a slightly run-down quality.

You'll most likely go to Chelsea for a specific purpose. The area's single largest concentration of retail clothing is at **Barney's** (Seventh Avenue and West 17th Street). Dance concerts are held at the **Joyce Theater** (175 Eighth Avenue, at 19th Street) and the **Bessie Schönberg Theater** (219 West 19th Street west of Seventh Avenue); theater is performed at the **Hudson Guild Theatre** (441 West 26th Street between Ninth and Tenth avenues) and the **WPA Theatre** (519 West 23rd, at 10th Avenue). Several interesting bars and restaurants—such as **Chelsea Trattoria**, **Man Ray**, and **Rogers and Barbero**—cluster around the Joyce Theater on Eighth Avenue. However, there are a few other sights that make Chelsea a pleasant enough stroll in its own right.

Start at the **Chelsea Hotel** at 222 West 23rd Street. One of the city's first cooperative apartment buildings when it was built in 1884, it is even more famous for the roster of celebrity artists who have lived there, from Mark Twain and O. Henry to Virgil Thomson, Janis Joplin, and Sid Vicious. The lives and deaths of these last two figures (Vicious was the subject of the Alex Cox film, *Sid and Nancy,* shot in the Chelsea) were eerily prefigured in a poem called "The Hotel Chelsea," written by another of the hotel's noted residents, Edgar Lee Masters:

> Today will pass as currents of the air that veer and die.
> Tell me how souls can be
> Such flames of suffering and ecstasy.
> Then fare as winds fare?

The pleasant eclecticism of the hotel's architectural style still extends to its guest roster; after inspecting its façade, take a look at the lobby to see its grand staircase and perhaps some of the regulars.

Walk down Eighth Avenue to West 20th Street, the heart of the Chelsea Historic District, a quiet area filled with late 18th-century residences ranging from town houses to large apartment buildings. On the north side of West 20th Street between Ninth and Tenth avenues is the General Theological Seminary, a conglomeration of 19th-century buildings, the oldest of which is the 1836 West Building at 5–6 Chelsea Square. Note the row houses on the south side of West 20th Street: 406–418, known as Cushman Row, dates from 1840; the Italianate houses at 446–450 from 1855.

Head up Tenth Avenue to West 23rd Street, where the entire north side of the block is taken up by a vast apartment complex called London Terrace, built in 1930. A more appetizing homage to the era is the **Empire Diner** at 210 Tenth Avenue at the corner of West 22nd Street, a 24-hour Art Deco–style eating establishment, which gets a glassy-eyed crowd (largely of the *Saturday Night Fever* variety) from the nearby discos during the wee hours. Just up Tenth Avenue at the corner of 24th Street is **Chelsea Commons**, a local hangout with good burgers, a fireplace, and an outdoor terrace.

## *LADIES' MILE*

Aficionados of cast-iron buildings should head back east at this point, where on Sixth Avenue between West 23rd and

West 18th streets they'll pass the cast-iron skeletons of the department stores that flourished in the area in the late 19th century, a part of town so devoted to shopping it was known as the Ladies' Mile. The northern part of the area is now given over to wholesale florists, on Sixth Avenue around West 28th Street, and garment manufacturing—one of New York's largest industries—centered slightly to the north on Seventh Avenue in the 30s: the **Garment District**. Seventh Avenue, in fact, is called Fashion Avenue between 26th and 28th streets, where the **Fashion Institute of Technology**, a school for those interested in the clothing industry as a profession, is located.

Begin back down at 32–36 West 23rd Street, the site of the 1878 Stern's Dry Goods Store. At 695–709 Sixth Avenue is what was originally the 1889 Erlich Brothers Dry Goods Store; 675–691 was the 1900 Adams Dry Goods Store (the third and final cemetery of the Spanish and Portuguese Synagogue, used between 1829 and 1851, is just around the corner from it at 98–110 West 21st Street); the former 1875 Hugh O'Neill Dry Goods Store is at 655–671 Sixth Avenue (across the street at 47 West 20th Street is the 1846 Church of the Holy Communion by Richard Upjohn, preserved for better or worse as the **Limelight discotheque**); 621 Sixth Avenue was the site of B. Altman from the building's beginning in 1876 until 1906; and the 1895 616–632 Sixth Avenue building housed the Siegel-Cooper Dry Goods Store.

To best get an authentic taste of the era, head back east over to the **Old Town Bar** near Union Square, at 45 East 18th Street, between Broadway and Park Avenue South. It serves inexpensive sandwiches and drinks in an original—though unpretentious—1892 setting. Once fortified, you might want to take a look at some more stores of the Ladies' Mile. Numbers 881–887 Broadway (at 19th Street), by Griffith Thomas, housed the Arnold Constable Dry Goods Store in 1869 (extensions were made in 1873 and 1877); a block north, 900 Broadway is an 1887 loft building by McKim, Mead & White; 901 Broadway was the Lord & Taylor Dry Goods Store in 1869; and finally, a block west at 153–157 Fifth Avenue, is the first headquarters of Charles Scribner's Sons publishing company, built in 1894 by Ernest Flagg.

## *THE EMPIRE STATE BUILDING*

With the demise of Pennsylvania Station, there is little of architectural interest in the 30s. The old station has been replaced with the present-day **Penn Station** and **Madison Square Garden**, which architecture critic Paul Goldberger calls "graceless, sloppy, cheap." You may be drawn to the neighborhood for any number of practicalities, however. You could be taking part in a gathering at the immense **Jacob K. Javits Convention Center** (at 655 West 34th Street, near the Hudson River). You may have business at McKim, Mead & White's classically inspired 1913 General Post Office at Eighth Avenue and 33rd Street, or at such stores as **Macy's** (Herald Square, at the intersection of Broadway and Sixth Avenue at West 34th Street) and **B. Altman** (Fifth Avenue at East 34th Street), and the variety stores along Fifth Avenue between 34th and 57th streets whose "going out of business" signs are such permanent fixtures they seem to announce the name of a local chain store. Or you may want to attend an exhibition from the extensive permanent collection of drawings and manuscripts at the **Pierpont Morgan Library**, a genteel 1907 McKim, Mead & White mansion (33 East 36th Street at Madison), followed by a stroll past the town houses on East 36th Street between Third and Lexington avenues. The 30s, in short, are a spotty area for sightseers.

One sight towers above it all, however: The Empire State Building. Though it opened in 1931 after a brisk two years of construction, by 1949 the Empire State Building had already accumulated enough history to be thus lauded by E. B. White in *Here is New York:*

> It even managed to reach the highest point in the sky at the lowest point of the depression. The Empire State Building shot twelve hundred and fifty feet into the air when it was madness to put out as much as six inches of new growth. (The building has a mooring mast no dirigible has ever been tied to; it employs a man to flush toilets in slack times; it has been hit by an airplane in a fog, struck countless times by lightning, and been jumped off by so many unhappy people that pedestrians instinctively quicken step when passing Fifth Avenue and 34th Street.)

In spite of the higher elevations of the Sears Tower in Chicago and the World Trade Center in their own city, to

New Yorkers the Empire State will always be the tallest building in the world—they are inhabitants of the Empire State, after all. Its observation deck is as popular for its views of the city as it was when the building opened, its power to amuse and excite as alive now with the bright lights—color-coordinated for the holidays—that illuminate its crown as it was when used for the final scene in the original 1933 *King Kong*.

So just enjoy it. Enjoy its superlatives, beginning with the **Guinness World Records Exhibit Hall** in its lobby. Enjoy the high-speed elevator ride up to the 80th floor, the shorter ride to the observation decks (open from 9:30 A.M. to midnight) on the 86th floor and the 102nd floor. And, above all, enjoy the views, which extend imperially 50 miles in every direction.

## *42ND STREET*

True to the lyric in the title song of its namesake 1933 Busby Berkeley musical, 42nd Street truly is "where the underworld can meet the elite." Its western end, particularly the area around Times Square, is still occupied by the underworld (though legions of pimps, prostitutes, and pornographers have replaced the Irish street gangs that gave the area the name Hell's Kitchen), while the apartment complex of Tudor City at its eastern end remains one of New York's most elite addresses.

### Times Square

Be prudent if you begin your visit in darkness before an evening at one of the area's Broadway theaters, because Times Square is every bit as "naughty, bawdy, gawdy," and "sporty" as it was when Ruby Keeler used those adjectives to describe it in the 1933 musical. However, it is also the optimal time to witness the dazzling effect of its lights, best described by British writer G. K. Chesterton in *What I Saw in America:*

> When I had looked at the lights of Broadway by night, I made to my American friends an innocent remark that seemed for some reason to amuse them. I had looked, not without joy, at that long kaleidoscope of coloured lights arranged in large letters and sprawling trade-marks, advertising everything, from

pork to pianos, through the agency of the two most vivid and most mystical of the gifts of God; colour and fire. I said to them, in my simplicity, "What a glorious garden of wonder this would be, to any one who was lucky enough to be unable to read."

There is plenty to read, of varying usefulness, on the signs as well as by way of the literature dispensed at the **visitor information center** at 158 West 42nd Street. Take a look at the building at its southern edge, 1 Times Square, which used to be Times Tower, the headquarters of *The New York Times*. The sphere that marks the beginning of the New Year still descends to a celebratory crowd each New Year's Eve, but if you're there at other times of the year you can still get into a celebratory mood at the bar-restaurant called **The View** (1535 Broadway, between 45th and 46th), the only revolving restaurant in New York, and true to its name, atop the Marriott Marquis hotel. More traditional amenities in the area range from hot dogs with the hoi polloi at one of Nathan's two locations in the vicinity (1482 and 1515 Broadway) to hobnobbing with show folk, either expensively at **Sardi's** (234 West 44th Street, between Seventh and Eighth avenues) or more moderately at **Joe Allen** (326 West 46th Street). This last place is on a block called Restaurant Row, a group of restaurants between Eighth and Ninth avenues in front of which you're likely to see a patrol of young men sporting red berets and tee-shirts. Called the Guardian Angels, they are part of a self-appointed peacekeeping force that keeps watch in the subways and other potentially dangerous parts of the city, and were recently hired by the street's restaurateurs to keep drug dealers off the block.

If you go under cover of daylight, you may want to look at specific pieces of architecture: The 1931 McGraw-Hill Building at 330 West 42nd Street (unfortunately located next to the squalor of the Port Authority Bus Terminal) is a modernist masterpiece, complete with jazzy Art Deco lobby and a blue-green terra-cotta skin. Returning to Times Square, you'll notice a long lineup of movie houses between Eighth and Seventh avenues. They were originally legitimate theaters when they were built in the 1890s, and if you venture into one of the action-adventure movies that predominate along with pornography, you can still watch a strangely theatrical phenomenon: The lively and largely harmless spectators scream and shout back at the screen as if the movie were an audience-participation theatrical performance.

Of the Broadway theaters still used for their original purpose in the **Theater District**, the oldest and most interesting is the 1903 **Lyceum** at 149 West 45th Street. Before leaving the area, note the **TKTS** booth at the north end of Times Square near the statue of George M. "Give My Regards to Broadway" Cohan. It sells half-price tickets to Broadway shows on the day of the event (after 10:00 A.M. for matinees, 3:00 P.M. for evening performances).

## New York Public Library Area

Walk east on 42nd Street to Sixth Avenue, where construction and drug dealers currently obscure Bryant Park, and you'll find another discount-ticket booth, specializing in music and dance. The park is named for William Cullen Bryant, who is commemorated there by a 1911 bronze.

Continue east along 42nd Street toward Fifth Avenue. The ski-slope building at 41 West 42nd Street is the W. R. Grace Building, Skidmore, Owings & Merrill's answer to the setback requirements of the zoning regulations. Its shape has been heavily criticized, but it does provide plenty of the requisite space for public amenities at its base (there is a passageway through it to West 43rd Street), and along with the plaza of the Graduate Center of the City University of New York next to it, at number 33, it is a popular spot for office workers to sun themselves during warm weather.

Office workers, scholars, and monumental lion sculptures alike sun themselves in front of the Central Research Division of the **New York Public Library**, between 40th and 42nd streets on Fifth Avenue. The wonders of the 1911 Beaux Arts masterpiece by Carrère & Hastings can be pointed out to you by the volunteers who conduct free tours of the building (Monday through Saturday, 11:00 A.M. and 2:00 P.M.). You may also inspect its lavish interior yourself, and test the strength of its research collection of over six million volumes by calling up a title on the computer system recently installed in its main reading room, number 315. Exhibits of works from its collection are often held throughout the building.

122  NEIGHBORHOODS

## East 42nd Street

Continue across East 42nd Street to another Beaux Arts landmark, the 1903–1913 **Grand Central Terminal** by Reed & Stem and Warren & Wetmore, at 42nd and Park Avenue. The Municipal Arts Society gives enthusiastic tours of the building free of charge on Wednesdays at 12:30, but at other times feel free to wander its expanses on your own. It only becomes "as busy as Grand Central Station" during rush hour; at most other times it is almost a refuge, as the homeless people inhabiting its bowels will attest. Its most intimate cranny is near the entrance to the Oyster Bar restaurant on the lower level. Stand in one corner of the brick vault and whisper sweet nothings: Through an acoustic oddity, they can be heard clearly in the opposite corner. The **Oyster Bar** is also an excellent place for a meal, the expense of which may be mitigated by ordering a simple bowl of clam chowder at the lunch counter. Upstairs, note the constellations twinkling on the ceiling before you venture outdoors onto 42nd Street to admire the 1912–1914 sculpture group by Jules-Felix Coutan entitled *Transportation* above a stately clock. Mercury's flight seems somewhat grounded by the Pan Am Building, a 1963 monolith by Pietro Belluschi and Walter Gropius rising behind it over Park Avenue and dwarfing everything in sight.

There is more art across the street at the branch of the **Whitney Museum of American Art** in the Philip Morris Building (entrance on the southwest corner of West 42nd Street and Pershing Square). Another Midtown refuge, it mounts exhibits of contemporary art on a temporary basis, but permanent fixtures are the creditable cappuccino and espresso served at its counter.

Continue east on East 42nd Street for more architectural marvels, each of which sports a highly decorative lobby. At 110 East 42nd Street is the 1923 Romanesque Bowery Savings Bank. At 122 East 42nd is the 1929 paisley-skinned Chanin Building, and across from it another familiar shape on the New York City skyline, the **Chrysler Building**. Designed by William Van Alen and built in 1930, it was the tallest building in the world until the Empire State surpassed it, but it is detail, not height, that makes it New York's quintessential skyscraper. Admire the African marble and chrome steel of its lobby, and the detailing of gargoyles and automobiles on its upper floors. On its ground floor is Con Edison's Conservation Center, a didactic display of common energy-saving concerns popular with energetic children and their energy-conscious parents. At 200 East 42nd Street is New York's last authentic Horn & Hardart Automat; this branch was built in Art Deco style in 1958, long after the first one opened in Philadelphia in 1912. The cafeteria-style restaurant dispenses food out of glass-covered pigeonholes, opened with coins or special tokens available at the cashier.

At 220 East 42nd Street is Howells & Hood's 1930 Daily News Building, with a globe in its lobby right out of Superman's *Daily Planet* (it was, in fact, used in the *Superman* films). Between First and Second avenues on the north side of the street is the 42nd Street entrance to the Ford Foundation, a 1967 building by Kevin Roche, John Dinkeloo & Associates with an elaborate atrium garden that inspired many others throughout the city. Across the street from it is Tudor City, the exclusive 1925–1928 apartment building where you can have a discreet picnic in the park or a meal in **Cinco de Mayo** (45 Tudor City Place), an uptown version of a moderately priced Mexican restaurant on West Broadway in SoHo.

At First Avenue and East 42nd Street begins United Nations Plaza, the main attraction in an otherwise quiet and elegant residential neighborhood. The visitors' entrance to the **United Nations** is three blocks north, at East 46th Street, which is where you begin the one-hour guided tours conducted seven days a week from 9:15 A.M. to 4:45 P.M. They are the best way of seeing the 18-acre site, designed by an international team of architects between 1947 and 1953. The Secretariat Building is the tall box of a building that rises above the scoop of the General Assembly Hall to the north; the library sits to the south, and the conference building stretches east beyond the Secretariat. Artworks from all member nations decorate the complex. Besides the architectural and artistic highlights that will be shown to you by the tour guides, note the UN Craft Shop and post office, both in the basement of the General Assembly building. After the tour you can rub elbows and forks with diplomats in the **United Nations Delegates Dining Room** (for reservations, Tel: 212-754-7625) on the fourth floor. A less official place in the vicinity, popular with the diplomats and trysting couples (sometimes one and the same), is the cocktail lounge on the top floor of the **Beekman Tower Hotel**, at 3 Mitchell Place on the northeast corner of First Avenue and East 49th Street.

## *PARK AVENUE*

Head back west across East 45th Street. Across Lexington Avenue, on the south side of the street in front of the entrance to the Pan Am Building, you'll find another international lineup, this time of sidewalk food vendors. The Pan Am lobby was recently remodeled at great expense if not taste, removing the Josef Albers mural and sculptures that once graced the space. Go in anyway, for a laugh. The hideous sculptures resembling enormous earrings that replaced the artwork will prepare you for the oddball art to come. From the Pan Am building go north through the arch marked "Helmsley Walk East" (where the cloud paintings on the ceilings are accompanied not by a Baroque concerto as you might expect, but by elevator music). You emerge in neither heaven nor a disco, but on Park Avenue, a stretch of which has some interesting architecture and rather unusual art. In the plaza before 245 Park Avenue is *Performance Machine, Big O's,* a 1986 kinetic sculpture by Lowell Jones, which is solar-powered and twists around like a giant chromosome. On the southeast corner of Park Avenue and East 48th Street is *Taxi!* Though it is actually a lifelike 1983 bronze by J. Seward Johnson, Jr., depicting an executive in the act of hailing a cab, frustrated New Yorkers have interpreted it as the petrified result of waiting for one. The **Waldorf-Astoria**, still one of the city's most prestigious hotels, is at 301 Park Avenue, between East 49th and East 50th streets. A block north, between East 50th and East 51st streets, is St. Bartholomew's Church, the parish church of the city's most affluent Episcopalian congregation. The church's Romanesque entrances, by McKim, Mead & White, were relocated from its earlier incarnation, and attached to the Byzantine building designed by Bertram G. Goodhue. A block north, in front of 345 Park Avenue, is *Dinoceras,* a 1971 abstract sculpture by Robert Cook that looks like a ball of wax, and in fact was an enormous lump of beeswax stretched on a bamboo frame before it was cast into bronze.

In the next uptown block is the **Seagram Building**, the 1958 modernist masterpiece designed on the outside by Ludwig Mies van der Rohe and on the inside by Philip Johnson. It houses Johnson's **Four Seasons** restaurant (entrance at 99 East 52nd Street), a sleek and expensive eatery that best exemplifies the New York phenomenon of combining dining with business deals known as the "power lunch." At 100 East 53rd Street, between Park and Lexington, is the **Brasserie**, a more modestly priced establishment to which patrons seeking only caloric power come at all hours, since it is one of the few places in town open around the clock. Two other imaginative examples of Johnson's architecture, done in collaboration with John Burgee, are nearby: the building at 885 Third Avenue (East 53rd Street), called the Lipstick Building because of its slick cylindrical shape; and the 1984 AT & T Building at 550 Madison Avenue (East 56th Street), which has been referred to as the Chippendale Building because of the similarity of its broken pediment to the furniture style.

Across the street from the Seagram Building, at 370 Park Avenue, is McKim, Mead & White's 1918 Racquet and Tennis Club, one of many private clubs in the area. At 390 is Skidmore, Owings & Merrill's 1952 **Lever House**, a glass box that spawned many less successful spinoffs. Next, take a look at the Chase Manhattan Bank branch at 410 Park Avenue (East 55th Street), which has a mobile by Alexander Calder on the second floor, visible from the street when the curtains are not drawn. The final piece of Park Avenue architecture worthy of inspection is the Mercedes-Benz Showroom at 430 Park Avenue (East 56th Street). It was Frank Lloyd Wright's first work in New York, designed in 1955. From here, look back toward the Pan Am Building for the full effect of its dwarfing the New York Central Building (now called the Helmsley Building), a 1929 Warren & Wetmore skyscraper that once grandly marked the end of the avenue.

## *FIFTH AVENUE AND ENVIRONS*

For an appropriately commercial crescendo to your Midtown promenade, return to the busy intersection of Fifth Avenue and 42nd Street and head uptown. Interesting sights fill practically all of the side streets to the west toward Sixth Avenue. On West 43rd and West 44th streets are some of Midtown's private clubs. The Palladian-style Century Club is at 7 West 43rd Street; the boxy Princeton Club is at 15 West 43rd Street. On West 44th Street is the sedate Georgian Harvard Club (by McKim, Mead &

White) at number 27; the fanciful Beaux Arts New York Yacht Club is at number 37; and the **Algonquin Hotel** is at number 59. Though not a private club per se, its **Oak Room** was the setting for the Round Table—Robert Benchley, Heywood Broun, Edna Ferber, George S. Kaufman, and Dorothy Parker were among its most famous "members"—a group of self-styled wits (or, as Anita Loos called them, "a boring set of exhibitionists") who gathered there regularly to engage in banter and boozing. A drink or tea in the lobby lounge is a must.

At 551 Fifth Avenue, on the northeast corner of East 45th Street, is the 1927 French Building, designed by Fred F. French. Note the multicolored faience on the building's upper floors, and the jazzy lobby.

Except for a branch of the **International Center of Photography** at 77 West 45th Street, just east of Sixth Avenue, West 45th and 46th streets have been virtually taken over by Brazilian shops and restaurants. Among the best restaurants is **Via Brazil** (34 West 46th Street), the only place in town that serves the all-you-can-eat meat extravaganza called churrasco. It is traditionally accompanied by a strong herbal tea called *erva mate,* which may be bought along with many other Brazilian products at **Coisa Nossa** down the street at 57 West 46th Street. Incidentally, if you look east on 46th Street, you'll get an idea of how imposing the New York Central Building must have once looked on Park Avenue, because it, rather than the Pan Am building, dominates the view from that angle.

West 47th Street is the heart of New York's **Diamond District,** where predominantly Jewish merchants trade their precious wares in noisy negotiations reminiscent of the Lower East Side. Scattered among them is the equally energetic **47th Street Photo** (67 West 47th Street), where great savings, if not service, may be had on electronic equipment when you know what you're looking for. It is but the most prominent of many such stores in the area. More relaxing is the **Gotham Book Mart** (41 West 47th Street), perhaps the city's most revered literary emporium, with hardly a current best seller dirtying its dusty shelves.

For best sellers (and at a discount) you'll have to go to **Barnes & Noble,** around the corner at 600 Fifth Avenue, between West 48th and West 49th streets. The former Scribner bookstore, an ornate iron-and-glass building across the street at 597 Fifth Avenue, was designed by Ernest Flagg in 1913 for the specific purpose of housing a bookstore (his brother-in-law's). The store was sold recently, but the exterior of the building—which has landmark status—will remain unchanged.

Up the avenue, between East 50th and East 51st streets, is **St. Patrick's Cathedral**, the seat of the Roman Catholic archdiocese in New York. Though built in 1879 to the designs of James Renwick, Jr., its Gothic-style spires work well with the modern towers of Rockefeller Center across the street, and are nicely reflected in the brown glass of Skidmore, Owings & Merrill's 1976 Olympic Tower a block north. The block of brownstone buildings on the east side of Madison Avenue facing the cathedral once housed the offices of the archdiocese, though they were built in 1884 by McKim, Mead & White as a mansion for Henry Villard. Developer Harry Helmsley later purchased them with the intention of demolishing them, but was convinced to preserve them as the entrance to the **Helmsley Palace Hotel**. Number 457 Madison Avenue, the northernmost of the group, houses the city's best architectural bookstore, **Urban Center Books**.

## Rockefeller Center

On the west side of Fifth Avenue, from West 47th to West 51st streets between Fifth and Sixth avenues, is Rockefeller Center, the sculpture-studded Art Deco business and entertainment complex that inevitably draws crowds of visitors and office workers alike. Built between 1931 and 1940, it was given landmark status in 1988 by the National Trust for Historic Preservation. It is most effectively approached on the promenade called **Channel Gardens** (because it separates the British Building from the Maison Française), between 49th and 50th streets. Channel Gardens, with its bronze fountainhead figures by René Paul Chambellan, is either elaborately planted or decked out with Valerie Clarebout's heraldic angels, depending on the season. It leads to a sunken area occupied by café tables in warm weather or an ice-skating rink in the winter, when it and its golden statue of *Prometheus,* by Paul Manship, is towered over by a gigantic Christmas tree. Behind it looms the 70-story RCA Building (note Lee Lawrie's 1933 panels depicting Wisdom, Light, and Sound at the entrance), where one-hour tours may be taken of the NBC television studios. (Television enthusiasts should note that tickets to tapings are often handed out free on the Fifth Avenue side of Rockefeller Center, and that the

**Museum of Broadcasting** is located nearby at 1 East 53rd Street.) The RCA Building also houses the **Rainbow Room** (65th floor), a newly renovated Art Deco restaurant ideal for romantic dining, dancing, or drinks.

The most traditional spot for entertainment at Rockefeller Center, however, is **Radio City Music Hall**, at 1260 Sixth Avenue at the northeast corner of West 50th Street. There, a seasonal stage show featuring the leggy Rockettes takes place in the huge auditorium. The building was also recently restored to its Art Deco splendor, and may be full appreciated by taking one of the music hall's special hour-long tours; Tel: (212) 246-4600.

At the new McGraw-Hill Building (1221 Sixth Avenue), the multimedia extravaganza **The New York Experience**, which for many years has been the best condensation of the touristic aspects of this part of town, has been temporarily closed. To see its equivalent in contemporary art, take 51st Street west (where art furniture by Scott Burton sits squatly on the north side of the sidewalk) to see one of the temporary exhibits usually held nearby at the **Whitney Museum at Equitable Center**, 787 Seventh Avenue, between West 51st and West 52nd streets. Its permanent sculpture collection includes *Hare on Bell* (1983) and *Young Elephant* (1984) by Barry Flanagan. Back to the east, on the northeast corner of Sixth Avenue and West 52nd Street (51 West 52nd Street), is the CBS Building. Built to the plans of Eero Saarinen in 1965, it is the only skyscraper the Finnish-born architect ever designed.

Farther ahead on West 53rd Street are two more museums, the **American Craft Museum** at 40 West 53rd Street, and the **Museum of Modern Art** at 11 West 53rd Street, both between Fifth and Sixth avenues. MoMA (as the latter is called in the acronym-obsessed art world) was the world's pioneer institution for the exhibition of modern painting and sculpture, and initiated the first museum departments in photography, film, architecture, and design as well. Its own buildings are noteworthy pieces of architecture: Museum Tower, at 15 West 53rd Street, is a condominium erected in 1983 to the designs of Cesar Pelli as a fund-raising adjunct to the museum. The original building dates from 1939, and was designed by Philip L. Goodwin and Edward Durell Stone; Philip Johnson added extensions in 1951 and 1964, and Cesar Pelli doubled the gallery space with extensive renovations in 1984.

Brochures explaining the highlights of the collection, which range from French Impressionist paintings to a hovering 1,380-pound helicopter, are available at the front desk: Among its most popular attractions are Pablo Picasso's *Les Demoiselles d'Avignon,* Claude Monet's *Water Lilies,* and Andrew Wyeth's *Christina's World.* The museum also has some of the most interesting shops in town: an extensive art bookstore and a shop specializing in modern design objects. MoMA is open every day except Wednesday, unlike most of the rest of the city's museums, which close on Monday.

If you haven't ended your tour of MoMA with a visit to its sculpture garden, cross Fifth Avenue and walk to **Paley Park** at 3 East 53rd Street. The tiny enclave of seats, trees, and a waterfall is swarmed by office workers during the lunch hour, but provides welcome respite the rest of the day.

Before you continue up Fifth Avenue, if you're well dressed and well heeled (and have a reservation) you might want to backtrack to pause for some refreshment at the **"21" Club**, at 21 West 52nd Street. The last remnant of the many speakeasies that once lined 52nd Street during Prohibition, when the street was also known for its jazz and swing clubs, the veritable institution was recently refurbished and given a trendy gallicized menu. But many New Yorkers continue to swing with the punches, and pay $21 for its venerable hamburger. On the way there you'll pass 666 Fifth Avenue on the west side between West 52nd and West 53rd streets. Go into its lobby arcade, where sculptor Isamu Noguchi has installed a waterfall and a white louvered ceiling. At the other end of the building, on the 39th floor, is **Top of the Sixes**, a mediocre bar-restaurant with marvelous views to the north.

Head back toward Fifth Avenue, where at 1 West 53rd is St. Thomas Church and parish house, designed by Bertram Goodhue in 1914. The reredos over the altar is just one noteworthy element of its lavish Gothic-style interior. At the northwest corner of Fifth and 54th Street (1 West 54th Street is the address) is the grandest private club of them all, the University Club, designed by McKim, Mead & White in 1899 along the lines of a Florentine palazzo. A private club of a different sort across the street, the Elizabeth Arden beauty salon at 691 Fifth Avenue, inspired the following lines from poet-humorist Ogden Nash:

In New York beautiful girls can become more beautiful
by going to Elizabeth Arden,
And getting stuff put on their faces and waiting for it to
harden....

The stepped-back building at the northeast corner of Fifth Avenue and East 56th Street is the 1983 Trump Tower, a rather garish newcomer. The imposing effect is somewhat softened by the trees placed in its recesses high above the street. Its pink-marbled, gilded lobby propels you immediately (if unintentionally) into the connecting lobby of the *next* building, Edward Larrabee Barnes's 1983 IBM Building (590 Madison Avenue), where free concerts may often be heard (Tel: 212-745-3500 for information) and the **IBM Gallery of Science and Art** usually has an interesting exhibition taking place.

Back at 727 Fifth Avenue is **Tiffany's**, which has lovely displays of gems in its tiny windows on the avenue and around the corner on 57th Street. Cross 57th Street and walk two blocks north on Fifth toward the southeast corner of Central Park. On the west side of the street is **Grand Army Plaza**, an open square modeled on Paris's Place de la Concorde. In its center is Karl Bitter's 1913–1916 Pulitzer Fountain, in which Scott and Zelda Fitzgerald once romped. Behind it looms Henry J. Hardenbergh's 1907 **Plaza Hotel**, one of the most romantic in the city. Its **Oak Bar** is a popular Midtown wateringhole, and its **Palm Court** is a cozy place for tea, especially attractive to shoppers from the elegant shops and department stores nearby.

## *WEST 57TH STREET*

One such department store is **Bergdorf Goodman**, on Fifth Avenue between West 57th and West 58th streets. Take a look at its windows, and if you can resist the temptation to go in, turn west on 57th Street. In addition to its shops, the area is known for its art galleries. (The art and antiques area extends for a couple of blocks east on 57th from Fifth as well, and way up Madison from 57th. If you'd like to see some shows, ask for a copy of *Art Now Gallery Guide* at one of the dealers in the closest gallery building, 20 West 57th Street, for an up-to-date listing.) The galleries—along with such other commercial attractions as another slope-façaded building (number 9), the **Henri Bendel** up-market department store (number 10), **Hacker Art Books** (number 54), the plush and fashionable **Russian Tea Room** restaurant (number 150), and the boisterous **Hard Rock Café** (number 221, with the line in front and the rear end of a Cadillac above)—will keep you busy on West 57th Street as you make your way to **Carnegie Hall**, at the southeast corner of West 57th Street and Seventh Avenue. The 1891 building was recently refurbished, some say to the detriment of its famous acoustics, but it's as popular a concert hall as ever, and New Yorkers still need not ask how to get there, for fear of the wisecracking answer, "Practice, practice, practice!"

You'll likely hear that Borscht Belt chestnut and others if you end your visit to Midtown with a corned beef or pastrami sandwich at the **Carnegie Delicatessen and Restaurant** around the corner at 854 Seventh Avenue, used extensively as the scene for such banter in Woody Allen's *Broadway Danny Rose,* though with the death of owner Leo Steiner the place is rumored to have relaxed its standards. If you'd rather finish with a flourish of higher culture, walk across West 57th Street past the ornate Osborne Apartments at number 205 to the Art Students League, an 1892 French Renaissance structure by Henry J. Hardenbergh at number 215, and thence to **Coliseum Books** at Broadway and 57th Street—at the gateway to the Lincoln Center/Upper West Side area.

# THE UPPER WEST SIDE

*By Stephen Brewer*

*Stephen Brewer, who was formerly an editor at* GEO *and* Connoisseur *magazines, now manages his book and magazine editorial service in New York City.*

You have probably read and heard of the Upper West Side many, many times. Theodore Dreiser's Sister Carrie lived here, in a fifth-floor flat on Amsterdam Avenue. J. D. Salinger's fictional Glass family occupied a roomy apart-

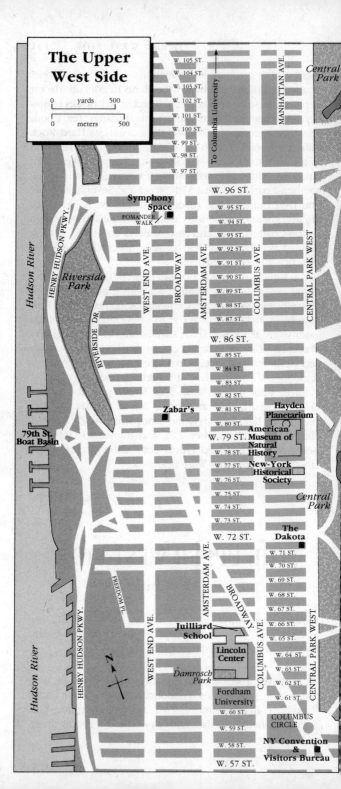

ment on Central Park West, not far from the Morningstars, that parvenu clan of Herman Wouk's *Marjorie Morningstar,* or, for that matter, from Oscar and Felix of "The Odd Couple." The tough denizens of *West Side Story* walked the same streets that you will if you choose to travel just north of Midtown to see this neighborhood, and you certainly should.

One reason to go to the Upper West Side, of course, is to see its major attractions, the Lincoln Center for the Performing Arts and the American Museum of Natural History foremost among them. The neighborhood's location is in itself an attraction. These 200-some blocks occupy a narrow strip of land between the Hudson River on the west and Central Park on the east, running from Columbus Circle north to Columbia University at 114th Street. This means that an Upper West Sider who steps out for a bit of air can stroll along the shores of the river that the writer Thomas Wolfe found so comforting ("like long pipes and old tobacco"), walk across the neighborhood to sit for awhile on a bench in Central Park, the most successful of all urban greenswards, and be back in the apartment in less than an hour.

You may also want to go to the Upper West Side to see for yourself traces of the reputation it has won over the years for harboring New Yorkers of artistic temperaments. Edgar Allan Poe wrote much of *The Raven* on West 84th Street, a Herculean task given that he had on his hands a tubercular wife and a brood of starving children. Two houses on the block bear plaques marking the site where the poor man allegedly lived, and no one really knows which is accurate. Enrico Caruso took up residence at the Ansonia on Broadway and 73rd Street. The maestro's golden voice penetrated even the building's three-foot walls, prompting his musical neighbors to stomp on the well-polished parquet floors in a futile attempt to hush the fellow up.

The neighborhood still attracts many writers, musicians, and actors, and an Upper West Sider who returns home from a night at the theater on the M 104 bus may have the pleasure of sitting next to one of the performers he has just seen on stage. (The M 104 begins at the United Nations on the East Side, crosses 42nd Street to Times Square, then proceeds north along Eighth Avenue and Broadway; if you are staying in Midtown, it is an excellent way to reach any of the sights on the Upper West Side.)

The mainstays of the neighborhood, though, have always been the bourgeoisie. As soon as the neighborhood began to develop, which was not until the late 19th century, the prosperous middle classes fled from the cramped downtown neighborhoods to take up residence on the West Side in what are still some of the city's best apartment houses and in brownstones. Edith Wharton, as much an elitist as the inhabitants of her novels about New York life at the turn of the century, thought these high, narrow houses were simply hideous.

The real reason to go to the Upper West Side, though, is not to partake of literary traditions or take in famous sights. Rather, even a brief walk here will give you the chance to see a quintessential New York neighborhood, a place where New Yorkers eat and sleep and go about their daily business, however eccentric that may be compared to quotidian activities elsewhere.

### MAJOR INTEREST

Lincoln Center for the Performing Arts
The Dakota and other grand apartment houses
Central Park West
American Museum of Natural History
Columbus Avenue shopping and street life
Zabar's and other food shops on Broadway
Riverside Drive and Park and the Hudson River
Columbia University and neighborhood
Cathedral Church of St. John the Divine
The Cloisters and other north Manhattan museums

## COLUMBUS CIRCLE AND LINCOLN CENTER

If you walk north from Midtown, you will approach the Upper West Side from its southern boundary, Columbus Circle. This vast, open space could have the monumental presence of, say, the Place de la Concorde—that is, were it not almost always full of a rush of traffic roaring around a tiny statue of the explorer, perched atop an 80-foot pedestal. Pedestrians scurry around the circle's periphery, first past the white marble pseudo-Islamic mosque at the southern tip of the intersection that has inspired jokes about Persian brothels since A & P heir Huntington Hart-ford put it up as a gallery of modern art in 1965. The building's saving grace is its current tenant, the **New York Convention and Visitors Bureau**, which distributes pamphlets and maps of the city from its ground-floor office.

As you make your way around the circle in a counterclockwise direction, you will pass the extravagant, white marble *Maine* Memorial, which commemorates the incident that sparked the Spanish-American War in 1898 and marks one of the main entrances to Central Park. You will then come to the foot of the Gulf & Western Building, an utterly banal office tower whose only mark of distinction is a pronounced tilt to the east, suggesting that it might one day have the good grace to topple out of sight. If you are in the mood for a drink, brave the pompous lobby and take an elevator to the top-floor cocktail lounge. The views of Midtown and the park are stunning, and, given the building's relative isolation on the far side of the Circle, you will usually be able to get a table next to the windows.

From the Gulf & Western Building begin the walk north on Broadway. As you leave the Circle, you will see on your left the old New York Coliseum, an ugly, functional structure that became dysfunctional when the five million some conventioneers that New York hosts every year moved their shows to the new Jacob K. Javits Convention Center in Midtown near the Hudson. No sooner had the city announced plans to demolish the hall than New Yorkers, who had never paid any attention to it before, began to protest, fearful that the two snazzy skyscrapers that are to go up in its place will cast mile-long shadows over the Circle and, worse, the southwestern corner of Central Park. Some variation of these buildings will undoubtedly go up, but the protest gives you a good idea of just how protective New Yorkers are of their land and the air above it, even when the space in question is as unremarkable as Columbus Circle.

Follow Broadway north for just seven blocks to the **Lincoln Center for the Performing Arts**. New Yorkers have been taking pot shots at the pedestrian appearance of this 12-acre complex since it opened in 1962. (You can see the neighborhood that once stood in its place in the film *West Side Story;* it was shot in the deserted streets and buildings of the slum that the center replaced just before the wreckers moved in.) To fuss about the appearance of Lincoln Center is to miss the point. The world's best performing artists grace its theaters, which surround a large marble plaza that is irresistibly charming despite its cold formality. The best time to take a seat on the rim of the central fountain is 10:30 P.M. or so, when the performances end and the audiences spill out onto the plaza, looking much happier than New Yorkers usually do en masse.

Perched atop one of the buildings across Broadway is one of New York's favorite unheralded landmarks, a miniature Statue of Liberty. When the designs for Lincoln Center were being laid, there was a movement afoot to tear down this and other surrounding buildings to extend the plaza all the way to Central Park—a dream that soon faded in the face of the realities of Manhattan real estate.

Anyone who comes to New York for even a short stay should try to buy a ticket and step off the plaza into one of the surrounding halls. **Avery Fisher Hall**, on the north side of the plaza, was originally called Philharmonic Hall. But when the esteemed New York Philharmonic moved into its new quarters and sounded its first notes, the acoustics were so bad that the audience made a beeline for the doors. The symphony made a plea to electronics czar Avery Fisher, and the hall was lined with oak paneling. As a result, Mr. Fisher is immortalized in one of the world's favorite venues for classical music, and the rest of us are treated to the best acoustics to be found anywhere.

The **Metropolitan Opera House** occupies center stage at the far western end of the plaza. This hall, home to the Metropolitan Opera Company and the American Ballet Theater, wins the prize for showmanship even before the curtain goes up. From the six-story height of its glass-fronted lobby hang two murals by Marc Chagall—they are visible even from a bus passing by on Broadway, except in the morning when they are shrouded to protect them from the sun. Inside, the theatrics begin when the huge crystal chandeliers float into the ceiling just before curtain time so they won't interfere with the sight lines, which are unobstructed from all but a dozen or so seats. The **New York State Theater**, where the New York City Opera and the New York City Ballet perform, occupies the south side of the plaza. The theater is the property of the state, and when the governor comes to the city he often throws official parties in the foyer and on the second-floor loggia.

The rest of Lincoln Center stretches to the north behind

the Metropolitan Opera House. The **Vivian Beaumont Theater**, which stages plays and musicals, most recently an enormously popular revival of Cole Porter's *Anything Goes,* shares a building with a branch of the New York Public Library, the **Library and Museum of Performing Arts**, with changing exhibits, an amazing collection of books on the performing arts, sheet music, and—its real treasure—some 12,000 recordings that musically inclined New Yorkers can borrow. Both face a reflecting pool that contains a Henry Moore sculpture, and is a good place to sit. Just beyond is the esteemed **Juilliard School**, whose well-trained graduates often return to perform on Lincoln Center's stages. Excellent tours, taking in the center's stages and labyrinthine costume storage rooms, leave frequently from the Metropolitan Opera House; Tel: (212) 582-3512. Across Broadway from Juilliard the Columbus Avenue strip begins its northward run.

The Hotel des Artistes, just one block east of Lincoln Center at number 1 West 67th Street, has been popular with creative types since the earliest days of this century. Its double-height apartments were built to accommodate painters, but it has been years since any normal boheme has been able to afford them. Isadora Duncan, Norman Rockwell, Rudolph Valentino, and Noel Coward have called the des Artistes home, but it was the debauched Harry Crosby who gave the place its racy élan. One evening in 1929, this nephew of J. P. Morgan and founder of the Paris-based avant-garde Black Sun Press locked the door to an apartment here, made love to and then shot his lovely mistress, and put the gun to his own handsome young head. You, too, can enter these bohemian portals and partake of a fine meal at the extremely attractive **Café des Artistes** on the ground floor. One of the café's famous neighbors is the equally popular **Tavern on the Green**, set just inside Central Park at 67th Street. Festooned with Christmas lights and decorated in an eclectic style that you will remember in nightmares for years after eating here, the place makes even regulars feel like tourists out for a night on the big town; it's another good place to stop in for a drink, though. Many of the buildings here in the West 60s house television studios. ABC has just moved into its sleek new semicircular headquarters at 66th and Columbus—just across the street from the studio where "All My Children" is shot, attracting to its stoop every day a faithful group of fans.

## THE 72ND STREET AREA

If instead you continue north on Broadway you will soon come to its busy intersection with 72nd Street, where just 100 years ago stood the ramshackle homestead of Jacob Harsen, whose farm was one of many on the Upper West Side. Less than 200 years ago Washington Irving described vast tracts of this area as "a sweet rural valley... enlivened here and there by a delectable little Dutch cottage." At the very center of the intersection you will see a brick kiosk, the entrance to the subway that, when it opened in 1904, finally brought civilization to the Upper West Side.

New Yorkers had already begun to take up residence in huge new apartment houses on Broadway in the decade or so before the arrival of the subway. One of these, The Dorilton, at 71st Street, opened to an onslaught of sour reviews, the most dire of them claiming "the sight of it makes strong men swear and weak women shrink afrightened"; New Yorkers have survived a full century of the building's ornate, Beaux Arts presence and have become quite comfortable with its hideous appearance. When **The Ansonia** opened at 73rd and Broadway in 1901, it sported two swimming pools, a lobby fountain populated by seals, and a roof garden where a bear roamed freely. These trappings, as well as its apartments of as many as 18 rooms, have wooed some of New York's most flamboyant citizens over the years, including Theodore Dreiser, Florenz Ziegfeld, and Babe Ruth. The building's most shameless tenant, though, was a recent one: a tawdry club called Plato's Retreat to which couples retired for the peculiar purpose of copulating in public, next to bubbling whirlpools. The place finally closed a few years ago, but will long be remembered—if only as proof that the West Side is bohemian at heart.

You should leave Broadway now and walk east on 72nd Street, toward Central Park. If you want a snack, you can do no better than **Gray's Papaya**, a gaudy stand-up counter on the southeast corner of the 72nd Street and Broadway intersection. A dollar and change here will get you two of New York's best frankfurters ("better than filet mignon," their motto claims) and a fruit drink, and will also bring you closer than you may want to be to some very seedy clients. Many of them are habitués of Verdi Square across the street. This tiny patch of greenery has long been known as Needle Park, in part because of its triangular shape but more so because of the lively drug trade that goes on beneath a statue of composer Giuseppe Verdi, put up by New York's Italian citizenry in 1906.

Seventy-second Street's few remaining kosher restaurants and butchers have long served the neighborhood's large Jewish population. The most notable of these is the **Eclair**, between Broadway and Columbus Avenue, a pleasant restaurant and pastry shop that is still a gathering spot for European Jews who came to New York half a century ago.

**The Dakota**, New York's first great apartment house, is at the corner of 72nd and Central Park West. When Edward Clark, heir to the Singer Sewing Machine fortune, put up this yellow-brick building in 1881, it was so far from the rest of Manhattan that his detractors said it may as well have been in the Dakota Territory, giving the house its now very famous name. The well-to-do were then still wary of apartments, considering it vulgar to share halls and elevators, invented only a few years before, with strangers. So Clark fashioned the Dakota in the style of a château, even surrounding it with a moat. So convincing is the effect that the Russian composer Tchaikovsky, visiting music publisher Gustav Schirmer here, thought that his host owned the entire house and that Central Park was his alone. The Dakota has also been home to such other musically inclined tenants as Theodore Steinway, the piano manufacturer, and, most recently, Leonard Berstein and Roberta Flack, the latter of whom fell out of favor with the neighborhood when she stripped her apartment of its mahogany woodwork and replaced it with stainless steel.

The building's most famous tenant, of course, was John Lennon, who was shot to death outside its gates in 1980. You can pay tribute to the musician across the street in **Strawberry Fields**, an acre of Central Park that Yoko Ono had landscaped in her husband's memory. This is a very nice place to enjoy the park, sitting beneath the arbor that leads off 72nd Street or wandering down to one of the gazebos alongside the rowing lake. If you come here at night you will notice a curious phenomenon: New Yorkers do not enter the park after dark (except in large groups of half a million or so to attend concerts on the Great Lawn), even in the hottest days of summer. They are heeding the advice of Ogden Nash, who warns anyone who finds himself in the park after dark to "hurry, hurry to the zoo, and creep into the tiger's lair, frankly you'll be safer there."

From the Dakota walk north on Central Park West, a handsome avenue whose big apartment houses facing the park are some of the neighborhood's best addresses. Aside from the Dakota, the most impressive buildings are the San Remo, which you'll pass at 74th Street, and other twin-towered apartments that went up in the 1930s to house, among others, well-to-do Jewish families who had arrived on the Lower East Side from Europe only a generation before.

## The West Side Museums

At 77th Street you will come to the **New-York Historical Society**, a quiet, stodgy institution-cum-museum that gave into temptation recently and arranged to sell its side garden to a developer of high-rises. The neighborhood set up a roar that rattled the society's rich collection of Tiffany glass and portraits, and made its point—this part of Central Park West, at least, will not soon be overshadowed by an apartment tower. The society is now fending off accusations that is has allowed much of its enormous collection of historic art and documents to molder beyond repair in a suburban warehouse.

Just across 77th Street is the **American Museum of Natural History**, a wonderful if rather musty collection totaling 37 million items—the world's largest—of bones, gems, and just about any other object relating to natural history. Anyone who grew up in New York counts among his or her happiest school days those field trips here, parading past dioramas of African scenes and dark rooms lined with mummies to the top floor galleries, where the dinosaurs are exhibited. The museum has expanded haphazardly and somewhat confusedly since it opened in 1877, so you may want to stop at the information desk at the main entrance and join one of the excellent tours. The Hayden Planetarium is adjacent, just to the north.

## *COLUMBUS AVENUE*

If you leave the museum by the 77th Street exit, you will be just a few steps away from Columbus Avenue. On the evening before and early morning hours of every Thanksgiving, Macy's uses this stretch of 77th Street as a staging ground for its parade, blowing up the huge balloon figures that will float down Central Park West and then Broadway to the department store in Herald Square. Many Upper West Siders stand here through the night, watching the familiar figures take shape.

Columbus Avenue from Lincoln Center to 86th Street is almost always crowded with the well-dressed patrons of its fancy shops and restaurants. Until recently, though, Columbus was decidedly middle class. The elevated subway, the "El," rushed above it, and the stores below did a lively business supplying the apartment houses of Central Park West. Of all these long-gone shops, the best remembered is Hellman's delicatessen, whose homemade mayonnaise has achieved fame far beyond the Upper West Side. The avenue now belongs to suburbanites in for a day's or evening's jaunt, and to the well-reared, well-dressed, well-educated young New Yorkers who pay as much as $2,000 a month rent for a few rooms in a brownstone that their grandparents could have rented in its entirety for $100. Seeing these well-heeled young people crowd into the neighborhood's bars and restaurants on weekend evenings, it is hard not to be cynical and recall what Dorothy Parker said when she once looked upon just such a crowd almost 50 years ago: "If all those sweet young things were laid end to end... I would not be at all surprised." Keep in mind, though, that young professionals like those who now inhabit so much of the Upper West Side have always formed a sizable portion of Manhattan's population. Keep in mind too, that the difference between the haves and have nots is shockingly distinct in New York. Within blocks of this affluent strip are sordid tenements housing welfare families, and it is impossible to walk these streets without seeing, and often being approached by, at least a few of the city's 50,000 homeless citizens.

## *SHOPPING AND DINING ON THE UPPER WEST SIDE*

Of the many good shops and restaurants that line Columbus, some of the best are those that have been here for a decade or more. On 71st Street, just east of the avenue, is **Café La Fortuna**, a pleasant little coffee house where you will be encouraged to linger over your cappuccino and Italian pastry. **Victor's**, a Cuban restaurant, 240 Columbus at 71st Street, is a holdout from the 1960s, when as many as 100,000 Cubans and Puerto Ricans settled in the neighborhood. Many have resettled in other boroughs, but Victor's continues to serve the best Latin food in the city. Nathan Cohen, a former network cameraman, sells his favorite toys, both antiques and reproductions, at **The Last Wound-Up**, on the west side of the street near 74th. **Mythology**, on the same side of the avenue at number 370, north of 77th Street, also sells toys, as well as a tastefully eccentric collection of books, posters, and other bric-a-brac. **Maxilla and Mandible**, across the avenue just north of 81st Street, takes advantage of its proximity to the natural history museum to stock a gruesomely fascinating collection of bones and taxidermic specimens.

The natty building across the avenue is the Endicott, an expensive cooperative apartment house that typifies the renovation that has reshaped so much of the Upper West Side in recent years. Before its conversion, the Endicott was a hotel of dubious distinction, losing on the average a guest a month to homicide. In an irony typical of this neighborhood, **Endicott Bookseller**, one of the smart new shops on the ground floor, is a gathering spot of local literati. There is still a hotel nearby, a very good one, the **Excelsior**, overlooking the museum on 81st Street between Columbus and Central Park West. A large double room here still costs less than $100, and slightly more will put you in a suite with a kitchenette; Tel: (212) 362-9200.

You will probably notice that a number of the shops on Columbus stand empty. Their former tenants learned a lesson: However high the aspirations of Upper West Siders may be, they are unwilling to pay $200 for a shirt—and you have to sell a good many shirts at that price to meet rents that average as much as $10,000 a month for even a small space.

To shop the way Upper West Siders do, walk west two blocks to Broadway. Like residents in European cities, New Yorkers tend to shun supermarkets—some in Manhattan maintain standards of cleanliness and service that would send Betty Crocker into a swoon—in favor of specialty shops. **Fairway**, 2127 Broadway at 74th Street, is a pleasure, even if New York's largest selection of greens and fruits isn't high on your New York shopping list. The store serves some 30,000 customers a week, many of whom stop in every day on their shopping rounds. Just up Broadway, at 75th Street, is **Citarella's**, a fishmonger that is as noted for its piscine window displays as it is for its exquisite selection of fresh fish. Even if you can't accommodate a red snapper rotting in a corner of your hotel room, you can partake of local shellfish at Citarella's stand-up clam bar.

**La Caridad**, at 78th and Broadway, is the best of a breed of Cuban-Chinese restaurants unique to New York. These places are run by Chinese who immigrated to Cuba, then fled to New York after Castro's takeover; La Caridad is frequented by a weird mix of taxi drivers (their favorite Manhattan hangout) and affluent young newcomers to the neighborhood. The large, white apartment house across 78th Street is the Apthorp, one of New York's best addresses, occupying an entire block and built around a dark though luxuriously quiet courtyard.

The Upper West Side's, and New York's, most famous food store is **Zabar's**, north on Broadway at 80th Street. The store's 160 employees sell 10,000 pounds of coffee, 10 tons of cheese, and 1,000 pounds of salmon a week—for total sales of $25 million a year—and Zabar's charges the lowest prices in New York for every item it stocks, be it a vacuum cleaner or a loaf of bread.

There is still much else to see on the Upper West Side, and you would do well to fortify yourself with coffee and pastry in Zabar's busy little coffee room. After that you might continue to pursue the neighborhood's two passions, food and books. For yet another sample of the former, walk across 80th Street to **H & H Bagels**, the city's largest manufacturer—70,000 a day—of this New York staple. **Shakespeare and Company** bookstore, north of Zabar's on Broadway at the corner of 81st Street, has only slightly less character than its Paris namesake and is very well stocked. **Gryphon**, just across Broadway, has a very fine, rather dusty collection of secondhand books (and an annex around the corner).

For New York's best smoked fish, you need walk only a few blocks north and one block east to **Barney Greengrass the Sturgeon King**, a deli and restaurant at 541 Amsterdam Avenue just north of 86th Street that counts among its past and present clientele the likes of Franklin D. Roosevelt, Groucho Marx, and Woody Allen. Some of the neighborhood's nicest restaurants are also on this shabby avenue, which is succumbing to gentrification only slowly. The real find here is **Ariba Ariba!**, on the west side of Amsterdam between 81st and 82nd; the Mexican fare here, served at a few cramped tables or delivered to neighborhood residents, is considered to be some of the best in the city.

## *RIVERSIDE DRIVE AND THE PARK*

It would be a shame to come to the West Side without having at least a glimpse of the Hudson River, and there is no better vantage point than Riverside Drive. Walking west from Broadway above 72nd Street, you will first cross West End Avenue, a street of tall, handsome apartment buildings that seems more typical of a residential quarter of Paris or old Berlin than of New York. What makes West End Avenue unique is the absence of shops—oddly enough, when the West Side was being laid out in the late 19th century, Broadway was to have been the residential street, serviced by businesses on West End—and the uniformity of its architecture. Most of these solidly middle-class buildings went up in the 1930s. In New York, leases are often passed from generation to generation, and many of these apartments are still occupied by the original tenants or their children and grandchildren. In recent years many of the buildings here and elsewhere on the Upper West Side have become cooperatives, and a comfortable two-bedroom apartment selling for less than $250,000 is a bargain. The same size apartment rents for $2,500 a month or more.

If you follow West End as far north as 94th Street, you will find one of the West Side's hidden treasures: **Pomander Walk**, a row of little town houses that look for all the world like cottages in a British village. Indeed, the Walk, built in the 1920s, was modeled on stage sets from a then popular British play of the same name. Suitably, these tiny rooms have been home to Humphrey Bogart, the Gish sisters, and many other actors.

**Riverside Drive**, one block to the west of West End, curves gently above the banks of the Hudson, which flows a hearty stone's-throw away on the far side of narrow Riverside Park. This lovely, exclusively residential, noncommercial avenue was originally lined with mansions, none more exquisite than the 65-room French château, complete with private chapel, that steel tycoon Charles Schwab built at Riverside Drive and 74th Street in 1904. Alas, in an uncharacteristic show of modesty, the city fathers decided not to buy the palace and make it the official mayor's residence, and the house came down to make way for an apartment building in the 1940s.

There are still a few survivors from the old days, though, including a dilapidated mansion at the corner of 89th Street and a whole block of fine French town houses between 105th and 106th. For the most part, the apartment buildings that have replaced the private homes are very pleasant places to live. As for **Riverside Park** itself, laid out, like Central Park, by Olmsted and Vaux in the 1870s, you will find it decidedly shabby or utterly romantic. It is both, and, given its isolation next to the river, you should confine your daylight exploration to well-trodden footpaths, and at night venture no farther north than the Soldiers and Sailors Monument, perched above the park on the drive at 89th Street.

A good place to see both park and river is the **79th Street Boat Basin** (just follow 79th Street all the way west). It may be hard to believe, but this shabby little marina often harbors the fleets of Donald Trump, Malcolm Forbes, and other rich and famous yachtsmen. It is also home to the few New Yorkers who live on houseboats, and the grassy lawn stretching up from the broad, noble river is as peaceful a place as any in New York for a picnic.

# COLUMBIA UNIVERSITY AND ITS NEIGHBORHOOD

Many residents of the Upper West Side went to school here, at Columbia University. You can walk to the campus, a straight shot up Broadway to 114th Street, or you can board the M 104 bus anywhere along Broadway.

Columbia bows to its Ivy League status with a large green quadrangle, but this is a decidedly urban, overbuilt campus. The university's major real-estate holding is not here but in Midtown—Columbia owns the land upon which Rockefeller Center was built. Like most universities, Columbia is surrounded by some good bookstores and inexpensive restaurants. Of the former, the best is **Barnard Book Forum**, just across Broadway from the main entrance to the campus and especially strong in history, philosophy, and literature, as well as books published by the Columbia University Press.

The students' favorite eateries are next to one another on Amsterdam Avenue between 110th and 111th streets. The **V & T Pizzeria** serves a pie that alone justifies a trip this far north. The **Hungarian Pastry Shop** allows its patrons to sit and read, downing strong coffee and rich poppy-seed rolls, as long as they wish, and the **Green Tree**, next door, serves hearty Hungarian fare in a homey atmosphere.

Just up the street here at 112th Street and Amsterdam is the **Cathedral Church of St. John the Divine**, which will be the world's largest cathedral if it is ever completed. The monstrous Episcopal edifice has been so long in the making, since 1892, that no one would recognize the site if it weren't buzzing with stone carvers. The neighborhood's other two monuments are west, on Riverside Drive. New York cab drivers are wont to ask out-of-towners if they know who is buried in **Grant's Tomb**. The answer lies at Riverside and 122nd Street, where the former president, who retired to New York four years before he died in 1885, lies next to his wife in a pompous marble mausoleum. The even colder, more imposing structure next door is Riverside Church, built by John D. Rockefeller in the 1920s.

# *THE MUSEUMS OF NORTH MANHATTAN*

Some of New York's finest smaller museums are north of Columbia in Harlem and elsewhere in upper Manhattan, and you needn't let the area's deservedly bad reputation keep you from seeing them. On Madison Avenue you can board an M 1 bus, which will deposit you at the **Schomburg Center for Research in Black Culture**, at 135th Street and Lenox Avenue. This amazing collection of materials relating to blacks, the world's most extensive, counts among its holdings some 50,000 prints and photographs, a small portion of which are on display at any one time.

**Audubon Terrace**, to the west at 155th Street and Broadway—you should take a cab from the Schomburg or, if travelling from areas farther south, the number 1 subway or M 4 or M 5 Madison Avenue buses—is a pleasant cluster of Neoclassical buildings that houses a delightfully eclectic mix of exhibitions: the **Museum of the American Indian**, the nation's largest collection of

Native American artifacts; the **Hispanic Society of America**, which owns a collection of paintings by Goya, Velázquez, and El Greco that is the envy of many a larger museum; the **American Numismatic Society**, the world's largest collection of coins; the **American Geographical Society**, the Western Hemisphere's largest collection of maps; and the **American Academy of Arts and Letters**, which has changing exhibits of American art.

If you travel still farther north, to the tip of Manhattan, your reward will be **The Cloisters**. You can reach the museum on the M 4 Madison Avenue bus, which will afford you a good look at Harlem and Washington Heights, a middle-class Jewish and Hispanic neighborhood whose lower rents have in recent years attracted the young writers, artists, and actors who once settled in Greenwich Village and on the Upper West Side. A faster route is the A line of the Eighth Avenue subway.

The Cloisters is a collection of five Medieval European cloisters, a 12th-century Chapter House, and other substantial treasures collected piecemeal in the early years of this century by George Bernard, a sculptor and architecture enthusiast. Mr. Bernard often had to pry discarded pillars and stones away from European homeowners who were using them as garden ornaments. He managed to reassemble the lot upon his return to New York, and sold it to John D. Rockefeller, who in turn presented the artifacts and a building to house them to the Metropolitan Museum of Art.

The cloisters are now handsomely planted with herb gardens and flowers, making it very easy for you to imagine you are in Europe and not in Manhattan—which will, nonetheless, lure you back after a pleasant afternoon here.

# CENTRAL PARK

*By Steven K. Amsterdam*

*Steven K. Amsterdam has been a resident of New York City for over 20 years and has written extensively about Central Park. Formerly editor of Chicago's* Grey City Journal, *Amsterdam is currently a travel editor in New York City.*

The New York legislature, in the 1850s, wanted to create some pleasant grounds for walking, something along the lines of London's manicured and formal Kensington Gardens. An area was chosen, covering 66th to 72nd streets and Third Avenue to the East River. Most of the land was city-owned and could have been easily landscaped. But William Marcy "Boss" Tweed, then city council president, argued for a larger and more central park, on some of the island's swampiest, rockiest land, which the city purchased from Tweed's friends at the absurdly inflated price of $7,500 an acre. A contest was held to find the best original plan for the central park. Frederick Law Olmsted (landscaper) and Calvert Vaux (architect) submitted their winning plan, which provided a naturalistic sanctuary within the city. Hills and valleys would be created so that the footpaths would meander instead of march across the landscapes. Transverse roads would be constructed to pass underneath the footpaths so visitors would not have to see the horse carriages. The style—the revolutionary idea of creating a wilderness—became a model for parks around the world.

More than a century later, Central Park is a full-service city park with midnight jogging, Polish folk dancing, ice-skating, bike racing, gondola rides, free performances of Shakespeare, tree climbing, and even some quiet places to sit and appreciate the flowers. In fact, recent commissioners of the Parks Department have restored much of what Olmsted and Vaux intended, and the park is looking more rustic now than it has in 50 years.

You should give Central Park at least an afternoon, to relax and watch the changing landscapes. Start at the new **Central Park Zoo** at 65th Street on the East Side. Its small but high-tech habitats took five years to complete. Best bets are the penguins (whose squawks are amplified over

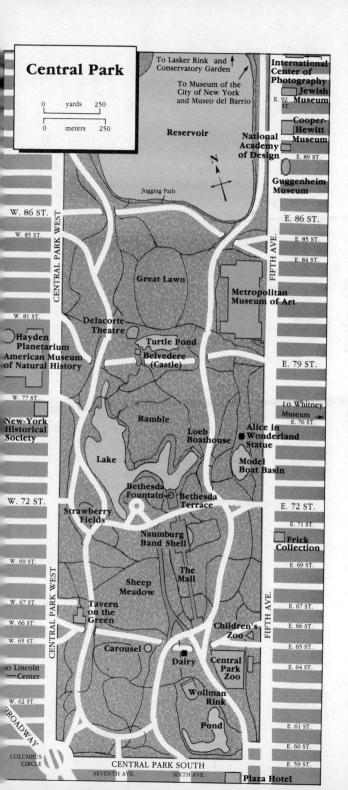

the speaker system), the playful seal feedings, and the Tropic Zone, an indoor rain forest complete with monkeys, snakes, free-flying birds, and bats.

Other sites in the southern portion of Central Park have given it a reputation as "The Children's District." Originally a distribution spot for fresh milk, the **Dairy** is now the visitors' center and usually has interesting exhibits and events. **Wollman Rink**, which was renovated a few years ago with funds from Donald Trump, offers ice-skating or roller-skating under the trees, depending on the season (rentals are available for $2.50). The nearby **Carousel**, built in 1908 (making it one of the oldest in North America), has been completely overhauled. One ride around, accompanied by organ music, will make you feel as if you're in either Old New York or a Hitchcock movie.

A walk along the elm-lined **Mall** to the north is likely to bring you to a free-lance magician, accordion player, or clown. Nearby, a company volleyball game and a flamboyant circle of disco skaters are usually on display. The Naumberg Band Shell's stage is given over to experimental musicians, actors, and artists as long as the weather permits. More organized events, such as jazz, blues, and reggae shows, go on each weekend of the summer.

The **Sheep Meadow**, just east of the Mall, hasn't had sheep on it since the Great Depression, when Mayor La Guardia decided the city couldn't afford their upkeep at a time when Hoovervilles were being built on the same grass. In the 1960s and 1970s, too many lively peace rallies and well-attended New York Philharmonic concerts threatened to destroy the terrain. The meadow, replanted, is currently fenced and occasionally off limits to visitors, in order to let the grass grow greener. When it is open to the frisbees of the public, it is a central spot in which to stretch out and enjoy a thick, well-tended lawn and a panoramic view of the city.

At 68th Street on the West Side a picnic lunch can be bought at the Tavern on the Green bus, a concession stand for picnickers outside the pricey but picturesque restaurant of the same name (the building was formerly a sheep hold). The box lunch, or a hot dog, for that matter, can be savored while watching skaters and skateboarders brave a tin-can obstacle course along the West Drive. At dusk, even the lights of the city don't cloud the sky over Sheep Meadow.

From there make the obligatory pilgrimage to the John

Lennon memorial, **Strawberry Fields**, across from the Dakota at the West 72nd Street entrance. New Yorkers may be too jaded to appreciate the *Imagine* mosaic at the center of the newly landscaped hill, but until the gift from Yoko Ono this area was not nearly as fashionably populated. Now every imaginable couple and crowd chooses this as a meeting ground. There are no strawberries here, by the way, but there are plants donated by more than 20 countries, including a cluster of white birch trees from the USSR.

The **Bethesda Fountain**, just off 72nd Street at the edge of the lake, is a meeting place for dog walkers and poets. Across the Lake, the **Loeb Boathouse** rents rowboats and is the departure point for gondola rides. There are two eating establishments here, one providing *nouvelle cuisine* and the other sandwiches. Behind the boathouse is the extensive and uncharted **Ramble**, a maze of small overgrown paths and streams and a haven for the adventurous who enjoy solitude—as well as watching others enjoy solitude. Recently a few log shelters have been built here, with complete loyalty to Olmsted and Vaux's original plans.

A spot for younger visitors is the **Model Boat Basin**, where, except in the dead of winter, toy sailboats, motorboats, and subs sail every weekend. A statue with magnetic charm is situated at the northern end of the pond: **Alice in Wonderland**, sitting on a mushroom, usually covered with all the children who can climb on.

If you are not ready to brave the Ramble, you can walk north along the Drive, through the back end of the Ramble, and up to **Belvedere Castle**. From here you can see the busy Midtown skyline—Victorian and Postmodern on the same block—as well as the more majestic and less congested views of Central Park West and Fifth Avenue. Just to the north are the somewhat murky Turtle Pond and the Great Lawn.

The open-air **Delacorte Theatre**, just under the cliffs of Belvedere Castle, offers free performances of Shakespeare's plays all summer long (Tel: 212-861-PAPP). Last year's program included Kevin Kline and Blythe Danner in *Much Ado About Nothing*. Do not pass up an opportunity to see the plays, with the backdrop of Belvedere Castle, the pond, and the stars; Broadway cannot offer an experience as evocative or as inexpensive. When the reviews are good, however, getting a seat involves sitting out on the Great Lawn for the afternoon until the tickets are distributed at 6:00. However, with a few trips to Zabar's delicatessen at Broadway and 80th Street for sustenance, this is not an altogether painful experience.

Currently, the **Great Lawn** is what the Sheep Meadow was in the 1970s—a playing field and gathering spot. As a result, the lawn itself is not so great. Still, baseball games, kite flying, ice-sculpture competitions, and all sorts of performances (from *La Bohème* to Elton John) can make the Great Lawn a memorable place to visit.

The **Conservatory Garden** at 105th Street and Fifth Avenue is a northern point well worth the exploration, as it is a reminder of what the park is not. When Olmsted began importing trees and bushes to the agriculturally barren region—before the project was launched there were only 42 species on the site—a nursery had to be established. Over time, 1,300 varieties of trees and shrubs were planted here in orderly rows, resembling a formal garden. Once the park was completed, they decided to keep the nursery as it was. The Conservatory Garden now has a perfectly timed procession of flowers in bloom throughout the spring, summer, and fall. The symmetrical paths of the garden circle around two delicate fountains.

For skating, the **Lasker Rink** (just in from the 110th Street entrance to the park) is cheaper and less crowded than the Wollman, though the clientele is a bit more rowdy. On the park's northernmost edge, the Harlem Meer looks like a city dump and beyond it is a burned-out building. But the Parks Department is not far behind. By 1991 they expect to have the water completely dredged and relandscaped, and the building will be fixed up and turned into an activities center for children.

All of Central Park can be done on foot, but you will be exhausted. Possibilities to explore are: biking, (212) 861-4137; boating, (212) 517-2233; group jogging, (914) 439-5155; group running, (212) 860-4455; horseback riding, (212) 724-5100; horsedrawn carriage riding, (212) 246-0520; any other kind of information, (212) 397-3156.

# THE UPPER EAST SIDE

## By Susan Farewell

*Susan Farewell, a longtime resident of Manhattan and until recently associate travel editor of* Bride's *magazine, is now a free-lance writer. She is a contributor to* Travel and Leisure, Diversion, *and* Caribbean Travel and Life *magazines.*

It's been called the "Yupper East Side," and indeed, the area east of Central Park, roughly between 59th and 96th streets, may have Manhattan's largest concentration of young urban professionals. Many of them live in expensive luxury towers with names like Highgate and Normandie Court. Many work out in clubs that cost as much as $1,000 a year; add another three grand for tennis at the "you've arrived" Vertical Club. But then there are the young adults who make less than $30,000 a year and wouldn't dream of living anywhere but the Upper East Side. What do they do? It's not uncommon to find two—sometimes even three—singles sharing studio apartments that rent for up to $1,500 a month.

New York's Upper East Side is also where old, established money lives, especially between Park and Fifth avenues. The scrubbed streets are lined with stately town houses, opulent mansions, and solid apartment buildings. Here's where you'll see limos, an occasional Daimler or Rolls, Swedish au pairs walking apricot-white poodles, and everyone else looking as though they might be somebody.

The museums and galleries in the area could keep you occupied for weeks, but so could the antiques shops (it's the largest antiques center in the world), the European boutiques that line Madison Avenue, and the architecture, an endlessly fascinating forest of buildings. Like the rest of New York City, the Upper East Side is best seen à pied.

### MAJOR INTEREST

Frick Collection
Temple Emanu-El
Antiques shops and boutiques
Art galleries

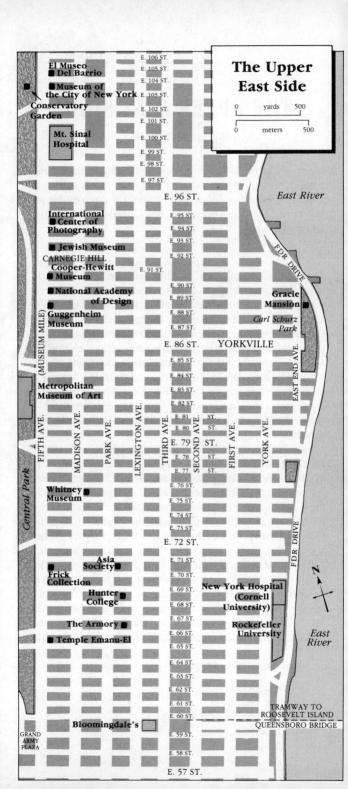

# UPPER EAST SIDE

Whitney Museum of American Art
Asia Society
Bloomingdale's
Restaurants and bars

**Yorkville**
Carl Schurz Park
Gracie Mansion
Henderson Place Historic District
Church of the Holy Trinity
Sotheby's auction house
The night scene

**Carnegie Hill**
Millionaires' Row mansions and town houses
View down Park Avenue
Façade of the Squadron A Armory
Shops and boutiques

**Museum Mile**
Metropolitan Museum of Art
Guggenheim Museum
Cooper-Hewitt Museum
Jewish Museum
International Center of Photography
Museum of the City of New York

As you move north of Midtown on the East Side (above 59th Street and east of Central Park), you'll notice that the buildings get increasingly shorter (with the exception of the residential high-rises in Yorkville); the streets are less crowded, and the energy level isn't as frighteningly high—especially on summer weekends, when the whole Upper East Side population seems to flee to the Jersey Shore, upstate New York, Connecticut, or the Hamptons.

Where to start is always a good question. Basically, you can hopscotch back and forth between avenues and hit the most worthwhile attractions. Start by caffeinating yourself with a cup of coffee at **Caffè Strada**, a state-of-the-art pushcart parked at Grand Army Plaza (Fifth Avenue and Central Park South, in front of the Plaza Hotel). In a city where the coffee served is often as transparent as tea, this is a real find. The proprietors saw the need for some decent coffee in New York, especially for people on the run. So here you have it, $1.00 for decaf or regular, $2.25 for cappuccino. Steps away are the **Strand Book Store kiosks**, where you could spend an hour or more looking through books, tapes, and maps spread out on tables and in large kiosks on the sidewalk.

Continue north up Fifth to the **Temple Emanu-El** (1 East 65th), the largest Reform synagogue in the United States, and then to the **Frick Collection** (1 East 70th), a superb collection of European paintings, antique furniture, and decorative arts in an elegant Fifth Avenue mansion. Unless you want to do upper Fifth Avenue's Museum Mile the same day, turn right on any cross street and head over to **Madison Avenue**. The city's biggest concentration of toney boutiques, antiques shops, and galleries are located on this stretch between 59th and 79th streets. And, because of zoning, all are in attractive town houses or brownstones, and often have residences on higher floors. Among the shops, you'll find Villeroy & Boch, Ralph Lauren Polo, Saint Laurent Rive Gauche, and Kenzo-Paris, all lined up like contestants in a beauty contest. (See the Fashion section for more on Madison Avenue shopping.)

You'll also find on the East Side the fine-arts auctioneer **Christie's** (502 Park Avenue, at 59th Street) and its branch, **Christie's East** (219 East 67th Street, between Second and Third; Tel: 212-546-1000 for information).

At 75th Street and Madison stands the **Whitney Museum of American Art**, which you might want to save for a Tuesday night when admission is free and it becomes a buzzing hive of mingling singles. Veer off to Park at 70th Street if you're interested in seeing the **Asia Society** (725 Park), founded under the guidance of John D. Rockefeller III, who wanted to increase American awareness of Asian culture. Back on Madison, you'll pass the **Carlyle Hotel** (35 East 76th Street), which is worth returning to for dinner: The **Carlyle Restaurant** serves classical French cuisine in one of New York's most elegant and sophisticated rooms. Farther down Madison you'll come to **Le Relais** (712 Madison between 63rd and 64th), a fashionable bistro packed with Europeans. It's a great lunch spot, especially if you sit outside on a beautiful day.

At some point in the 60s, start inching your way east, so you can sample a bit of Lexington Avenue. It's chockablock with a variety of boutiques and shops (not all as prohibitively expensive as those on Madison) and Greek-owned coffee shops where you can still get a meal for less that ten dollars (today, in New York City, that's close to a miracle). Look up to the second stories on Lexington and you'll see lots of nail salons, some called nail sculptors. Look down to the sidewalk and you'll see sneakers donned by young professionals. The suit-cum-sneakers ensemble has become totally acceptable, even in high-fashion circles.

Next stop: **Bloomingdale's** (Lexington Avenue at 59th Street). One of the most amusing things about this department store is that absolutely every visitor includes it on his or her sightseeing list. It's right up there with the Empire State Building and the Statue of Liberty. Whatever you do, though, don't call it Bloomie's. You will immediately be identified as an out-of-towner. You might also want to go there with your defenses up; otherwise you'll walk out smelling like a five year old who played dress-up with mommy's perfumes. Mannequinlike men and women stand with index fingers ready to tap the sprayers of different fragrances as they call out the names of their products. Bloomingdale's is *always* busy, so don't go when you're feeling cramped, and don't go on Sunday, when it is usually closed.

Some of the East Side's best restaurants are in the Bloomingdale's area, including **Arizona 206** (206 East 60th, near Third Avenue; Southwestern cuisine); **Contrapunto** (200 East 60th at Third Avenue; great pasta); **Arcadia** (21 East 62nd, between Madison and Fifth; down-home American food); and **The Sign of the Dove** (1110 Third Avenue at 65th Street; a costly brunch spot). And of course there's **Le Cirque** (58 East 65th, between Madison and Park), the ultimate French restaurant in New York City—very expensive and very difficult to get reservations.

# *YORKVILLE*

You have to have a really great imagination to picture what this shore of Manhattan Island looked like in the late 18th century. At that time it was considered "upstate New York," where only the fabulously wealthy could afford to have country homes. With the advent of the railroad linking New York City with Harlem in 1834, Yorkville was "suburbanized" and attracted Eastern European and German immigrants. Though many of the Germans, Czechs, and Hungarians have since migrated to the suburbs, there are still traces of their heritage—especially in small restaurants and businesses from the low to mid-70s and up to 96th Street, between Park Avenue and the East River. Today's Yorkville residents are predominantly young working couples and singles.

Although 86th Street and Second Avenue are the main streets of Yorkville, a good starting place for a walking tour is **Carl Schurz Park**, which is built directly over the Franklin D. Roosevelt Drive, smack-dab on the East River and stretching from 90th Street to Gracie Square at 84th Street.

The centerpiece of the park is the mayor's official residence, **Gracie Mansion**. The original part of the house was built as a country home for merchant seaman Archibald Gracie; it later passed through a series of wealthy owners, each of whom eventually lost his fortune. In 1924 it was taken over by the Museum of the City of New York and later—during Mayor La Guardia's term—turned into the official mayor's residence. Mayor Koch is to thank for opening it up to the public. Tours are conducted on Wednesdays (Tel: 212-570-4751 for an appointment). The house as it stands today is actually a historic re-creation, not a restoration, of the Federal style. Many of the interior pieces are on loan from museums and private collections, or are reproductions. There is a perennial exhibit called "Merchants to Mayors" in the basement, and a gift shop where you can buy memo pads that say Gracie Mansion.

The park's waterfront esplanade—the John Finley Walk—is a fine place to perch yourself for a rest. Grab a bench that looks out at the churning East River and you'll have a hard time leaving. This is one of those places that keeps all New Yorkers in love with the city. You see sparkling white sailboats temporarily disappearing from sight behind swelling waves, sturdy tugboats shoving the water out of the way like snow plows, and hundreds of lenses pointing in your direction from the Circle Line sightseeing boats. At the same time, a helicopter might sputter into view, or a blimp, casting a shadow like a cloud. You also see Roosevelt, Wards, and Randalls islands, the Triborough Bridge, and Hell Gate Arch. And of course there's a soufflé of New Yorkers sharing the scene: the dog walkers, the stroller pushers, the sunbathers, the New York *Post* readers, the lunch eaters, the school groups, and an aggressive collection of squirrels and pigeons looking for handouts.

Just outside the park (86th Street) there's a stunning block of Queen Anne–style row houses, the **Henderson Place Historic District**, with slate roofs, charming windows of all shapes and sizes, turrets, and double stoops. Continue on west through Yorkville and you'll pass hundreds of row houses (each one is usually just 20 to 25 feet wide), stately town houses (fancy row houses for people who could afford to have pieds-à-terre), and innumerable nondescript high-rise apartment fortresses. Sadly, these towers are eating up the old neighborhoods.

On sight of the **Church of the Holy Trinity**, between First and Second avenues on 88th Street, you'll think you're in the Loire Valley. The church is French Gothic style with gargoyles, flying buttresses, arches, and ornate copper work. The inside is just as impressive, with Medieval-style stained-glass windows and an incredible rank of organ pipes. Check the newspapers for information on Holy Trinity's winter organ recitals and classical-music concerts.

Also in Yorkville, you'll find Sotheby Parke Bernet, known as **Sotheby's** (1334 York Avenue at 72nd Street), the American branch of the world's oldest firm of arts auctioneers. This is the auction house that sold most of Andy Warhol's estate, and van Gogh's *Irises* for $53.9 million (Tel: 212-606-7000 for information).

For dining in Yorkville, consider **Jams** (154 East 79th, east of Lexington), an expensive California-style restaurant with a fascinating menu that changes quite frequently. Hope that they'll still be offering the cornmeal-coated catfish. **Le Refuge** (166 East 82nd, between Third and Lexington) is a quiet, refined bistro with country French decor. Its clientele is made up largely of Upper East Siders who show up dressed in anything from casual weekend clothes to Brooks Brothers suits. If you want to do a little celebrity watching, try **Lusardi's** (1494 Second Avenue, between 77th and 78th), where the Italian cuisine is unfailingly good. Though everyone will tell you that **Elaine's** (1703 Second Avenue, between 88th and 89th) is where to go stargazing, don't bother. Not only is the food lamentable, but ordinary people are made to feel like real nobodies. However, it used to be a bastion of New York literati, including Woody Allen, who used it as a location in *Manhattan*. A good Italian find is **Remi** (323 East 79th, between First and Second avenues), a bustling little ristorante with at least half a dozen out-of-the-ordinary pasta dishes. One of the last remaining Eastern European restaurants in Yorkville is **Vasata** (339 East 75th, between First and Second avenues), which serves New York City's best Czechoslovakian food in an old Bohemian setting.

The Upper East Side is famous for its profusion of bars, mostly on First Avenue in the 60s and on Second and Third from 72nd to 94th streets. If you want to sample the bar scene here, drop in at **Jim McMullen** (1341 Third, between 75th and 76th). In a city where bars open and close like flowers, this one has managed to stay hot for years. The clientele is made up of many regulars, most of whom are fashion models and professional athletes. Tops on the list of trendy spots is **The Outback** (between 93rd and 94th on Third), a scuzzy-looking bar with cigarette butts on the floor and much too loud music. Pour down an Aussie beer, pull out all the Down Under phrases you know, and you'll fit right in. On weekend nights it's so popular that the spillover crowds bide their time across the street at **The Launch Café** until they can get in. The Upper East Side is also home to two very good comedy clubs: **The Comic Strip** (1568 Second, near 81st Street) and **Catch a Rising Star** (1487 First, near 77th).

## *CARNEGIE HILL*

Carnegie Hill is more a state of mind than an actual neighborhood. It stretches from about 86th to 96th streets, from Fifth to Park, but sometimes reaches over as far as Lexington and Third, as indicated by some shop and building names. You won't find it marked on most maps and will come across few—if any—New Yorkers who can tell you exactly where it begins and ends.

The area became known as Carnegie Hill in 1901 when Andrew Carnegie built a mansion (now the Cooper-Hewitt Museum) on 91st and Fifth. Up until that point, the socially acceptable place to live was south of 59th Street. His bold step set off a trend, and before long several mansions sprang to life along a section of Fifth facing the park. The Astors, the Vanderbilts, and other wealthy families began migrating up to the area, which soon became known as **Millionaires' Row**. The growth of Madison Avenue and the side streets between Madison and Fifth followed. Today, Carnegie Hill continues to be one of the most exclusive neighborhoods in the world (Richard Nixon couldn't get in after his presidency).

To get a feel for the area, just wander aimlessly. Most of the mansions and lavish town houses line Fifth (many now house small museums or consulates) or are tucked away on side streets, especially in the lower 90s between Fifth and Madison. Make a point of getting over to see 120 and 122 East 92nd Street, two wooden town houses that were built in the late 1800s, complete with shutters and columned front porches. Over on Park at 92nd, there's a Louise Nevelson sculpture called *Night Presence,* a 22-foot-high steel work donated to the city by the artist in 1972. A block north is the headquarters building of the Synod of Bishops of the Russian Orthodox Church Outside of Russia, which was owned in the late 1920s by banker George F. Baker, who had a private railroad car that would stop directly beneath the building (the railway tracks for Grand Central Station run under Park here). It's not open to the public, but you can peek in at a garden courtyard that leads to a ballroom that Baker added to the original 1918 structure.

The view south down Park Avenue from Carnegie Hill is spectacular. The avenue dips down like a rolled-out carpet, with building cornices lined up, drawing your eye to what used to be the New York Central Building (now the Helmsley) between 45th and 46th streets, with the Pan Am Building looming over it. And though the color gray predominates, there's a central divider planted with a colorful profusion of flowers, trees, and bushes in fair-weather months. During the winter season, delicate white lights strung in the trees give the avenue a delightful carnival spirit at night. Most Park Avenue buildings are compatible in size (from 15 to 18 floors) and materials (all are brick, many have limestone trim), with the exception of the occasional town house or church.

In contrast to the present-day vista, before 1900 Park Avenue was not a very coveted address. The railroads ran above ground and were lined with rather humble dwellings and unattractive factories. Beginning in 1872 the tracks were moved below street level as far north as 56th Street. It was not until after the completion of Grand Central Terminal in 1913, however, that the tracks were depressed as far north as 96th Street. By the 1920s, the avenue had become very desirable real estate, with one luxury residential building after another. Today it continues to be one of New York's most fashionable areas—up to 96th Street, where Spanish Harlem abruptly begins.

If you follow 93rd Street back west toward Madison, you'll pass a classical mansion with Palladian and bull's-eye windows and a discreet sign identifying it as the Smithers Alcoholism Treatment Center. It was originally a house built for William Goadby Loew, a stockbroker, and later was owned by Billy Rose, a producer and art collector, and a husband of Elizabeth Taylor. The façade of the former **Squadron A Armory** between 94th and 95th on

Madison is hard not to notice. It's a massive fortresslike building with arched doorways, towers, and battlements. Walk through the entrance and you'll find yourself in the middle of a playground that serves next-door Hunter High School.

Carnegie Hill architecture can keep you mesmerized for hours, but so can the shops along Madison Avenue. Forget about buying anything; most of the shops belong to exclusive name chains and are here just for show. But if you're in the market for antiques this is where to find them. If money is no object, you can have a glorious time. Many of the small boutiques and shops sell European imports, including shoes in European sizes (they're displayed as if they are precious objets d'art) and handbags the size of paperbacks for $300 and up. You never have to walk more than a few blocks to find a gourmet shop in the neighborhood, where chances are good that you will find that rare mustard you thought you could only get in Lyon.

Consider brunching at **Sarabeth's Kitchen** (1295 Madison, between 92nd and 93rd). The setting is delightful, with high ceilings, light floral wallpaper, small round tables covered with crisp white tablecloths, and vases spilling over with daisies. The food is wholesome and good: specialties such as whole-wheat pancakes topped with fruit and wheatberries, pumpkin waffles, and cheddar and apple-butter omelets. It's connected to the **Hotel Wales**, a longtime favorite among loyal guests, with some of the most reasonable rates in town (see Accommodations section). The **Bistro du Nord**, Madison at 93rd, is very European and comfortable, and across the street is the fashionable restaurant **Island**. Carnegie Hill is not generally known for its restaurants, though. If you're looking for a dinner place, you're better off elsewhere on the Upper East Side.

## *MUSEUM MILE*

Museum Mile is a consortium of ten cultural institutions on Fifth Avenue between 82nd and 104th streets. The grande dame is the **Metropolitan Museum of Art** (The Met), a gargantuan building on the edge of Central Park between 80th and 84th streets (closed Mondays). Especially impressive is its Egyptian Wing. The American Wing is rich with over 3,000 paintings and decorative arts from the Colonial period to the 20th century. Other outstanding collections, each worth at least half a day, are the European Painting rooms, the Meyer Galleries of 19th-century European paintings, the new modern-art wing, and the Rockefeller primitive-art collection. The museum shops are spectacular, too. You'll need a break afterward, so stop for tea at the Stanhope Hotel's **Terrace**, a pleasant sidewalk café directly opposite.

The nine other museums are spread out along Fifth on the east side of the street. Walking north, you'll pass them all. First, you'll come to **Goethe House New York** (1014 Fifth), a Beaux Arts building that houses a branch of Munich's Goethe Institute. In addition to exhibitions, it offers film programs, lectures, and theatrical performances. Next is the **Yivo Institute for Jewish Research** (1048 Fifth at 86th Street), housed in one of Fifth Avenue's most exquisite mansions, with Ionic pilasters, balustrades, rosettes, and bull's-eye windows. The museum is devoted to the history of Eastern European Jews. Frank Lloyd Wright's **Solomon R. Guggenheim Museum** (1071 Fifth, between 88th and 89th streets) is one of the city's most distinctive buildings. It contains painting and sculpture from the Impressionist period to the present; most of the exhibit space is devoted to temporary exhibitions. (Closed Mondays.)

A block north, between 89th and 90th streets, is the **National Academy of Design** (1083 Fifth), which holds a rich collection of 19th- and 20th-century American art. At 90th stands the Protestant Episcopal **Church of the Heavenly Rest**, a Gothic church with a tiny side chapel. Directly across the street is the main meeting place for joggers warming up to do "the loop"—a run around Central Park's Reservoir. The entrance of the **Cooper-Hewitt Museum**, the Smithsonian Institution's museum of design, is at 2 East 91st Street. This was millionaire Andrew Carnegie's home, a 64-room mansion with elaborately carved woodwork throughout. The exhibits change regularly, but always focus on some aspect of design. Directly across the street is the Convent of the Sacred Heart (1 East 91st), a neo-Italian palazzo, now a girls' school. (This area contains many of the city's private schools, most on the side streets.) Continue up Fifth and you'll come to the **Jewish Museum** (1109 Fifth) in a French Renaissance–style mansion. In addition to its permanent collection of Judaica it runs temporary exhibits.

**The International Center of Photography** (1130 Fifth) has changing exhibits by 19th- and 20th-century photographers and photojournalists. Several blocks up (at 103rd Street) is the **Museum of the City of New York**, where the city's history is re-created. Call for information (Tel: 212-534-1672) about their Sunday walking tours. At 104th Street, **El Museo del Barrio** (1230 Fifth) completes the Museum Mile. It's the only museum in America devoted to the cultures of Puerto Rico and Latin America.

# BROOKLYN

*By Randall Short*

*Randall Short is a cultural journalist who writes on books and theater for* The New York Times, New York Newsday, *and* Spy *magazine.*

"When the sun is shining and the wind is right," says a character in Richard Condon's *Prizzi's Honor,* "there ain't no place like Brooklyn!" If Manhattan is flash and glitter, Brooklyn (perhaps recalling its origins as Dutch-colonized farmland in the 1600s) is the gentler side of urban living in New York. Although Manhattanites used to regard Brooklyn simply as a bedroom community across the river, that attitude has given way in recent years to a vigorous, renewed sense of local pride perceptible even to the casual visitor. The borough owes much of its character to close-knit neighborhoods, a diverse ethnic mix—West Indies blacks, Hasidic Jews, Norwegians, Russians, and Middle Easterners barely begin to exhaust the list—and a superbly preserved heritage of 19th-century architecture.

Older Brooklynites still joke about a time when "fine dining" meant one thing: chow mein and egg rolls in one of the borough's numerous Chinese restaurants, a Canarsie kid's usual introduction in the 1930s and 1940s to foods more exotic than bagels or corned beef. At that time the borough was home to working-class Irish, Italian, and Jewish families, whose distinctive accents and don't-try-to-bullshit-me attitudes still characterize the Brooklynite. Now, however, Brooklyn offers variety in dining comparable to that in Manhattan—often at significantly lower prices—and its row houses are being snatched up by

Manhattanites for a relative song, compared to prices across the East River.

Brooklyn lies to the east and south of Manhattan, connected to it by three bridges and a network of subways. Prior to its annexation into New York City in 1898 ("the Big Mistake," one Brooklyn-born writer calls it), the borough's 77 square miles formed a separate city composed of six principal towns and numerous small independent villages. Much of the area still has a strong regional feel; inhabitants consider themselves Bay Ridgers or Williamsburgers or Park Slopers first, Brooklynites second, and the neighborhoods bear strong witness to several successive waves of immigrant history.

### MAJOR INTEREST

Brooklyn Bridge
Promenade view of Manhattan skyline
Brooklyn Heights's Brownstone Belt
Atlantic Avenue Middle-Eastern community
Brooklyn Academy of Music
Prospect Park
Brooklyn Botanic Garden
Brooklyn Museum
Brighton Beach's Little Odessa
Greenpoint

Subways and cabs will take you from Manhattan into Brooklyn with no trouble, but it may be more difficult to hail a cab going the opposite direction—drivers tend to prefer the crowded Midtown district for pickup business. However, there are numerous car services to ferry you around. Or—an alternative solution—rent a bike and make the trek from Manhattan over the pedestrian walkway atop Brooklyn Bridge, from which there's no finer view anywhere.

Take the IRT number 2 or 3 train to the Brooklyn Heights stop (20 minutes from Midtown Manhattan), walk two blocks to the small park square at the end of nearby Montague Street, and you're at a natural point of entry to the borough, the Esplanade, commonly called the **Promenade**, a pleasant bench- and tree-lined walkway built by legendary city commissioner Robert Moses. Fronting the East River and lower Manhattan, it offers an unparalleled view of the harbor, the Financial District, and the borough's best-known symbol, **Brooklyn Bridge**, the 1883

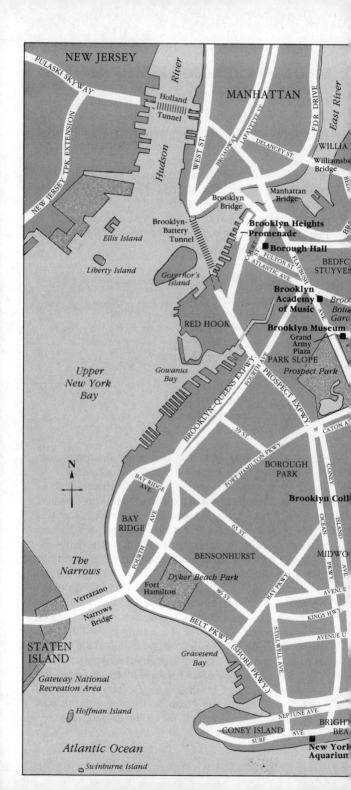

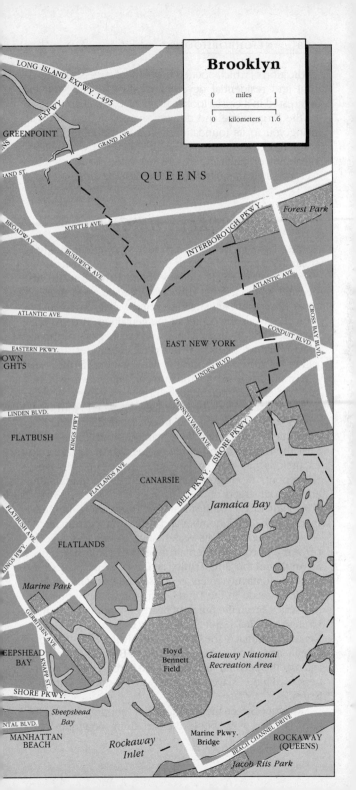

dedication of which opened Brooklyn to large-scale industrial and residential development. If you find yourself interested in a closer look at the bridge, a walk to the end of the Promenade and down a sharply sloping hill will bring you to its foundations—and to the **River Café** (1 Water Street; reservations, Tel: 718-722-5200), which offers pleasantly elegant (and expensive) waterside dining from a French-style menu featuring American classics.

## *BROOKLYN HEIGHTS*

Some 70 years before the bridge's completion, when steam-ferry service between Brooklyn and Manhattan was begun, the riverbank neighborhood **Brooklyn Heights** became America's first suburb, conceived as an oasis of genteel *rus in urbe* living for harried Wall Street businessmen. Today it's the center of the gentrified "Brownstone Belt," a swath of magnificent urban architecture rediscovered in the late 1950s by young professionals resisting the call of Levittown-style housing developments farther out.

A walk down any of the surrounding streets will reveal dozens of meticulously preserved Greek Revival and Federal-period brownstones crowned with gargoyles, oriel windows, and finely detailed ornament. A convenient route might be to start out south down Hicks near the northern end of the Promenade and make side excursions, as the whim takes you, on Middagh, Pierrepont, Montague, Henry, Strawberry, Joralemon, and Warren streets.

Brooklyn acquired the nickname "Borough of Churches" in the 1800s for the number and distinction (both architectural and clerical) of its ecclesiastical institutions; several of the most prominent remain in central Brooklyn Heights. **St. Ann's and the Holy Trinity**, an Episcopal parish at Clinton and Montague streets, possesses the first stained-glass windows made in the United States and hosts a popular arts series. From the pulpit of nearby **Plymouth Church** at Orange and Hicks streets—formerly known as "the Grand Central Terminal of the Underground Railroad"—the clergyman and abolitionist Henry Ward Beecher preached against "the peculiar institution" and harbored large numbers of fugitive slaves on their way to sanctuary in the North.

Montague Street, the Heights' main shopping thoroughfare, is filled with bookstores, clothing boutiques, art galleries, and lots of convivial, moderately priced places for a bite and a swallow. The bars at **Peter Hilary's Bar and Grill** (174 Montague Street), **Slade's** (107 Montague Street), and **Montague Street Saloon** (122 Montague Street) draw a young professional crowd from the nearby downtown City Hall and court districts; try **Foffe's** (155 Montague Street) down the block for lovingly prepared traditional Italian specialties. If you're in the mood for game, **Henry's End** (44 Henry Street) regularly features dishes like pheasant, quail, bear, buffalo, and reindeer; a 52-selection beer list is available to help wash them down. And, after a few anxious months spent in the shadow of the wrecker's ball, the classic wood- and mirror-paneled 1870s salon of **Gage & Tollner** (372 Fulton Street, in the nearby downtown shopping district; Tel: 718-875-5181) has been rescued by restaurateur Peter Aschkenasy and restored to its full gastronomic glory. "Brooklyn's Landmark Restaurant," as it bills itself, now offers both its hallowed seafood specialties (try the clam bellies) and Virginia-style dishes (Smithfield ham, homemade breads and preserves) by the renowned Southern chef Edna Lewis.

## *ATLANTIC AVENUE*

Nearby Atlantic Avenue is lined with shops and restaurants, many of them operated by and catering to the recent wave of Middle Easterners that have relocated in Brooklyn. An antique district with dozens of small independent stores has recently sprung up here to service the growing crowd of new home buyers. It offers prices substantially lower than those in Manhattan. After you've loaded up on porcelain and sconces, try the kebabs, curries, and couscous at **Adnan** (129 Atlantic Avenue) or **Tripoli** (156 Atlantic Avenue), two of the area's more elegantly appointed Arab restaurants. Slightly more modest, but just as good, are **Son of Sheik** (165 Atlantic Avenue), featuring Lebanese specialties, and **Near East** (136 Court Street), whose motto hangs on a sign over the door: It Pays To Eat Well.

## Brooklyn Academy of Music

Avant-garde performance is alive and flourishing just off the intersection of Atlantic and Flatbush avenues at the **Brooklyn Academy of Music** (20 minutes from Midtown

Manhattan on the D train to the Atlantic Avenue station; box office, Tel: 718-636-4100), America's oldest continuously operating performing arts center. BAM, as it's commonly known, operates out of a superb 1908 opera house and offers New York's largest ongoing concentration of experimental dance, music, and theater. The fall Next Wave festival regularly premieres new work by the likes of Pina Bausch, Philip Glass, and Robert Wilson. Around the corner, BAM's newly opened **Majestic Theater**, a turn-of-the-century variety stage, has been renovated in the Postmodern manner by director Peter Brook, who makes his American creative home here.

# *PARK SLOPE*

From BAM, Flatbush Avenue runs through a renovated commercial district, into Park Slope, a magnificent enclave of late Victorian homes developed in the 1880s for Brooklyn's prosperous English and German upper middle classes. The houses' satisfying combination of sober practicality and fancifulness (elaborately carved stone detailing, delicate cast-iron filigree, decorative castings) today seems more modern—certainly more popular—than ever.

The neighborhood's focal point is the center of old Brooklyn, **Grand Army Plaza** (40 minutes from Midtown Manhattan on the number 2 or 3 West Side IRT train to the Grand Army Plaza station; 20 minutes on the D train to the Seventh Avenue station), a European-style traffic circle with a memorial arch built in 1892 to honor Brooklyn's Union Army war dead. The group of statues at its summit, featuring Columbia (the pre–Uncle Sam symbol of America) at the center of a victory quadriga, are by the prominent 19th-century American sculptor Frederick MacMonnies; relief panels over the inner entrance doorways by Thomas Eakins are the only public Eakins sculptures in New York City.

Walk from the plaza down the wide, pleasant spaces of Eighth Avenue and its side streets (Carroll, Garfield, Montgomery Place) for a look at the comfortable gentility of the 19th-century good life; then skip over for drinks on Seventh Avenue, the main shopping drag, at **McFeely's** (847 Union Street), a Victorian-style saloon from which waitresses (such as Kelly McGillis) routinely go on to become movie stars, or **Rex** (222 Seventh Avenue), an old

Irish bar with a new Caribbean flair. **Cousin John's Café**, with two Seventh Avenue locations, makes its own pastry and fresh ice cream on the premises. And, a little farther down, the kitchen of **Aunt Suzie's** (247 Fifth Avenue between Carroll and Garfield) turns out inexpensive trattoria fare in a homey atmosphere.

From the plaza, three of the borough's proudest attractions are within a few minutes' stroll of one another. **Prospect Park**, a pastoral, 526-acre expanse of trees, grass, and water (its Long Meadow offers the largest green vista unbroken by buildings in New York City), is the masterpiece of urban designers Frederick Law Olmsted and Calvert Vaux, who also created Manhattan's Central Park. Begun in 1866, it was built on land from the estate of city father Edwin Litchfield, whose palatial Italianate villa is the park's headquarters. Contemporary Brooklynites of every stripe now come from all over to picnic, ice skate, play ball, and enjoy concerts in the band shell, site of the popular Celebrate Brooklyn summer festival. Across from the band shell is **Raintree's** (142 Prospect Park West), a restaurant in a converted drugstore with tile floors and stained-glass windows that open onto the park. Regulars drop in after park concerts for an eclectic range of entrées based on Italian home cooking. A couple of blocks down, **Aunt Sonia's** (1123 Eighth Avenue), named for the neighboring Ansonia Clock Factory, is a newcomer serving classic American dishes with a piquant twist in an intimate, friendly atmosphere.

Dismayed by the intrusion of not entirely appropriate buildings (like the Metropolitan Museum) into their design for Central Park, Olmsted and Vaux didn't make the same mistake twice: They insisted that the Prospect Park commissioners set aside a tract of land separate from the park proper to accommodate subsequent developments. So cross the street and you're in the **Brooklyn Botanic Garden** (1000 Washington Avenue; Tel: 718-622-4433). The botanic garden, with a design reminiscent of an English estate and grounds, contains a Japanese scholar's garden, a cherry esplanade that bears great clouds of soft pink blossoms in the spring, the Cranford Rose Garden (third largest in the United States), and the new Steinhardt Conservatory of tropical and desert plants. The number 2 and 3 subway line stops at its door and that of the **Brooklyn Museum** (200 Eastern Parkway). The museum's stately Beaux Arts building is undergoing expansion these days.

## BRIGHTON BEACH

If you're in the mood for a longer trip, 40 minutes on the D train from Midtown Manhattan will land you in Brighton Beach, just up the boardwalk from Coney Island and until the last decade best known as a fertile breeding ground for Jewish-American comedians and humorists (Moss Hart, Neil Simon, Woody Allen). It's now familiarly known as Little Odessa for the massive numbers of Russian nationals who relocated to this seaside neighborhood when Soviet emigration restrictions eased in the early 1970s. On **Brighton Beach Avenue**, the area's commercial center, bookstores (biggest seller: Gorbachev's *Perestroika*), restaurants (caviar, *shashlik*), and omnipresent balalaika music attest to its status as America's largest Russian community. Check out the Saturday crowds shopping for smoked fish and garlicky sausage at **M & I International Foods** (number 249); then cross the street for a lunch accompanied by vigorous Slavic renditions of American pop tunes at **Primorski** (number 282). (You've never heard Elvis till you've heard him in Ukrainian.) Fifteen dollars here will bring more food than one human being can reasonably consume; Russians, explains the owner, "like good value for their money." **Café Europa** (number 306) and **Café Zodiac** (number 309) offer slightly lighter fare in the same vein, but dinner visitors to **National Restaurant** (number 273) should be prepared to do things in a big way: For $25, you get dinner, drinks, dancing, a nightclub show, and the chance to participate in the most passionate audience singalongs this side of Kiev. You might want to plan a walk in the salty air of the boardwalk along the beach first in order to whet your appetite.

## GREENPOINT

In 1862, the ironclad *Monitor* emerged from the Continental Ironworks in Greenpoint to fight for the Union against the Confederate *Merrimac*. At the northernmost point of the borough, this area was responsible for the development of Brooklyn's international reputation as an industrial center by the 1890s. Its numerous factories and plants specialized in cast-iron manufacture, pottery, printing, and petroleum. Although all of those enterprises have long since departed, the neighborhood is still populated by the descendants of the Polish, Italian, and Irish immigrants who came over to work in them. The Polish community has recently expanded to include a large number of Solidarity activists who left the homeland when martial law was imposed in 1981. Many of the community's activities are centered about St. Stanislaus Kostka Church (607 Humboldt Street), where a brass plaque commemorates the 1969 visit of Polish Cardinal Karol Wojtyla before he became Pope John Paul II.

If you go to Greenpoint (a ten-minute trip from lower Manhattan on the M or J subway to the Marcy or Lorimer stations), try the Polish pastries at the **White Eagle Bakery** (600 Humboldt Street) or **Little Europe** (888 Manhattan Avenue). **Bamonte's** (32 Withers Street) and **Crisci** (593 Lorimer Street) are landmark Italian restaurants, each boasting several generations of family ownership.

There's no real debate about this area's most exceptional dining experience, however: **Peter Luger** (178 Broadway; Tel: 718-387-7400), under the shadow of the elevated train in neighboring Williamsburg, is by itself worth the trip—from anywhere. This Teutonic *keller*, with worn wooden floors and an atmosphere redolent of more than a century's worth of beer, tobacco, and red meat, serves the finest steaks in New York City, aged to perfection in the restaurant's own warehouse and served in classic German-American style by waiters in high, white, starched aprons. The way there via subway (D or N lines from Midtown) is slightly inconvenient, so take a cab; there's not a driver in greater New York who doesn't make the trip regularly.

# QUEENS

*By Barry Lewis*

*Barry Lewis, an architectural historian, has created tour programs and produced lecture series for New York City's 92nd Street Y. He has also written articles on the city's architectural history for many publications, and was a contributing writer to the Municipal Art Society's* Juror's Guide to Lower Manhattan. *He lives in the borough of Queens.*

Queens: To residents of Manhattan it's New York's Midwest, the Archie Bunkerville where dwell the cab drivers, the firemen, the secretaries, and the plumbers of New York City. Built up half before World War II and half after, Queens was considered, in the 1950s and 1960s, the "suburbia" to Manhattan's "city." But things change—New York always does—and this borough of nearly two million has changed with it.

Queens is New York's London. It doesn't look like London, but it acts like it. Its dozens of small towns and small cities are instinctively independent and terribly insular. If nuclear testing were planned for Flushing, the people in Jackson Heights—two "towns" away—would wonder what it had to do with them. Each neighborhood is different in class, in ethnic texture, and even in architectural scale. From the Brooklyn-style row houses of Ridgewood to the upstate, small-town atmosphere of College Point, from the modernistic factories of increasingly artsy Long Island City to the bustling Hong Kong–like downtown of Flushing, Queens is a mosaic of how New York is really lived in, away from the media-soaked atmosphere of Manhattan.

### MAJOR INTEREST

Garden-city planning
The Seven Sister neighborhoods
Queens melting pot
Greek Astoria
Latin American and Indian quarters in Jackson Heights
Flushing's Little Asia

Forest Hills' Russian enclave
Corona Avenue's Italian enclave
Long Island City's Socrates Sculpture Park
Isamu Noguchi Museum
Museum of the Moving Image
Queens Museum

Queens, originally a patchwork of different towns and of developments begun after the Civil War, was annexed to New York in 1898 and achieved full throttle with the opening of the Queensboro (59th Street) Bridge and the Long Island Railroad (LIRR)/Penn Station complex around 1910. In the next 30 years Queens boomed. The city had arrived, but it was a verdant city, where architects and developers often tried to thread gardens and greenbelts around their apartment buildings and private homes. Some neighborhoods were built up in the repetitive patterns of Archie Bunker-type developments. Others, however, like Astoria in the northwest or the older sections of Rego Park in the center of the borough, were built with the kind of garden-style apartments and row houses that give much of prewar Queens a leafiness absent in over-bricked Manhattan.

A word about the Queens street system: There appears to be a "system," but there really isn't. After the 1898 consolidation, city hall imposed a Manhattan-style grid on the new borough. Old names were replaced by numbers with, theoretically, 1st Street at the East River end and 250th Street at the Nassau County eastern end; and First Avenue along the northern Long Island Sound shoreline and 150th Avenue at the southern end near what is now Kennedy Airport. But the old patchwork of separate street systems resisted easy codification. The result is a crazy quilt of numbers pretending to be organized. One hint: An address like 83-10 125th Street means, theoretically, the building is on 125th Street near 83rd Avenue (and likewise for vice versa addresses), but usually that's only the beginning of your quest. The best advice is to call ahead to the restaurant or museum and get explicit directions. When you get there, you can then set out to explore the surrounding neighborhood.

The western half of the borough is mostly prewar, except for the huge 1960s apartment complexes in Rego Park and Forest Hills. The northeast quadrant of the borough was built up after the war and resembles any postwar suburb; but don't overlook the older communi-

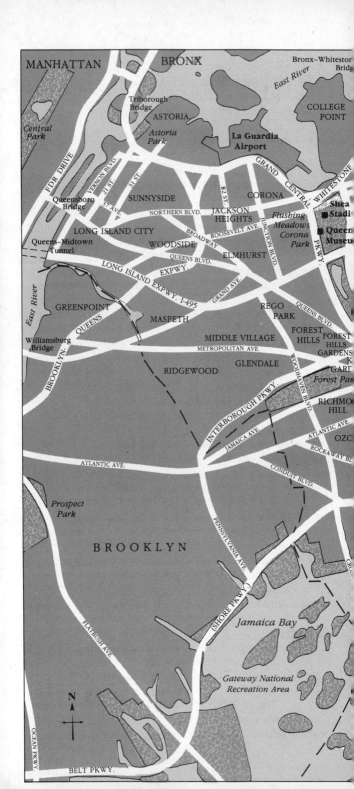

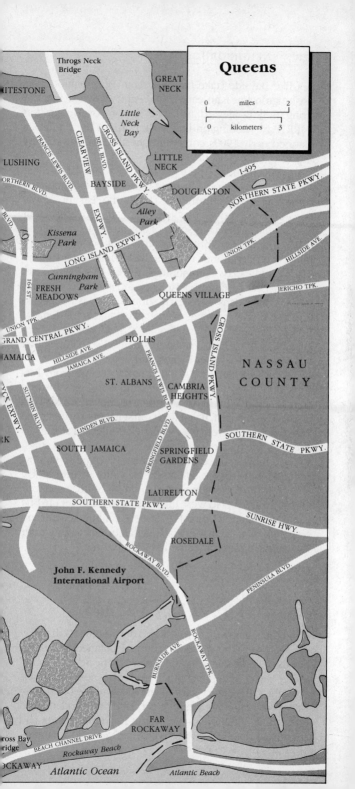

ties like **Bayside** (take the LIRR from Penn Station, Port Washington line), an early 20th-century town strung out along Bell Boulevard near the station, or **Douglaston** (LIRR, Port Washington line, walk north of the station), a planned early 1900s community nestling on the marshy shores of Little Neck Bay.

In the southeast there is another series of verdant 1920s neighborhoods, most of these black or integrated communities like Laurelton (LIRR, the Far Rockaway line). The one serious problem here is the poverty belt of South Jamaica that runs south of downtown Jamaica along Sutphin and New York boulevards. But South Jamaica's plight too often blinds us to the handsome solidity of the black middle-class communities nearby. The row-house-lined streets of Cambria Heights and the eclectic mansions of St. Albans were early suburban areas opened to upscale blacks coming out of Manhattan's Harlem or Brooklyn's Bedford-Stuyvesant area. St. Albans in particular had, in the 1950s, a stellar residents' list that included Roy Campanella, James Brown, and Count Basie.

Downtown Jamaica (along Jamaica Avenue from Parsons Boulevard to 169th Street), the borough's historic county seat, is now, like many other old downtowns, struggling to revive itself. If you find yourself there try to see the Tabernacle of Prayer (90-07 Merrick Boulevard at Jamaica Avenue), the former Loew's Valencia, a grand 1929 atmospheric movie palace in the Spanish Baroque style, now remade, with a new color scheme, into an evangelical church, where everyone is welcome for Sunday services. Or visit, a few blocks west, the **Jamaica Arts Center** (161-04 Jamaica Avenue, at Union Hall Street), a cultural center and art gallery housed in the small but flamboyant City Register Building built soon after the 1898 annexation.

## *THE SEVEN SISTERS*

Amid the patchwork of towns and developments that covered Queens there was a group of planned neighborhoods of real quality. Today known as "The Seven Sisters," these seven independently developed neighborhoods brought 19th-century garden-city ideals to the often crass New York real-estate scene. Sports facilities, parkland, and community clubhouses were built for homeowners and apartment dwellers, giving residents "rest and recuperation" from the frenzy, noise, and dehumanizing congestion of modern industrial life.

The Seven Sisters began with **Richmond Hill**, an 1880s speculative development, whose Shingle-style "Meet-Me-in-St. Louis" Victorians fan out from a village center and town common clustered around the intersections of Hillside, Jamaica, and Myrtle avenues and Lefferts Boulevard (take the E or F subway line to Union Turnpike, Kew Gardens, and the Q-10 bus to Hillside Avenue). Some of the best houses stand north of Myrtle Avenue between 112th and 115th streets; a few blocks farther on Myrtle is the 500-acre, densely wooded Forest Park. The 1890s town center is nostalgic (if slightly run-down), and the tiny common became, in 1905, the campus for a Carnegie library (at Lefferts Boulevard and Hillside Avenue). Inside, in one wing of the library, is a 1937 WPA mural by Philip Evergood depicting in exuberant 1930s optimism, *The Story of Richmond Hill*. For a meal, there is the **Triangle Hofbrau**, at 117-13 Jamaica Avenue at Myrtle, a long-standing German restaurant—Mae West frequented it when she lived nearby—whose premises were originally an 1860s way station on the Jamaica Turnpike (now Jamaica Avenue). For just a hamburger, across the street at 117-33 Myrtle Avenue is the **Junction Diner**—streamlined inside, 1980s remodeling outside—a *real* diner, not one of the cleverly packaged mock-ups so popular in Manhattan.

To the north, developed in the 1910s, is **Kew Gardens** (LIRR Main line to Kew Gardens, or the E and F subway lines to Union Turnpike, Kew Gardens), with its Neo-Tudor "village" centered around the railroad station at Lefferts Boulevard and Austin Street. Its eclectic mixture of apartments, row houses, and especially private homes that range from modest to mansion, dominated by the 80-year-old pin oaks that line the streets, fit respectfully into the rolling, hilly landscape.

Adjacent and to the west of Kew Gardens is the most famous of the Sisters, **Forest Hills Gardens** (take the LIRR to Forest Hills, or the E and F lines to Continental Avenue, Forest Hills, and walk south), the "fairy tale suburb" of Sinclair Lewis's *Main Street,* a superb example of garden-city planning. Lushly landscaped by Frederick Law Olmsted, Jr. (his father designed Central Park), the "Gardens" include housing of all types, from apartment towers to mansions to experimental poured-concrete row houses made friendlier with Neo-Tudor detailing. Station Square, the 1912 "town center" by architect Grosvenor Atterbury that clusters around the LIRR station, is a fine example of urban design, as much Expressionistic as it is Medieval Revival, evincing character and a sense of place without ever being cloying or cute. While visiting the Gardens, you might want to try the well-prepared nouvelle cuisine at closet-sized **My Kitchen** (72-24 Austin Street, between Continental and Ascan avenues) in the bustling shopping district near the railroad station.

Closer to "the city" (always meaning Manhattan) is **Jackson Heights** (number 7 IRT subway line from Times Square or Grand Central to 82nd Street; walk north), built in the 1910s and 1920s with apartment-house blocks of imaginative historic revival designs, threaded with greenbelts running through the blocks, and with superior apartment layouts boasting three and four exposures, floor-through plans, and separate service and bedroom wings. (Restaurants in Jackson Heights will be mentioned below in the ethnic section.)

Farther west, with Midtown's skyline rising in the background, is **Sunnyside Gardens** (number 7 IRT subway line from Times Square or Grand Central to 48th Street, and walk north; for information contact the Sunnyside Foundation, Tel: 718-392-9139), a utopian experiment of the late 1920s designed by the gifted team of Clarence Stein and Henry Wright. Home for many years to urban critic and *New Yorker* columnist Lewis Mumford, and once known as the "Nursery of Greenwich Village" for the number of ex-Village artists who moved there to raise their families, Sunnyside was built as a model housing complex, including verdant commons within the blocks and a still extant Community Park that is New York's only private park besides Manhattan's Gramercy Park. The two remaining Sisters are Douglaston, already mentioned, and **Fresh Meadows**, two miles east of Forest Hills Gardens, a moderate- and middle-income garden-city complex built in 1949 by the New York Life Insurance Company as a low-rise, more spaciously laid-out sibling of Manhattan's Stuyvesant Town. These seven communities are now being rediscovered and reevaluated as classics of American urban and suburban design.

## THE QUEENS MOVIE INDUSTRY

Queens was America's first Hollywood. During the days of the silents and the early talkies, before producers discovered Los Angeles, Astoria Movie Studios was one of the principal centers of the movie industry. Today that studio, renamed **Kaufman/Astoria Movie Studios**, is thriving again, and its new addition, **The Museum of the Moving Image** (at 34-31 35th Avenue at 36th Street) has itself become a box-office smash, giving visitors a multimedia understanding of TV, video, and film production. The museum, which also hosts screenings in both its main and experimental theaters, is four blocks from the R train's Steinway Street station—that's three stops from Bloomingdale's in Manhattan. Call the museum for directions and hours; Tel: (718) 784-0077.

Queens was also the first Beverly Hills; the stars of stage and screen (and jazz as well)—including Charlie Chaplin, Al Jolson, Will Rogers, Billie Holiday, Bix Beiderbecke, and the immortal Louis Armstrong—settled in from Corona to Forest Hills to Bayside, some to lead quiet lives away from Manhattan's din and others to lead the North Shore Long Island lifestyle that would soon move to "West Egg" and be immortalized in *The Great Gatsby*.

## *ETHNIC QUEENS*

Queens is today's melting pot, serving New York as the Lower East Side once did, only here the number of people is far larger, their origins more exotic, and their lifestyles more prosperous than those of their 19th-century predecessors along Manhattan's Rivington, MacDougal, and Mott streets. Queens is one of the most densely mixed ethnic melting pots in the world. Los Angeles has a mix, but they're all in cars and only fenders brush, not people. In Hong Kong it's largely Asian, while in Queens there are Greeks, Latins, Middle Easterners, West Indians, and Russian Jews besides denizens from the entire arc of eastern and southern Asia.

Queens is the place where almost any kind of ethnic foodstuff, cooking gadgetry, or ethnic restaurant can be found. But this is not Manhattan, where retail stores and eateries are often slickly packaged and merchandised. Restaurants and food stores in Queens are not written up; you simply have to know about them. They're not glitterized with Postmodern decor; they just have plain cloths on the tables and simple pictures on the walls. The food, however, is excellent, cheap, and abundant. The atmosphere is home-style—home, that is, to a Greek, an Indian, or an Argentine. Queens is where you can see an Indian woman in a sari eating Italian pizza made by an Argentine in what is basically an Oriental district, where churches announce services in Korean, and an Indian temple rises among the Victorian homes of old Flushing.

Here is Greek **Astoria**, clustered around the stations of the elevated N line (from Bloomingdale's) that rumbles above 31st Street. Once German, then Italian, now one of the largest concentrations of Greeks outside of the home country, Astoria's major activity is at the N line's terminus, Ditmars Boulevard, where Greek coffee and pastry shops (and Italian pastry shops as well), Greek-language newsstands, and a Greek-language movie house serve the local population. **Nea Hellas Restaurant** (31-15 Ditmars Boulevard, east of 31st Street), **Tony's Ristorante** (33-12 Ditmars Boulevard, two blocks east of 31st Street), **Lefkos Pirgos Bakery** (at 31st Street and 23rd Avenue, one block south of Ditmars), and **Europa Delicacies** (22-42 31st Street, under the "El"—or elevated train—just south of Ditmars) are just the appetizers to a culinary feast. Broadway, near the El station, is another frenzy of food shops, with **Roumely Taverna** (33-04 Broadway, east of the El) and **Karyatis Restaurant** (35-03 Broadway, two blocks east of Roumely's) being two excellent restaurants in that stretch.

Latin American **Jackson Heights** is centered at 82nd Street and intersects 37th Avenue, which is one block north of the IRT number 7 El train route, Roosevelt Avenue. Exit at the 82nd Street station and bring your Spanish phrase book with you. Two wonderful Colombian restaurants nearby are **Tierras Colombianas** (82-18 Roosevelt Avenue, east of 82nd Street) and **La Pequeña Columbia** (83-27 Roosevelt Avenue, one block farther east). On Baxter Avenue, south of Roosevelt Avenue and 84th Street, is **La Fusta**, 80-32 Baxter Avenue, an Argentine restaurant specializing in *parrillada,* Latin American–style barbecue. And under the El on Roosevelt are several Latin nightclubs and elegant eateries, including **Uncle Peter's** (76-18 Roosevelt Avenue at 76th Street), an excellent, upscale restaurant with adjoining bar and music room. Farther east on the number 7 line, at the Junction Boulevard station, is an expatriate Cuban restaurant, **Rincon Criollo**, at 40-09 Junction Boulevard, just south of the El. On the western side of Jackson Heights is one of New York's Little Indias (number 7 IRT line to the 74th

Street station, or the E and F lines to the 74th Street Roosevelt station): 74th Street, north of Roosevelt, is a veritable "Saree Alley," and it and the surrounding area are filled with Indian saree shops, restaurants, and grocery stores.

Then there is downtown **Flushing**'s Little Asia (Main Street from Sanford Avenue to Northern Boulevard, and side streets, including Union Street, parallel to and east of Main Street), where the intense small-scale retailing, billboards in foot-high Oriental letters, and mixture of Koreans, Chinese, Indians, and Japanese will make you feel that you have just flown across the China Sea.

The entry to Flushing is via the IRT number 7 line, nicknamed "The Orient Express," from Times Square and Grand Central to its terminal at Main Street (the LIRR's Port Washington line also stops there). When you exit from the subway at Main Street and Roosevelt Avenue you will be right in the heart of the business district. **Cho Sun Ok** (136-73 Roosevelt Avenue, upstairs, one block east of the subway terminal) is a Korean restaurant specializing in hibachi-based barbecue. **Flushing Yuet Tung** (136-11 38th Avenue, two blocks north of the subway and east of Main Street) serves *Haka*-style Chinese dishes (Haka is the soul food of China) such as salt-baked chicken. **Crystal Garden** (136-40 39th Avenue, three blocks north of the subway and east of Main Street) prepares excellent *dim sum*. **Hwa Yuan** (41-97 Main Street, two blocks south of the subway) specializes in Szechwan dishes such as cold noodles in sesame sauce.

Asian supermarkets and food stores also dot Flushing's streets. Nippan Daido is a Japanese supermarket (with an attached Dosanko fast-food restaurant) at 137-80 Northern Boulevard at Union Street; several excellent Chinese and Korean supermarkets line Main Street near Sanford and Maple avenues (about three blocks south of the subway), and Indian grocers and delis cluster on Main Street another block farther south. Nearby, to the east of Main Street, a Hindu temple, built by Indian craftsmen flown over from the subcontinent, sits beside the surrounding Victorian houses. Home to the Hindu Society of North America (45-57 Bowne Street at Holly Avenue; Tel: 718-961-1199), the temple has a richly decorated interior of shrines and Hindu gods and goddesses, and always has a welcome mat out for strangers. It's best to call for hours and directions.

In **Forest Hills** on 108th Street north of 65th Avenue

(it's about 20 blocks north of Forest Hills Gardens; the nearest subway is the 63rd Drive, Rego Park station of the R and G lines; walk east from the station) Russian Jews have established a small colony far from the better-known settlement in Brighton Beach, Brooklyn. Two Russian delis, **Misha & Monya's** and **Loxtown**, face each other across 108th Street at 65th Avenue, duelists in the game of freshly made sour cream, dried fish, pickles, and pirogi. A block north, at 64th Road, **Carmel Middle Eastern Grocery** (64-27 108th Street), serving the local population of Sephardic Jews, specializes in freshly made hummus, *babaganouj,* olives, pickles, and Middle Eastern grains and spices.

## *CULTURAL INSTITUTIONS*

The list of neighborhoods and their specialty stores could go on and on. Yet Queens is also beginning to attract the kinds of cultural institutions that people—even Manhattanites—will go out of their way to visit. Housed in a fortresslike 19th-century school, **P.S. 1** (46-01 21st Street at Jackson Avenue; Tel: 718-784-2084) is a combination of art gallery, artists' working lofts, and sometime performance space that pioneered Long Island City's role as a new center for the "downtown" art scene. The number 7 line's Court House Square/45th Road station (three stops from Grand Central) and the E and F's 21st Street/Ely Avenue station (one stop from Citicorp Center) are only a few blocks away.

Farther north, along Long Island City's industrial riverfront, is the **Socrates Sculpture Park** (31-29 Vernon Boulevard at Broadway and the East River), where large-scale modern sculpture can be seen against the spectacular backdrop of the Manhattan skyline. From the N line's Broadway station it's an eight-block walk west to the riverfront and Socrates. The park is open daily during the summer but only on weekends in the winter, and is near the food shops and restaurants of Astoria's Broadway. Just two blocks south of the Socrates, at 33rd Road, is the **Isamu Noguchi Museum** (32-37 Vernon Boulevard, which is the riverfront road; Tel: 718-204-7088), in the sculptor's former studio. Open only Wednesdays and Saturdays, Noguchi displays at any one time dozens of the artist's works in a redesigned industrial loft of almost monastic simplicity. Nearby, on the other side of Astoria, is the aforementioned **Museum of the Moving Image**. From Noguchi or Socrates you would have to walk back east on Broadway, five blocks past the El to 36th Street and turn right, or south, two blocks to 35th Avenue to reach the Moving Image. It's a "schlepp," as New Yorkers say, but the sights and aromas of Astoria's Broadway might make the walk less taxing than you think.

In Flushing Meadow Park, once the dusty "ash heaps" of F. Scott Fitzgerald's *The Great Gatsby* and subsequently the site of two world's fairs, stands **Shea Stadium**, home of the Mets, and, just to its south, the **National Tennis Center**, site of tennis's U.S. Open championships. Both are reached from the number 7 line's Shea Stadium station, and both are only a few minutes away from the gustatory delights of both downtown Flushing and Jackson Heights. Just south of the tennis center is the **Queens Museum**, with excellent art and photography shows; within the museum (housed in the New York City pavilion of the 1939 World's Fair) is the **New York Panorama**, a Lilliputian-scaled model of the entire New York City, including every building and street within the five boroughs.

On Flushing Meadow's western edge, in Corona Park, is the **New York Hall of Science** (in the park, 47-01 111th Street at 48th Avenue, Corona; Tel: 718-699-0005), a tremendously popular hands-on experience of applied science and high technology housed in a reinforced concrete "amoeba" originally built for the 1964 World's Fair. If you're visiting just the Hall of Science, it's best to take the number 7 line to the 111th Street station and walk south eight blocks to 48th Avenue.

Getting hungry? From the Hall of Science walk south on 111th Street (that's a left on exiting the hall) three blocks to 51st Avenue and turn right one block to 108th Street (only in Queens is 108th one block from 111th). There, where Corona Avenue intersects 108th and 51st, is Joseph Lisa Square, the heart of an Italian neighborhood. On the square the **Lemon Ice King of Corona** (52-02 108th Street) still makes New York's best Italian ices in an endless variety of flavors. The **Parkside Restaurant** (107-01 Corona Avenue, on the 51st Avenue side of the square) serves Italian cuisine in a posh style that attracts people from all over the city; for more modest but still excellent dining, nearby is **Army's Italian Cuisine** (51-01 108th Street at 51st Avenue). Take-out sandwiches and heros with fresh Italian cheeses and deli meats can be had at the **Corona Park Salumeria** (14-46 122nd Street), and for cappuccino and pastry there is **Baldi's Italian Pastry Shop** (108-15 Corona Avenue at 53rd Avenue). Don't be fooled by Corona's small-town atmosphere. It was the longtime home of jazz great Louis Armstrong, whose house is now a national historic site and archives (34-56 107th Street; Tel: 718-478-8274). Nearby, though long closed and picked clean of "debris," was Louis Comfort Tiffany's studio (96-18 43rd Avenue), where many a Tiffany lamp and Favrile glass vase was fabricated.

All this gives you a few good reasons to cross the East River and chart "the unknown borough." Don't be fooled by what your Manhattan friends tell you; being Manhattan people, they really don't know New York. Queens is worth the trip.

# DAY TRIPS FROM MANHATTAN

## By Eleanor Berman

*Eleanor Berman is a widely published travel writer. Her guide* Away for the Weekend: New York *has been a regional bestseller since 1982. She has contributed to all the major metropolitan daily newspapers, as well as to such national magazines as* Harper's Bazaar, Savvy, Modern Bride, *and* Diversion.

For visitors caught up in the Manhattan maelstrom who wonder, How does anybody live here? here's the secret: New Yorkers get away—often—to some of the most appealing day-trip destinations offered by any city in America. Why not join them? Greenery, scenery, history, prime beaches, ivy-clad campuses, and even early American charm are waiting nearby to add a new dimension and a refreshing change of pace to a New York stay. Here are some of the escapes the natives favor.

MAJOR INTEREST

**The Bronx**
Bronx Zoo

New York Botanical Garden
Wave Hill mansion and grounds

**Hudson Valley**
Philipsburg Manor's early Dutch farm grounds
Washington Irving's retreat, Sunnyside
Van Cortlandt Manor colonial house
Union Church of Pocantico Hills
Franklin D. Roosevelt National Historic Site at
  Hyde Park
United States Military Academy at West Point

Yale University
Litchfield, Connecticut, historic New England town
The Hamptons beaches and resort towns
Princeton University

# *BRONX OASES*

The city's northernmost borough, generally better known for its Yankee baseball team than for its beauty spots, offers three magnificent leafy retreats less than an hour from Manhattan. Contact each attraction for routes by subway, public bus, or Metro-North train. Liberty Lines express buses go to all three (Tel: 212-652-8400 for routes and schedules).

**The Bronx Zoo**, the nation's largest urban zoo, founded in 1899, still has its famous central court of stately exhibit buildings, but the rest of the 265 wooded acres is undergoing a renaissance. Cages are being replaced with spectacular natural habitats for the 4,000-plus animal residents, to create new excitement for the human beings who come to call.

Siberian tigers, Asian elephants, Indian rhinoceroses, and red pandas roam the plains of Wild Asia, while rare and beautiful snow leopards are in residence in the Himalayan Highlands, a habitat that re-creates the high passes and remote mountains of their homeland. Lions, gazelles, giraffes, zebras, and cheetahs roam the African Plains, where predator and prey are safely separated by moats. The environments are authentic down to the fencing and signs based on native art. In good weather the monorails and trams make it easier to cover ground, and bring you right into some of the habitats.

The most lavish of the new environments is the indoor Jungle World, a 55-foot-high, glass-enclosed complex that

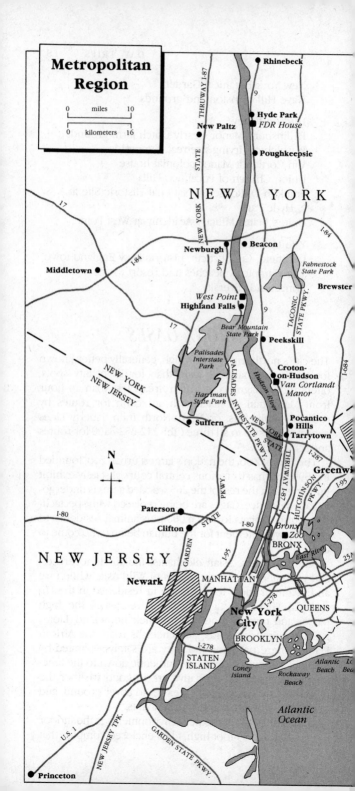

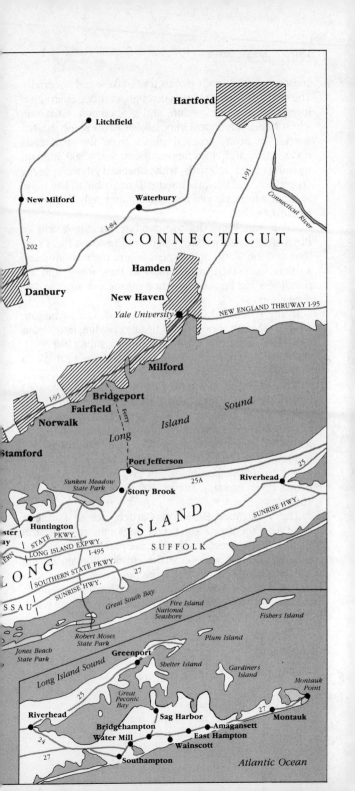

comes complete with clouds, rain, lakes, and waterfalls. The wooden walkway leads through an Indonesian scrub forest, a mangrove swamp, and a Southeast Asian rain forest where it is almost impossible to distinguish the 100 species of actual tropical plants from the man-made rocks, trees, and vines among them. Some 800 animals, including black leopards, white-cheeked gibbons, sleepy crocodiles, and brightly hued Bali myna birds, live here, separated from people and one another only by ravines, streams, or cliffs.

Other innovative indoor exhibits are the World of Birds, a three-story space where multicolored fliers soar free, and the World of Darkness, where night is simulated so that such nocturnal animals as bats, foxes, and supergliders can be seen in action during our regular daytime hours.

In the whimsical Children's Zoo, kids can participate while they learn about animal life, by crawling into a giant snail shell, exploring a giant spider web, sitting in a child-size nest, or comparing their jumping ability to that of a frog.

To reach the zoo (and the New York Botanical Garden) by car, start from Manhattan, take the Triborough Bridge and Bruckner Expressway east to the Bronx River Parkway northbound. From the exit marked Bronx Zoo, turn left to the Bronxdale parking field. The botanical garden is directly opposite, across Fordham Road.

The New York Zoological Society, Fordham Road and Bronx River Parkway, Bronx, NY 10460. Tel: (212) 367-1010.

**The New York Botanical Garden**, across Fordham Road from the Bronx Zoo (enter on Southern Boulevard; see above for directions by car), are part of the same vast urban park that was once the private domain of the Lorillard family. Since 1891 it has been devoted to showing off nature at her exuberant best. The 250-acre site is part unspoiled woodland with nature paths along a winding river, part formal gardens.

The undisputed star of the botanical garden is the Enid A. Haupt Conservatory, 11 shimmering pavilions of glass around a courtyard and reflecting pools. The glass dome over the central pavilion, inspired by London's Crystal Palace, soars 90 feet over a leafy palm court below. The conservatory also houses desert and tropical plant collections, a fern forest, and showy seasonal floral displays.

Outdoors there are formal gardens planted with more

than 200 varieties of roses, a perennial garden, herb and rock gardens, a conifer garden, and a garden of native New York plants. In spring, flamboyant bulb displays and clouds of pink and white flowering trees greet the season.

The massive stone museum building on the grounds contains exhibitions, an herbarium with an enormous collection of dried plant specimens, and a shop that is a treasure trove of horticultural items. The extensive plant literature collection at the Harriet Barnes Pratt Library is open to all.

New York Botanical Garden, Southern Boulevard and 200th Street, Bronx, NY 10458. Tel: (212) 220-8777 or 220-8700.

**Wave Hill** is a small, perfect jewel, a 28-acre enclave of velvet lawns, gardens, greenhouses, two manor houses, and an incomparable view of the Hudson River and the geological wonder beyond: the stony cliffs of the New Jersey Palisades. The astonishing beauty of this setting in the Riverdale section of the Bronx has drawn a roster of rental tenants that includes Theodore Roosevelt, Mark Twain, and Arturo Toscanini.

The main house at Wave Hill was built in 1843 by jurist William Lewis Morris as a summer home away from the heat and noise of a growing city. In 1866 it was acquired by publishing mogul William Henry Appleton, who transformed it into a Victorian estate, building a greenhouse and stable and bringing in exotic plants. It became an intellectual center where people like William Thackeray and Thomas Henry Huxley were likely to stop by for tea.

Wave Hill and the neighboring manor house of Oliver Harriman, called Glyndor, were bought by George F. Perkins in 1903. Perkins brought in Albert Millard, a royal landscape gardener from Vienna, to help him further develop the gardens. The estate remained in the Perkins family until 1960, when the property and the two houses were donated to New York City as a public park. Nature trails connect it to Riverdale Park, a 97-acre sanctuary along the Hudson with three miles of hiking trails. A perfect time to visit is on Sunday afternoon, when chamber-music concerts are offered in the Wave Hill house.

Wave Hill is a short drive from Manhattan by car. From the East Side take the Major Deegan Expressway northbound. Exit at Henry Hudson Parkway and take the first right to H. Hudson Parkway, *southbound*. Take the 254th Street exit, turn left at the stop sign, left again at the light, right at 249th Street to Wave Hill. From the West Side take the West Side Highway/Henry Hudson Parkway northbound. Get off the parkway at the 246th–250th Street exit; continue north to 252nd, go left at the overpass, left again, and right at 249th Street.

Wave Hill, 249th Street and Independence Avenue, Bronx, NY 10471. Tel: (212) 549-2055.

## *HISTORIC HUDSON VALLEY*

Farther north, much of the early history of New York was forged in the great manor houses along the river. Historic Hudson Valley, a nonprofit corporation, was formed over 35 years ago, with financial aid from John D. Rockefeller, Jr., to preserve some of the most important properties. Three of their four beautifully restored estates are within easy day-tripping range in suburban Westchester County. Costumed guides give an excellent overview of their history, which spans three centuries. An art treasure also under Historic Hudson auspices is the Union Church of Pocantico Hills, with windows by Marc Chagall and Henri Matisse.

**Philipsburg Manor** in North Tarrytown is a farm that was the domain of a Dutchman who came to the New World in the early 1650s as Peter Stuyvesant's carpenter and amassed his own fortune through the clipper trade and a good marriage. The Upper Mills site, built in 1682, was a trading and shipping center where tenant farmers brought grain to be ground, bagged, and shipped. It has been restored to approximate its appearance during its most prosperous period, 1720 to 1750. The mill still grinds, the garden grows the same kinds of plants that were cultivated in the 18th century, and the cows, sheep, and chickens roaming the farm have been "back bred" to reproduce the breeds of an earlier day. The simple stone farmhouse with its whitewashed walls contains samples of rustic, early New York furniture and Dutch Delft ceramics.

Nearby **Sunnyside**, three miles south on Route 9, Tarrytown, is the quaint Victorian cottage and gardens of author Washington Irving. The estate, which he accurately called his "snuggery," contains Irving's furniture, possessions, and library.

Antique lovers should definitely plan a visit to handsome **Van Cortlandt Manor**, about ten miles north of Sunnyside, in Croton-on-Hudson. This was also the domain of a Dutchman, Oloff Stevense Van Cortlandt, who arrived in New Amsterdam in 1638 and sired a prominent family that boasted a mayor of New York City and a lieutenant governor of the state. The house has been restored appropriate to the elegant period between 1790 and 1814. Most of its fine furnishings were made in New York and belonged to the Van Cortlandts, who remained in residence here until 1945. Open-hearth cooking is demonstrated daily in the downstairs kitchen.

Other highlights here are the fruit orchards, the flower gardens along the brick "long walk," and the display gardens filled with herbs, flowers, and vegetables used in this country prior to 1814. The ferry house looks as it did when it served as a rest stop for travellers on the Albany Post Road to New York City; it was at this spot that stages were ferried over the Croton River. The smoke house, necessary house, ice house, and other estate buildings also have been restored.

The **Union Church of Pocantico Hills**, Route 448, North Tarrytown, the final select Westchester County property, still has an active congregation, and is the worshiping place of the Rockefeller family, whose estate is nearby. It boasts the only cycle of church windows created in this country by Chagall, including eight luminous side windows in blues, greens, and golds and an enormous rear window dedicated to John D. Rockefeller, Jr.; its vivid colors fill the small sanctuary with light even on the darkest of days. The small circular rose window by Matisse, his final work before his death, shimmers over the altar with cutouts in green, yellow, pale blue, and white. It is a memorial to Abby Aldrich Rockefeller, John D., Jr.'s, wife, who was a patron of the arts and an active member of the church. Visiting hours are limited, so phone Historic Hudson Valley for information (see below) before you plan a trip.

**Tappan Hill**, Highland and Benedict avenues, Tarrytown (Tel: 914-631-3030), is the place for dining with a hilltop Hudson view after you've seen the sights.

All of the Westchester properties are off Route 9 on the east side of the Hudson and can be reached by taking the New York State Thruway (Route 87) to exit 9, Tarrytown; follow Route 9 south one mile to Sunnyside, north two miles to Philipsburg, north another nine miles to Van Cortlandt Manor. To reach the Union Church, go east on Route 448 from Route 9 in North Tarrytown. Signs mark the turnoffs clearly. To see all the sites, a car is necessary, but Metro-North Commuter Railroad offers packages to several properties; Tel: (212) 340-3408.

Historic Hudson Valley, 150 White Plains Road, Tarrytown, NY 10591. Tel: (914) 631-8200.

## *FRANKLIN D. ROOSEVELT NATIONAL HISTORIC SITE*

It was in the mid-Hudson highlands farther up the east side of the river that the lavish mansions of a later era were built. The best known of these is Franklin Roosevelt's home, officially called Springwood, but usually referred to simply as **Hyde Park**.

The popularity of this much-visited site is warranted. Few memorials offer such personal glimpses of public figures. Touring the main house (overlooking the Hudson River), the Roosevelt Museum and Library, and Eleanor Roosevelt's own modest home, Val-Kill, gives new awareness of the public and private lives of one of our most remarkable presidents—and his equally remarkable wife.

The museum of the Franklin D. Roosevelt Library contains a series of photos and displays about the life of the only man elected for four presidential terms, who guided the nation through its worst depression and most perilous war. Franklin's bout with polio, his campaigns and presidency, and the worldwide mourning at his death in 1945 are all recorded.

The library contains Roosevelt's study (where he gave some of his famous radio fireside chats) and his presidential desk, preserved just as it was on his last day in office, covered with "toys"—miniature Democratic donkeys and replicas of his pet Scottie, Fala. Eleanor's costumes and her knitting, Franklin's collection of ship models, some of the many gifts he received in office, and his elegant Ford Phaeton convertible with hand controls are some of the many personal mementos displayed.

The Roosevelt home is where Franklin grew up and returned every summer with his wife and family. It remains as it was after the 1915 remodeling done by Franklin and his mother, Sara, and has an uncanny lived-in quality.

Both Franklin and Eleanor are buried in the rose garden beside the house. Eleanor, however, never felt at home at Hyde Park, where Sara Roosevelt reigned. With Franklin's blessing, she built a small retreat on the estate two miles away from the big house in 1926. It was often her weekend escape, and it was in this unpretentious pine-paneled house, Val-Kill, that she lived from 1945 until her death in 1962—the years when she became known as First Lady of the World.

Hyde Park is a two-hour drive from New York City. Follow the New York Thruway (Route 87) to exit 19, cross the Rhinecliff Bridge to Route 9G south and make a right turn to Route 9 south. While in Hyde Park, enjoy a meal prepared by the soon-to-be-greats at the **Culinary Institute of America** on Route 9, the nation's top training ground for chefs. For the formal lunch or dinner, reservations are needed far in advance (Tel: 914-471-6608), but no reservations are required for a light lunch weekdays in their St. Andrew's Café.

The Roosevelt home is modest compared with such palatial neighbors as the Vanderbilt Mansion. The Hudson Valley merits an overnight stay to explore the great estates along the river: Montgomery Place, Clermont, Mills Mansion, and Olana north of Hyde Park, and the Vanderbilt and Boscobel to the south. An excellent guide to the area is *The Hudson River Valley: A History and Guide* by Tim Mulligan. The most pleasant overnight accommodations are at the **Beekman Arms**, a stagecoach inn dating back to 1700, ten miles north of Hyde Park on Route 9 in Rhinebeck (Tel: 914-876-7077).

Franklin D. Roosevelt National Historic Site, Route 9, Hyde Park, NY. Tel: (914) 229-9115.

# *THE UNITED STATES MILITARY ACADEMY*

Standing on a crest on the west bank of the Hudson River, the gray stone buildings of the United States Military Academy at West Point are impressive. There's a strong sense of rich history here, and the pride of the young cadets who are carrying on the "long gray line" of patriots who marched before them is tangible.

West Point is also one of the Hudson Valley's great beauty spots. The same site from which colonial troops kept watch for British ships up and down the river still provides an unsurpassed Hudson overlook.

The visitors' center at Thayer Gate supplies all the information needed for a rewarding visit, including a self-guiding tour map and a movie about cadet life. Battle buffs will find one of the largest collections of military history in the Western Hemisphere at the West Point Museum in Thayer Hall, complete with models of famous battles.

A favorite spot for all is Trophy Point, where you can see the links of the Great Chain that was stretched across the river during the Revolution as a barrier to enemy ships. In days when America's highways were its rivers, the Hudson was a vital artery. In fact, if Benedict Arnold had succeeded in turning strategic West Point over to the British, they might have won the war.

The Cadet Chapel, noted for its Gothic architecture, contains the largest church organ in the world (18,000 pipes) and outstanding stained-glass windows donated by past graduating classes. Beyond the chapel are the gracious 19th-century homes of the superintendent and the commandant, facing the parade ground known as The Plain. On the roster of cadets who have marched here are Ulysses S. Grant, Robert E. Lee, Thomas J. "Stonewall" Jackson, Douglas MacArthur, Dwight Eisenhower, and astronauts Buzz Aldrin, Frank Borman, and Michael Collins.

Dress parades on The Plain with cadets in full regalia are a colorful sight. They are held on football weekends in autumn and at various times throughout the year (phone for current schedules).

There are many other buildings and monuments to be seen at West Point, including Fort Putnam, the original 1778 garrison constructed under the supervision of General George Washington. In the warmer months there is also the opportunity to take a one-and-a-half-hour Hudson Highlands river cruise (Tel: 914-446-7171 for reservations). Metro-North Commuter Railroad also offers day excursions (Tel: 212-340-3408). While you are at West Point the **Thayer Hotel** on campus is the best place for meals.

West Point is 50 miles from New York City, and can be reached by car by taking the George Washington Bridge to the Palisades Interstate Parkway northbound, to Bear Mountain Circle, then Route 9W north, following signs to Highland Falls and West Point.

United States Military Academy, West Point, NY 10996. Tel: (914) 938-2638.

## YALE UNIVERSITY

Founded by ten clergymen in 1701 and named for an Englishman who saved the fledgling school from bankruptcy, Yale University has grown from its puritan beginnings into one of the nation's great centers of learning. The Gothic-spired campus, an attraction in itself, boasts cultural treasures that are a more than ample incentive for a visit. Among them is America's top collection of British art.

Guided tours of the campus leave twice daily from the information office at Phelps Gate on College Street, off the green, or you can wander on your own, armed with the center's walking-tour map. Touring begins with the green itself, one of nine squares laid out in 1638 in America's first planned city. Among its three notable churches, the 1838 Center Congregational Church is considered a Georgian masterpiece.

Though it is now a sprawling university of 11,000 students, the historic heart of the school remains the old campus bounded by Chapel, High, Elm, and College streets. Nathan Hale, Noah Webster, Eli Whitney, and William Howard Taft all lived in Connecticut Hall, a 1752 Georgian structure that is the oldest on campus. It is now the Department of Philosophy, and the rest of the old campus buildings serve as freshman dormitories.

From sophomore year, Yale undergraduate life centers around a college plan similar to that of English universities, dividing the students into 12 colleges, each a separate entity under the guidance of a master. The first of the distinctive Gothic colleges came into being in 1933, and eight of the first ten quadrangles were designed by one architect, James Gamble Rogers. The newest buildings, Ezra Stiles and Morse, completed in 1962, were designed by Eero Saarinen.

The misty sea- and landscapes of Constable and Turner, the bawdy London of Hogarth, and the portraits of Gainsborough and Reynolds are all found at the **Yale Center for British Art**, the 1977 gift of philanthropist Paul Mellon. Mellon, who had amassed the largest collection of British art outside England, endowed a modernistic building designed by Louis Kahn to show off his paintings with natural radiance from skylights in the ceiling.

Yale also boasts the nation's oldest college art museum,

the **Yale University Art Gallery**, whose eclectic exhibits span the continents and the centuries. The Yale collection of musical instruments is world renowned, numbering some 850 antique and historical instruments from the 16th to 19th centuries. The **Beinecke Library** has its own displays of rarities, including a Gutenberg Bible, original Audubon bird prints, and Medieval manuscripts.

New Haven is a theater lover's haven. In addition to excellent productions at the **Yale Repertory Company**, the **Long Wharf Theater** is an outstanding regional company where many Broadway hits have been born.

**Robert Henry**, 1032 Chapel Street, is the acknowledged gourmet headquarters in town. Wooster Street is famous for its Italian restaurants; the pizza at **Sally's** and **Pepe's** is legendary in Connecticut; come early or late to avoid the lines.

New Haven is a 1-hour-and-45-minute train ride from New York via Amtrak or Metro-North; take a cab or buses A, J, or U for a short ride from the station to the campus. By car, follow Route 95 north to exit 47.

New Haven Convention and Visitors Bureau, 900 Chapel Street, Suite 344, New Haven, CT 06510. Tel: (203) 787-8367.

## *LITCHFIELD, CONNECTICUT*

You may recognize the steepled Congregational Church on the green in Litchfield. It has been featured in countless photographs of the typical New England town. And indeed, it would be hard to find a more idyllic setting than this community, which is considered by many to be the finest authentic 18th-century town in America.

Once a prosperous stage stop between Boston and New York, Litchfield attracted political and intellectual leaders from the time of its founding in 1720. The nation's first law school and first women's academy were founded here, and the Reverend Lyman Beecher first preached against the evils of intemperance in the Litchfield village meetinghouse. His son, abolitionist Henry Ward Beecher, and his daughter, Harriet Beecher Stowe, were born in the 1787 parsonage next to the church.

The three dozen or so choicest homes, those forming the central historic district around the village green, can easily be seen on foot because they are concentrated on two long blocks, North and South streets, radiating from the green. Little restoration has been necessary; many of Litchfield's homes have been continuously occupied—some by their original families—since they were built.

Most are still privately owned, but you can visit the 1773 home where Tapping Reeve opened the nation's first law school, with his brother-in-law Aaron Burr as his first pupil. Eventually, the pupils outgrew the house and a one-room school was erected next door in 1784. Among its alumni were three Supreme Court justices, 28 senators, over 100 congressmen, two vice presidents, 14 governors, and 16 chief justices of Connecticut.

John C. Calhoun was a student here, lodging in the rectory next door and planting some of the elms that remain along the street. Farther down the street is the 1736 home where Ethan Allen, Revolutionary War leader of the fabled Green Mountain Boys, is believed to have been born. Also on South Street is a white clapboard house, circa 1775, that was the home of Oliver Wolcott, Sr., a signer of the Declaration of Independence who became governor of Connecticut. And there is the obligatory structure boasting "George Washington Slept Here"—in this case the former Elisha Sheldon Tavern.

Another building open to the public is the Litchfield Historical Society Museum, where exhibits cover 250 years of local history. Displays of locally made furniture include the tall case clocks for which Litchfield was famous.

**Toll Gate Hill Inn** on Route 202, a 1700s Colonial, is the appropriately historic spot for a meal or lodging (Tel: 203-567-4545). And while it is strictly 20th century, gardeners won't want to miss a stop at Litchfield's White Flower Farm, on Route 63 south, nationally known for its 1,200 varieties of unusual perennials.

Litchfield is 85 miles from New York. Take the New York Thruway (Route 87) north to Route 287 east to Route 684 north, then Route 84 east into Connecticut. At Danbury pick up Route 7 north and at New Milford follow Route 202 into Litchfield.

Litchfield Hills Travel Council, P.O. Box 1776, Marbledale, CT 06777. Tel: (203) 868-2214.

# THE HAMPTONS

If you think you spy your favorite actor or your favorite author sitting across the room in a restaurant in the Hamptons, you are probably right.

This chain of half a dozen towns on the east end of Long Island (South Fork) is summer home to countless celebrities. Socialites live in shingled mansions behind the tall hedges in Southampton; artists, writers, and publishing executives tend to settle in East Hampton; and prominent faces from the arts and entertainment world are legion in either town or nearby villages such as Bridgehampton, Water Mill, Amagansett, or Sag Harbor. Many of them show up in July for fellow resident George Plimpton's annual fireworks show, a benefit for Guild Hall, the arts center in East Hampton.

But celebrity watching is only part of the lure of the Hamptons for visitors. The main attraction is what brought everyone here in the first place—miles of magnificent, unspoiled, dune-backed white-sand beaches that are among the finest in the east. The ocean beaches are wide and beautiful all the way from Southampton to Montauk; each town also has bay beaches with calmer waters. Most popular are **Main Beach** in East Hampton and **Atlantic Avenue Beach** in Amagansett, both favored by the many young single New Yorkers who share summer homes in the area. All beaches are free, but beach-parking permits are an absolute necessity if you go by car. Permits are expensive for short visits, since the price is the same whether you buy for a weekend or a season. They are also a bit complicated because each area has its own rules and regulations. In Southampton apply at the Parks and Recreation Department, Hampton Road; Tel: (516) 283-6000. East Hampton Village runs the five local ocean beaches (parking costs ten dollars a day at Main Beach—pay at the Beach Office—or apply for permits at the Village Hall, Main Street; Tel: 516-324-4150). The rest of the beaches are under the umbrella of the Town of East Hampton (apply at Town Hall, Pantigo Road, East Hampton; Tel: 516-324-4140). Many lodgings make parking permits available to their guests; it pays to ask before you reserve.

In addition to the beauty of the beaches, these are historic towns that still bear the windmills, village greens, and clapboard homes of their 300-year-old colonial heritage. Southampton, the first settlement in New York, dates back to 1640, and its Old Halsey House is the oldest frame house in the state. Along East Hampton's picturesque green are half a dozen notable homes including the Studio, the home of watercolorist Thomas Moran, and, two doors down at 217 Main Street, the Summer White House of President John Tyler.

Hook Mill, at the end of East Hampton, is a town landmark. The wind-powered mill is still grinding and is open for tours. It is not unusual to find people taking rubbings of the ancient stones in the nearby Hook Mill Burying Ground.

The Hamptons are also known for the many stylish boutiques, antiques shops, art galleries, and excellent restaurants that have sprung up to serve such a distinguished clientele.

For Hamptons dining, **Gordon's**, Main Street, Amagansett, just east of East Hampton, is a longtime favorite, as is the **1770 House**, 143 Main Street, East Hampton—and there are two branches of Manhattan's pricey **Palm** steak house in East Hampton, at the **Huntting Inn**, 94 Main Street, and **The Hedges**, 74 James Lane. Trendy favorites opened recently by New York restaurateurs are **Sapore di Mare**, Route 27 and Wainscott Road, Wainscott, and **Mel's**, Main Street, Bridgehampton. For the best lobster, drive to the very end of the island and join the waiting line at **Gosman's Dock** at Montauk harbor.

If you choose to stay and enjoy the beach, East Hampton's 1770 House (Tel: 516-324-1770) and The Hedges (Tel: 516-788-7269) are among the most appealing lodgings, along with the **Mill Garth** (Tel: 516-267-3757), cottages in a garden, on Windmill Lane in Amagansett.

Southampton is 96 miles from Manhattan—but it feels like 296 in summer Friday-night traffic. Drive *only* at nonpeak hours. Take the Long Island Expressway to exit 70, go right for three miles to Sunrise Highway (Route 27), then follow 27 east. Long Island Railroad has frequent service from Manhattan (Tel: 718-739-4200), as does the Hampton Jitney bus (Tel: 212-936-0440).

Southampton Chamber of Commerce, 76 Main Street, Southampton, NY 11968. Tel: (516) 283-0402. East Hampton Chamber of Commerce, 4 Main Street, East Hampton, NY 11937. Tel: (516) 324-0362.

## PRINCETON UNIVERSITY

Princeton would merit a visit even if it were not home to one of America's great universities. The shaded lanes of this historic town are lined with outstanding Colonial and Federal architecture. Add the beautiful ivy-clad campus that dominates the center of town, and its extraordinary outdoor art collection, and the trip becomes a double pleasure.

First stop is Maclean House, just inside the main campus gate, to sign up for a free one-hour Orange Key guided tour or to pick up a do-it-yourself tour guide. Either way, the place to begin is where Princeton began—at **Nassau Hall**. The building, one of the largest in Colonial America, housed the entire college for nearly 50 years beginning in 1756. It also played an important part in the nation's history, serving as home to the Continental Congress for six months in 1783.

Move on to Firestone Library, where students need road maps and compass points in the floor to find their way around the three million volumes on the shelves. Whig and Clio halls, twin Greek temples to the west of the library, are reminders of the rival societies where two 18th-century students, James Madison and Aaron Burr, honed their debating skills (the two groups merged in 1929).

Princeton's University Chapel boasts glorious stained-glass windows, oak pews, and a 16th-century pulpit from France. It took 100 men a year to carve the choir and clergy stalls, which are made of wood from England's Sherwood Forest.

The striking Woodrow Wilson School of Public and International Affairs and the **Princeton University Art Museum** show the progression of campus architecture. Chinese paintings, and prints and drawings are among the special strengths in the museum's fine collections, which range from African ritual masks to paintings by Cézanne and van Gogh. The Picasso sculpture just outside is part of the outstanding outdoor collection that covers the campus, and includes dozens of works by such masters as Louise Nevelson, Henry Moore, Alexander Calder, and Jacques Lipchitz.

For information on other historic sites in and around town, stop for a guide at Bainbridge House, the headquarters of the Princeton Historical Society on Nassau Street.

Among sights worth seeing are Rockingham, George Washington's onetime headquarters; Morven, the former official residence of the governor of New Jersey; the Stony Brook (Quaker) Meeting House; and the homes of Woodrow Wilson, Albert Einstein, and Aaron Burr. There are dozens of fine historic homes to be viewed on Nassau Street and its side streets Alexander, Mercer, and Stockton. Nearby (ask for directions) are the attractive Neo-Gothic Graduate School and the world-famous **Institute for Advanced Studies**.

Princeton's fine dining choices include **Le Plumet Royal** in the Peacock Inn, 20 Bayard Lane, and **Lahiere's**, 5 Witherspoon Street. The **Nassau Inn** in Palmer Square is newer than you might expect, but is pleasant and convenient for lunch (accommodations reservations 1-800-922-3432 or 609-921-7500).

New Jersey Transit (Tel: 201-762-5100) runs frequent trains to Princeton from Penn Station, with a change at Princeton Junction. The trip takes an hour and the center of the university is a three-minute stroll from the station. Bus service is available via Suburban Transit (Tel: 212-868-7367) from the Port Authority Bus Terminal to the center of town. To reach Princeton by car, take the New Jersey Turnpike south to exit 10, then route 287 north to another exit 10, then Route 22 west. Continue about two-and-a-half miles to the exit marked Flemington-Princeton. Follow Route 206 south to Princeton.

Princeton Chamber of Commerce, P.O. Box 431 (entrance 2–4 Chamber Street, Suite 127), Princeton, NJ 08542. Tel: (609) 921-7676.

# THE CITY'S SPECIALTIES

## ART

### By Eleanor Heartney

*Eleanor Heartney is a writer and critic specializing in contemporary art. She is a regular contributor to* Artnews, Art in America, Contemporania, *and* The New Art Examiner.

New York City is haunted by the ghosts of art worlds past. You can stroll around Union Square and nod to the spirits of Isabel Bishop and Reginald Marsh as they toss off rapid sketches of the inhabitants of a quieter America between the wars. Then, heading south along University Place, you pass near the sites of such legendary wateringholes as the Cedar Tavern and the 10th Street Bar, where Jackson Pollock, Willem de Kooning, Philip Guston, and their cronies tipped their bottles in the raucous hours between their solitary labors. A detour along Washington Square takes you past the Judson Church, which during the 1960s served as a stage for happenings, experimental dance and theater productions, and environmental installations by such avant-gardists as Red Grooms, Allan Kaprow, Allen Ginsberg, and Yvonne Rainer. Of course, the most obvious places to partake of New York's rich artistic heritage are the city's many art museums, covered in our Neighborhoods section.

However, to penetrate the heart of *today's* art world, you must continue on across Houston to SoHo, that once shabby warehouse district that now boasts what is undoubtedly the richest concentration of artists, artworks, and art talk in the world. There are, by conservative estimate, roughly 500 art galleries in New York City, over one-half of them in SoHo, and perhaps as many as 90,000 artists living in the city and its immediate environs. Such sheer numbers, at once the cause and effect of the burgeoning art market, have re-created the art world in ways that would have seemed unimaginable even 15 years ago. As art, money, and hype mix here in a sometimes unwholesome stew, bohemia today wears a distinctly modern face, and though black remains the sartorial color of choice, the notion of starving in garrets or repulsing the bourgeoisie is definitely passé.

You can chart the rising respectability of respectability by the changing fortunes of the late, lamented East Village art scene. Back in the already distant early 1980s, an enterprising group of young artists decided to challenge the hegemony of the art establishment by opening their own collection of motley storefront galleries on the then unfashionable Lower East Side. This guerrilla action, begun almost as a lark (one trailblazer opened her first exhibition in her bathroom), evolved into an astonishingly successful assault on the taste-making process, and for a few short years it was not uncommon to see limos parked along the garbage-strewn streets of Alphabet City (Avenues A, B, and C) while their owners hopped from tiny storefront to tiny storefront in search of the latest manifestation of the avant-garde.

Times change, and in the end the East Village art scene has been undone by its own success. The influx of dedicated and well-heeled art lovers lured new restaurants and real-estate developers to the neighborhood, rents shot up, and gallery owners found themselves edged out of the market. Meanwhile, the more successful artists and art dealers discovered that they had outgrown both the cramped quarters and the aggressively raunchy style that had been the signature of the East Village art scene.

## *THE GALLERY AS SHOWCASE*

Ensconced in clean white exhibition spaces, and equipped with an open-door policy, revolving schedule of exhibitions, and a quasi-educational function, most galleries today attempt to duplicate the museum experience. Yet, unlike museums, they support themselves through the sale of work. This lends them a slightly schizophrenic character, a fact forcefully brought home last year when the New York Department of Cultural Affairs decreed that galleries, like all other retail businesses, must display an up-to-date price list of all items on display. Some galleries quietly complied, others protested vigorously that too much emphasis on commerce would detract from aesthetic contemplation—and a few evaded the regulation entirely by preselling entire shows.

The price-list furor dramatizes the complicated role galleries play in the contemporary art world. Commercial galleries today are the primary mechanism through which artists emerge into the art mainstream (thanks in part to the decline of the alternative space; see below). Hence a gallery exhibition is far more than a display of wares for sale; it is a crucial milestone in an artist's career, a way to enter the art dialogue, to get reviewed, to be considered for museum exhibitions. Therefore, it is important for everyone involved that the exhibition be open to the general public and be seen by a larger audience than that composed of potential buyers.

At the same time, however, the gallery is a place of sale. Typically, each gallery represents a "stable" of artists, whose works are available for viewing and sale at all times in the back room. Most galleries support themselves as much or more through the back room as through sales of exhibited work. In theory, at least, this allows them to present work that may be risky and potentially unsalable out front.

## *DOING THE GALLERIES*

Given the number of galleries and the varieties of art currently on display, "doing" the galleries in New York can seem a somewhat daunting task. Once an activity that might fill a pleasant afternoon, gallery going now threatens to overwhelm the unselective visitor. In order to survive a day of gallery hopping, begin with a definite plan of attack. The indispensable tool is the *Art Now Gallery Guide,* a monthly listing of the exhibitions currently on view in more than 500 galleries and museums around the city. The *Gallery Guide* is available free from the listed galleries (though toward the end of the month they tend to become a very scarce commodity) or at select bookstores. The guide divides the city into areas, and each section is accompanied by a small map.

Because they benefit from spillover traffic, galleries tend to cluster together. The greatest concentrations exist in **SoHo**, of course, where you can expect to find the work of the most hotly debated new artists and styles. The galleries on **57th Street**, with several lively exceptions, focus on artists of more solidly established reputations. And those on the Upper East Side along **Madison Avenue**, in elegant converted brownstones, present art of historical and contemporary importance with a quiet decorum that contrasts strikingly with the downtown scene's noisy self-promotion.

The first-time visitor wanting to get the flavor of New York art could do worse than focus on the various multi-gallery buildings, such as those at: 420 West Broadway and 560, 568, and 578 Broadway in SoHo; and 41 East 57th Street, 50 West 57th Street, and 724 Fifth Avenue in the 57th Street area. Those with more time or specific interests will want to venture as well to the more dispersed galleries listed in the *Gallery Guide*.

Though distinctions have begun to blur somewhat, the old division between haughty uptown and hip downtown remains largely in force. What follows are a few thumbnail sketches of some notable galleries in the three major art zones. No effort is made here to be comprehensive (an impossible task anyway), and this selection should be taken as a mere starting point for gallery exploration. (You'll find exact street locations in the *Gallery Guide*.)

## SoHo Galleries

Less an art purveyor than a tourist attraction in her own right, **Mary Boone** has almost single-handedly redefined the gallery business in the 1980s. Her talent for showmanship and marketing and her uncanny ability to position herself at the crest of whatever wave is breaking over the art world at the moment make her gallery must viewing for casual observers and cognoscenti alike.

By contrast, the grand old man of the New York art scene is **Leo Castelli**, who made his reputation in the early 1960s with his unwavering support of the then-brash newcomers like Andy Warhol, Roy Lichtenstein, and Jasper Johns. The work of these artists can still be seen in Castelli's newly remodeled West Broadway gallery, along with that of several younger generations.

One of the elegantly apportioned East Village transplants, **Jay Gorney Modern Art** is a showcase for the conceptual-based, opulently appointed New Object art. Both artworks and setting resonate with the aura of temperate luxury that marks the spirit of the late 1980s.

For the "old" austere Conceptual and Minimal art, the place is **John Weber Gallery**, whose stable includes such venerable names as Sol LeWitt, Alice Aycock, and Robert Smithson, as well as younger artists with a compatible outlook.

**Ronald Feldman Gallery**, one of the more independent and idiosyncratic galleries in town, offers artists as different as the elegantly restrained Conceptualist Arakawa, the boisterous Russian expatriates Komar and Melamid, and the self-appointed nouveau Andy Warhol, Mark Kostabi.

A cryptic, cerebral, ironic aesthetic is to be found at **Metro Pictures**. Home of the so-called Pictures Generation, whose politically attuned media explorations offered a counterpoint to Neoexpressionism in the early 1980s, Metro shows artists credited with spawning the currently ultra-trendy "Neo Geo" movement.

The core of the **Phyllis Kind Gallery** are the brash aesthetics of the Chicago "Hairy Who" artists who Kind discovered and promoted when she was centered there in the 1970s. In most cases, Kind's other artists are faithful to the gallery's orientation toward fantastic figurative painting.

The only gallery in New York specializing exclusively in work that celebrates the marriage of art and architecture, **Max Protetch** offers architectural drawings and models as well as quasi-functional and architecturally inspired sculpture.

For relief from too much seriousness, there is **Gracie Mansion Gallery**, which, as one of the first East Village galleries and the last bastion of that scene's original cartoon-inspired funky energy, continues to resist the subsequent sobering of the art world.

## 57th Street Galleries

A gallery with a venerable history (its proprietor was linked to the discovery of Pop art in the 1960s), **Sidney Janis Gallery** is noted for the museum quality of its exhibitions of the art of such historical figures as Giacometti, Mondrian, and Albers as well as its surprising embrace of the ill-fated graffiti movement of the early 1980s.

New work by the major figures of the color-field school is frequently the fare at **André Emmerich Gallery**, whose stable boasts, among others, Jules Olitski, Lawrence Poons, Kenneth Noland, Helen Frankenthaler, and Sam Francis.

The decorative movement, which had its great moment in the mid-1970s, remains the inspiration for many of the artists represented at **Holly Solomon Gallery**, while ambitious installations, provocative theme shows, and a taste for the fashionably eccentric are the hallmarks of **Kent Fine Art Gallery**.

The focus at **Marian Goodman Gallery** is on the European avant-garde, with an emphasis on *arte povera*, Conceptualism, and large-scale sculpture projects. This is the place to see the work of artists who have achieved major reputations in Europe but are still little known here.

## Uptown Galleries

**M. Knoedler & Co.**, one of the oldest and most elegant galleries in New York (founded in 1846), is home to a distinguished stable of artists that includes such illustrious names as Frank Stella, Nancy Graves, and Richard Diebenkorn as well as historical figures such as Adolph Gottlieb, David Smith, and Alexander Calder.

Also offering uptown's characteristic mix of old and new, **Hirschl & Adler Modern** focuses on 20th-century modernists as well as contemporary artists concerned with figuration. Meanwhile, the gallery's original branch, **Hirschl & Adler**, concentrates on historical material from the 18th through the early 20th century; newly opened **Hirschl & Adler Folk** presents 19th-century American folk art from paintings to weather vanes to quilts.

## *HANGING OUT*

The best experience of the art world as theater is to be obtained at gallery openings. Ostensibly, the purpose of these receptions is to inaugurate a new exhibition, but they are actually opportunities to see and to be seen, to network, to party. Once the gallery begins to fill up with artists, collectors, and well-wishers, the art becomes invisible anyway, so anyone seriously interested in viewing the exhibition is advised to return another day.

On any given night through the art season (which lasts from September to June or July) there are likely to be multiple openings, so that a determined opening aficionado can take in quite a variety of different scenes. Times and dates of openings are listed in the back of the *Gallery Guide* or can be obtained from the galleries.

One warning: Most galleries long ago abandoned the practice of serving food at openings, and most offer only the most inferior wine. Plan instead to stop off afterward at such art hangouts as **Fanelli** (at Prince and Mercer) or the **Spring Street Bar** (at Spring and West Broadway) in SoHo, where post-opening crowds gather.

# *BUYING ART*

Buying a work of art is not always a simple proposition. Some of the tonier galleries, maintaining that they have a responsibility to place their artists in only the most important, most visible collections, practically require an audition before they will part with a work of art. Other dealers, especially those specializing in non-superstars, younger, or emerging artists, or in specialty items such as prints, photographs, drawings, or old master works, are more than willing to steer potential collectors through the art labyrinth. A listing of reputable dealers, which includes information on their areas of specialization, can be obtained by writing or calling the Art Dealers Association, 575 Madison Avenue, New York, NY 10022; Tel: (212) 940-8590.

Other important sources of information for a novice art collector are the major art magazines: *Art in America, Artnews, Arts,* and *Artforum,* which publish reviews of recent exhibitions and articles on important contemporary artists and trends. The Friday edition of *The New York Times* and the weekly *Village Voice* may be even more helpful, because they contain reviews of shows currently on view.

Once you have determined what kind of work you are interested in purchasing, it may help to focus on galleries specializing in that medium or approach. A short (and once again, by no means comprehensive) list of various specialties includes:

*Photography:* Marcuse Pfeifer Gallery, Light Gallery, Laurence Miller Gallery, Pace/MacGill Gallery.

*Prints:* Castelli Graphics, Multiples, Pace Prints, Diane Villani Editions, Crown Point Press, Editions Ilene Kurtz, Pelavin Editions.

*Old Master and Period Works:* Richard L. Feigen & Co.,

Barry Friedman, Daniel B. Grossman, Hirschl & Adler, Coe Kerr, David Tunik.

## Art Auctions

For those who like a little adventure with their art hunting, it is also possible to purchase art at auction. Prices are not always lower than those attainable at the galleries, but the astute collector can find some bargains. Contemporary art auctions are held twice a year, in November and May. The evening sales are for the heavy hitters, but the daytime sales focus on younger artists with shorter track records and on smaller works. Also of interest to the novice collector are the weekend previews held before the major auctions, at which the works to be auctioned off can be viewed.

The two major auction houses are **Sotheby's** (1334 York Avenue; Tel: 212-606-7000 or 606-7245) and **Christie's** (502 Park Avenue at 59th; Tel: 212-546-1000 or 371-5438). Neck and neck in competition for the best offerings, Sotheby's and Christie's are practically indistinguishable in the range and quality of their art lots. A distant third is **Phillips** (406 East 79th Street; Tel: 212-570-4830).

In order to participate in the auctions, you will want to subscribe to the catalogs for the sales you are interested in (contemporary, modern, prints, etc.). The catalogs, distributed before every sale, cost about $20 each and contain pictures of the works to be auctioned and the high and low estimates of the sale price, along with information about the work's ownership history. Generally there is also an unstated reserve price below which the seller will not go.

One interesting development of recent years is the tendency for collectors and dealers to use the auction as the testing ground for the prices of works by younger artists. When a work by someone like Julian Schnabel or David Salle goes at auction for as much or more than the gallery price, this confirms the validity of those prices. Thus, astute collectors follow the auctions closely to gauge the ups and downs of major reputations.

A final bit of advice: A lot of ink has been spilled in recent years about art as investment, but for most collectors the old advice is still the best—buy only the works you truly love. Then, whether their value rises or falls, you will still be a winner.

# ALTERNATIVE SPACES AND UNORTHODOX INSTITUTIONS

During much of the 1970s, the art market seemed to be running on empty. In response, artists began to organize their own not-for-profit, cooperatively run exhibition spaces to provide commercially unviable and emerging artists with a means of exposure. Many of the most prominent artists today were first presented to the art world under the auspices of the alternative space, as these institutions came to be known. With the resurgence of the art market in the early 1980s, commercial galleries began to reassert their role as taste makers and talent scouts. The alternative movement faded—but did not die away completely. Those few alternative spaces that survived have had to carve out a new place for themselves in today's art landscape. One common strategy is to show work that is by nature unsalable—installations, performance art, and the like—or that is politically sensitive or otherwise unsuited to the commercial gallery. Other spaces have begun to function in a quasi-museum fashion, putting together theme exhibitions that explore a particular aspect of contemporary art or life. As a result, some of the most provocative shows in town are to be found in these stalwart survivors of the 1970s. Among the most interesting:

**Artists Space.** One of the most respected alternative spaces, both for the innovative quality of its exhibitions and for the intelligence of its choices, Artists Space (223 West Broadway between Franklin and White in TriBeCa; Tel: 212-226-3970) boasts that the artists who received their first exposure in its modest galleries include such contemporary heavyweights as Laurie Anderson, Jonathan Borofsky, Robert Longo, David Salle, and Cindy Sherman. It has long focused on such noncommercial forms as video art and installation, and maintains a computerized slide registry that outside curators, dealers, and critics may peruse to locate artists who do not necessarily have a gallery affiliation.

**P.S. 1 and the Clocktower.** Two outposts of the same organization, the Institute for Art and Urban Resources, P.S.1 is located in a rambling red-brick schoolhouse (at 46-01 21st Street) in Long Island City, Queens (Tel: 718-784-2084), while the Clocktower occupies the top two floors in the old courthouse building (including the rather spectacular clock tower itself) at 108 Leonard Street, between Broadway and Lafayette in lower Manhattan (Tel: 212-233-1096).

Both offer a schedule of provocative special exhibitions, but their most innovative feature is the studio program. Each year a group of local, national, and international artists are awarded working space in the P.S.1 and Clocktower buildings. Visitors may catch glimpses of artists at work, especially during the three or four openings a year, when resident artists transform their small cubicles into exhibition spaces for their work. As the artist stands by ready to discuss his or her work with curious passersby, it is possible on these occasions to view a dizzying variety of work, ranging from traditional painting and sculpture to video works, environmental installations, and multimedia performance art set side by side in jolting juxtaposition. Not to be missed as well at P.S.1: James Turrell's *Meeting,* a permanent site installation that is one of the most serene, contemplative spots in the city. (To get to P.S.1 take the number 7 subway line from Times Square or Grand Central Station to the 45th Road/Courthouse Square exit; or the E or F line to the 23rd Street/Ely Avenue exit.)

**The Dia Art Foundation.** The Dia Foundation, founded in 1976, reflects the expansive ambitions of the art of that era. Dedicated to the encouragement of projects "which cannot obtain sponsorship or support from other public or private sources because of their nature or scale," Dia has exhibited a commitment to long-term installation and environmental projects in New York and elsewhere in the United States. In SoHo, Dia has maintained two works by Walter De Maria since 1977: *The New York Earth Room,* at 141 Wooster between Prince and Houston, and *The Broken Kilometer,* at 393 West Broadway between Spring and Broome. In 1987 it opened a huge new exhibition space on the far West Side (548 West 22nd Street, between 10th and 11th avenues) that will present a series of year-long exhibitions of specially commissioned works by important contemporary artists. Dia is unique among New York's not-for-profit art institutions both for the high-profile nature of the participating artists (the 1987/1988 exhibitions involved Joseph Beuys, Imi Knoebel, and Blinky Palermo, while the 1988/1989 roster was composed of Robert Ryman, Francesco Clemente, and Jenny Holzer) and the generous financing it provides for its contributors' projects.

In addition to the commissioned works, Dia maintains an exhibition space in SoHo (77 Wooster Street, between Spring and Broome) that features changing shows often drawn from the foundation's extensive holdings. For all Dia locations, Tel: (212) 431-9232.

**The New Museum of Contemporary Art.** In a category all its own—not exactly an alternative space, but not a traditional museum either—is the New Museum. Founded in 1970 by former Whitney Museum curator Marcia Tucker, the New Museum, at 583 Broadway between Houston and Prince (Tel: 212-219-1222), was originally run in a spirit of radical egalitarianism. Eventually the idea of paying all employees the same rate and rotating jobs proved impractical, but the institution's resistance to orthodoxy remains strong. Shows tend to be conceptual, political, or for one reason or another on the fringes of the mainstream. Despite, or perhaps because of, its antiestablishment stance, the New Museum was one of the first institutions to seriously consider the art of commodity critique that eventually was dubbed "Neo Geo" and swept the art scene for a season. It is also one of the few museums in New York that makes a concerted effort to incorporate works by regional artists in its group shows.

The offerings at the New Museum tend to be a mixed bag: The museum can be excessively leery of popular themes or artists. Nevertheless, the New Museum remains a remarkable and admirable experiment.

Other not-for-profit spaces worth a visit are White Columns, 325 Spring Street (Tel: 212-924-4212), 55 Mercer (Tel: 212-226-8513), and the Storefront for Art and Architecture at 97 Kenmare Street in SoHo; the Alternative Museum, 17 White Street (Tel: 212-966-4444), in TriBeCa; and Fashion Moda, 2803 Third Avenue (Tel: 212-585-0135), in the Bronx.

## ART AND CRAFT SUPPLIES

**David Davis**, 346 Lafayette, is revered among artists for its informed help, selection of imported materials, and overall quality.

**Pearl Paint**, 308 Canal Street, is generally cheaper, though not quite as comprehensive for the fine artist. Pearl also carries hardware and supplies for designers and crafts people.

Just a step below the above (by overwhelming consensus the best art-supply outlets in the city) is **New York**

**Central Art Supply**, 62 Third Avenue at 11th Street, which also carries an excellent selection of papers.

**Utrecht**, 111 Fourth Avenue, between 11th and 12th streets, is also popular among fine artists. It carries its own line of paints, which are less expensive but not as high in quality as the name brands.

## OTHER ART AND CRAFT SPECIALTIES

**Arthur Brown**, 2 West 46th Street, carries materials of interest to designers and art directors.

**Charrette**, 212 East 54th Street, offers a variety of fine-art and commercial materials, with a particularly good selection of architectural and drafting supplies.

**Jam Envelope and Paper**, 621 Sixth Avenue at 19th Street, is a wholesale outlet specializing in paper.

**Polk's Model Crafts**, 314 Fifth Avenue at 32nd Street, carries wood products.

**CK & L Surplus Store**, 307 Canal Street, carries metal screening, wire, and the like.

**AIN Plastics**, 300 Park Avenue South, between 22nd and 23rd streets, and **Industrial Plastic**, 309 Canal Street, specialize in plastics, acrylic, acetate, buterate, and so forth.

See also Bookstores in the chapter on Literary New York for shops that specialize in **art books**.

# ANTIQUES, ANTIQUITIES, AND COLLECTIBLES

*By Lynn Yaeger*

*Lynn Yaeger is the author of a biweekly column in the* Village Voice *on antiques and collectibles, and was also a contributor to* The Village Voice Guide to Manhattan's Shopping Neighborhoods. *A resident of New York City for over 15 years, she has written on fashion for* Cosmopolitan, Australian Woman, *and other publications.*

Whether the collector is visiting New York for a few months or a fortnight, whether he or she is an avid accumulator of objects from the past or maintains a purely academic, scholarly interest in such items, New York City provides a scope and variety of antiques, antiquities, and collectibles probably unrivaled in the world today. (Did somebody say London? But London is full of old English things. New York City is full of old things from *all* over.)

Anywhere you go in New York you are likely to run into antiques and collectibles shops, whether nestled in the shadows of the Washington Square Arch or buried in the small streets radiating from the major museums. Certain areas, however, have clusters of stores, and the serious shopper should head to these places first to get an idea of what is currently popular in the Manhattan antiques world and what prices the New York City market will bear.

Serious money might begin its tour with the axis of 57th Street and Madison Avenue. On **57th Street** proper, between Fifth and Lexington avenues, are a number of antiques dealers with internationally known names, displaying goods (mostly furniture and decorative accessories) of exquisite manufacture and rigorous provenance. Turn up **Madison Avenue** and you will find a number of additional prestigious shops, most at their addresses far longer than the foreign fashion stores snuggling up next to them. Their aristocratic presence is felt in varying intensity up to about 96th Street, where Madison Avenue sheds its golden glow and begins its rapid decline.

A visit to the Madison Avenue antiques shops stuns all but the wealthiest traveller into shocked, impoverished silence. Jump on the Lexington Avenue downtown local subway (number 6) and alight in **SoHo**, which, while not inexpensive, gives the ordinary working person at least a fighting chance at shopping survival. The mood down here is rampant Art Deco and French bistro, and there is a growing enthusiasm for mission oak and the Arts and Crafts movement. The atmosphere is relaxed, and even when the price tag is astronomical the salesroom will lack the pin-drop hush of 57th Street.

From SoHo, the inexhaustible visitor might walk northwest to **Greenwich Village**, where on Hudson Street or Greenwich Avenue he or she will find lots of furniture stores with jumbled-up stock that looks inexpensive but isn't, really. Higher priced things are for sale on Bleecker between Christopher and Bank, where for some reason the shops seem equally divided between delicate, austere

French and Biedermeier furniture on the one hand, and folk-art galleries full of quilts, Beacon blankets, and moth-eaten dolls on the other.

Those young urban professionals who do not mind being identified as such can hop on the Seventh Avenue train (number 1, 2, or 3) to 72nd Street and stroll with their compatriots up **Columbus Avenue** (to about 92nd) and back down **Amsterdam Avenue**, where a selection of stores sell old and antique furniture and accessories that are appropriate for the furnishing of one's new co-op or first home in Westchester.

Heartier souls not intimidated by Wholesale Only or To the Trade signs might want to check out the huge repositories of furniture, lamps, bronzes, and so on in the **wholesale antique district** located up and down Broadway and University Place and intervening streets between 8th and 14th streets. Though you are neither dealer nor decorator, a tough-talking demeanor and the willingness to pay quickly and in cash may succeed in getting you past the door.

Specific recommendations regarding individual antiques and collectibles stores have built-in limitations, because stock may vary enormously and the buyer tends to rely on the inspiration of the moment. Furthermore, the assiduous antiques shopper is ever on the lookout for that one-in-a-million baby in a five-and-ten store, and may in fact turn up nothing of interest in any store described below, but rather find his or her heart's delight in some alleyway hovel unknown to us. (Note: Be sure to check the other shopping sections of this guide, where a number of additional stores specializing in collectibles are described. Vintage-clothes wearers, for instance, will find their haunts listed in the Fashion Shopping section.) Still, keeping all of the above in mind, we suggest the following.

## Furniture

A huge and intense variety of styles, ages, countries of origin, and prices exists. (In fact, it is difficult to ascertain which preoccupation is more intense among New Yorkers: their personal appearance, or the way their houses look.) The market groans with everything from 19th-century Portuguese and Spanish furniture at **Cobweb** (116 West Houston Street) and French working-class pieces at **T & K French Antiques** (120 Wooster Street) to American oak and English country pine at **Pony Circus Antiques** (381 Second Avenue at 22nd Street).

Collectors of the newly fashionable vintage furnishings from the 1930s through the postwar era will be serviced by **First 1/2** (131 Thompson Street), **Fifty-50** (793 Broadway between 10th and 11th streets), **Retro-Modern** (214 East 10th Street), and **Depression Modern** (135 Sullivan Street). **Alice's Antiques** (552 Columbus Avenue) specializes in 19th-century American iron beds, and the nearby **Better Times Antiques** (500 Amsterdam Avenue) can provide likely companion pieces. In SoHo, **Bertha Black** (80 Thompson Street) sells small pieces of hand-painted furniture that evince a Hudson River school influence. At **Peter Roberts Antiques** (134 Spring Street) the hunky, chunky look of mission oak is much in evidence.

Those preferring sleek, polished examples of the Art Deco movement should dip around the corner to **Alan Moss Studios** (88 Wooster Street) or travel to the Village to **Maison Gerard** (36 East 10th Street). If you have money to burn you should proceed uptown in a taxi to where the finest of the finest English and French 17th- to 19th-century antique furniture is for sale, at such establishments as **Stair & Co.** (942 Madison Avenue), **Didier Aaron, Inc.** (32 East 67th Street), and **Dalva Bros.** (44 East 57th Street). Highly desirable American furniture, pre-Revolutionary to early 19th century, is available from the eminent **Israel Sack** (15 East 57th Street). Those whose eyes gaze wider than their pocketbooks can open should not despair but rather visit **ABC Antiques** (880 Broadway at 19th Street) or the **Salvage Barn** (523 Hudson Street between 10th and Charles streets), both of which sell interesting pieces (mostly late 19th and 20th century) from various countries for reasonable prices. In SoHo, **Fleur de Lis Antiques** (489 Broome Street) is a big, friendly warehouse sort of place, open only Friday through Sunday, where bargains can be hunted and where famous faces have been known to pop out from behind dusty armoire mirrors.

# Jewelry

Jewelry is one collectible category traversed even by those who otherwise shy away from antiques and collectibles. Much interesting jewelry is available from the variety of dealers at the **New York Center for Art and Antiques** (fairly affordable) and at its more glamorous sister, the **Place des Antiquaires** (less so)—see below under Antiques Centers for locations. Edith Weber, in Antiquaires, has a distinguished collection of English lovers' eyes (painted on ivory, under glass) from the turn of the 18th century. **Fred Leighton** (Trump Tower and 773 Madison Avenue) has Cartier Art Deco diamonds and other signed pieces of early 20th-century jewelry, as does **Primavera** (808 Madison Avenue) and **Macklowe Gallery and Modernism** (667 Madison Avenue). **A La Vieille Russie** (781 Fifth Avenue) carries jewels that look as if they would have fallen out of the czarina's Gladstone had she crossed the border into Finland. **James Robinson** (15 East 57th Street) has wonderful fine jewelry in its street-level store, but take the elevator up to six for relatively more affordable Edwardian and Victorian paste, cut steel, and Scottish agate.

Those interested in acquiring a vintage wristwatch are advised to visit **Time Will Tell** (962 Madison Avenue) or **Chiuzac Gallery** (510 Madison Avenue). (Prices will be higher here than at the flea markets, but the shopkeeper will at least provide a guarantee.) Shoppers in search of fashionable, less expensive vintage merchandise might like the 1930s Bakelite bracelets at **The Good, The Bad and The Ugly** (143 East 13th Street). Fans of the rather overblown costume jewelry of Miriam Haskell will want to know that there are always many pieces available at **Norman Crider Antiques** (Trump Tower, Fifth Avenue at 56th Street).

## Folk Art

American folk art has burgeoned in popularity over the last several years, and with it has come an attendant boom in fakes and reproductions. Foreign visitors, who may never have seen a drunkard's path quilt or yellowware bowl close up, should exercise special caution when considering items such as these at outdoor markets. The following shops will of course provide annotated receipts assuring the quality and provenance of your purchases.

**Susan Parrish** (390), **Cynthia Beneduce** (388), and **Kelter-Malce** (361) are all near one another on Bleecker Street in the Village, and among the three of them their stock approximates a veritable museum of hooked rugs, indigenous textiles, Adirondack furniture, Indian souvenir beading, and various other items in the folk-art fashion. **Laura Fisher**, in the New York Center for Art and

Antiques, is a nice person who sells hundreds of quilts and knows a lot about them. **Hirschl & Adler Folk** (851 Madison Avenue) is a serious gallery where browsing is expected and purchasing is a more private affair.

## Clocks

A man walked into a New York City clock shop some years ago, looked around, saw something he favored, and brought it over to the shopkeeper. "I'll give you $300 for it," the man said. "Well, I'll tell you," said the proprietor, "I'm not going to sell it for that—Mr. Fanelli on Madison Avenue will give me at least $400 for it." "I am Mr. Fanelli," said the first gentleman, "and I will give you $300." Mr. Fanelli's shop, **Fanelli Antique Timepieces, Ltd.**, is located on Madison Avenue, near 85th Street.

## Silver

**Tudor Rose** (28 East 10th Street) has a sizable stock of English and American silver, including many small items (boudoir accessories, picture frames), and exceptionally reasonable prices. **Sutton Place Mews**, next door, has an interesting selection as well. **Alice Kwartler**, in the Place des Antiquaires at 125 East 57th Street, sells a rigorously curated collection, with a lot of things at the level of signed Tiffany dresser sets. Antique silverplate and sterling coffee and tea services, along with early flatware (sold individually or in sets), are among the specialties at the venerable **S. Wyler Inc.** (941 Lexington Avenue at 69th Street).

## Antiquities

Strong as it is in most areas of collecting, the New York market collapses a bit when it comes to purveyors of ancient art and objects of antiquity. Nonetheless, take time out to visit **Royal Athena Galleries** (153 East 57th Street), where over 1,500 ancient sculptures, vases, and other objects (Greek, Roman, pre-Columbian, etc.) are for sale by an enthusiastic staff. In the rarefied upper reaches of Madison Avenue, **Antiquarium Fine Ancient Arts** (948) or the **Safani Gallery** (960) might be worth looking into as well. And **Ares Rare** (961), among its other jewelry offerings, features authentic ancient Greek and Roman bibelots.

## Rugs and Textiles

**Cora Ginsburg** (819 Madison Avenue, Suite 1-A) is usually whispered to be the high bidder at textile auctions, and presents a scholarly collection of early examples (including rare 18th- and 19th-century day clothing, shoes, and lingerie) at her gallery. For carpets and tapestries, the toney name is **Doris Leslie Blau** (15 East 57th Street), where exceptionally high tariffs justly reflect the quality of the merchandise. Across town, shoppers with less money who are forced to be more flexible in their requirements might find an acceptable antique floor covering at the **Rug Warehouse** (2222 Broadway at 79th Street), or around the corner at **Central Carpet** (424 Columbus near 80th Street). Both these places usually have on hand an assortment of desirable 1920s Chinese Art Deco rugs.

## China, Glass, and Porcelain

A revival of interest in Tiffany, Galle, Daum, and other art glass has priced most examples right out of the market, but those who like to look at these things should visit **Minna Rosenblatt** (844 Madison Avenue). French and English cameo glass and highly collectible glass paperweights are specialties at **Leo Kaplan** (967 Madison Avenue). **Meisel-Primavera** (141 Prince Street) in SoHo holds down a corner of the world market of the British Art Deco chinaware by the bizarre Clarisse Cliff.

Flea markets and travelling antiques shows remain excellent sources for early 20th-century glass and porcelain, but a careful and prudent eye is advised. (The tiniest chip, of little interest to the casual user, can devalue the object considerably.) Shoppers desiring depression-era proto-American Fiesta ware dishes are advised to visit **Mood Indigo** (181 Prince Street), where stacks in several colors and sizes are always on hand at reasonable prices.

## Orientalia

Bargains on authentic examples in this area may be ferreted out by experts—we only have the ability to recommend highly reputable if costly outposts. **Ralph M. Chait** (12 East 56th Street) specializes in Chinese pottery, porcelains, and handstones dating from the Neolithic period

(2500 B.C.) through the heady days of the early 18th century. **Flying Cranes Antiques** (1050 Second Avenue) sells cloisonné, satsuma, bronzes, and the like from both Japan and China from 1690 to 1890. Nestled in a corner of the Carlyle Hotel is **Michael B. Weisbrod** (987 Madison Avenue) and his fine Chinese works of art, including inlaid lacquer, though you may require a few stiff ones at the hotel's well-known Bemelmans Bar before you garner the confidence to sign the enormous check.

## Decorative Accessories

Almost every antiques store in town sells items that may be construed as decorative accessories, so suggestions in this area will necessarily be cursory and eccentric.

Those wishing to decorate their domiciles in the manner of the American home circa 1935—be it a cottage with sagging porch and cabbage-rose wallpaper or an oilcloth-covered Sears & Roebuck–furnished Bronx apartment—will find authentic rolls of wall-covering and linoleum at **Second Hand Rose** (270 Lafayette Street). Appropriately humble linens, boudoir accessories, and esoterica such as funny old aprons are for sale at **Ellen O'Neill's Supply Store** (242 East 77th Street) at surprisingly reasonable prices. Lamps by which to curl up with the latest issue of *The Smart Set* may be located at **Louis Mattia** (980 Second Avenue at 52nd Street) or **Barry of Chelsea** (154 Ninth Avenue), both of which sell earlier, higher priced examples as well. If you live permanently out of a suitcase, visit **Eclectiques** (483 Broome Street), where you will find a large selection of rare vintage Louis Vuitton trunks as well as antique hatboxes, Pullman cases, and other bags covered in a variety of exotic animal skins, from ostrich to elephant.

You may find a vintage pedestal sink or tub for sale—along with old columns, mantels, staircases, and the like—at **Great American Salvage Co.** (34 Cooper Square), a place that claims it has 25,000 items in its computer memory bank. Furnishings that once graced the interiors of now-defunct barbershops, saloons, and ice-cream parlors now grace **Urban Archaeology** (285 Lafayette Street). Smaller items in a similar vein (world's fair standing ashtrays, old Coney Island peep-show machines) can be found at **Lost City Arts** (275 Lafayette Street).

## Toys and Memorabilia

Aficionados of old toys, games, dolls, and assorted childhood memorabilia are among the most zealous visitors to flea markets and antiques shows, where genuine bargains may still surface and careful searching can really pay off. Those interested in visiting stores that specialize in this sort of thing should take in **Second Childhood** (283 Bleecker Street) for tin toys, soldiers, and interesting small Celluloid dolls, and **Darrow's Fun Antiques** (309 East 61st Street). In the shadow of the 59th Street Bridge, under the intermittent gaze of the Roosevelt Island tram, Darrow's sells vintage games and rarer items like big 1930s toy zeppelins. Older, saucier children might fall for a vintage gaming machine from the **Antique Supermarket** (86 Wooster Street).

A jumbled-up but excellent selection of dolls is for sale at the **Antique Doll Hospital of New York** (787 Lexington Avenue), where the proprietor is a real craftsman. ("Can I repaint a doll's eye? I can fix anything. I am an artist.") Boyish types of any age will probably like the **Soldier Shop** (1222 Madison Avenue between 88th and 89th), specializing in highly collectible, not inexpensive antique toy soldiers and military miniatures. Readers less partial to the martial might prefer **Lionel Madison Trains** (105 East 23rd Street), a one-of-a-kind railroadiana shop. Those evincing unlimited enthusiasm and funds to match should visit **Monde Magique**, in the Place des Antiquaires, for museum-quality 19th-century automata, dolls, toys, and early games.

## Markets

Of course, many people eschew conventional antiques stores entirely in favor of flea markets, antiques shows, and public auctions. For these collectors, the thrill of the chase is all, and the heart leaps as they sidle up alongside shopkeepers at markets, ready to buy what has momentarily been replaced on the shelf, or, even better, succeeding in outbidding these same merchants at auction houses all over town.

There are a number of year-round weekend markets in Manhattan, the most recommended being the one located in two adjacent parking lots on Sixth Avenue between 24th and 26th streets. Although there has been an attempt to open this market on Saturdays, the offerings are paltry, since for 22 years this has operated as a Sunday market, and dealers are by nature creatures of habit. Half the market is cordoned off and requires that you pay one dollar admission, presumably to discourage diamond thieves who might otherwise enter and have a field day. Other markets include one in the schoolyard of Public School 183 (York Avenue and 67th Street) on Saturdays, and its superior cousin on Sundays at P. S. 87 (Columbus Avenue and 77th Street). Both of these also have small, depressing indoor sections in school cafeterias still redolent of lunches but transformed for the weekend into collectibles dens.

## Shows and Street Fairs

There are any number of specialty shows (paper ephemera, dolls, baseball, etc.) and street fairs that make their way to New York City. For current listings of these, buy the Friday and Sunday editions of *The New York Times* and check the antiques classified advertisements. Shows of a more general, eclectic nature spring up all the time as well. Highbrow ones take place in fall, winter, and spring at the Park Avenue Armory (winter, in January, is the fanciest), and there is a wonderful show of more than 600 dealers held on three Hudson River piers each year in November and March. Once a year (March also) a huge and highly regarded collectibles show takes place on the boardwalk in Atlantic City, easily accessible from New York City by the buses that shuttle thousands of unregenerate gamblers to and from Atlantic City on a daily basis.

## Antiques Centers

Somewhere in the shadowy world between a table of junk for sale in the broiling sun and a full-fledged antiques store lies the province of the antiques center—a collection of glass-enclosed booths owner-operated by individual dealers. There are two major centers in New York City. **The New York Center for Art and Antiques** (1050 Second Avenue at 55th Street), with 104 galleries, sells everything from toys to rugs and objects of virtue, with a heavy concentration on fine jewelry. The newer, smaller, and very elegant **Place des Antiquaires** (125 East 57th Street) contains 64 expensive miniature shops showing admittedly expensive merchandise. There are also a number of small, less diverting antiques malls in town. You might choose to visit the indoor center on Canal Street off West Broadway, where, among much undistinguished merchandise, one woman sells a spectacular collection of antique powder compacts, vinaigrettes, and other early purse accessories, and another has a showcase full of excellently priced, exceptionally attractive gentlemen's vintage wristwatches.

## Auction Houses

Those visitors possessed of steel nerves who disdain paying preordained prices for anything might care to try their hand at a Manhattan auction. These take place at **Christie's** and **Sotheby's** at least weekly, and there are often interesting items at **Doyle Galleries** and **Phillips** as well. (See the Art section, above.) Check the advertisements in *The New York Times,* paying careful attention to notices of Christie's Collectibles or Sotheby's Arcade auctions, as these often feature lower priced, more amusing merchandise.

# ARCHITECTURE

*By Barry Lewis*

*Barry Lewis, an architectural historian by profession, has created tour programs and produced lecture series on New York City architecture for New York's 92nd Street Y. He has also written articles on the city's architectural history for many publications, and was a contributor to the Municipal Art Society's* Juror's Guide to Lower Manhattan.

New York is a great maw for architecture. Throughout its existence New York has built itself up as a city, played out history in that city, and then ripped it out a generation later only to replace it with another. Some downtown lots have been redeveloped five times since 1800. In Europe, buildings stand for centuries; in New York, a lifetime for a building might be only 30 years.

And yet, peruse certain neighborhoods and it would seem as if time has stood still: the brownstone-lined streets of Chelsea, the Greek Revivals of Greenwich Village, the 19th-century row houses of the East 50s hard by the soaring towers of Midtown. Ghostly department stores of the Victorian Ladies' Mile still line Broadway above Union Square, and Federal row houses still stand among the industrial buildings of SoHo. So much of New York is surprisingly old; so much of it can be harshly new.

New York's buildings are eclectic beyond imagination. The city has the well-deserved reputation of trying to mimic the airs of European aristocracy, and is often unfavorably compared to Chicago and California, where a fresh American originality was encouraged. Nonetheless, New York's buildings are far more varied than historians will admit. To see this, roam the streets around Union Square, where a modern commercial style was hammered out in turn-of-the-century loft buildings; or the Upper West Side, where from the 1880s to the 1930s new forms for urban residences were developed in row houses and apartment houses. Walk the Grand Central Terminal area, where in the 1920s the image of the skyscraper was indelibly etched in the world's imagination—and you can see that New York was no slouch in forging its own original style and flair.

New York, being completely American, is the product of private speculators, some of whom demanded architectural quality, most of whom demanded the cheapest product. This resulted in a good deal of banality and some extraordinary exceptions, but the sum total is quite impressive. The city's buildings, like its people, are numerous, jammed together, and at times rise to dizzying heights making an estimable silhouette—especially from afar. That's why some of the best views of Manhattan are from "offshore" looking back: from atop the Jersey Palisades in Weehawken's Hamilton Park, along the Brooklyn Heights promenade, or from the Socrates Sculpture Park on Long Island City's East River shore. But walking the city's streets and seeing it in detail is rewarding as well. The new, the old, and the older are layered along the same block. New York may seem to be a chaotic jumble of buildings, but actually there is an order, a sequence, and a logic. Like any archaeologist, you only need to know the "key" in order to understand the hieroglyphics.

## THE ROW HOUSE

Back in the 1810s New York was a town clustered hard by the Battery and extended no farther than the brand-new **City Hall** (1802–1811; Mangin & McComb). City Hall, a delicate Federal gem, is still one of America's most impressive city halls, but it was plagued by extended deadlines and cost overruns, proving that certain civic practices have a deep-rooted tradition. The city's merchants were fast making their town America's busiest port and most populous metropolis. Earning their money from the sailboats lining the East River docks—parts of today's **South Street Seaport** are all that remain—they lived in handsome town houses along lower Broadway and along Greenwich Street near the verdant Hudson River shoreline, where they could stroll in evening promenades and "take the air." Built in the Federal style, with fanlights in their entrances, brick and marble-trimmed fronts, and delicate interiors, these houses represented a simplified, "Yankee" version of England's richly ornamented, brilliantly colored late Georgian or Adams style. Although hundreds of these town houses were built for the newly prosperous lawyers, merchants, and bankers, all that remains intact is a relative handful, among which the most elegant is the **James Watson House** (1793–1806; John McComb, Jr., 7 State Street, opposite Battery Park), now a Roman Catholic shrine.

As the city grew, the wealthy residential district pushed northward to Canal Street and, by the 1820s, beyond. Federal row houses scattered among the circa 1900 tenements and factories of Chinatown, Little Italy, and SoHo attest to those areas' former roles as the Upper East Side of a bygone era.

The Erie Canal, opening in 1825, put New York over the top. First the canal and then the railroads funneled America's—and the world's—raw produce and goods through New York's harbor. In the 1830s the city began an explosion of growth that, until the troubles of the 1970s, seemed to be without end. By 1835 the city had reached and engulfed the rural town of Greenwich, and the emerging Greek Revival style would embellish the new precincts of Washington Square and lower Fifth Avenue. Especially distinctive are the houses of West 10th Street (between Fifth and Sixth avenues) and **The Row** on Washington Square North (numbers 1–13 and 21–26;

1831; Martin Thompson, architect), which, though slightly altered, evoke the stiff-backed restraint of antebellum society.

Though larger and more monumental than the Federal houses, the Greek Revivals followed the same basic elevation and plan. The configuration of the New York row house had been essentially set by 1800. The stoop had already appeared, a New York phenomenon dictated by the lack of back alleys (New York developers balked at cutting alleyways through expensive real estate). No back door meant deliveries, garbage, and honored guests all had to pass through the front. The stoop allowed for an "upstairs-downstairs" double entry, with service personnel entering the ground-floor servants' quarters and guests entering the first-floor parlor and dining room. The stoop was actually a poor solution to the problem of a double front entry, dictating clumsy exteriors and a cramped interior layout, but rich New Yorkers loved them as their descendants would love Cadillacs; a house with a stoop indicated that the family within had finally arrived. Designers of the day, from James Renwick (architect of St. Patrick's Cathedral) to Olmsted and Vaux (creators of Central Park), railed against the stoop, but New Yorkers turned a deaf ear. They would not give up their stoops until the later, more sophisticated generation of the early 1900s would be persuaded by the likes of Stanford White and Edith Wharton to adopt the more graceful, stoopless townhouse designs of London and Paris.

Around 1845 a war of styles broke out, as the Greek Revival was challenged by the newer Neo-Gothic and Italianate. Within five years the dust had settled and the Italianate had won. It was obvious that New Yorkers, preferring the Renaissance palazzo look, identified themselves with Medicis and Sforzas rather than Medieval prelates or ancient Athenians. But the New York palazzo was of brownstone (a material native to Connecticut and New Jersey, not Tuscany), and the streets were soon lined with what Edith Wharton disparagingly called a "chocolate sauce." Thousands of these new town houses were built along the streets of Chelsea, Longacre Square (now Times Square), Turtle Bay, and Murray Hill. So many brownstone-fronted houses went up in New York, Brooklyn, and the Jersey towns atop the Palisades that to this day New Yorkers habitually call any old row house—of whatever material or style— a "brownstone."

Behind the brownstone façades a revolution in domestic technology was unfolding. Modern water systems, sewers, and gas lines meant indoor bathrooms, gas-fed globes to replace dripping candles, modern kitchens with stoves, hot and cold running water, and "refrigerators" (they were actually iceboxes), and, thanks to cheap coal from Pennsylvania, central heating systems. The "modern" house had arrived. By the 1860s the average New York bourgeois could boast of a high-tech domesticity, smugly knowing that the great palaces of Europe still remained cold and unplumbed. It's no wonder that the people of those times thought theirs was truly "The Century of Progress."

After the Civil War the French mansard style, with all its nouveau-riche flamboyance, became popular, though often all New Yorkers did was take a prewar brownstone and stick a mansard on top of it. Instead of the Italianate, the new rage was a mechanistically rendered Neoclassicism, called the Neo-Grec, reflecting the growing Victorian interest in an honest, machine-age style. These Neo-Grec, mansard-roofed brownstones lined the streets of the Upper East Side, a new district opposite newly built Central Park. Thoroughly middle class—the rich then lived on Fifth Avenue in the 50s—the neighborhoods' breadwinners commuted down to Wall Street on the equally new elevated railroads.

In the 1880s brownstone fell out of favor and Eclectic styles ranging from the Queen Anne to the Neo-Romanesque became popular. It was the age of Richardson, Sullivan, and Furness; their intuitive genius for the simple rendering of materials is reflected in the glorious palette of stone, brick, tile, and terra-cotta that New York architects used for this new generation of city houses. Streets from the West 70s to the West 130s, just then being developed, were alive with brilliant coloration and texture. The Eclectics were also interested in new interior layouts (it wasn't easy squeezing a home into a narrow row house plot), and they introduced bay windows, interlocking balconies, terraces, and towers to make the rooms inside both more interesting and more open. There are superb examples of this era's accomplishments on West 76th Street off Riverside Drive and around the corner on West End Avenue. Likewise is Harlem's **Striver's Row** on West 138th and 139th streets between Seventh and Eighth avenues.

Of all the thousands of row houses built since the 1830s only two remain totally intact and open to the public as house museums. One is the 1832 **Old Merchant's House** at 29 East 4th Street (between Bowery and Lafayette), a late Federal gem, and the other is the **Theodore Roosevelt Birthplace**, 28 East 20th Street (between Broadway and Park Avenue South), a rebuilt, Neo-Gothic brownstone from 1848. Go first to the Old Merchant's House and notice its spare Yankee simplicity, then visit Roosevelt's boyhood home to see firsthand the growing Victorian penchant for decoration and embellishment.

By 1900 the price of Manhattan real estate had made row house living prohibitive for the middle class. Between 1900 and 1930, the last major era of the Manhattan town house, these houses went up almost exclusively in the new wealthy precincts of the Upper East Side. The rich had been displaced by the growth of Midtown, so they moved north of 59th Street, where they built Beaux Arts–style town houses and freestanding Fifth Avenue mansions reflecting the Neoclassicism of Italy, France, England, and colonial America. Of the town-house-lined side streets, East 79th Street off Fifth is an excellent example. As for the mansions, few are left and almost all have been recycled for other uses. Among the earliest and the best are the **Villard Houses** (1883; McKim, Mead & White) at Madison Avenue and 50th Street, a group of six houses expertly arranged to give the look of a Renaissance palazzo. (How different they are from the provincial brownstones of the 1850s!) The gem of the group was Villard's own house, today the south wing of the Palace Hotel. The clarity, simplicity, and sophistication of the interior, which is now well restored, was 20 years ahead of its time. Other grand mansions still extant are the French 18th-century-style Duke mansion (1912; Horace Trumbauer; Fifth Avenue at 78th Street), now the **New York University School of Fine Arts**; the Loire Valley–style Warburg mansion (1908; C. P. H. Gilbert; Fifth Avenue at 92nd Street), now the **Jewish Museum**; and two Neo-Georgian houses that are today the homes of the **Cooper-Hewitt Museum** (Andrew Carnegie's home; 1902; Babb, Cook & Willard; with its interior beautifully restored) at 91st Street; and the **International Center of Photography** (Willard Straight's house; 1914; Delano & Aldrich) at 94th.

Built to last forever, many of these houses were demolished within a few decades. In typical New York fashion they were removed by the 1930s to make way for a new city, one of elegant department stores south of 59th Street and elegant apartment houses north of it.

## THE APARTMENT HOUSE

Middle-class Americans of the 19th century insisted, like the English, on living in their own private homes. Tenements were fine for the immigrant poor, but the middle class would have nothing to do with multiple dwellings.

Tenements first appeared before the Civil War in the ethnic slums like the Irish Five Points (now Chinatown) and the German Bowery district (now the Lower East Side), but middle-class New Yorkers were adamant. They would not adopt the Continental style of apartment-house living until they had to. By 1900, they had to. Real-estate prices made town houses a luxury commodity, and the New York bourgeoisie began moving into new "apartment-hotels."

The luxury apartment house first appeared en masse on the Upper West Side and in Harlem, the two New York districts most associated with the solid middle class. The famous **Dakota** (Henry J. Hardenbergh) at Central Park West and 72nd Street, opening in 1883, was a bit ahead of its time. By the 1900s the city's first subway line, the IRT, linked upper Broadway with Wall Street—and the apartment-house boom was on. **The Ansonia** (1904; Graves & DuBoy; 2109 Broadway at 73rd), **The Apthorp** (1908; Clinton & Russell; Broadway between 78th and 79th streets), and **The Belleclaire** (1903; Emery Roth; Broadway at 77th Street, southwest corner) were typical of the new breed. The Ansonia especially, with its blowsy Neo-Baroque style, reminds us of a Parisian extravagance of the Belle Epoque. But the New York version was far taller and contained more high-tech gadgetry than any Parisian apartment house.

These new high-rise residences were state-of-the-art palaces with garages (equipped with outlets for electric cars), underground shopping centers, and health clubs. Elevators, built-in refrigerators, pneumatic mail-delivery systems, and miles of piping and wiring for gas, electricity, water, and heat made these new luxury apartment houses the equivalent of oceangoing steamships anchored to the New York streets. To assuage the "shame" of living in a ten-room flat, these early apartment houses offered hotel-like services including maid service, room service, elegant in-house restaurants, and rooftop gardens and pavilions for private soirees.

The super rich finally capitulated as well to apartment-house living, but they insisted on doing it in their own aristocratic manner. McKim, Mead & White's elegantly proportioned **998 Fifth Avenue** (1910; 81st Street, northeast corner) set the pattern. Rejecting the West Side's middle-class flamboyance, the East Siders preferred the subtleness and simplicity of a Renaissance palazzo. This restrained academicism took hold, and when New York went apartment-house wild after World War I, when Park Avenue on the East Side, Fifth Avenue opposite Central Park, and West End Avenue on the West Side were rebuilt to the new scale, it was flat-topped, porticoed Neoclassicism that prevailed.

In the 1930s the new Moderne or Art Deco style emerged. It was especially popular in the new apartment towers of Central Park West, such as **The Century** (1931; the Chanin Co.) at 62nd Street, **The Majestic** (1930; the Chanin Co.) at 72nd, **The San Remo** (1930; Emery Roth) between 74th and 75th streets, and **The Beresford** (1929; Emery Roth) at 81st—though the last two are a mixture of Moderne and Mannerist. The new skyscraper-style apartment houses emphasized wraparound corner windows (only possible in a steel cage building), spacious foyer-plan interior layouts, and soaring towers housing magnificent apartments with four exposures—literally "mansions in the sky"—making that era seem, by today's standards, the golden age of the New York apartment house.

Though undecorated brick boxes predominated after World War II, interior layouts continued their prewar spaciousness. Beginning in the 1960s, however, apartments and their rooms began to shrink, and materials seemed to "shrink" as well. Today's elaborate Postmodern decor, concierges' desks, and in-house health clubs cannot hide the fact that often the apartment itself, considering the price, is a pale shadow of its magnificent Beaux Arts and Art Deco predecessors.

## *DEPARTMENT STORES, THEATERS, AND COMMERCIAL BUILDINGS*

Traditionally, New York's downtown (Wall Street) was where the money was made and Midtown—the city's retail, theater, and café district—was where the money was spent. Downtown remained stationary, though growing taller every generation, but Midtown followed the northward expansion of the luxury class that frequented it and moved constantly farther uptown.

In the 1840s Midtown settled at Broadway near City Hall Park, producing America's first department store, **A. T. Stewart's** (Snook & Trench), which rose at Chambers and Broadway (northeast corner) in 1845 and is still standing. (It is now called the Sun Building after a newspaper tenant of later years; being city owned, it is in terrible shape.) Stewart's was not only a new phenomenon in retailing, it also brought the Italianate style to New York, sparking a fashion in architecture that would sweep the city during the next two decades.

By the 1850s Midtown had moved to what is today called SoHo, with Tiffany's at 550 Broadway (now altered) and Lord & Taylor (now demolished) at Grand Street. Cast-iron construction, a modern modular system for erecting buildings (much like a kid's erector set) became all the rage; and so many cast-iron department stores in the guise of Venetian palazzi rose along Broadway that New Yorkers dubbed that thoroughfare "the Grand Canal." The Venetian Renaissance style was not popular for mere sentimental reasons. Its open, well-fenestrated arcading allowed architects to exploit cast iron's possibilities, creating Victorian "glass boxes" framed in Neoclassical packaging. The 1857 **Haughwout Store** (J. P. Gaynor) still stands at Broadway and Broome Street (northeast corner). Though today painted black, its windows were originally transparent and its cast-iron framing was a glistening white painted with faux marble veining to give the illusion of antiquity. It mattered little to New Yorkers that their "palazzi"—bigger and glassier than anything in Renaissance Venice—would have been impossible to build before the age of iron.

After the Civil War, Midtown jumped north to the Ladies' Mile: Broadway and Sixth Avenue from 14th to 23rd streets. Grand department stores in the French Second Empire style, with cast-iron framing and iron-crested mansard roofs, lined Union and Madison squares and Sixth avenue from 18th to 23rd streets. Many still stand, like so many ghosts from a vanished past. The new money of the infamous Gilded Age, an era expertly captured in Jack Finney's novel *Time and Again,* had a chance to display itself strolling fashionable 14th or 23rd streets. The department stores were generally built with skylit interior atriums, open-cage elevators, and acres of glass windows and skylights, making each store a veritable Crystal Palace. **Tiffany's** (now severely altered to house a labor union) moved to Union Square West and 15th Street in 1869; **Arnold Constable** (1869; Griffith Thomas) opened at Broadway and 19th Street (southwest corner), and serves today as the home of ABC Carpets (across the street ABC also occupies the old 1881 W & J Sloane store); and **Lord & Taylor** (1869; James Giles) settled in at Broadway and 20th Street, part of it (the altered part) now occupied by Saint Laurie Clothiers. The opening of Lord & Taylor prompted Teddy Roosevelt, Sr.—whose brood, including the future president, lived just down the block—to exclaim that the neighborhood was changing, and it was time to move. That they did in 1873, to the new address of note, West 57th Street.

By 1910 Midtown had moved again, this time to Fifth Avenue north of 34th Street. **B. Altman & Co.** (Trowbridge & Livingston) opened in 1906 at 34th Street, where it still stands. Acknowledging the Beaux Arts fashions of the day, Benjamin Altman wrapped his 11-story steel-cage department store in the elegant detailing of a Renaissance palazzo (a far more sophisticated version than A. T. Stewart's back in 1845), and the other great shopping emporia followed suit. In the same year **Tiffany's** moved into McKim, Mead & White's glass palazzo at the southeast corner of 37th Street (it's now the Reverend Moon's printing plant); **Lord & Taylor** (Starrett & Van Vleck) opened at 39th Street in 1914; **Arnold Constable** moved to 40th (now the Mid-Manhattan Library); and **Saks Fifth Avenue**'s "palazzo" (Starrett & Van Vleck) capped the trend when it opened in 1924—way uptown!—at its current location at 50th Street. By this time a distinct middle-class shopping district had blossomed at Herald Square (Macy's opened there in 1902), and the theater district had followed its own path up Broadway, settling down around 42nd Street and Times Square in the 1900s.

Midtown shifted slightly again—to 57th Street—in the 1930s and 1940s. **Bergdorf Goodman** (Buchman & Kahn) moved into its streamlined headquarters on 57th Street in 1928. **Tiffany's** (Cross & Cross), moving again, built a Classical-Moderne "safe" for its jewels at 727 Fifth Avenue in 1940. This time, however, the central business district was moving northward as well, and for the first time in the city's history corporate skyscrapers joined the department stores and retailers to share Midtown's streets.

The Beaux Arts–embellished Heckscher Building (Warren & Wetmore; now the **Crown Building**, recently restored and spotlit) opened at Fifth Avenue and 57th

Street, southwest corner, in 1922, and ten years later Rockefeller Center rose opposite Saks Fifth Avenue and St. Patrick's Cathedral. Midtown, continuing to shift, had always been moving up the island's spine. In 1910 people assumed that by the 1950s (way in the future), Midtown would probably reach 125th Street—but it never happened. Midtown New York, having moved northward for over 100 years, finally stopped at the southern gates to Central Park.

## *PUBLIC BUILDINGS*

New York's unrelenting grid gives few public buildings a chance to shine—no vistas or grand boulevards here. But when New York entered its great age of civic design, the Beaux Arts era between 1890 and 1930, its architects produced a handful of buildings whose qualities of planning and design we had not seen before and may never see again. The 1898 consolidation of New York created a five-borough city of four million people that demanded new public facilities. The New York architectural establishment rose to the occasion by producing buildings of extraordinarily skillful planning and outstanding civic presence. This new generation of professional, Beaux Arts–trained American architects married the sublimity of European Neoclassicism with the pragmatism of the Yankee mind. The result was great Neoclassical palaces fine-tuned to become machines for modern life, criticized by a later, so-called Modern generation for stylistic irrelevancy. In today's Postmodern era we have put aside those prejudices to appreciate once more the masterworks of that earlier generation.

**The American Museum of Natural History** and the **Metropolitan Museum of Art** (both begun in the 1870s) received new Beaux Arts fronts, though in these instances the Neoclassical faces, though skillfully done, masked decades of willy-nilly additions. There were, however, four public buildings built from scratch that became instant landmarks for all times. In typical American fashion, indicative of how we build our cities, three of these four "public" buildings were in fact built by private corporations.

The former **United States Custom House** (1907; Cass Gilbert) on Bowling Green is the only true public building of the group. Reminiscent, in its palatial guise, of the deep-rooted traditions of Western architecture, behind its

Beaux Arts façade it is a paradigm of skillful functionalist planning. Separation of freight and people was achieved by giving cars and trucks a street-level basement entrance in back and pedestrians a first-floor monumentalized entry in front. The statue-flanked Neo-Baroque grand entrance (Daniel Chester French did the *Four Continents*—and are they kitsch!) made New Yorkers understand instantly where the customhouse was and where they should enter. The grand stair leads, in the Neoclassical tradition of an architectural promenade, to the nerve center of the building, a skylit rotunda where the customs officials waited for the business at hand. In 1937 Reginald Marsh, under the auspices of the Work Projects Administration, embellished the ceiling of the rotunda with gritty scenes of New York Harbor showing its piers bustling with passengers and freight. In 1973 the United States Customs Service moved to the World Trade Center (where, thanks to the Modern idiom, you can't even find the customhouse and, if you do, you can't figure out how to get in), and the 1907 customhouse came close to being demolished. Saved after a preservation battle, it has recently been proposed as the future home of the Museum of the American Indian. At present it is sometimes used for temporary exhibits, and if it is open don't miss the chance to see it.

The **New York Public Library** (1902–1911; Carrère & Hastings; actually a private institution) rose on Fifth Avenue between 40th and 42nd streets in the same decade as the U.S. Custom House. Though it is usually compared unfavorably to its inspiration, the Boston Public Library (1890; McKim, Mead & White), people often forget that Boston's library, though aesthetically richer and more sophisticated, is a building that never worked. The New York Public Library, on the other hand, was designed by librarians with the help of architects (an unusual shift in architects' priorities) and is as superbly functional today as it ever was—and is undergoing a badly needed restoration program (by Davis, Brody & Associates with Giorgio Cavaglieri).

The library's practical layout, ingenious use of natural light, and its deft mixture of specialized libraries and the more modern stack system (via a 1911 pneumatic-tube system that is still state-of-the-art today) make it a working machine for everything from scholarly research to casual reading. Its varied rooms, as they come out from under the restoration wraps, are a marvelous synthesis of sensibility and function. Its newly restored (1987) Bartos Forum, originally the circulating library, skylit and metal-framed, is a gem of Beaux Arts–influenced, machine-age design. The main entrance plaza, facing Fifth Avenue, is one of the city's great public spaces, its steps and flanking terraces a constantly shifting scene of street theater and schmoozing. Its exhibitions in the reopened Gottesman Hall are usually first rate, and the daily tours by trained docents worth attending. No city can call itself civilized without a great library at its heart, and New York's, after years of sad neglect, is again becoming the vibrant core it once was and should always be.

**Grand Central Terminal** (1902–1913; Reed & Stem, Warren & Wetmore) shares kudos with the library. Replacing an earlier terminal on the same site, the new GCT is actually a city-within-a-city, mixing long-distance and commuter trains, subways, taxis, automobiles, and pedestrians. The steel-framed Beaux Arts building sits atop a double-deck underground railroad yard that stretches from Lexington to Madison avenues, from 42nd to 50th streets. As Park Avenue developed in the 1920s and 1930s, every building on the avenue, from the terminal to the Waldorf-Astoria, was positioned on the roof of that yard, one of our earliest examples of "air rights" development. An iron-framed highway, planned in 1904 and one of the nation's first, carries Park Avenue traffic around the building, and underground "streets" link the terminal to over half a dozen skyscrapers and two major hotels.

The terminal itself is an ingenious interlocking of specialized spaces, lit by a system of skylights and interior windows that fully exploit its steel frame. Its monumental concourse is one of the city's great plazas, a roofed piazza San Marco, serving the dashing commuter and the casual pedestrian alike. The Municipal Art Society (Tel: 212-935-3960) conducts tours of the terminal every Wednesday at 12:30 P.M. Few complexes today combine with such skill the efficient and the humane. It is truly one of the nation's great architectural works.

The same could have been said of its sister railroad complex, Pennsylvania Station. McKim, Mead & White's 1910 architectural wonder (Seventh and Eighth avenues, 32nd to 34th streets) modeled its concourse in front on the Baths of Caracalla, and built its train platforms in back in a totally functionalist idiom of exposed iron and glass. No one could accuse these architects of using historical styles for lack of imagination. As in the three other public buildings we've mentioned, the station's designers used history where they felt its symbolism was appropriate, and utilized modernity where the building program demanded it. But Penn Station is gone, buried under the cracker-box skyscrapers and garish arena of Madison Square Garden. The station's demolition in 1960–1963 so infuriated the New York public that it led to the establishment of the New York City Landmarks Commission, given authority to prevent that kind of vandalism from ever happening again.

The great tradition of public architecture might be revived in the Postmodern era, but that remains to be seen. Fans of high-tech will be interested in the new **Jacob Javits Convention Center** (1987; I. M. Pei's James I. Freed; the Hudson River at 37th Street), whose steel-and-glass superstructure has given New York City its own Crystal Palace. But the great public buildings of the Beaux Arts period have yet to be surpassed—or even equaled—in their skillful integration of function, beauty, and humane concern for the private citizen. That kind of architectural largesse might in fact be a lost art.

## *THE SKYSCRAPER*

The skyscraper, invented in Chicago in 1885, arrived in New York in 1890. The first New York skyscraper, at 50 Broadway, lasted less than 30 years, and, characteristically for New York, was torn down to make way for a bigger building. In the ensuing generations Chicago and New York vied with each other for superlatives of height. The Chicago style often won the acclaim of critics for its no-nonsense, flat-topped rationality; New York came in a poor second, criticized for its costume-y historicism and "vulgar" flamboyance. But if the scholars preferred Chicago, the public preferred New York, and a new generation of critics is beginning to swing around to give New York its due.

New York's first steel-cage buildings popped up downtown in the Financial District and in the wholesale belt from Canal to 34th streets. Using a Neoclassical formula, the New York architects artificially divided their buildings' façades into a base-shaft-capital arrangement based on the parts of a classical column—even though steel-cage construction is modular and uniform from bottom to top. The critics charged "façade-ism" and "artifice," but on closer look we find that the New York architects were not such dummies.

The tripartite formula allowed for a decorative base at the sidewalk level where pedestrians can relate to it (no one ever looks above the third floor—unless you're on a walking tour); an austere midsection to keep the decorativeness in check; and a fanciful top that announced the building's presence in the city's skyline. The romantic top, later so despised by the Moderns, often served parenthetically as a "billboard" for the corporation located within. Chrysler's spire, Bankers Trust's ziggurat (at Wall and Nassau streets), and Standard Oil's oil lamp (22 Broadway, seen best from New York Harbor) were the best advertisements a company could buy.

In the Wall Street area the designs were largely Neoclassical, because prestige and "image" were so important to financial institutions. The narrow streets, soaring towers, masonry street walls, and the recurring Beaux Arts formula encouraging decoration disciplined by a rhythmical order created streetscapes not seen anywhere else in the world. Midtown, with its broad avenues and river-to-river streets opening up views in all directions, does not compare. Downtown New York is its own special place. Typical is lower Broadway, where Bowling Green, framed by the 1907 customhouse, and the Beaux Arts–era skyscrapers create one of the city's finest vistas.

Around 1900 a satellite office district emerged uptown in the Madison Square area (23rd Street and Fifth Avenue). After part of the old Ladies' Mile was ripped out, the new construction produced two of New York's more notable skyscrapers, the **Flatiron Building** (1902; Daniel Burnham; Fifth Avenue at 23rd Street) and the **Metropolitan Life Tower** (1909; Napoleon Le Brun & Sons; Madison Avenue at 24th Street). The latter briefly held the record as the world's tallest building.

In the wholesale district, east and west of Broadway from Canal to 34th streets, the buildings were more anonymous but no less interesting. Perhaps feeling less restrained, the architects gave the façades of their loft buildings eclectic treatments that melded (Louis) Sullivanesque modernity with Beaux Arts formality. Brick, stone, iron, glass, and terra-cotta were used to create high-rise tapestries of incredible originality. Blocks to notice include West 12th and 13th streets between Broadway and University Place. Down in SoHo, the "little" **Singer Building** (1904; Ernest Flagg; 561 Broadway) and the **New Era Building** (1893; Alfred Zucker; 495 Broadway) both give Chicago stiff competition in the game of high-rise aesthetics.

As buildings grew to astronomical heights it became obvious that their massiveness would have to be pruned back—if only to allow light and air to penetrate the streets below. Ernest Flagg's magnificent Singer Building (1908; Broadway and Liberty Street; now demolished!) pointed toward a solution with its narrow, ornamented tower rising from a stubby base, but it was the **Woolworth Building** (1913; Cass Gilbert; Broadway at Barclay Street–Park Place) that gave the basic formula to the next generation of skyscraper designers. Its secular Neo-Gothicism made the building's unprecedented 795 feet soar into the clouds. Its multiuse base included shops, a luxury restaurant, a health club (still in operation), and a direct link with the new BMT Broadway subway line, making it more a "city" than just a building. Its two-story-high mosaic-tiled lobby served as grand entrance and interior "court" (a must-see; the Woolworth personnel are very hospitable), giving access to all the building's multiple functions. The world's tallest building until 1930, it still remains today—thanks to the Woolworth Company's vigilance—one of the finest skyscrapers of its day and a template for all times.

When in 1916 New York adopted America's first zoning code requiring setbacks and narrow towers, the Woolworth Building was its prototype. In the unparalleled building boom of the 1920s the city's skyline was reshaped largely in the Woolworth image. The great Art Deco skyscrapers of the 1920s were built mostly in Midtown on the "new Wall Street" (as the area around Grand Central was then called). Skyscrapers such as the **Chanin Building** (1929; Sloan & Robertson; Lexington Avenue at 42nd Street, southwest corner), the **Chrysler Building** (1930; William Van Alen, Lexington Avenue at 42nd Street, northeast corner), and the **Empire State Building** (1931; Shreve, Lamb & Harmon; Fifth Avenue at 34th Street, southwest corner) gave the world its definitive image of what a skyscraper should look like. No Chicago skyscraper ever captured so intensely the public's imagination.

They borrowed their silhouette from the American skyscraper gothic, their details from the German Expressionists, and their nomenclature from the French Exposition des Arts Décoratifs of 1925. Traditional materials such as marble and stone were mixed with new materials like stainless steel and Monel Metal, so that references to both the past and the future were interwound. The Chrysler Building with its Art Deco marble lobby, elevators paneled with inlaid wood, and stainless steel tower is the epitome of its time. Its top was planned to be brilliantly lit (finally achieved in 1985) as in Fritz Lang's Expressionistic film *Metropolis*.

Downtown Art Deco skyscrapers were pinstriped and bankerish, though one of the finest, the **Irving Trust Co.** at 1 Wall Street (1932; Voorhees, Gmelin & Walker) houses a brilliant red and gold mosaic banking hall, now used as an office but accessible to the public. Uptown the Deco buildings were more colorful, both outside as well as inside, whether serving as a corporate headquarters—like the **Fred F. French Building** (1927; Fred F. French Co.; Fifth Avenue at 45th Street, northeast corner)—or as commercial loft space, such as **2 Park Avenue** (1927; at 33rd Street), Ely Jacques Kahn's confection of Vienna Secessionist color and form.

The boom went bust as we all know, but the depression era produced one of the finest skyscraper complexes the world has ever seen. Pushing the Midtown office district farther north to around 50th Street between Fifth and Sixth avenues, **Rockefeller Center** (1931–1938; the Associated Architects) put slab towers atop low-rise bases (for more light and air both in the building and on the street) and tied its buildings together with a vast underground shopping center. The center gave the public an unprecedented pedestrian promenade and sunken plaza (used for ice-skating in the winter), direct access to the new IND Sixth Avenue subway, and provided for underground truck deliveries (below the skating rink), making its streets more civilized to negotiate.

Its two music halls (one is now gone) and cinema (the Guild, at 50th Street) provided entertainment, while sculpture, art works, and museums (the latter are now all gone) provided culture. Raymond Hood, the project's chief architect, melded Le Corbusier's insistence on light, airy slabs with the German Expressionists' insistence on symbolism. The result was a then-unique type of "city" that was friendly and familiar, light-filled and open in spite of its gargantuan scale. Yet it gives us "character" as few Modern buildings ever do: The RCA Building (newly spotlit), the center's visual focus, anchors the city as Medieval cathedrals once anchored old European cities. Many complexes have tried to emulate Rockefeller Center, but few have achieved its balance of size, scale, and civility.

After World War II the Modern "glass box" school came into vogue. Skidmore, Owing & Merrill's Gordon Bunshaft shocked New York with his Manufacturers Hanover Trust glass bank (1954) at Fifth Avenue and 43rd Street (southwest corner) and the floating glass slabs of **Lever House** (1952) at Park Avenue and 53rd Street (northwest corner). Here was an urban world of shimmering glass, light, air, and sun. Glass skins began to be wrapped around old-fashioned setback silhouettes.

Mies van der Rohe and Philip Johnson's **Seagram Building** (1958; Park Avenue at 53rd Street, southeast corner) changed the shape of the skyscraper radically and created the template for a generation. Mies's brilliant rendering of bronze, glass, and marble expressed perfectly that generation's search for a new functionalist, machine-age style. The building's pristine glass tower, set in a podium-style plaza, was reproduced superficially by the thousands in cities across the country. In New York itself, as Midtown pushed up Park, Third, and Sixth avenues, and as downtown expanded from Water Street to the World Trade Center, the Seagram's imagery permeated everything.

The Seagram is perfection both as a piece of sculpture and as an aesthetic statement. But its popularity among developers did not stem from its refined proportioning. Rather, because the building is actually fatter and more complicated than it first appears to be, the Seagram gave them a sleek corporate image while allowing them to stuff a good deal of office space behind the glass façade. Its pristine lobby had no room for messy retail tenants, and the tower-in-a-plaza siting was the perfect expression of the Suburban Decade's dislike of anything remotely urban.

The Seagram is a work of art, but what turned out to be a prototype for mass production was itself, ironically, not truly capable of being mass produced. Most of the building's features—from its bronze mini I-beams, used as decorative mullions, to its bronze-tinted glass windows and special interior lighting (which gives the Seagram at night a totally different effect)—were custom designed and custom made. This classic image of a machine-made product was in fact a custom-made arts-and-crafts artifact costing twice as much as other buildings. Knocked off cheaply, it lost the genius that made its minimalism work.

When repeated on a large scale the Miesian city was lifeless, boring, and scaleless, giving 1960s cityscapes an almost fatal case of visual anomie.

Everything the Seagram eschewed has come back in the Postmodern 1980s. Decoration, romantic silhouettes, flamboyant tops, intensely active plazas all are now *de rigueur*. One of the first of the Postmodern towers, the **Citicorp Center** (1977; Hugh Stubbins; Lexington Avenue at 53rd Street), is still one of the best, creating a truly urbane interior court that has consistently attracted the public. Others of note are the **AT & T Building** by Philip Johnson (1979; Madison Avenue at 55th Street, northwest corner), known for its Chippendale top (which is probably the building's best part), the **IBM Building** next door (1983; Edward Larrabee Barnes; Madison Avenue at 57th Street, southwest corner), with its own quite popular glassed-in court and the excellent **IBM Gallery** downstairs, and **Trump Tower** (1979; Swanke Hayden Connell; Fifth Avenue at 56th Street, northeast corner), whose opulent, marble-swathed, vertical shopping center is a fitting altar to New York's worship of the loud and the flashy.

Downtown, **Battery Park City** (BPC) gives us in one fell swoop all the Postmodern standards on a single stage. Cesar Pelli's **World Financial Center** has mosaic-domed lobbies, a shop-lined walkway system, and the glass-enclosed, café-filled **Winter Garden**, which give us the commercial side, while BPC's new residential districts, with their traditional city streets and apartment buildings reminiscent of prewar designs, show us Postmodernism on the domestic front. The open-space planning and landscaping here is the most imaginative in years, and includes a new version of Gramercy Park as well as waterfront esplanades and parks designed with a refreshing sensibility.

Though it is too early to tell, the Postmodern style is probably the beginning of a new Eclectic era, when romantic silhouettes, decoration of whatever kind, intense urban activity, and design sources from both the past and the future will predominate. But Postmodern decor cannot mask the changing facts of city life. In the service economy of the postindustrial world, our buildings are being built for computers more than for people. Though Midtown office buildings might be slender and notched to give each member of their corps of corporate executives a corner office, most skyscrapers are now built on a massive scale to give the computerized back-offices and trading floors the immense amount of room they need. Large floors mean fat buildings: Though the World Financial Center's towers average 40-odd stories, each contains at least the square footage of the 102-story Empire State Building.

In addition, record-breaking real-estate costs mean gargantuan towers, whether commercial or residential. Every one of Manhattan's desirable residential sections is being glutted with apartment houses of unprecedented size.

Whither goes Manhattan? Nobody knows. Looking back over the previous 20-year period, we can with hindsight see that no one could have predicted the changes that would take place five years down the road from any particular time. Who knows when we'll see the next masterpiece—or the next abysmal flop. Whenever it is, you can be sure it won't be long in coming.

## MUSEUMS AND BOOKSTORES FOR ARCHITECTURE

**The Museum of Modern Art.** Books, galleries, and occasional exhibitions on, of course, modern-movement architects. Don't miss the gallery highlighting modern consumer products. 11 West 53rd Street (between Fifth and Sixth avenues). Museum bookstore.

**The Metropolitan Museum of Art.** Period rooms including French 18th-century salons, an American Neo-Gothic library, and a Frank Lloyd Wright living room. Fifth Avenue at 82nd Street. Museum bookstore.

**Cooper-Hewitt Museum.** The Smithsonian's decorative arts branch, which often has architectural exhibitions. Its building is a major exhibit in itself: the 1901 mansion for Andrew Carnegie. Check the bookstore's inventory. Fifth Avenue at 91st Street.

**The Urban Center.** Located in the south wing of the 1883 Villard Houses, with the rest of the complex now functioning as the Helmsley Palace Hotel. Often has small exhibits on architectural and city-planning topics especially relating to New York and/or historic preservation. 457 Madison Avenue at 51st Street. **Urban Center Books**, located in the Urban Center, is *the* New York bookstore for architecture, city planning, and urban design.

**Rizzoli Bookstore.** As handsome a bookstore as the books it sells. Its design section features lush volumes on art and architecture. 31 West 57th Street between Fifth and Sixth avenues. There are also branches at 454 West Broadway in SoHo and in the new World Financial Center in lower Manhattan.

## GALLERIES

**Max Protetch.** Devotes one of its galleries full time to architectural exhibits, and has original architectural drawings for sale. 560 Broadway at Prince Street at the edge of SoHo.

**The Drawing Center.** This nonprofit gallery occasionally has smashing shows on architectural drawings. 35 Wooster Street, between Broome and Grand streets, SoHo.

**Storefront for Art & Architecture.** Offbeat, interesting architectural shows. 97 Kenmare Street, near Lafayette Street, not far from SoHo.

For up-to-the-minute schedules of gallery and museum shows of architectural interest, see the listings in *Blueprint* magazine, a British publication that covers the New York scene, or *Metropolis* magazine, published locally, devoted to architecture, urban design, and the decorative arts. Both are available at Urban Center Books and Rizzoli Bookstore.

# FASHION

*By Lynn Yaeger*

From its earliest days as a metropolis, nascent New York displayed an enthusiasm for the culture of beauty, the cult of fashion, and the vagaries of style quite out of proportion to the circumstances of most of its residents. "I have known young ladies supporting themselves," wrote one Anne Royall in the early years of the 19th century, "sit up til 12 o'clock at night, to complete a suit of clothes, the proceeds of which was to purchase a fine cap, or a plume of feathers, to deck herself for church. Hundreds of those females thus maintain themselves in a style of splendor; no ladies in the city dress finer. A ten dollar hat, a thirty dollar shawl, with silk and lace, is common amongst the poorer class of females."

By the middle of the 19th century, A. T. Stewart, considered the first true department store in the United States, had opened on lower Broadway, employing good-looking gentlemen to shepherd the ladies from counters of the finest European laces and linens to the revolutionary displays of ready-made cloaks and mantles. Other dry goods stores were also expanding (many dispensing with the traditional custom of selling "wet" goods—rum—on one side of the establishment and necessities for the ladies on the other), including Lord & Taylor, which had a great currency during the Civil War years at the now almost irredeemable intersection of Grand and Chrystie streets.

As the century progressed the big stores moved uptown, and by about 1885 the "Ladies' Shopping Mile," or "Fashion Row," as it was called—Sixth Avenue from 14th to 23rd streets, with some offshoots on Broadway—was filled with towering cast-iron emporiums. ("Meet you at the fountain!" shoppers said to one another in 1895, referring to the waterworks in front of Siegel-Cooper Dry Goods Store, Sixth Avenue at 18th Street, years before the Biltmore clock came into fashion.)

No sooner had the Ladies' Mile become firmly entrenched in the shopper's imagination than the stores pulled up stakes and moved again. (Lord & Taylor, having left the Lower East Side in 1869 for Broadway and 20th Street, packed up again in 1906 and relocated to its present Fifth Avenue location.)

Of course, not everyone dressed in silks and proper bonnets, genteelly attempting to ape their betters. There were those, then as now, who stuck their stylistic tongues out at the passing show and elected a wildly bohemian style. The Bowery G'hirls of the 1840s, with their garish yellow shawls, scarlet dresses, and giant feathers and boas, scandalized society with bold manners and ankle-length skirts (floor-dragging being the only respectable length). Now their spiritual descendants, in torn black leather, nose rings, and spiked hair, tread the same streets with identical *épater les bourgeois* intentions occupying their youthful minds.

Why is it that New York remains at the crossroads of style and fashion, century after century? Is it because for 150 years Manhattan has been a center of clothing manufacture, of design, of intense wholesale and retail activity? By the 1920s the clothing business had moved from its squalid cottage-industry origins to large-scale factories in the neighborhood once known as the "Tenderloin." A noon visit to this **Garment District**—Sixth to Eighth avenues in the 30s—will dispel any doubts the reader may harbor that Manhattan has somehow passed its peak as the apex of the fashion industry. Choking racks of clothing impede all but the hardiest pedestrian, trucks with screaming drivers stall aggressively at loading docks, and the whir of 10,000 sewing machines is dimly audible in the distance.

Today as yesterday young designers rush from fashion school to Manhattan, where they apprentice themselves to established designers or set up storefront couture houses on their own. And when the time comes to show the fashion collections of the major designers, there are no "American" or "United States" collections for the press and society to flock to. The only important fashion showings this side of the Atlantic are the appropriately named, aptly situated, and justly famous "New York" collections.

## SHOPPING

### *The Upper East Side*

Eclipsing Fifth Avenue, challenged by SoHo, but still holding strong at the center of the shopping firmament, *Madison Avenue* is the street of dreams for those who dream of the best clothes, from the fanciest shops, offering the most uncompromising service. Although there are a few interesting outposts below 59th Street (**Itokin Plaza**, at 520 Madison, contains some serious contenders), the real action begins north of the new AT & T Building. The only way to canvass the area properly is to walk uptown along the avenue (or down from 96th Street), since several stores are scattered on each block. Take plenty of breaks for coffee—or sherry—and grab a taxi home.

Not in geographical order, but rather grouped according to tastes, some of the interesting shops are as follows: For the youthful shopper, **Fausto Santini** (697) has flat-heeled, peculiar, amusing shoes at (given the location) surprisingly reasonable prices. This shopper will also like the brightly colored clothing at **Kenzo** (824) as well as the judiciously edited collection of European items at **Betsey, Bunky, Nini** (746). **Joseph Tricot** (804) can provide properly unserious knitwear; visit **Stewart Ross** (754) for shelves crammed with hand-knitted bulkies—some wacky, some ditsy, most originating in the British Isles.

The marginally more mature shopper might prefer to

buy her pullover at **Cashmere/Cashmere** (840), where styles are casual but the materials at hand are almost insufferably elegant. At **Missoni** (836) the stock features unique jaquard wool items, from socks to coats. **Sonia Rykiel** (792) plies her snug, knitted costumes (considered quite revolutionary at their introduction 20 years ago) from a comfortable, busy store nearby.

Although the well-fixed but not unhip matron will probably head next for **Giorgio Armani** (815) and **Gianni Versace** (816), both of which sell famous luxuriously appointed Italian separates, she should also consider a visit to **Milan D'Or** (910), which offers less well known Italian designs, so she won't see herself coming and going at embassy cocktail parties. For Francophiles, **Yves St. Laurent** (855), **Pierre Balmain** (795), and **Emanuel Ungaro** (803) offer their labels in relatively close proximity to one another.

Americans experiencing a burst of civic pride (and foreign visitors weary of encountering similar designer merchandise in all the major cities on the globe) should visit **Polo/Ralph Lauren**, sequestered in the old Rhinelander mansion at the corner of 72nd Street (867), of interest to students of architecture and interior design as well as those in search of fashion. The old mansion still sports its original interior, the lower floors being full of Lauren clothing interspersed with antiques (both fine and homely), while the upper floors, where Ralph sells furniture and decorative accessories, stand ready with their old-fashioned bedsteads, travel trunks, lace panels, and even the occasional birdcage to accommodate a long-lost Rhinelander princess, as she rushes to the window to catch the sunrise over Madison Avenue.

### *Fifth Avenue–57th Street Area*
The corner of 57th Street and Fifth Avenue, sunk deeply in myth from the time that Zelda swam in the Pulitzer Fountain and the morning Holly broke fast at Tiffany's, remains for many the cosmopolitan center of the universe, and the shops fanning out in all directions do nothing to disabuse them of this notion.

Those who wish to approach this zenith from a southerly direction should begin their walking tour at **Saks** on 50th Street, or perhaps make a brief visit to St. Patrick's Cathedral before setting off. Though this stretch of Fifth lacks the stupendous allure it once held, there are still some excellent shops, including **Mario Valentino** (745) and **Ferragamo** (663 and 717, the latter selling shoes only), both featuring Italian clothing and leather goods. Readers as yet unconvinced that Mr. Mencken spoke the truth when he asserted that "no one ever lost money underestimating the taste of the American people" can dispel any lingering doubts with a visit to Trump Tower. This pink marble and waterfall-encrusted edifice, attended by embarrassed-looking security guards dressed in Gilbert and Sullivan costumes, actually contains a few not uninteresting shops (Aspry, Charles Jourdan, etc.).

Now turn west briefly, where half a block away stands **Charivari 5**, the newest and for many connoisseurs the best of the Charis, with four floors of designer merchandise plus the video screens, good-looking salespersons, and blaring music some people consider indispensable company when they spend their money. East of Fifth Avenue, 57th's reputation as a shopping street is confirmed. **Chanel**, at number 5 East 57th Street (the company waited a long time for this particular address), sells its famous collarless brass-buttoned suits, but there is also a full range of makeup and accessories available (including the quilted bag) for those wishing to commit a few hundred rather than a few thousand. The popular **Ann Taylor** (3 East 57th) has reasonably priced stylish clothing, a glass elevator, and a highly regarded shoe department. **Laura Ashley** (21 East 57th) specializes in the maid-of-the-moors look, with its flowery prints, high-waisted dresses, puffy sleeves, and sashes. Those preferring a more androgynous appeal should turn instead to **Burberry's** (9 East 57th) or **Jaeger** (19 East 57th), both of which will accoutre the serious person, with not a sprig in sight.

On the next block (between Madison and Park) you will find, among the many other high-priced offerings, shoes by **Maud Frizon** (49 East 57th), internationally renowned for their blend of grown-up gamin (round toes, bows) and glamor girl (gold kid, high heels). At **Matsuda** (465 Park Avenue) the clothes are World War I as filtered through the artistic sensibility of modern Tokyo; while the palette is sober and conservative, the prices are not.

## *Upper West Side*

Once, not so long ago, the Upper West Side was a shabby-genteel neighborhood, full of butcher, hardware, liquor, and shoe-repair shops. Then came the co-ops, and the traditional stores found themselves replaced by places selling antiques and tostadas. Lately the more esoteric of these shops are beginning to disappear, in favor of branches of European chain clothing stores and fancy ice-cream depots.

**Charivari 72**, on the corner of 72nd Street and Columbus Avenue, deals in high-priced men's and women's big-name European clothing from its triplex shop. (The Charivari shops were among the first fancy stores to open on the Upper West Side and have since reaped the profits of their prescience.) Among the other offerings, spread out along Columbus Avenue, you might like **Caroll** (256) and **Alain Manoukian** (301), both of which sell working women's French sweaters; **Sacha London** (294), interesting shoes with low prices; or **French Connection** (304), hip, collegiate clothing. Those with more exotic tastes should look into **Zoo** (267), expensive, avant-garde items; or **Street Life** (422), a house line of oversize cotton shirts and smocks, with a lot of items in the rare under-$100 range. **Charivari Workshop** (441 Columbus Avenue, across the street from the American Museum of Natural History) is especially strong in the area of gender-neutral clothing from Japan.

## *Chelsea*

Though it has experienced something of a renaissance lately, Chelsea still does not qualify as a serious hunting ground for the fashion-minded tourist. **Barney's** (Seventh Avenue and 17th Street) remains the only real reason to travel to Chelsea for shopping, and although its six floors of very stylish, very desirable European and American clothing, shoes, and accessories for men and women are intriguing, the consistently high tariffs have left tourists and natives alike stampeding to the elevators and into the street. Still, all the major (and a lot of the minor) labels are represented, and the physical setting is impressive.

After Barney's, you can walk east a few blocks to Fifth Avenue in the teens, an area that is experiencing a bit of a retail revival. Here you will find **Folklorica** (89 Fifth Avenue), with clothing and decorative objects from South America, Africa, and other Third World locales; **Willie Wear** (119), stylish and casual reasonably priced clothing; and the excellent **Royal Silk** (79 Fifth Avenue), three floors of silk blouses, dresses, skirts, shirts, nighties, and so forth, all dramatically underpriced.

## West Village

For almost a hundred years "Greenwich Village" has conjured images of bedraggled painters starving in attics, bearded poets ranting in parks, and bohemian wine parties of astonishing debauch. Those in search of this lost world will reel in horror at the reality of streets full of squeaky clean suburban teenagers and nice respectable couples pushing baby carriages where once the middle classes feared to tread.

Still, it is possible, with a little determination, to uncover a few interesting shops in these confines. **Patricia Field** (10 East 8th Street), despite its unassuming name, has some of the weirdest, most uncompromising getups to be found around town, and **Capezio**'s upper floors (177 MacDougal Street) can still outfit the aspiring ballerina or black-clad modern dancer. **Modern Girls** (169 Thompson Street) has an ever-changing stock of punk-influenced items, many one-of-a-kind (well, it might be difficult to sell more than one of most of these things). At **Untitled** (26 West 8th Street) the items are upper-crust British rock star, and the designs lean heavily to the brocaded waistcoat and the odd, displaced ruffle. Both **Ibiza** (42 University Place) and **Lo: New York** (22 Greenwich Avenue) sell clothing suited for the rich hippie whose taste is rooted in yesteryear—the former specializing in printed rayon 1930s-influenced dresses and long skirts, and the latter featuring a unique line of drippy, drooping flaxen-knitted garments that can be dyed any color desired and would have been the perfect thing to wear to the long-ago wedding of John and Michelle Phillips, had you been invited.

For reasonably priced, stylish, youthful clothes, you should not miss the huge and justly famous **Reminiscence** (74 Fifth Avenue), located at the very northernmost tip of what is considered Greenwich Village, but well worth the walk.

## East Village

The undeniably shabby East Village, with its tottering tenements, luncheon counters, and crackpots of every persuasion, nonetheless pulls like a magnet at the heart of every would-be hipster from Bangkok to Bailey's Beach. The shops, as you would expect, are tiny, eccentric, ever-changing holes-in-the-wall—some cluttered, some streamlined by recent art-school graduates, all selling things either stitched up on the home sewing machine or hammered together in a garret (or perhaps special ordered from the wilds of punkdom in the United Kingdom). At **109 St. Mark's Place** a number of neighborhood designers show their work, ranging from the borderline wearable to the outrageous, such as a fringed Saran Wrap burnoose. **Enz** (5 St. Mark's Place) is home to the heavy-metal aficionado, though it may be possible to turn up something like a fuchsia mohair sweater mixed in with the spikes and chains. **Ponica** (325 East 5th Street), comfortably located next to the local police precinct house, sells transparent, drifting dresses suitable for the Mad Hatter's tea party. Both **Lilla Lova** (117 East 7th Street) and **Shrimpton & Gilligan** (70 East 1st Street) have storefront couture items that someone might actually wear to work—assuming she toils for, say, a struggling theater troupe rather than the president of General Motors.

## SoHo

Once purely a center for painting, sculpture, and performance art (and, for a century before that, a warehouse district with a lingering reputation of 19th-century licentiousness), SoHo in the last few years has come to rival Madison Avenue as a place to view, purchase, and parade around in expensive, interesting clothes. Stores open, close, and replace one another with dizzying rapidity down here, because of the spiraling rents and the shifting buying moods of the crowd.

Visitors to SoHo will probably arrive and proceed on foot, as this is preeminently strolling territory. Most people start at West Broadway, which between Houston and Canal streets is full of fashionable shops selling predictably fashionable, avant-garde items. Neighboring streets (Greene, Wooster, Thompson, etc.) also contain many interesting stores, some of which, due to the cheaper rents obtained by moving off the main drag, feature rather more esoteric merchandise.

On West Broadway proper, shoppers can visit **If** (470) for an outstanding selection of European clothing, with labels running the gamut from Azzadine to Zoran, with Clergerie shoes and Gaultier corsets wedged between. Across the street, **Victoria Falls** (451) presents a collection of the Southern France–influenced white-silk-and-straw-boater variety, while **Nicole Farhid** (435) has clothes for women from the same country of origin who work as executives in the towering glass monsters of Montparnasse. (Suitable clothing for this entrepreneur's secretary, or her lycée-attending daughter, is available at **Agnès B**, off West Broadway at 116 Prince.)

One block west, Thompson Street features a number of smaller shops with growing reputations. **Bomba de Clercq** (98 Thompson Street) may have the best sweaters in the city (Italian, capacious, often cashmere), but the prices will discourage all but the most jaded shopper. **Peter Fox** shoes (105 Thompson Street), with their curved court heels and delicately laced napes, appeal to a faithful coterie, as do the offerings of **FDR Drive** (109 Thompson): its fine gabardine 1930s- and 1940s-influenced separates, and its oversize, unisex printed rayon shirts, are made from authentic vintage fabric. **Betsey Johnson** (130 Thompson) sells weird skintight clothes for shoppers young enough to be amused by such things.

Readers anxious to spend more money should now proceed west to Wooster Street, where **Comme des Garçons** (116) holds forth with its world-renowned collection of Rei Kawakubo–designed Japanese esoterica, including oddly shaped and sized coats, shirts, dresses, and accessories. **Yohji Yamamoto** (103 Grand Street) has similarly priced and draped oddments (though fans of the two will turn purple with rage at the allegation that these two giants are at all comparable). **Tootsie Plohound** (110 Prince, women; 124 Prince, men) sells clunky beribboned clodhoppers, many with the obligatory serrated rubber sole, which lots of people think look great with droopy, flappy Japanese costumes.

Those who wish to lurk near the heart of fashion darkness might like the black belted overcoats with shoulder pads and epaulets that, along with a full line of other seasonless items, are usually available at the huge and loftlike **Parachute** (121 Wooster).

## *Department Stores*

A visitor overwhelmed by the number of small stores in New York, or desiring a crash course in the scope, price ranges, and general diversity of merchandise in Manhattan, should plunge headlong into Manhattan department-store shopping. Those who desire hair-raising excitement can elect to visit **Macy's** at 34th Street and Sixth and Seventh avenues first—purportedly the world's largest department store and containing departments covering all of humankind's basic needs in every price range and to suit every taste. There are floors of inexpensive merchandise, but lots of less democratically priced high-fashion goods as well. At Christmas, gangs of inebriated-acting children roam through the toy floor, crashing into sky-high piles of miniature robots, computer weapons, and leering Donald Ducks.

Those reeling from the mobs at Macy's might seek refuge down the block at **B. Altman** at Fifth Avenue, which, despite a barrage of recent publicity touting its new, up-to-the-minute image, still exudes a dignified dowager atmosphere. Farther up Fifth, **Lord & Taylor** tries valiantly to hang on to its superlative reputation, but the inelegance of the surrounding neighborhood has taken its toll, and the old girl (despite an excellent collection of American country-style clothing) is a shadow of her former self. **Saks Fifth Avenue**, luckier in its location at 50th Street and Fifth Avenue across the street from Rockefeller Center and St. Patrick's Cathedral, offers a predictable cross-section of high-quality merchandise.

**Bloomingdale's** at 59th and Lexington, which started life as an East Side bargain basement, has transformed itself over the past 20 years into the epitome of glamorous, new-wave fashion. The entire fourth floor is given over to individual boutiques, and the big names—Chanel, Ungaro, St. Laurent, plus more obscure avant-gardists like Romeo Gigli and Workers for Freedom—evince a merchandising sensibility not to be trifled with.

A number of the traditional, carriage-trade department stores have updated and upgraded recently as well. **Bergdorf Goodman**, for years a dependable if fading flower on the corner of 57th and Fifth, has recently blossomed with a burst of excellent European and American designer merchandise (Gaultier, Donna Karan) in its newly renovated interior. A new, smaller **Bonwit Teller** at 4 East 57th (the old one was destroyed by Donald Trump several years ago) is trying mightily to compete with interesting merchandise. **Henri Bendel**, 10 West 57th, longtime home of the moneyed anorexic set, still features lots of one-of-a-kind obscure merchandise in its innovative street-of-shops format, but the store has recently been taken over by the comparatively lowbrow Limited corporation, and change hangs ominously in the air.

## Discount Shopping

Visitors who are incorrigible, incurable bargain hunters, or those temporarily overawed by the bold, unblinkingly high price tags that pass for normal in Manhattan, will be happy to know that there is a shadow world of shopping in New York, where bare metal racks and dusty linoleum floors yield delectable merchandise at genuinely encouraging prices.

In these hidden districts of the city, no one ever pays full price for anything. Tentatively acclimate yourself to lower prices by visiting the area of lower Fifth Avenue (between 16th and 23rd streets) for off-price men's wear (**Moe Ginsburg** at 162 is prototypical) or visit West 14th Street for extremely cheap, appealing children's clothes (try Bunnie Baby Wear or Jacks Bargain Store). Thus primed, plunge headlong into the land that time forgot, the bargain center of the universe—the creaking but thriving ancient Lower East Side neighborhood of **Orchard Street**, where the impoverished and the savvy bargain hunter have met for the past 100 years. (The entire district is open every day but Saturday; Sunday is the day for lovers of hyperactive crowds and screeching, henpecked proprietors.) Lots of Orchard Street stores confine themselves to ordinary merchandise, but a few break out with high-class, high-style European designer goods. Investigate **Chez Aby** (77–79 Delancey Street) and **Opium** (104 Orchard Street) for likely French and Italian items, or visit the slightly more prosaic **Breakaway** (125 Orchard Street), where American designers mingle with European closeouts. Extraordinarily chic shoes, all heavily discounted if not absurdly cheap, are carried by the **Lace-Up Shoe Shop** (110 Orchard Street). Shoppers willing to stand in line (sometimes extending outside the door) may reward themselves with a name-brand off-price handbag from the famous **Fine & Klein** (119 Orchard Street).

Of course, there are those who blanch at the highly charged atmosphere of the Lower East Side. These visitors might prefer several of the other discounters scattered throughout Manhattan. Young women, or those who have preserved the physiques of their younger selves, might like the offerings at **Strawberry** (all over town) or **Joyce Leslie** (20 University Place and numerous other locations), both of which specialize in very inexpensive, up-to-the-minute imitations of designer merchandise. The more bohemian reader will prefer **Unique Clothing Warehouse** (718 and 726 Broadway, between Washington and Waverly places) or **Canal Jean Co.** (504 Broadway between Spring and Broome streets), two cavernous holes in the wall near New York University with immense collections of hip, cheap things. (Young gentlemen of the painter-writer-filmmaker persuasion can purchase suitable outfits at these places as well.)

Fashion connoisseurs with more taste than money might wish to investigate two shops lurking in the very heart of the fancy Madison Avenue shopping district: **Damages** (768 Madison at 66th Street) and **22 Steps** (746). The former specializes in off-price Italian fashions, with a strong selection of silk afternoon dresses and blouses. The latter features discounted items from illustrious designers (with label intact), including the likes of Yves St. Laurent, Sonia Rykiel, and Comme des Garçons. (Neither of these shops is breathtakingly cheap, but they do feature impressive merchandise.)

Shoppers who wish to experience a genuine Third-World bazaar atmosphere while remaining on the isle of Manhattan should head for one of the **Conway** stores (225 West 34th Street and other locations), where overstuffed hausfraus and irascible teenagers compete for groaning racks of ridiculously inexpensive merchandise. The offerings spill right out of the giant plate-glass, garage-type doors, covering adjacent sidewalks, and encroaching on neighboring storefronts. The resultant bulging pink paper shopping bags can be seen draped over the arms of bus and subway riders all over town.

## Accessories

If, as has been alleged, God is in the details, then surely your outfit, whether at home or abroad, would benefit from a few distinguished accessories. These popular items (scarves, hats, gloves, handbags, etc.) have an additional benefit as souvenirs, since any size will fit the recipient; they are available over the complete spectrum of prices, and, most important, they are usually small and travel well.

Due to their currency as both business and fashion, *handbags and briefcases* of surprising beauty and interest are available all over town. If utility is paramount: **Coach** (710 Madison Avenue at 63rd Street) has American softly tailored leather products, or visit **Lederer** (613 Madison) for classic French styles. At the old-line **Crouch & Fitzgerald** (400 Madison), traditional styles crowd the first floor, while upstairs the complete line of Louis Vuitton items waits in chains. (Crouch was the first place in town to carry L. V., years before it assumed its current popularity.)

Higher priced fashionable bags are available from **Bottega Veneta** (635 Madison between 59th and 60th); this place also carries especially impressive small leather goods (wallets, card cases, etc.), but beware of scorching prices. More youthful designs are sold by the famous French house **La Bagagerie** (727 Madison at 64th Street), and the even more ambitiously stylish should seek out the Italian **Furla** (705 Madison). Among an impressive array of items made up from quilted printed Provençal fabrics, **Pierre Deux** (870 Madison at 71st Street) offers commodious duffle bags, suitable for weekends in Westhampton. And for those willing to cash in their airline tickets and stow away for the trip home, **La Jeunesse** (989 Lexington between 71st and 72nd streets) sells incomparable evening reticules, composed of antique frames (some inset with semiprecious stones) with new leather purses added.

*Shoes.* It sometimes seems that even if each resident owned a thousand pairs, they would not be able to support the number of shoe stores flourishing in Manhattan. Although quite a few booteries are scattered elsewhere throughout this guide, the true shoe enthusiast should not fail to visit West 34th Street between Fifth and Sixth avenues and West 8th Street between the same avenues. Both thoroughfares are crowded with shoe shops, and while styles there are always up-to-date, corresponding price tags are unassuming.

*Lingerie.* Visitors who possess a sentimental longing for underthings of the past will enjoy the neo-Victorian, neo-hippie look of lingerie at **Michelle Nicole Wesley** (126 Prince Street in SoHo). Plenty of pristine white cotton, tiny satin bows, and seed pearls are in evidence, and there is usually a corner piled high with crushed velvet items as well. Those who crave handmade pure silk camisoles and drawers will like **Montenapoleone** (789 Madison between 66th and 67th streets), popular with daughters of deposed dictators, or **La Lingerie** (792 Madison), beloved by movie stars and/or wives of movie moguls. Those lacking sufficient funds should visit **Victoria's Secret** (34 East 57th), where items in satin and faux silk materials are glamorously cut and reasonably priced. Over at **R. Jabbour & Sons** (51 East 58th), a lonely holdout of a near-vanished way of life, nightgowns brandishing the sleeper's monogram can still be ordered.

*Scarves.* For that prototypical souvenir, the silk scarf, many travellers visit **Hermès** (11 East 57th) or **Gucci** (683 Fifth Avenue), where the haute bourgeois merchandise is always dependable. The slightly more original shopper might prefer to travel down to the Orchard Street area, where **Bernard Krieger & Son** (316 Grand Street) has been offering cotton and linen men's and women's handkerchiefs by the dozens (that's the only way they're sold) at ridiculously low prices since 1936. In the East Village, a few surviving nativist shops still sell brightly colored floral printed Ukrainian wool challis peasant scarves out of piles of cardboard boxes stacked up on ancient, creaking showcases.

*Hats.* Though only a decade ago it seemed as if the custom millinery business in New York was all but dead and buried, the corpse has in fact been resuscitated over the past few years, and a couple of establishments can actually be described as thriving. **Victoria Dinardo** (68 Thompson Street in SoHo) has a number of appealing designs—ranging from the winsome to the downright strange—and will listen to and attempt to incorporate your suggestions into her work. **Suzanne Daché** (156 East 64th)—keeping the famous Daché hat name alive—offers plenty of personalized, old-fashioned service at her spacious uptown salon.

*Cosmetics.* **Boyd Chemists** (655 Madison Avenue between 60th and 61st streets), despite its elegant location, is anything but subdued—the wildly enthusiastic, overly made-up sales staff will push products on you no matter how reluctant you are to buy. The selection is very impressive (it includes hard-to-find foreign brands), and there is a spectacular array of hair accessories, leaning heavily toward the fake tortoise and rhinestone variety, and hailing mainly from France. For still more hair accoutrements, investigate **Halina's** (160 West 55th), an obscure hairdressing shop that sells vintage (and vintage-looking) tortoise barrettes, clips, and hard-to-locate dramatic Spanish-style combs.

Downtown at **Kiehl's** (109 Third Avenue between 13th and 14th streets), considerations of health outweigh those of glamor. The store sells a house brand of potions and ointments, and many New Yorkers swear by their efficacy. **Caswell-Massey** (Lexington at 48th), the oldest pharmacy in the city, also has a private label and the accompanying claque of enthusiastic fans.

To renovate your complexion with a complete and rigorous workout, call for an appointment at **Georgette Klinger** (501 Madison Avenue between 52nd and 53rd streets) or **Janet Sartin** (480 Park Avenue between 58th and 59th streets); either of these ladies will slather, slap, and massage your face in accordance with her particular expensive regimen.

*Furs.* The fur coat, once strictly the province of the moneyed classes and once emblematic of female sophistication and implied indolence, is no longer synonymous with the life of leisure. It has been embraced by the working woman, the gentleman stroller, and even the (fur) swaddled babe in arms. Reasonably priced middlebrow coats are available all over town, but the stoical of heart are urged to take on the area of Seventh Avenue in the high 20s, where office buildings bursting with innumerable showrooms and workshops sell coats in various price ranges, depending on the skins in question and the complexity of design. The fur district has an aura of a wholesale-only operation, but many (most) of the businesses are more than happy to entertain the retail customer. **Steven Corn Furs** (14 West 28th Street, ground floor) is huge and bustling and will keep the undecided customer occupied for hours; at **Harry Kirshner** (307 Seventh Avenue between 27th and 28th streets, fourth floor), a typical factory/salesroom operation, the service is unusually cordial and solicitous.

Uptown, **Jindo Furs** (41 West 57th) sells a wide range (from under $1,000) of fur jackets and coats; some of the less expensive models are conspicuously stylish. To examine the dramatic, ground-breaking designs that have left fur fanatics breathless over the past several years, don't hesitate to visit the Fendi coats at **Henri Bendel**, even when potential purchase (never under $10,000) remains remote.

## *Jewelry*

Many of the old-line jewelry houses may claim at least partial responsibility for lending the words "Fifth Avenue" their international connotation of wealth and glamor. **Cartier**, snug in its landmark building at the corner of 52nd Street, remains hushed and intimidating to all but the most brazen and well-heeled shopper. **Tiffany's**, by contrast, exudes a bustling, almost egalitarian air. (Take the elevator to two for less expensive silver items, still packaged in the famous Tiffany blue box and brought to you from the stockroom by an antiquated system of dumbwaiters and pneumatic tubes.) Upper Fifth also features branches of **Fred Joaillier** (703), very fine fashionable French jewelry, and **H. Stern** (645, across the street from St. Patrick's), Brazilian and a specialist in the innovative use of colored gemstones. The venerable **Harry Winston** (to whom Ms. Monroe alludes when she explains why diamonds are a girl's best friend) occupies a site at 718 Fifth.

Intersecting Fifth Avenue at 47th Street is the **Diamond District**—one solid block (to Sixth Avenue) of stores, booths, workshops, and showrooms dedicated to the design, renovation, repair, but mostly the sale of diamond, colored gemstone, and gold jewelry. Though it looks and behaves like a wholesale area, most of 47th Street talks retail enthusiastically. Bring cash and prepare to bargain. (A similar, but smaller, less boisterous wholesale-retail jewelry district exists downtown in the area of Canal Street and the Bowery; proximity to Chinatown accounts for its interesting supply of high-karat red-gold charms and chains.)

Shoppers attracted to Fifth Avenue gems but lacking corresponding funds should consider visiting **Kenneth Jay Lane** (725 in Trump Tower), who made his reputation with beautifully executed copies of high-priced pieces. Those who leave the real thing in the vault, or wish to appear as though they do, should stop at **Jolie Gabor** (699 Madison Avenue), where individual pieces can be copied or "fabulous fakes" bought off the shelf. Much less expensive is **S. Gould** (20 East 58th Street), whose imitation baubles would be perfectly illuminated by the dim light of dusk on board an ocean-liner deck.

If it's pearls you're after, there is **Mikimoto**, the veritable inventor of the cultured variety, at 608 Fifth Avenue between 48th and 49th streets. **Buccellati** (725 Fifth Avenue in Trump Tower) will seat you on a comfortable chair and spread before you individual specimens of heartbreaking luster and intensity, to be strung at your behest. Stagger out of Buccellati to the nearest magazine stand, from whose wooden frames many news dealers are selling one-dollar strands of ersatz pearls—just to make sure these things truly become you.

For a *wristwatch,* veer nominally off Fifth Avenue to **Tourneau Corner** (500 Madison Avenue at 52nd Street) for a staggering collection of watches, ranging from reasonably expensive to rarefied Rolex. An entirely different world of watches—namely, the oversize, comical, bubble-headed variety—is accessible to those willing to travel downtown to 8th Street, where **Savage** (59 West 8th) sells a likely selection.

Visitors interested in jewelry that no one back home has ever seen might wish to visit **Detail** (345 West Broadway) in SoHo for items like shellacked fried egg gyroscope earrings. At **Charles' Place** (234 Mulberry Street) rhinestone-bedecked animal earrings (the gamboling pigs are nice) can be custom tailored to your specifications or bought ready-made. Gentlemen who are looking for shops that will sell them a single earring will want to know that the stretch of 8th Street between Fifth and Sixth avenues, as well as eastern Greenwich Avenue, should prove particularly fruitful. **Einstein's** (96 East 7th Street in the East Village) can provide perverse, almost threatening pieces of jewelry to those in search of same.

People who want something unusual but still have to work for a living will find amusing but wearable examples at **Zoe Coste** (30 West 57th Street) and **Ylang Ylang** (4 West 57th). Modernists who don't mind spending a bit may prefer **Artwear** (456 West Broadway). Unusual metals like titanium are experimented with here; the results often decorate the mannequins at prestigious fashion shows. If your financial sky has no limit, there are interesting one-of-a-kind items for sale at the **Neil Isman Gallery** (1100 Madison Avenue near 83rd Street), where important new jewelry artists are represented.

Lastly, shoppers in search of something completely different (as well as those who find themselves temporarily in queer street) might benefit from a visit to **Gem Pawnbrokers** (608 Eighth Avenue), a classic place (three balls outside, glass window) with a surprisingly comprehensive display of "out of pawn" offerings.

### *Vintage Clothing*
The popularity of vintage clothing, which began its worldwide ascendance in the 1960s, has hung on with surprising tenacity in New York City. Many of the locals pride themselves on dressing funny and find that their innate taste and "ideas" about clothing, usually crippled by their lack of funds, can find full expression at the secondhand store.

There are fine antique clothes (1920s through 1940s, excellent condition and presentation) at **Panache** (525 Hudson Street between 10th and Charles streets), **Gwenda G.** (1364 Lexington Avenue at 90th Street), **O'Mistress Mine** (143 Seventh Avenue South), and the vintage racks at the always appealing **Reminiscence** (74 Fifth Avenue at 13th Street). **Harriet Love** (412 West Broadway between Prince and Spring), the grandmother of antique clothing stores in New York, now stocks a variety of new clothing along with the special old pieces (beaded jackets, cashmere sweaters, rayon dresses) for which she is so justly famous. At **Jana Starr/Jean Hoffman Antiques** (236 East 80th) there is a preponderance of Victorian white-work, and hard-to-find accompanying accessories like boudoir caps and early satin dancing shoes. (These ladies outfit a lot of weddings, graduations, and christenings, and thus provide a high level of service—with prices to match.) Madame Liza of **Liza's Place** (132 Thompson Street in SoHo), boasts that her shop sells authentic Chanels and Schiaparellis, and even when these are not in evidence you will find unparalleled beaded flapper dresses among her permanent collection.

Shoppers seeking to spend vastly less money will be happier visiting **Andy's Chee-Pees** (14 St. Mark's Place) or **Cheap Jacks** (841 Broadway betwen 13th and 14th Streets), two stores with lower priced rough-and-tumble merchandise, where condition is often dubious but you are sometimes able to uncover a diamond in the rough. At **Alice Underground** (481 Broadway downtown and 380 Columbus Avenue on the Upper West Side) the surroundings are more presentable and price tags are still extremely reasonable. The East Village contains a number of inexpensive possibilities, among them **Debris** (321 East 10th Street), the long-lived **Love Saves The Day** (119 Second Avenue at 7th Street), and the densely packed, filthy, and infamous **Bogie's** (201 East 10th Street).

### *Men's Clothing*

The main line of gentlemen's clothiers is in the area of Madison Avenue in the lower 40s. Here are **Brooks Brothers** (346 Madison Avenue at 44th Street), justly famous, predictably conservative, surprisingly affordable; **Paul Stuart** (Madison at 45th Street), more ambitious merchandise; and **F. R. Tripler** (336 Madison at 46th) for old-fashioned items including the hard-to-find gentleman's Edwardian nightshirt. If you are looking for the loud, off-center style peculiar to the American country-club denizen, investigate **Chipp** (342 Madison), club ties depicting 90-plus breeds of dogs; and **J. Press** (16 East 44th Street), indescribable madras-plaid patchwork baggy trousers. Farther uptown, at **Sulka** (430 Park Avenue at 55th Street), the extremely refined goods are strictly for the silk-undies set. Cashmere robes here are $700 plus, but an ascot might prove affordable—and makes a lovely souvenir.

The newly opened **Louis, Boston** (Lexington at 57th)

brings with it a well-established Boston reputation for exquisitely tailored overcoats and dress suits. **Burberry's Ltd.** (9 East 57th Street) has the plaid-lined raincoats synonymous with its name. The gentleman traveller should be aware that **Bergdorf Goodman** contains boutiques bearing two interesting old names, Hackett and Charvet, from Britain and France respectively.

For an amusing new shirt to wear home visit the English outpost of **Paul Smith** (108 Fifth Avenue) for oversize shirts with unusual details, or the **Custom Shirt Shop** (618 Fifth Avenue, between 49th and 50th streets, and other locations), which makes chemises to order, as the name would indicate. Profligate guys who must be the cynosure of all eyes can fulfill that intention with a new outfit from the wildly admired Italian, **Giorgio Armani** (815 Madison Avenue between 68th and 69th streets).

An entirely different sort of man, who looks as if he rolled out of a haystack dressed in the same black sweat shirt and jeans you've seen him in for 20 years, may also be a secret shopper—albeit of a radically different persuasion. His requisite leather jacket can be purchased at the **N.Y. Leather Co.** (33 Christopher Street in the West Village), and accompanying baggy, shapeless trousers are available from **Aca-Joe** (313 Columbus Avenue and other locations). On the rare occasion (his wedding day?) that this guy dresses up, he might consent to wear a neo-1940s outfit (pleated pants, gabardine shirt) from an excellent in-house collection at **FDR Drive Men** (80 Thompson Street at Spring Street in SoHo). **Trash and Vaudeville** (4 St. Mark's Place), which he will surely saunter past on his nocturnal treks to the East Village, will happily accoutre the aspiring rock star. If he suddenly wins the local lottery or has a successful day at the races, the visitor might enjoy a shopping trip to the elegant, austere **Comme des Garçons** (116 Wooster Street), **Yohji Yamamoto** (103 Grand Street), or **Matsuda** (465 Park Avenue), all of which feature expensive, extreme, avant-garde designs from Japan.

Finally, the man whose sartorial style was fixed for all time during his freshman year at the University of Wisconsin circa 1968 (or the University of London, or Sydney, or the Sorbonne) will find everything he requires down among the canteens, gas masks, and goggles at the **Army & Navy Stores** (221 East 59th Street and other branches) or at **Weiss and Mahoney** (142 Fifth Avenue at 19th Street).

## Children's Fashions

The fairly recent but undeniably virulent national obsession with childbirth, babies, and their attendant requirements has spawned a serious increase in the number of stores serving small persons in Manhattan. Wee shops with teensy, adorable names are springing up all over, and autos with Baby on Board signs trudge from the East River to the Hudson and back in search of the perfect snowsuit and the most elegant bunny pajamas.

If you are travelling with a child or know one at home you'd like to buy something for, you will soon find that the New York kiddie market divides itself into two distinct branches: one approximating the taste of the (pre–Fergie and Di) British royal family—a lot of tartan plaid, velvet collars, and patent-leather Mary Janes—and its polar opposite, a sort of 1960s redux, with the prevailing themes being tie-dyed or painted tee-shirts and bib overalls.

Those shopping for the former style should visit **Liberty of London** (229 East 60th Street), where printed smocked dresses with round collars and sashes are available for fruity little girls. **Cerutti** (807 Madison Avenue between 67th and 68th streets) has French and Italian items as well as things from England, and will suitably accoutre the luckless little pretender to one or another royal throne. The unpronounceable **Swantje-Elke** (1031 Lexington at 74th Street) sells similar items, albeit slightly less conventional and conservative. **Puss N Boots** (357 Bleecker in the West Village) will supply the necessary footwear (and remember: Tiny shoes are the perfect gift item for the person who can't walk yet). Readers who resent spending a week's wages on an outfit consisting of a quarter-yard of fabric should stop down at **Klein's of Monticello** (105 Orchard Street), where heavily discounted high-toned European children's clothes have been available for years.

Converts to the Woodstock school of children's fashion will find diminutive hipster clothing at **Space Kiddets** (46 East 21st Street). **Dinosaur Hill** (302 East 9th Street) is a preeminent tee-shirt source, and **Peanut Butter & Jane** (617 Hudson Street between 12th and Jane streets) will outfit a child appropriately for West Village life. Miniature Bianca Jaggers, who wear baby Maud Frizons and seek outfits to match, may like the selection at **Bebe Thompson** (98 Thompson Street in SoHo).

Parents who are suffering pangs of premature separation anxiety will be heartened to learn that there is a store in New York—**Danielle Like Mother Like Daughter**, 169 Sullivan Street in the Village—where anything mommy has sissy can have too, and vice versa.

Finally, if the child in question lacks only a set of horns and a tail to make his true character known, if this small person is driving you to the hotel balcony where you sip what you claim is your last gasp of Champagne and make threatening promises to the pedestrians below, attempt to mollify your tormentor (at least temporarily) with the gift of a kiddie Ninja suit, available from **Bok Lei Tat Trading Co.** (213 Canal Street).

# PHOTOGRAPHY AND FILMMAKING

### By Stephen R. Ettlinger

*Stephen R. Ettlinger is a free-lance picture editor and photography consultant in New York City, and is also an independent book producer. He was formerly associate picture editor at* GEO *magazine, and is currently an editor of* Photo Opportunity. *His most recent book project is* Vietnam: The Land We Never Knew, Recent Images by Geoffrey Clifford.

Visual artists of all stripes from all over the world make pilgrimages to New York City to do business, and thousands work, study, and live here. The main draw to the city for professional photographers is the concentration of major advertising agencies, magazines, and publishing companies. An editorial photographer from out of town may spend a week here, making appointments to see as many as six editors in a day at such publications as *Time, Life, Newsweek, Vogue, GQ, Connoisseur,* and the like. He or she may stop in to see any of the major photo agencies, all of which also have their headquarters here: Magnum, Gamma-Liaison, Contact, Woodfin Camp, Wheeler Pictures, Comstock, Image Bank, Freelance Photographers Guild, Photo Researchers, Associated Press, Bettmann Archives, and so on. The attendant organizations and associations are also here. There is no reason why a professional or even a devoted follower of photography could not stop in at any of these places to at the very least absorb some of the atmosphere.

There is not one main street or neighborhood for filmmakers, though groups of them are found in SoHo, TriBeCa, and the East Village, and a concentration of services is found near the television studios in the West 40s and 50s. However, photographers have definitely developed something akin to their own neighborhood, called the **Photo District**, anchored by the venerable Flatiron Building at Fifth Avenue and 23rd Street. Among the city's first skyscrapers, it was the location of a 1905 movie featuring the wind blowing women's skirts up in a revealing way. This windy locale gave birth to the phrase "23 skiddoo." Warren Beatty found it a perfect 1902 setting for Diane Keaton's New York City arrival in the film *Reds*. Although there are no official borders, the consensus is that the Photo District extends from 23rd Street to 14th Street, and from Park Avenue South to Sixth Avenue.

The area has been home to advertising and fashion photographers for years because of its commercial loft buildings and low rents. Recently, following the usual pattern of gentrification, rents and purchase prices have skyrocketed, forcing new photographers to look elsewhere for living or studio space, while professional-oriented stores and labs, on the other hand, have moved into the area. In fact, the equipment-rental business is growing rapidly in the area, which is good news for a visiting photographer: Everything from the studio to the camera can be rented. Some of the upward pressure on rents has been generated by the arrival of several of the major advertising agencies, who have taken over large loft buildings in the district after total renovations.

Photographers themselves are not as much in evidence in the streets of the Photo District as are the businesses that serve them. Beyond the obvious labs (the more established ones occupy entire buildings and have reception areas buzzing with messengers, assistants, and students—all displaying the latest in street fashion) are more traditional businesses that have adapted to serve their photographic neighbors—antiques stores have signs in the windows proclaiming that their goods are available as rental props, and a plethora of gourmet stores cater photo shoots.

For some reason there are not any famous, traditional

photographers' hangouts in the area, though if anything came close it would be the **Old Town Bar** at 45 East 18th Street, a resolutely dark, dingy, and inexpensive place that has vociferously resisted any attempts at gentrification. The owner has gone so far as to post signs in his dirty window that say his place is not for sale to any well-dressed developers (earlier signs used to say, "Don't stare at the artists," etc.). It is one of the few spots that regular photographers and assistants can afford. Nearby there are some elegant restaurants that cater to visiting art directors or celebrated photographers, but this clientele is apparently quite fickle, as the hot spots rise up in glory and go out of business in a flash with astounding regularity. Only one place has tried a definite photo orientation complete with ongoing displays of photography: **Portfolio Restaurant and Gallery**, 4 West 19th Street. The real action in the district is in the labs and photo stores concentrated around West 19th and 20th streets.

It is fitting that New York City would have a major museum devoted solely to photography: the **International Center of Photography** (ICP), 1130 Fifth Avenue at 94th Street, and a Midtown branch at 1133 Sixth Avenue at 43rd Street. Between the two locations ICP hosts about 20 major shows each year, accompanied by crowded and jolly opening celebrations (be sure to ask when the next one is). Photographers tend to work alone, and the editors and agents seem to have been colleagues since whenever they started in the business, so the openings smack of reunions. ICP offers a full program of courses, workshops, and lectures, all of which are open to the passing traveller.

Two other major museums, the **Museum of Modern Art** and the **Metropolitan Museum of Art**, have excellent photo exhibitions. MoMA's permanent collection is one of the most important things for any photographer to see, and the bookstore's selection supplements the experience.

In order to find out what's happening here, photographers can turn to a local monthly of some renown, *Photo District News*. (Filmmakers rely on the national paper *Variety*.) *PDN* is distributed free at various labs and photo stores, or may be had at the publication's offices, 49 East 21st Street. The classified ads would be of help to anyone planning a prolonged stay and in need of free-lance assistant work or a studio to rent.

# Films and Filmmaking

Film buffs need not look far in New York to find satisfaction: There are dozens of theaters and spaces showing absolutely every kind of film made, from the most experimental avant-garde to the most cherished classics. Listings are easily found in daily and weekly magazines such as *The New York Times,* the *Village Voice* (new issues on Wednesday), *New York* magazine, and *The New Yorker.* The Sunday *New York Times,* which is available around 11:00 P.M. Saturday evening, always has thorough reviews and news of festivals.

One of the best places to see the widest range of classics, including a good number of silent films, is at the **Museum of Modern Art**, which has a regular program (Tel: 212-708-9490 for the daily features). Through MoMA's Film Study Center, the complete archive and film library is open to qualified students and scholars who write in advance for an appointment in a private screening room.

The New York Public Library shows and circulates films, mostly from the comprehensive **Donnell Library branch** Media Center, across from MoMA (at 20 West 53rd). The Donnell Library is one of the more relaxed and yet complete branches in the city, excellent for someone in need of a convenient Midtown office for a few hours. The **Performing Arts Library at Lincoln Center** (111 Amsterdam Avenue) does not circulate films but has an amazing collection of world cinema books, clippings, periodicals, memorabilia of all kinds, posters, and a reference service at the Billy Rose Theater Collection that is open to all but is a particular boon to film scholars. They even have a catalog of film memorabilia from which you can call up items.

Each September and October there are two film festivals of note: the **New York Film Festival**, with the subgroupings of the New Directors series, and the **Independent Feature Project Market**, which also includes workshops and is oriented toward low-budget films, including documentaries. Well-known pros often participate in workshops at New York Women in Film (Tel: 212-512-8022). The New York University filmmaking, video, and broadcasting studies department at the School of Continuing Education, 721 Broadway, Tel: (212) 998-7140, offers weekend workshops as well.

While most people link Hollywood with the origins of

filmmaking, it all started over here. In fact, New York claims as many movie landmarks as Los Angeles. This is in part because Thomas A. Edison invented the whole idea in nearby West Orange, New Jersey; his laboratory and home is now a national park most definitely worth a pilgrimage (Tel: 201-736-5050). The first westerns were shot in New Jersey. These days movie and television productions bring New York almost $3 billion yearly in gross revenue, and a major studio, the Kaufman/Astoria Studios, has just reopened in Queens. Its clients past and present range from D. W. Griffith to Woody Allen. The city even has a one-stop department devoted to assisting filmmakers with permits and resources. The Mayor's Office of Film, Theatre and Broadcasting at 254 West 54th Street issues permits overnight and arranges for the police film unit to coordinate traffic and control bystanders during chase or fire scenes. They keep lists on hand of guides to services, cooperative hotels, and items like a penthouse apartment overlooking rooftops that give a 1930s feeling, or the one place in Manhattan where you can walk directly into a river (under the George Washington Bridge).

Filmdom has its own brand-new museum in New York City: the **Museum of the Moving Image**, located within the studio complex at 35th Avenue and 36th Street in the Astoria section of Queens, near the 59th Street Bridge. Unique in this country, it is a wonderful blend of education and entertainment and contains a small theater, a large screening room, and special and permanent exhibits on both the art and the business of movie and TV-show making. (See the Queens Neighborhood section for directions.)

## BOOKSTORES
**The Drama Bookshop**, 723 Seventh Avenue; the **Gotham Book Mart**, 41 West 47th Street; and the **Theatre Arts Bookshop**, 405 West 42nd Street, all go beyond film into theatrical work. **Applause Cinema Books**, 100 West 67th Street (near Lincoln Center and ABC Studios), is an excellent place to find elusive screenplays. Mainline art bookstores such as **Rizzoli** (main store at 31 West 57th Street) are good, too, but the best is probably the **New York University Bookstore**, 18 Washington Place, which supports all the courses in film theory and the like at their famous film school.

**A Photographers Place**, in SoHo at 133 Mercer Street, not only has a huge selection encompassing damaged bargains and old classics, but also has a regular mail-order catalog. Some antique paraphernalia is displayed, along with occasional shows. They will also search out a rare title for you on request. The **ICP** bookstore at 94th Street and Fifth Avenue has one of the most complete selections of contemporary work as well as related texts and technical books. Their Midtown store, at 1133 Sixth Avenue at 43rd Street, is more limited. Both feature photographer appearances from time to time, although at any time uptown you may find the photographer of the very book you are perusing looking over your shoulder—a good place to keep your criticisms to yourself.

Both the Met and MoMA have photo books for sale, but MoMA's selection is broader. Surprise bargains as well as regular discounts are found at both **Barnes & Noble** bookstores across the avenue from each other at Fifth Avenue at 18th Street, as well as at the nearby venerable secondhand store, **Strand** (828 Broadway at 12th Street). A newer store, **Untitled II**, across from New York University at 680 Broadway, has a growing reputation among serious photo-book collectors.

## PHOTOGRAPHY AND FILM SHOPPING

While there are no guides to New York City for photography buffs, there is something that is sort of a major photographers' Rollodex in book form, listing every conceivable potential supplier of goods or services to photographers: the *Professional Photo Source*. Available at a number of photography industry vendors in the Photo District for $12.95, it is also available by phone or mail order from 568 Broadway, New York, NY 10012; Tel: (212) 219-0993. There are 350 headings ranging from acrylic ice to walkie-talkies, including dealers specializing in various categories of cameras, such as "collectible" or "panoramic." The ads in *Photo District News* are also a decent guide (their articles are useful as well).

A concentration of large department-store-type camera stores developed in the early postwar period around Macy's, and some are still there. However, bargains take considerable digging to find, and little advice is given. The better stores, concentrated in the Photo District, include the ultimate bargain places as well as those that may not offer the best prices but make up for that considerably with personal advice, equipment loans, and excellent service. In those you will be rubbing shoulders with a genuinely professional crowd. A good number of places are open seven days a week (some close on Saturday but open on Sunday), and weeknights until quite late, some until midnight. Most advertise in *PDN* or are listed in *Professional Photo Source*. They attract an international clientele.

For the quintessential New York purchasing experience, two places stand out. **Gould Trading**, 41 Union Square West, Room 225, is found at the end of a long, dark corridor in a very dingy building. If they don't have what you want, with a little cajoling they'll find it for you through their network of dealer friends, especially used Nikon equipment. They'll also pay cash for your own equipment. Bargaining is a way of life here. Gould also makes excellent, inexpensive 35-mm duplicate slides and sells film in bulk at a terrific discount. Similar in atmosphere is **Adorama**, 42 West 18th Street, with old gadgets piled side by side with the latest Zeiss attachments. At both places it helps to have a good idea of what you want before entering, as neither has a display area for wandering. It is more like a bar where you belly up and order. Talking comes later.

The **Lens & Repro Equipment Corporation**, 33 West 17th, is noted for its large selection of used and new large-format cameras, including a Japanese brand made of ebony, and its own brand. Amazingly, they have a selection of the rare handmade Deardorfs. **Ken Hansen Photographic**, 920 Broadway at 21st Street, is more or less the Leica king, though he has a full range of other equipment and a huge lighting equipment display. But Hansen prides himself more on the personal service angle of the business, actually publishing the names of his salesmen in his ads, and having many telephone lines so clients can make appointments if they so desire.

Hasselblad maniacs will find therapy at **Gil Ghitelman Cameras**, 166 Fifth Avenue, especially if they are looking for trades. **Olden Camera**, 1265 Broadway between 31st and 32nd, is favored by students, which keeps the place lively in a pleasant way, and Olden carries a wide range of lines, including used equipment.

Every photographer has his favorite laboratory, but for quick service of all kinds the larger labs do an excellent job. **K & L** (222 East 44th Street), **Ken Leiberman** (13 West 36th), and **Duggal Color Projects** (9 West 20th Street) will do virtually anything you can think of, any way you want it. Duggal actually has an entire building and is something like the hub of the Photo District. Duggal is owned by a legendary Indian who has helped many of his countrymen immigrate, and they have in turn left to start their own smaller custom labs: Baboo, L & I, and Tony (acronym for "To New York," the only English this man knew when he came here). They are all very aggressive marketers, operating 24 hours a day, and anxious to please. K & L is in a building that houses services for the video and film industries as well.

## *Rentals*

**Photographics Unlimited**, at 17 West 17th Street, rents not only equipment but darkrooms as well, both color and black-and-white, and has something of a Woodstock-era feel to it.

Professionals in the Photo District tend to rent equipment at **Ken Hansen** (920 Broadway at 21st Street; especially good for lighting), **Lens & Repro** (33 West 17th), **Photo Marketplace** (11 West 20th), **Foto-Care** (170 Fifth Avenue), and **Profoto** (128 West 31st Street), which is actually a branch of a Hamburg store.

Probably the most amusing place to visit is **The Set Shop**, at 3 West 20th Street. Set Shop has one of the biggest and most cluttered bulletin boards, a direct line on the doings of the district, but, more importantly, has a superb display of foam-rubber rocks, plastic ice cubes, and rubber fish that fill out its line of props. They have a complete catalog, too, which includes backgrounds, building supplies, studio equipment, and all kinds of gadgets undoubtedly useful in all the visual or theatrical arts. **The Camera Mart, Inc.**, at 456 West 55th, rents any movie- or TV-related items you may need, whether for the usual use or as a prop.

## *Repairs*

For years, the pros have all gone to **Professional Camera Repair Service** at 37 West 47th Street.

## SHOPPING FOR PHOTOGRAPHY IN GALLERIES

New York City supports a wonderful range of galleries that show photography on a more or less regular basis, and you can easily buy pictures from day one of the medium to the absolute cutting edge. Many of the leading painting galleries show the latest "in" photographers, generally one with connections in the fashion or advertising world, and these would be featured in the standard gallery listings (see Art section). (Galleries are usually open Monday to Saturday from 10:00 or 11:00 A.M. to 5:00 or 6:00 P.M.)

Collectors who are interested in experimental work of both early and contemporary 20th-century photographers from both sides of the Atlantic and Latin America should visit **Lieberman & Saul**, at 155 Spring Street at West Broadway. A small space, they are credited among dealers as having some of the most exciting work in the city, though not in a style that attracts mainstream media attention. For example, a recent show featured portraits of Jean Cocteau.

Mid-century American work in the tradition of the Farm Security Administration and the Esso Collection is found across the street at **Photofind**, 138 Spring Street. Their emphasis is on reportage—modern for them means Robert Frank.

No doubt the gallery the farthest off the beaten track belongs to dealer Alan Klotz, who holds a very personal European-style salon in his Upper West Side apartment. His **Photocollect Gallery**, at 740 West End Avenue between 96th and 97th streets, features vintage 19th- and early 20th-century quality work, ranging from $200 to $20,000 in price. Although he maintains regular gallery hours, a phone call is recommended in case he has just dashed off to make a new acquisition; Tel: (212) 222-7381. A close second to Photocollect in terms of being small and personal is **The Union Square Gallery**, 32 Union Square East, which is photographer Todd Weinstein's studio. On Fridays and Saturdays he packs all his gear into his darkroom, hangs some terrific work, and sets up a table with wine and cheese in the hallway. His neighbors are his biggest fans.

The more expensive work of living and dead greats, such as Irving Penn and Brassaï, can usually be found in the main art gallery area at the **Marlborough Gallery**, 40 West 57th Street. Current stars are often exhibited at the **Pace/MacGill Gallery**, 11 East 57th Street, as are well-known painter-photographers.

The **Witkin Gallery**, at 415 West Broadway, is probably the most prominent of the commercial galleries featuring work by the best contemporary photographers, and it also sells a good selection of photo books. Openings are well attended by noted critics, writers, and, of course, photographers. **Ledel** and **Marcuse Pfeifer** are two other galleries showing consistently good work.

Probably the most exciting place to buy photography is at one of the auction houses. Four major houses organize among themselves to present a series of auctions for one week in late October or early November, and again in early May. The Friday and Sunday editions of *The New York Times* are the best places to see what is being offered. The venerable houses of **Christie's** (502 Park Avenue at 59th Street; Tel: 212-546-1000) and **Sotheby's** (1334 York Avenue on the East Side at 72nd Street; Tel: 212-606-7000) usually have the largest number of items, but often **Phillips** and **Swann Galleries** have excellent items for sale. Sales at these places are usually confined to three-hour sessions, and their expensive catalogs are very well produced. There is much greeting and cooing among the small group of dealers who find themselves moving from one seasonal event to another.

# CLASSICAL MUSIC

## *By Matthew Gurewitsch*

*Matthew Gurewitsch is a senior editor at* Connoisseur *magazine, specializing in the performing arts. He has written about music and dance for* Opus, The New York Times, Vogue, Opera News, The Wall Street Journal, *and other publications.*

A wild spirit haunts musical New York in the person of a gaunt, scruffy pianist with unsmiling eyes who turns up (usually after dark, usually near a brick-strewn vacant lot on the east side of Broadway south of the 1960s-monumental architecture of Lincoln Center) to bang out Liszt, Chopin, and Tchaikovsky above the din of the street. A tin can—he does not deign to pass it—stands at the ready for collections. As urban surrealism, nothing quite matches the sight of him dragging his instrument to work of an evening through Amsterdam Avenue's pre-theater gridlock or dragging it back homeward past midnight. The ruin of a fabulously ornate upright, decked out with candelabra and inky gorgons and mounted on casters, it follows him on a chain like a domesticated dragon. Making a living at music in this city takes nerve, resolve, and invention. That roving pianist is a heraldic device come to life.

Close to curtain time every day of the week, in buses and subways, you encounter other musicians en route to their jobs: men of all ages, lacking only bow ties to complete their evening dress, negotiating luggage in the telltale shapes of cellos and horns, or, more discreetly, attaché cases; women in long dresses and sneakers wrestling harps. A glance at their datebooks would confirm that, like our street player, they have to cobble together the existence that suits them. Artistic and economic necessities require it, even of the musicians with the greatest job security.

Thus, many principal players with the New York Philharmonic, with multiple-season contracts running 12 months a year, double as faculty at the Juilliard School, across 65th street from Avery Fisher Hall. Regular players in such busy Manhattan-based ensembles as the self-conducting chamber orchestra Orpheus or the Orchestra of St. Luke's free-lance regularly, in accord with their private interests, with groups dedicated to early or contemporary music. Some switch-hit as soloists (as in another country the flutist James Galway did before cutting loose from the Berlin Philharmonic) or establish trios or quartets. The studious-looking international crowd of children, adolescents, and young adults who disappear into Juilliard each morning are headed for careers checkered in just this fashion. The most precocious among them are already on the circuit.

## The Musical Places

Though guidebooks for travellers never mention it, **The Juilliard School** is well worth the musical visitor's attention. With recitals by students and faculty, concerts by student orchestras (often with students or illustrious recent graduates as soloists), master classes, and fully staged productions of operas both familiar and rare, the school offers more than 300 performances a year. Quality, as you might expect, varies; at best, it is superb. Prices, as you might also expect, are low (often, admission is free). And the Juilliard Theater, though obscurely situated—the entrance is from a dark underpass on 65th Street—is Manhattan's only opera house built on a human scale. (It seats 933, comfortably and with good sight lines.) For information, consult the billboards by the bus stop on the west side of Broadway between 65th and 66th streets, or call the concert office; Tel: (212) 874-7515.

**Lincoln Center for the Performing Arts**, of which Juilliard is a constituent, boasts the city's highest concentration of stages for music. At the center's epicenter is a fountain: a black marble circle enclosing vertical jets of water whose play, in its abstract fashion, is as ecstatic as any of the Baroque cascades of Rome. But in the summer, it, too, has been covered to double as a platform. Around the fountain spreads a rectangular plaza, bounded on three sides by grandly scaled houses for opera, dance, and concerts: the soothingly gleaming **New York State Theater** (2,737 seats), home to the New York City Opera and the New York City Ballet; the plush, crystal-studded **Metropolitan Opera House** (3,718 seats); and **Avery Fisher Hall** (2,738 seats), articulated like the inside of a cream-colored accordion, home to the New York Philharmonic. Add to these the open-air band shell of **Damrosch Park** at the southwest corner of Lincoln Center; **Alice Tully Hall** (1,096 seats) in the same building as Juilliard and to the north of Avery Fisher, home to the Lincoln Center Chamber Music Society; and impromptu outdoor spaces devised for free summer events—and it is hard to imagine that you would ever need to look elsewhere for musical enjoyment.

And to an extent, that is true now. Time was when the New York music scene was divided neatly into "uptown" and "downtown." Uptown meant little beyond mainstream classics from the Continent, a canon closed, after several largely wasted decades, when Richard Strauss finished his "Four Last Songs" and laid down his pen. "Downtown" meant the esoteric John Cage, pixieish guru for the few, heard in cellars, lofts, and assorted holes-in-the-wall; then it meant the minimalists from Terry Riley through Steve Reich and Philip Glass, who after a quiet start have entranced multitudes. Since have come fast-rising children of the tape age from A (Anderson, Laurie) to Z (Zorn, John).

In the late 1960s, downtown found its temple across the river, at the Brooklyn Academy of Music, whose success has been so phenomenal as to create demand for its artists where else but uptown? And Lincoln Center has come through, scheduling special events and even whole series (like the recent summertime creation "Serious Fun!") designed not to hurt a bit.

**Carnegie Hall**, a short walk away from Lincoln Center at 57th Street and Seventh Avenue, cannot compete for sheer quantities of programming, but after all, how many concerts can you attend at once? And it is still the incomparable prestige address. Since its construction in 1891, it has ranked not only as the nation's premier concert hall but as the concert hall's Platonic ideal. (You've heard the story: A man stops a man with a violin case on a New York street corner. "How do I get to Carnegie Hall?" asks the first. "Practice!" comes the reply. It has been correctly observed that the punch line is really the set up. Substitute any other concert hall and there is no joke.)

In 1986 the main hall (2,784 seats) was sumptuously refurbished, and so was the smaller space upstairs then known as Carnegie Recital Hall and since rechristened the **Weill Recital Hall** (268 seats). The public heard many assurances beforehand that the fabled warm acoustics, traditionally equaled only by the Amsterdam Concertgebouw, Boston's Symphony Hall, and the Vienna Musikvereinsaal, would be preserved intact. At the reopening, it was instantly apparent that the sound had changed—and the listeners were scarce indeed who thought it had changed for the better.

Most agree that the hall has become brighter, colder, more space age, more aggressive. Some have wondered whether the impression originates in what amounts to an optical illusion: Now that all the dowdy gray drapes and tacky screens have been removed from the stage area (and now that the palette has gone to ivory, rose, and gold and the ushers have been outfitted by Ralph Lauren), Carnegie Hall certainly *looks* brighter, in a Postmodern-retro way. Nevertheless, at the start of the 1988/1989 season cautious—to these ears, unavailing—experiments with acoustic panels began. Fine tuning is bound to continue for years. So is the bickering among the experts. Meanwhile, a time-honored flaw in the hall remains: The rumble of the subway is still plainly audible.

Since the departure of the New York Philharmonic to Lincoln Center in 1962, Carnegie Hall has had no resident orchestra. However, the symphonies of Boston, Philadelphia, and other major American cities provide continuity with their regular seasons there. In addition, the hall produces and presents dozens of series with leading international artists. On dates when the hall does not have plans of its own, it is available for rental, which will explain the presence of a decidedly second- or third-tier attraction from time to time. The monthly schedule, available at the box office, is color-coded to distinguish the rentals from Carnegie Hall's own offerings, which can give the critical concertgoer a useful signal when confronted with unfamiliar names. Book especially warily at Weill Hall, a venue much favored for once-in-a-lifetime vanity recitals. But here, too, Carnegie Hall as an institution grows more ambitious with each passing season.

So far, the talk has mostly been of the big venues. For more intimate material—solo recitals or chamber music—there are many smaller spaces, too, frequented faithfully by all but the hugest box-office stars. You would not expect to encounter Jessye Norman or Dietrich Fischer-Dieskau at the **92nd Street Y**, on upper Lexington Avenue, for instance, but Elly Ameling and Hermann Prey are regulars. The **Metropolitan Museum of Art**, for its part, has long presented, in its **Grace Rainey Rogers Auditorium**, such internationally acclaimed artists as the Guarneri Quartet, the Beaux Arts Trio, and Les Arts Florissants.

**The Frick Collection**, ten blocks down Fifth Avenue from the Metropolitan Museum, retains its character of a connoisseur's private mansion and boasts—apart from a glorious assemblage of paintings—a fine music room, where late-afternoon concerts are held once or twice a month. Important performers appear here with minimal fanfare. No advance notices are published in the newspapers, but they are broadcast on WNYC radio, and the audience is often extremely distinguished. Tickets are free with admission to the museum, but the procedure for obtaining them is Byzantine to the point of impossibility. For information on dates, phone (212) 288-0700. To get in, queue up a half hour or so before the concert and hope for the best. Your patience is likely to be rewarded; there are always plenty of no-shows. One more tip on high-class, free concerts: From October to June, the radio station WNCN broadcasts hour-long recitals each Tuesday at 8:00 P.M. A live studio audience attends. For information and reservations, call (212) 730-9629.

If you enjoy music in beautiful surroundings, you should know that the **Metropolitan Museum of Art** offers performances not only in the Grace Rainey Rogers Auditorium, which has no cachet, but also in its Medieval Sculpture Hall, the Temple of Dendur, the Velez Blanco Patio, and elsewhere—as well as at the Funtedueña Chapel at **The Cloisters**, its bastion of Medieval art, surrounded by a rambling park at the northern tip of Manhattan. Often the performances at the Cloisters coincide with church holidays; they almost always have a deliberately archaic cast. (To get to the Cloisters, take the uptown-bound A train to 190th Street and Overlook Terrace, exit by elevator, and walk through the park; or hop the M 4 bus marked "Fort Tryon Park, The Cloisters." The bus comes up from lower Manhattan via Madison Avenue, but it is a waste of several hours to take it from points downtown or Midtown.)

The **Museum of Modern Art** has adapted the Cloisters' example in its own way, offering end-of-summer concerts of small-scale 20th-century works amid the Nadelmans, Maillols, Picassos, and Oldenburgs in the outdoor sculpture garden. Splendid artists appear in imaginative programs. Alas, this is Midtown, and the urban racket intrudes. Ambient noise is a problem in **Central Park**, too, where the New York Philharmonic and the Metropolitan Opera—heavily amplified—play beneath the stars and the airplanes and the mosquitos to the picnicking multitudes on various midsummer nights.

The **Brooklyn Academy of Music**, better known as BAM, has already been cited in passing for its role in legitimizing downtown music. In the process, it has turned itself into something very like the Alternative Lincoln Center, housing under a single roof the festive Opera House (2,085 seats), a well-proportioned playhouse (1,011 seats), and a black box, reconfigurable any which way, called the **Lepercq Space** (seating 350 to 550). In addition, BAM has recently refurbished the Majestic Theater (875 seats), a dilapidated former vaudeville house several blocks closer to Manhattan, enshrining its very disrepair.

All of BAM's auditoriums serve many muses, notably the muses of music and dance. The **Next Wave Festival**, held each autumn, juxtaposes ground-breaking American work with adventurous work from abroad. Thanks to the festival's enduring success, BAM is associated above all with the commercially viable avant-garde. In the future, BAM may be equally famous for its contributions in opera. Plans call for importing front-line productions from innovative companies outside New York, for mounting challenging productions of lesser-known, smaller-scale pieces, and for commissioning new works. As of 1991, the Metropolitan Opera will be BAM's partner in this venture. In the meantime, BAM is determined to get off to a roaring start, and certainly operatic New York, notorious for its conservatism, desperately needs the shot of creativity.

All the BAM theaters are easily accessible by subway. From Manhattan, take the Broadway express lines (numbers 2 or 3) or the less-circuitous Lexington Avenue express (numbers 4 or 5) to Nevins Street for the Majestic; ride one stop farther, to Atlantic Avenue, for BAM proper. The Q, R, B, and N trains will also get you to BAM (though not to the Majestic) from Manhattan; the stop to look for on those lines is Pacific Street. Another convenient option is the BAM Bus, which departs from the Summit Hotel, Lexington Avenue and 51st Street, one hour before curtain time at the Opera House or the Majestic. On the way back the bus makes several stops, the first in Greenwich Village, the last on Broadway at 72nd Street. For BAM information, call (718) 636-4100.

## Listings and Tickets

The Arts & Leisure section of the Sunday *New York Times* is indispensable for long-range planning, but for a visitor the weekly magazines and newspapers provide more helpful calendars. The best-organized listings are in *New York* magazine (see the *Cue* listings section). In "Goings on about Town" *The New Yorker* gives just the facts (but often not enough of them) about a reasonable selection of smaller events and all the majors. Following the music columns, *7 Days* magazine offers a similar overview, with capsule descriptions that attempt with mixed success to be a little more judgmental.

Each day, the **Bryant Park Ticket Booth**, on 42nd Street behind the New York Public Library, sells half-price tickets for music and dance events taking place that evening. The very hottest attractions (Bernstein and the Vienna Philharmonic, Solti and the Chicago) will not be represented, but many first-rate ones often are. Call (212) 382-2323 to find out what is on offer—and what the booth's hours are; they vary from day to day.

Apart from this booth, ticketing is mostly decentralized. All the leading institutions and most marginal ones will take ticket reservations over the phone and charge them to the standard array of credit cards. Such sales are final. When ordering by phone, it is usually impossible to find out exact seat locations (you are generally promised "best available" within the price range). Fussy patrons are advised to go to the box office, *Stubs* in hand. *Stubs,* available at magazine stands in the Broadway Theater District, contains seating plans for all but the smallest of the city's theaters and concert halls. Though these plans are posted at theaters and concert halls, they are usually posted too far from the box office to be of any use.

## SHOPPING FOR MUSIC AND MUSICAL INSTRUMENTS

Not surprisingly, the prime shopping area for musical instruments is within a few steps' radius of Carnegie Hall. The **Steinway & Sons** showroom, at 109 West 57th Street, is an institution. Pianists who want to investigate legendary rarer makes—Feurich, Grotrian, Bösendorfer—should look in at **Artist Pianos**, 346 West 57th Street. **Jacques Français**, 250 West 54th Street, is the place to go for rare string instruments. Amatis, Guarneris, and Strads probably pass through here as frequently as anywhere in the world. For the keyboardist of the future, the **Yamaha** showroom, 142 West 57th Street, is a must. Apart from conventional concert-quality grands, Yamaha has acoustic pianos with brains that allow you to correct mistakes, transpose, speed up, or slow down your live performance, and then to play it back (cleaned up) with no hands. Other Yamahas produce sound electronically so that, if the occasion requires, you alone, in headphones, can hear what you are up to. The top-of-the-line synthesizers are virtual symphony orchestras in a console, awaiting their new age Beethoven. For band instruments, stroll down to West 48th Street between Sixth and Seventh avenues and browse.

Classical musicians shopping for scores head for **Patelson**, 160 West 56th Street, across from Carnegie Hall's stage door. The shop also stocks the city's best selection of books on classical music and musicians, and an interesting array of recordings. Another exclusive feature: The latest concert reviews from *The New York Times* (the only reviews in town that really matter) are pasted into a loose-leaf album by the door.

If you are after sheet music for show tunes, go to **Colony Records Center**, 1619 Broadway, where the bossy sales help can probably set you up with whatever you want—even private tapes of musicals never commercially recorded.

## SHOPPING FOR RECORDS

Compact discs are significantly cheaper in the United States than anywhere else, so it is not uncommon to see visitors from abroad loading up on them by the armful. For the latest classical releases (often issued here several months later than in Europe) the most reliable source is the **J & R Classical Outlet**, 33 Park Row, near City Hall. It is the store you can count on to order sufficient stock. Nevertheless, *the* name in this game is **Tower**, at two locations: 1965 Broadway, just north of Lincoln Center, and 692 Broadway (at 4th Street), downtown, in Greenwich Village. The downtown location has a more knowledgeable sales staff and a larger selection, though to find a specific title you may have to check both stores. For music lovers still interested in vinyl, an attraction at the downtown Tower is the sales annex, at 4th and Lafayette streets, where conventional LPs and cassettes are available at rock-bottom prices.

The LPs at **Gryphon Records**, 251 West 72nd Street, second floor, are often pricey, with good reason: They are collector's items. The pleasantly Dickensian emporium specializes in "Proudly Archival Sound," so audio fetishists will disapprove. But for anyone with a tolerance for a recently obsolete technology and an appreciation for historic performance, Gryphon is a gold mine. So is **G & A Rare Records Ltd.**, the new shop nearby at 139 West 72nd Street (another second-story outlet), which is a little sprucer to look at and charges more outlandish prices. Still, if they have what you've always been looking for.... Another stop for the serious collector of out-of-print records is the **Academy Book Store**, 10 West 18th Street—dusty, cramped, and full of surprises. **Footlight Records**, 113 East 12th Street, specializes in hard-to-find Broadway albums, movie sound tracks, big band music, jazz, country, and rock 'n' roll. For rare rock, drop in at **Midnight Records**, 255 West 23rd Street.

A word of caution: Examine all merchandise critically. While it is possible to find copies of fairly commonplace material in mint condition, many rarer items are decidedly worse for the wear. If you want to hunt further, consult the Yellow Pages of the Manhattan telephone directory under the heading "Records-Phonograph-Retail." Phone before going out of your way. Used-record shops are forever going out of business, as anyone who wants to sell used records quickly discovers.

# DANCE

*By Joanna Ney*

*Joanna Ney is a free-lance writer specializing in dance. She was formerly dance critic for* East Side Express *and* Other Stages. *She has contributed to* The New York Times, Cosmopolitan, Cue, *and* V. *She also reviews dance for WBAI radio.*

The sheer quantity and diversity of dance in New York guarantee that there is something for the visitor to see at any given time of the year. Whether you crave the formality of classical ballet or the improvisational quality of performance art, you are likely to find it in an opera house or a loft. Once considered an exotic art reserved for a select coterie, dance now appeals to a much wider audience in New York.

At the heart of New York's dance explosion is the **Lincoln Center** complex, which includes the New York State Theater, the official home of New York City Ballet (NYCB), and the Metropolitan Opera House, which plays host to American Ballet Theatre, as well as to a variety of other major companies from around the world.

When Lincoln Center was built 25 years ago the neighborhood was a wasteland dotted with tenements. Today it is packed with restaurants, cafés, boutiques, and much frenetic activity. Strolling up Broadway from Columbus Circle to 79th Street, you can see famous dancers and ballet students making their daily rounds. Dancers are easy to spot, walking briskly in ballet's proverbial first position. Their favorite hangout is the Plaza Fountain at Lincoln Center; it takes on a movie-set glitter when illuminated at night.

**New York City Ballet**, the creation of Lincoln Kirstein and George Balanchine, is now run by Peter Martins and Jerome Robbins. The company performs November through January and April through June, with December reserved for the perennial favorite, *The Nutcracker*. Traditionally, the company has stressed choreography, specifically that of George Balanchine, over a star system. Since Balanchine's death the company has faced an identity crisis, but the dancing, especially at the principal level, remains top-notch. NYCB also has its own professional school, and each June its graduating class performs on the stage of the Juilliard School, giving dance lovers an opportunity to witness dancers in the making.

Although NYCB has many faithful subscribers, some tickets are usually available the day of performance, unless it happens to be a company premiere or a dancer's debut in a particular role. Even when a performance is sold out, balletomanes know that if they wait outside the theater before curtain time someone is likely to sell them a ticket.

Across the plaza, the imposing Metropolitan Opera House, with its gigantic Chagall murals and red and gold trappings, is the unofficial home of **American Ballet Theatre** (ABT), now under the artistic direction of Mikhail Baryshnikov and associate director Twyla Tharp. Formerly a star-studded glamor company, it has become "Balanchinized" and now stresses ensemble dancing rather than star "turns." The company's corps de ballet is now virtually unparalleled, and many exciting principals (for example, Susan Jaffe and Amanda McKerrow) have risen from its ranks. The repertory includes 19th-century classics such as *Swan Lake* as well as contemporary works by modernists such as Twyla Tharp and Mark Morris. Baryshnikov's appearances are rare these days, but thanks to *glasnost,* one of the Bolshoi's most exciting dancers, Andris Liepa, is on loan to ABT for one year and should add some needed dazzle to its male contingent.

When ABT is touring the Met has no shortage of other illustrious guests. Internationally renowned ballet companies that appear there include the Paris Opéra Ballet, run by Rudolf Nureyev; Denmark's Royal Ballet; Germany's Stuttgart; and the Soviet Bolshoi and Kirov. It is an ironic fact that the formerly insular Russians have given new life to American ballet, beginning with Balanchine's contribution and continuing with such present-day idols as Nureyev, Baryshnikov, and Natalia Makarova.

The Moorish-style **City Center**, at 131 West 55th Street, is another major showcase for both ballet and modern dance. At various times of the year you can catch the spirited **Joffrey Ballet**, now under the leadership of Gerald Arpino, who succeeded its late founder, Robert Joffrey; the **Alvin Ailey Company**, with its unique blend of modern, jazz, and blues arising out of the black experience; the classical **Dance Theater of Harlem** (led by

NYCB alumnus Arthur Mitchell), which combines Neoclassicism with a flair for drama; and the twin masters of modern dance, **Paul Taylor** and **Merce Cunningham**. City Center is one of the most congenial dance spaces in the city and a favorite with dancegoers.

A newish addition to the dance scene is a former offbeat movie house converted into the **Joyce Theater**, at Eighth Avenue and 18th Street in the gentrifying Chelsea area. The Joyce offers works by established choreographers such as **Eliot Feld**, as well as many bold newcomers, all in an agreeably intimate setting. One of the pluses of the Joyce experience is the number of restaurants, both modest and chic, virtually on its doorstep. The Joyce season runs from September to May, and single performance tickets are often available.

Nearby, at 219 West 19th Street, is the **Dance Theater Workshop** (DTW), a haven for experimental dance. Up a narrow flight of stairs is the **Bessie Schönberg Theater**, a small, informal space with bleacherlike seating. Devotees don't mind the slight discomfort: DTW is known as a leading pioneer of new dance in the country. The theater is accompanied by an attractive gallery that presents solo art and photo exhibits.

Downtown in the East Village, at Second Avenue and 10th Street, is another showcase for new dance—**St. Mark's-in-the-Bowery**. This 200-year-old Episcopal church, built on land that was part of Peter Stuyvesant's estate, is the second oldest church in Manhattan. Seriously damaged by fire in 1978 but scrupulously rebuilt, this active church converts into a performance stage for Postmodern dance and poetry readings.

For the committed dancegoer, the **Brooklyn Academy of Music**, or BAM, as it is affectionately called, is a definite must. The main building has three theaters—the Opera House, the Carey Playhouse, and the smaller Lepercq Space. Bam's Majestic Theater is across the street. The turn-of-the-century Opera House is a spacious, beautifully appointed theater on whose stage appear some of the most exciting innovators in dance, performance art, and contemporary music. This is where you'll see the theater pieces of Robert Wilson and Pina Bausch and hear the work of Philip Glass and other minimalists.

BAM can be reached via the IRT subway line on the number 2 or 3 train on the West Side and the 4 or 5 on the East Side, as well as the Q, B, R, and N on the BMT line. The BAM stop for the IRT trains is Atlantic Avenue; for the BMT, Pacific Street. The BAM Manhattan Express Bus is an option available for events taking place at the Opera House and the Majestic Theater. It leaves Manhattan one hour prior to curtain time from the Summit Hotel at 51st Street and Lexington Avenue. On return it makes stops in the West Village, Midtown on the East Side, and the Upper West Side. For reservations and BAM information, Tel: (718) 636-4100, Monday to Friday 10:00 to 5:30; Saturday and Sunday on performance days, 12:00 to 3:00.

BAM has a concession area in the lobby where you can stave off hunger pangs with a hot or cold sandwich or salad and a cup of coffee or a soft drink. There is also a full bar. For something more leisurely try **Gage & Tollner** at 372 Fulton Street (a 15-minute walk from BAM; a dangerous excursion after dark). This old New York establishment has specialized in steaks, chops, and seafood since 1879. The dark wood paneling and colored glass lighting fixtures provide an authentic traditional flavor; Tel: (718) 875-5181 (closed Sunday). For a more informal, family-style restaurant you might choose **Junior's** at 386 Flatbush Avenue (Tel: 718-852-5257), known for its roast beef and brisket of beef and justly famous countrywide for its cheesecake.

Apart from the formal dance events, you can also experience New York's dance wave in many outdoor performances that take place all over the city in the summer. For basic information on all dance events, it's a good idea to check the listings in *The New York Times,* as well as the *Village Voice, The New Yorker,* and the new weekly arts magazine, *7 Days.*

## DANCE APPAREL AND EQUIPMENT
**Capezio**, in Greenwich Village at 177 MacDougal Street off 8th Street, is definitely the one-stop place to get outfitted for a dance studio or gym. Its dance shoe department on the second floor carries a full line of ballet, aerobic, character, and tap shoes. The salespeople are knowledgeable and helpful. The adjoining Dance Body Shop stocks every conceivable item you will need for a dance, exercise, or aerobics class. Styles range from traditional to the latest in spandex and decorated dancewear. The shop also carries socks, stockings, and lingerie. There are other Capezio stores in Manhattan: one at Steps Dance Studio at

2121 Broadway at 74th Street, and the big main branch at 755 Seventh Avenue at 50th Street (with a more hectic pace than the others).

For superior quality soft ballet shoes and pointe shoes there is also **Freed of London** at 922 Seventh Avenue at 58th Street. The footwear is of fine and durable leather. They also carry leotards, tights, and accessories. There are no bargains here, but the service is efficient and courteous.

**Barbara Gee Danskin Center**, a Danskin discount house at 2282½ Broadway (between 82nd and 83rd streets) and also at 2509 Broadway (betwen 93rd and 94th streets), is hard to beat for standard dancewear at reasonable prices. In this minuscule space you'll find cotton and lycra leotards, unitards, and spandex tights in all sizes—though color selection is limited. This is also a great place to buy name-brand hosiery such as Hanes, Berkshire, and Calvin Klein in a variety of shades. Also available are all-cotton tights and knee highs and intimate apparel. The sales help is patient and helpful, and there is a tiny dressing room.

In the basement, where most of the space is devoted to active sportswear for jogging and running, **Paragon Sporting Goods**, 867 Broadway (between 17th and 18th streets), also has a section devoted to dancewear. Traditional styles are limited, and the emphasis is on the aerobic and jazzy types. You'll find the top sports lines—Avia and Nike—and a full line of Baryshnikov dancewear, including spandex tights and sweatpants. Another line, Marika, offers basically the same merchandise at lower prices.

## DANCE MEMORABILIA AND COLLECTIBLES

**The Ballet Shop** at 1887 Broadway (at 63rd Street near Lincoln Center) is a one-of-a-kind establishment owned by Norman Crider, a former champion baton twirler and collector. For the past 16 years the shop has been on this site and managed by the knowledgeable Tobias Leibovitz and his assistant, Joe Marshall, a former ice skater. There is nothing these two don't know about *la danse*. Here you'll find rare prints and lithographs from the romantic era on, as well as out-of-print books, signed photographs, statuary dating back to the pre-1840 period of ballet, class records for ballet, modern, jazz, and tap, the largest video selection from technique to documentary performances, as well as the more mundane fare, such as tee-shirts and dance-related gift items. If you've been looking for an original signed Chagall sketch, a rare original Leon Bakst ballet design, or a 19th-century bronze statuette of Fanny Elssler, The Ballet Shop is likely to have it.

**The Performing Arts Shop**, underground at Lincoln Center, has a more limited and popular selection of items related to dance, such as tee-shirts, ceramic mugs, and books, records, and cassettes. Opera and music items are highlighted.

# THE THEATER

*By David Berreby*

*David Berreby is a member of the Outer Critics Circle. His work has appeared in the* Village Voice, V, Diversion, *and* New York Newsday. *He reviews theater for* The New York Law Journal.

One late summer afternoon in Midtown Manhattan, a film crew was carefully choreographing an attractive couple, a mounted policeman, a dancer in pink pants wearing headphones, a hot-dog cart with its distinctive umbrella, great clouds of smoke from a dry-ice device, and, in the center of it all, a gleaming red Ferrari. A happy crowd watched the crew shoot take after take in the glow of theater marquees and immense neon signs, ignoring the honk and roar of passing traffic. Meanwhile, across the street, a posse of young break dancers gyrated to the beat of a powerful portable radio, while, a couple of blocks up, a rival group danced to a live drummer. A block up from *them,* a duo played show tunes on a bongo and a steel drum. The whole honking, drumming, banging, yelling chaos seemed to harmonize into a single purposeful scene, over which hovered the electronic headlines of the Times Tower (where the ball drops at New Year's) and a perpetually wheeling flock of irritated pigeons.

This is Times Square, where Seventh Avenue and Broadway meet to form the Crossroads of the World, as it was known in the 1920s. In many ways, the square and the blocks of the West 40s immediately adjacent still form the heart of New York. And, not coincidentally, the neighborhood is also the heart of New York's **Theater District**.

You need only a few minutes here to see how New York's essence is bound up with the theater. It's a fact of geography (the world's greatest concentration of theaters is here, just off Broadway in the center of the center of town). It's a fact of economics (drama is a major industry and tourist attraction). But more important, it's a fact of the spirit. Like the theater, New York City is high-class yet not entirely respectable; artistic yet crass; insular yet eager for attention and approval from outsiders. Perhaps that's the reason why when the city works, it acts like a well-choreographed show.

Of course, the Broadway Theater District (especially at its southern boundary, 42nd Street, and at Eighth Avenue) has its low-down, sleazy, and menacing blocks, where drugs and sex are sold. And it's also true that the cost of putting on a Broadway show nowadays is so immense that "Broadway" to many people stands for safe dull plays and homogenized international musicals imported from London. Nonetheless, this part of town remains the repository of the city's theatrical tradition, where you can have cheesecake at **Lindy's** on Broadway near 45th (a strictly Disney version of the original haunt of show biz, bootleggers, and wise guys immortalized by Damon Runyon), get in a gawk at **Sardi's** (234 West 44th), where opening-night parties are still held, and contemplate the Brill Building farther up on Broadway, where Kern and Gershwin once toiled.

The city has embarked on a multimillion-dollar office development plan to tone up the area. The neighborhood is already pocked with construction sites, and the lights may not stay bright as the corporate towers go up. See it while you can.

## Getting Tickets

Times Square is a good place to start hunting for a show to see, even if you've decided to skip the astonishingly high costs of Broadway, where the top ticket price is now $50. Many non-Broadway theaters are in the neighborhood, and it's easy to reach others from this central location.

The best way to cut your ticket expenses is to go to one of the booths where the Theatre Development Fund sells seats for Broadway and off-Broadway shows for *half price* (plus a $1.50 fee per ticket). The catch is you have to take what's available the same day you buy your ticket. There are three in the city, all marked with a big **TKTS** sign (it's pronounced "tickets," as in "I'll meet you on the tickets line"). The largest is right in Times Square, at 47th Street. It opens at 3:00 P.M. and doesn't close until curtain time, 8:00 P.M. (It's within sprinting distance of a number of theaters, and hence is still selling at three minutes to the hour.) On Wednesdays and Saturdays, when there are matinee performances at 2:00 P.M., the booths open at noon, close at curtain time, and reopen an hour later for the evening shows. Any show that isn't a sold-out hit will turn up on the TKTS listing of available shows (even *Cats* has been sighted occasionally). Naturally, you'll have a better chance (and a much shorter wait) if you go on a Tuesday or Wednesday rather than a Friday or Saturday, and the earlier you turn up, the better. (On Mondays, most theaters are "dark"—closed—so if you go then you'll have little to select from.) Count on waiting in line 30 minutes or so if you come midweek before people escape from their offices; it'll take longer if you arrive at, say, 6:30 P.M., or if you come on a weekend.

Unless the weather's bad, the Times Square TKTS line is not an unpleasant place to wait. You've got a perfect perch for watching Times Square go by, and you'll likely be approached by hawkers trying to interest you in less-than-sellout shows. Often, they'll offer you a "twofer"—a ticketlike slip that allows you to purchase two tickets for the price of one. You can then leave the line and go directly to the theater box office. (Twofers are also widely available in stores, hotels, and at the city's Department of Cultural Affairs, at 2 Columbus Circle, 59th Street and Broadway.) Naturally, the more popular a show, the less likely it is that you'll find twofers for it.

If you hate to wait, the lines are generally shorter at the other TKTS booths: One, in the financial district, is in 2 World Trade Center (the south tower); the other is in Brooklyn Heights, at the foot of Montague Street in front of the state court building.

If the show you're living to see is sold out until next Christmas, you might consider foregoing a seat. Most Broadway houses sell standing room for a fraction of the usual ticket price; inquire at the box office. You can also get on line to buy the seats of people who have cancelled (be early, though, because the cancellation line for a hit show will start to grow at least two hours before curtain time).

If you want to be sure of seeing one exact show on one exact date, you can always reserve with a ticket agent: **Golden and LeBlang** at 1501 Broadway, Tel: (212) 944-8910, for example, or **Hickey's** at 251 West 45th, Tel: (212) 586-2980. If you're staying in the area, your hotel can put you in touch with a ticket agency, too. Their nominal fees are set by law.

## What to Look For

If you've arrived in New York without a show in mind, you can find listings for all major productions in *The New Yorker* or in *New York* magazine, both sold at newsstands. If you're more adventurous, buy *Theaterweek,* which lists every production being given in the city. There you'll find the smaller shows not mentioned elsewhere.

Shows are listed as "Broadway," "off-Broadway," and "off-off-Broadway"; knowing these categories can give you a good idea of what to expect.

"Broadway" is not really a geographic term (most Broadway theaters aren't on Broadway). Broadway is a type of contract, covering a big house, providing big salaries, and generally portending high ticket prices and a certain sumptuousness of staging that visitors expect from one of the city's premier tourist attractions. "Off-Broadway" contracts cover the kind of smaller productions that sprang up 25 years ago in reaction to Broadway's expense and conventionality. These days, though, off-Broadway itself is part of the mainstream. (Many off-Broadway shows are offered at TKTS.) Still, it's free of the immense financial pressures of Broadway, and it's less expensive (with a top ticket price of about $30 versus Broadway's $50). Off-Broadway in turn engendered off-off-Broadway—smaller, more experimental, more daring (in theory), and cheaper still. Many small off-off-Broadway shows are actually "showcases," in which the actors aren't paid at all, but play because it's a chance to do something professional and (you never know) the show might get discovered. Such plays may run only on weekends, take place in a church basement, and charge you a mere ten dollars, but they can be excellent theater, and they give you a chance to get off the beaten path.

Directly adjacent to the Broadway area is one of the city's

happier urban renewal efforts, **Theater Row**. It's a long block of off-Broadway theaters and restaurants stretching from Ninth to Tenth avenues on 42nd Street. Here you can usually find something worth seeing—and a good meal. (It's also the site of the Manhattan Plaza Garage, which offers one of the lowest parking rates in the area.) A ticket center for all Theater Row productions operates on the southern side of 42nd Street just west of Ninth Avenue.

Elsewhere in the city, a number of off- and off-off-Broadway productions are sponsored by long-standing theatrical institutions with records of offering high-quality interesting work. Perhaps the foremost of these is **The New York Shakespeare Festival**, founded and run by the legendary Joseph Papp, who produced *A Chorus Line, Pirates of Penzance,* and *The Mystery of Edwin Drood,* among other unconventional hits. In the 1960s Papp successfully overcame the objections of megabuilder Robert Moses and won permission to stage free plays every summer in Central Park. Summer visitors can still enjoy free Shakespeare at the Delacorte Theatre in the park—but be warned: If the show's a hit, you should arrive in the late morning and spend the afternoon picnicking under the trees on line, until the 6:00 P.M. ticket distribution.

These days most of Papp's lively, often controversial productions of both classics and new works are to be seen indoors, at **The Public Theater**, 425 Lafayette Street near 8th Street/Astor Place. The huge building is a converted library that houses legitimate theaters and a movie house. Appropriately enough for a combative, controversial theater, nearby Astor Place is where, in 1849, a different theatrical *contretemps*—the fight between supporters of the American tragedian Edwin Forrest and fans of English actor William Macready—led to 31 deaths in the infamous Astor Place Riot. (New York theatergoers have always been passionately opinionated.)

Not far from Papp's empire is one of the most venerable avant-garde theater groups in the world, the **La MaMa Experimental Theater Company**, 74A East 4th Street, in the East Village. Founder Ellen Stewart's ideal is to create a genuine world theatrical community, and so La MaMa's offerings have ranged from Andrei Serban's stunning reinterpretation of the Trojan War to Eskimo drama performed by Eskimos (Stewart would have had pygmy dancers come, too, but the government of Zaire refused). Another bastion of innovation is **The Brooklyn Academy of Music**, 30 Lafayette Avenue, Brooklyn, where Ingmar

Bergman, Peter Brook, Robert Wilson, Peter Sellars, and Laurie Anderson, among others, have presented their work. BAM, as it's known, has been many an experimentalist's ticket into the mainstream. It's the place to go to see work the year before everyone else learns about it. (See Classical Music or Dance for directions, or call BAM; Tel: 718-636-4100.)

Several other companies are worth seeking out. The **Circle Repertory Theater**, at 99 Seventh Avenue South, on Sheridan Square in Greenwich Village, was long the home company of Lanford Wilson, and has presented many fine new American plays. **The Roundabout Theatre Company**, 100 East 17th Street, sticks staidly to classics and revivals, and does them well. The **Jean Cocteau Repertory**, 330 Bowery, likes to stage neglected works in its tiny theater on the city's traditional skid row. Performance art meets theater at **The Performing Garage**, 33 Wooster Street. **Mabou Mines** is an experimental troupe with a commitment to language as well as image. Headquartered at P.S. 122, a former public school at 150 First Avenue, they often perform elsewhere, and their work is worth hunting for in the listings. And finally, when you get fed up with the wonder of it all, go see **Forbidden Broadway**, a hilarious, constantly updated spoof of the theater scene and of the latest hits. After five years in a cabaret, it's now lodged at the Theater East, 211 East 60th Street.

## Theatrical Hangouts

If you haven't gotten enough of the cast at the show, you can try to rub elbows afterward. Waiting at the stage door for an autograph is a venerable Broadway tradition, and well worth it if you have the patience. Not only could you meet your favorite performer, but you'll encounter a curious cast of regulars—autograph hunters and photographers—who live in a subculture all their own.

There are also a number of Theater District restaurants where you'll likely find actors unwinding after shows. If you want to go in comfort, **Orso**, at 322 West 46th (near Eighth Avenue) is a pleasant Italian restaurant where you might find the stars of major shows and visiting celebrities. Immortal Sardi's (see above) still gets its share of the prominent and would-be prominent. And **Café Made-**

**leine**, at 43rd and Ninth Avenue, gets after-show clientele from both Broadway and Theater Row.

On the other hand, if you'd like to see how most actors really live, try **Barrymore's**, 267 West 45th (between Seventh and Eighth avenues), a large, dark bar where you'll see a lot of people wearing the nylon jackets emblazoned with logos that Broadway shows issue to their casts and crews. Nearby is **Charlie's Restaurant**, 705 Eighth Avenue between 44th and 45th, another good bet. Neither of these will send you to gastronomic nirvana, but you won't get ptomaine either, and you'll be seeing life as it's lived by the majority of actors (or at least actors who are working—to see life as it's lived by most New York actors, you'd have to go to an unemployment line or become a waiter).

Finally, if you're not satisfied to see the show, wear the sweatshirt, buy the album, get the autograph, and eat next to one of the cast, you can always follow the actors home. The M 104 bus goes up Eighth Avenue to the Upper West Side, haunt of many actors (though fewer these days, since rent has skyrocketed). The Seventh (numbers 1, 2, and 3) and Eighth (A, B, C, and D) Avenue subways are the closest to Theater Row and Broadway. Between 11:30 P.M. and 1:00 A.M. these public conveyances bear many actors (looking incongruous without their makeup, costumes, and stage auras) back to their homes. Try not to stare.

## THEATER BOOKS AND MEMORABILIA

Many a city has theaters, but New York has a theater culture. With a little effort, you can find a book on Kabuki, a 1964 Broadway poster, or the script of the new play you saw last night. The city's major bookstores have well-stocked drama sections, but the best place to start hunting (especially for a new play) is in one of the bookstores that cater to the trade. They make an effort to have available everything currently showing, as well as the thousands of other plays, memoirs, works of scholarship, and such books as *Foreign Dialects* and *How to Market Your Play*.

Many new scripts are quickly published in inexpensive, pamphletlike editions by one of two major publishers: Samuel French and Dramatists Play Service. **Samuel French** maintains a bookstore of its own, at 45 West 25th Street (between Fifth and Sixth avenues), where you can purchase its own editions and other theater books. Another publisher, **Applause Theatre Book Publishers**, bills itself as "the unavoidable source" and offers everything from the essays of Eric Bentley to recently published Australian plays as well as a wide selection of other publishers' titles at its store at 211 West 71st (between Broadway and West End Avenue). Cinema books are offered at their second store, at 100 West 67th, between Broadway and Columbus.

For rare theater books and old prints of theater productions, an excellent source is **Richard Stoddard Performing Arts Books**, 18 East 16th Street, Room 202 (between Fifth Avenue and Union Square). In the theater district itself there are three comprehensive bookstores: **The Drama Bookshop**, 723 Seventh Avenue near 48th Street; **Theatrebooks**, at 1600 Broadway, Room 1009 (near 48th Street); and the **Theatre Arts Bookshop**, 405 West 42nd Street (just west of Ninth Avenue, on the north side of the street). A good place to hunt for show scores and sheet music is **Colony Records Center**, 1619 Broadway (at 49th).

New York's theater culture offers a wide selection of souvenirs and memorabilia, ranging from the plastic *Phantom of the Opera* masks sold everywhere around Times Square to framed, original drawings by Hirschfeld, *The New York Times*'s indestructible caricaturist of 50 years.

The most "touristy" of places to hunt memorabilia (but worth a look, nonetheless) is **One Shubert Alley**, a tiny shop tucked into an outside wall of the theater where *A Chorus Line* has been playing for as long as anyone can remember. (Shubert Alley extends between 44th and 45th streets, in the block between Broadway and Eighth Avenue.) This is the place for tee-shirts, mugs, the latest posters, postcards, and the like. Slightly to the west on 44th Street is **The Actors Heritage**, at number 262; here they have photographs, movie stills, programs, posters, scripts, and some records and scores. The Theatre Arts Bookshop, mentioned above, also has a decent collection of posters, and offers more memorabilia around Christmastime.

The biggest seasonal break for souvenir hunters, though, is early October, when Lincoln Center's **Performing Arts Library** has its annual sale. Every conceivable kind of memento relating to theater, dance, opera, and music is offered at prices that begin at 25¢. The sale items are not merely the library's castoffs: Theater people often donate things (the proceeds help the library). The library's sale is one of the best sources in the city for one-of-a-kind theatrical souvenirs. For information, Tel: (212) 870-1670.

Finally, for the serious collector (spending serious money) there are a number of galleries that offer posters and original drawings. Two that have a strong emphasis on theater are the **Triton Gallery**, at 323 West 45th (between Eighth and Ninth avenues), featuring Broadway and foreign posters; and **Margo Feiden Galleries** (11th Street and University Place, in Greenwich Village), which has, among other things, those Hirschfeld drawings.

# LITERARY NEW YORK

## By Ingrid Nelson

*Ingrid Nelson, formerly an editor of GEO magazine, is a free-lance writer living on Manhattan's Upper West Side.*

Few writers have character strong enough to write in New York. For all the hoo-haw that surrounds it, writing is the least glamorous of professions: It is slow, laborious, and ultimately solitary work. To attempt it in a city as distracting as New York can be disastrous, and while there have been times when writing has flourished here, the names of the talented writers who have died from overindulging in Manhattan's fleshpots could also serve as a reading list for a survey course in American literature. Writers with sense head for tamer spots, like Chicago, when there's work to be done.

Nonetheless, New York is essential to American writers for two reasons: It provides inspiration and it promises fame. Nowhere else is such a variety of human beings and human pursuits packed into such a small area; the inspirational potential of this pure human concentrate is boundless. And once words have been set down on paper the city becomes the writer's marketplace.

New York is the seat of publishing, the home base of most important magazines and journals, the headquarters of the country's largest wire service (the Associated Press), the stage upon which playwrights make or break their reputations, and the country's chief arena in which

## THE CITY'S SPECIALTIES

literature is dissected, analyzed, and judged. The novelist Thomas Wolfe, whose relationship with New York was as ambivalent as any writer's has ever been, described the city he adopted in *From Death to Morning:* "The great vision of the city is burning in your heart in all its enchanted colors just as it did when you were twelve years old and thought about it. You think that some glorious happiness of fortune, fame, and triumph will be yours at any minute, that you are about to take your place among great men and lovely women in a life more fortunate and happy than any you have ever known—that it is all here, somehow, waiting for you."

In the beginning—that is, before 1850—there wasn't much that was literary about New York. Publishers lived in Boston. Most American writers were from elsewhere. An exception was Washington Irving, who had been born in lower Manhattan in 1783. This was merely a coincidence of birth; after he gained his early and considerable fame from humorous essays about New York society, Irving moved to Europe, which he far preferred, and stayed there for much of his adult life. When it came time to retire, he installed himself and his extended family in an eccentric mansion called Sunnyside in Tarrytown, about 25 miles north of Manhattan. (Sunnyside is now a museum, open to visitors; see Day Trips chapter.)

Around 1850, however, publishers began to migrate south, drawn by New York's growing population (and thus, pool of book purchasers). With them came editors, illustrators, and the usual literary hangers-on. The city was ripe for them. Having made money in trade, wealthy New Yorkers were ready to put it into less tangible investments: They were endowing museums, amassing art collections, and reading for pleasure.

At the time, New York was also the occasional home of two genuinely great writers: Herman Melville and Edgar Allan Poe. Neither prospered from his writing, nor did either find the city to be a sympathetic place. There was something about New York, even in those early days, that didn't like writers.

Herman Melville was born at 6 Pearl Street in lower Manhattan in 1819. When he was 12 his father died. A few years later, Melville ran off to sea and lived the adventures he described in two early books, *Typee* and *Omoo*. Both were wildly successful, and Melville purchased a farm near Pittsfield, Massachusetts, and settled in to write his masterpiece, *Moby Dick*. It was a complete flop. Destitute and discouraged, Melville returned to New York. He moved into a one-family brick house at 104 East 26th Street, and took a job as a customs officer at a dock on the East River. The pay was about four dollars a day. He died 28 years later, in 1891, having written a series of brilliant but unrecognized novels and stories. Melville is buried at Woodlawn Cemetery in the Bronx. During his career, he earned less than $8,000 from his writing; in his obituary, *The New York Times* called him Henry.

Edgar Allan Poe was a Bostonian, but in 1844 he moved to Greenwich Village with his child bride, Virginia, and took a job at the *Evening Mirror* newspaper. Although a collection of his tales was published during this period, and he wrote several poems, including "Annabelle Lee," the Poe family was impoverished, and Poe himself was regarded more as a hack critic than a real artist. Virginia suffered from consumption, and in 1846 her condition had worsened so much that Poe rented a house (now open to visitors) in Fordham in the Bronx, where the air was clean. The rent was $100 a month. This put such a strain on his precarious finances that Virginia's mother (who lived with them) had to beg for food from the neighbors. Virginia died in 1847. Two years later Poe himself died during a trip to Baltimore. He was found in an alcoholic stupor outside a voting booth where presumably he had been earning a few dollars as a repeating voter.

Fortunately for literature, New York City's next great writer chose to live abroad. Edith Wharton was born here in 1862 and lived in a brownstone at 28 West 25th Street. She was married in a church across the street, went to Europe, and eventually settled in Paris. Her novels, however, are wickedly critical dissections of New York, set in and around her old neighborhood. In *The Age of Innocence,* the Archer family lived in a brownstone on West 28th Street, where similar buildings still stand. Of them Wharton wrote in *A Backward Glance:* "the narrow houses so lacking in external dignity, so crammed with smug and suffocating upholstery . . . the little low-studded rectangular New York cursed with its universal chocolate-colored coating of the most hideous stone ever quarried."

Whatever it was about early New York that drove these writers to Europe or to their deaths—perhaps the city's crass materialism or its stuffy provincialism—was about to change. The first wave of European immigrants arrived in Manhattan in 1860 or so. The contribution they made is incalculable—they brought vitality to New York, and they formed a bond between America and Europe, a kind of vibrating chord linking the Old World to the New. They also created a whole new social climate, one in which teeming slums existed cheek by jowl with uptown brownstones. The city became a different place altogether, and as such it was the geographical center for a remarkable group of writers, men and women of enormous energy, sophistication, optimism, and humanity, all imbued with a strong social conscience.

An early member of this group (actually, a precursor) was Walt Whitman of Long Island. Whitman was an editor of the *Brooklyn Eagle,* among other newspapers, for many years. In his free time he roamed through lower Manhattan and composed some of the poems that would eventually make him one of the best-known and most acclaimed of all American poets; poems about the Brooklyn Bridge and "Mannahatta," written with exuberance, sensuality, and a strong sense of individualism. Unfortunately, the New York curse on writers was still partially in evidence, for Whitman never achieved in his lifetime the fame that came to him after his death.

The writers of the next few decades did, however. O. Henry (William Sydney Porter), who lived on Gramercy Park, wrote a story a week for the *New York World* newspaper, and earned $100 for each—remarkable affluence for a New York writer. The legend goes that he wrote "The Gift of the Magi" in Pete's Tavern, still just around the corner from the park on Irving Place.

Something of a writer's colony grew up around Washington Square in Greenwich Village, the New World's closest equivalent to the Latin Quarter. Theodore Dreiser and Sinclair Lewis both struggled with naturalistic novels there early in their careers. Lincoln Steffens, the New York journalist for whom the word "muckraker" was invented, lived in the village too. Proclaiming that "the city is human nature posing nude," he travelled throughout the country recruiting like-minded writers to join him in New York. One who did was John Reed (author of *Ten Days that Shook the World*). Reed lived at 42 Washington Square (now the address of New York University's law school), and wrote a poem about his apartment:

> In the winter the water is frigid,
> In the summer the water is hot;
> And we're forming a club for controlling the tub

> For there's only one bath to the lot.
> You shave in unlathering Croton,
> If there's water at all, which is rare—
> But the life isn't bad for a talented lad
> At Forty-Two Washington Square.

Reed belonged to a small theater group called the Provincetown Players. It may have been the most talented amateur theatrical group in history—other members were Edna St. Vincent Millay, Sherwood Anderson, E. E. Cummings, and Eugene O'Neill.

Another group of writers, critics, and wits congregated uptown, at a round table in the Rose Room of the Algonquin Hotel on West 44th Street. (The hotel is now owned by a Japanese conglomerate.) Robert Benchley, Alexander Woollcott, George S. Kaufman, and the riveting Mrs. Dorothy Parker formed the inner circle. One afternoon, Mrs. Parker was asked to use the word "horticulture" in a sentence. "You can lead a whore to culture," she instantly replied, "but you can't make her think."

And, farther uptown, the Harlem Renaissance was just getting underway. It was, as the name suggests, a new birth of black writing. Countee Cullen was an early leader; the poet Langston Hughes was an usher at Cullen's wedding in a Harlem church, and a disciple of his work.

All these literary stirrings and rumblings in New York attracted more writers, some of whom came here to write about someplace else. The novelist Willa Cather lived on the Upper East Side and wrote about Nebraska; at the Society Library on East 79th Street she once ran into Truman Capote, another young writer from elsewhere (Alabama) who had come to make his reputation in New York. Sherwood Anderson was physically present in New York City while his imagination populated small towns in the American Midwest, and evoked them in several novels.

The subjects and styles of these uptown, downtown, and out-of-town writers differed; they were not always familiar with one another's work, or even aware that one another existed. Nevertheless, they fermented together in this city, and together they created a literary community, the first New York had known. They were drawn here by New York's growing sophistication and variety; they in turn gave to the city the two essentials of poetry and passion.

Of course, where there are writers there are also editors, and New York's publishing industry continued to thrive. Practically every important American publisher was based in Midtown New York, close to former speakeasies turned literary wateringholes. (The "21" Club on West 52nd Street is one, but it has since degenerated into an expensive see-and-be-seen hangout, and is best avoided.)

Publishing for the most part is a fairly dull business conducted by penny-pinching businessmen, but occasionally an editor will come along who is as much an artist as the writers he works with; great editors, it has been said, are artists whose medium is the work of other artists. One was Maxwell Perkins who, during much of this period, worked for Scribners. Perkins's other artists included Ernest Hemingway, F. Scott Fitzgerald, and Thomas Wolfe.

New York's literary community would prove to be lasting, although its hospitality to writers turned out to be a fleeting thing. After World War II, rents began to rise, and many of the writers who had been dispersed by the war moved to cheaper places. But the template of a literary community remained, and it wasn't too long before a new group of New York writers emerged.

The term *beatnik* seems curiously outdated; its literary equivalent, beat, is hardly ever heard now. And Allen Ginsberg and his fringy, offbeat contemporaries—Gregory Corso, Jack Kerouac, and William Burroughs—are practically grand old men of mainstream American letters today. When they started out, however, they shuttled between the Upper West Side (where Ginsberg was a student at Columbia University) and the Lower East Side (where they took their various pleasures) like ragged urchins. Nobody believed that the free-form, experimental writing they were touting as poetry would ever last. It did, of course. However, the Beat poets did not stay for too long in New York; the whole movement shifted to the West Coast and San Francisco.

In postwar Harlem, James Baldwin, the son of a preacher and a preacher himself for a brief period, brought the original Harlem Renaissance into a more militant phase with his first book, *Go Tell It on the Mountain*. Baldwin too left New York, and settled in France.

The handful of writers who did stay in New York to work had, often as not, sadly truncated lives. Notable among them are the poet Delmore Schwartz, who died an alcoholic in 1966, and Dylan Thomas, who perished in 1953 in St. Vincent's Hospital in the Village after a monumental drinking binge. Clearly there is still something about New York that drives certain writers to Europe or to their deaths.

It's worth mentioning that the exact opposite is true of New York's intellectual community. The city is and has long been a haven for thinkers of all persuasions. Edmund Wilson and Lionel Trilling are two American critics who found employment and success in New York. Philosopher Hannah Arendt and art critic Meyer Schapiro were both refugees from Europe; Arendt taught at the New School for Social Research in the Village, and Schapiro at Columbia University; both became essential parts of the New York intellectual landscape.

What of the current literary situation in the city? Where are the presses hottest, the writers most talented, the poetry most modern? For one thing, publishing houses have moved downtown in recent years, to the lofts and low office buildings around Union Square.

Lunching is a large part of the business. If you were to wander into the **Union Square Café** at one o'clock or so and see a pair of diners, one casually but carefully dressed, the other looking slightly disheveled, you are probably witnessing an expense-account meal between editor (or maybe Roger Strauss of Farrar, Strauss & Giroux) and author. If that evening you wish to go to a real literary wateringhole, you should know that there aren't any left in New York. There are those with historic interest—the **White Horse** in the West Village, where Dylan Thomas hung out, and the **Lion's Head** at 59 Christopher, which has long been a meeting place for journalists from the *Village Voice*. But young writers in New York today tend to frequent the posh restaurant and club scene—those establishments that are photographed for the latest issues of *New York* magazine, *Vanity Fair,* and *Details*.

Instead, one of the best ways to get a good feel for literary New York is to go to the city's bookstores. No city, London included, has so many that are so good. Almost any are worth wandering into and through; below is a highly selective if not idiosyncratic list of some of the best.

## BOOKSTORES

### Downtown

The **Academy Book Store** (10 West 18th Street) is a used bookstore. It is not nearly as large as the Strand (see below) and, as a consequence, the books out on the shelves (about 100,000 at any one time, with 200,000 in reserve) are carefully chosen and rotated regularly. The tone here is generally quite serious; humanistic subjects such as philosophy and history are stressed. The Academy also has a superb collection of used records, including some classic recordings that are elsewhere unavailable.

**Barnes & Noble** (105 Fifth Avenue at 18th Street; 128 Fifth Avenue at 18th Street; and at Columbia University) has about a dozen branches around town, but these three are the only ones worth going to. The main store, at 105 Fifth, has a really remarkable collection of books: shelf upon shelf of the newest fiction and nonfiction in both paperback and hardcover; a large room full of the latest in medical books; and a rear annex of university texts. The sales annex across the street has terrific prices on current books, and an uneven, but immense, selection of overstocks and out-of-prints that are even cheaper. The uptown branch is actually the Columbia University bookstore, but nonstudents are welcome, and the paperback fiction collection is wonderful.

**East West Books** (78 Fifth Avenue at 14th Street) deals in philosophy, spiritualism, and self-help. The emphasis here is on Eastern writers and thinking; the atmosphere in the small store is suitably serene and contemplative.

**Forbidden Planet** (821 Broadway at 12th Street) doesn't look like a bookstore. In fact, it looks a bit like the alien bar in the first Star Wars film. The resemblance must be intentional, for the specialty here is science fiction and fantasy (with a sideline in comics).

The **Strand Book Store** (828 Broadway at 12th Street) claims to have eight miles of books—used, overstocks, out-of-prints, reviewer copies, and some of the oddest paperbacks that have ever been printed. But how anyone could measure anything in this rabbit-warren of a place is a mystery. Whatever the mileage, this is New York's biggest used bookstore, and thus the biggest in the country. By mysterious means, previously owned books from as far away as China end up here. They are arranged by subject, the staff is adept at negotiating the maze of shelves to find what you may be looking for, and you can spend hours browsing through the splendid selection. There is also a section of fine bindings and rare books.

**University Press Books** (65 Fifth Avenue near 14th Street) stocks only a selection of those books published by American, Canadian, and British university presses. Not all are thick, academic tomes; on the contrary, some university press books are quite current. Normally, they are hard to find, but this store makes it easy.

## Midtown

**The Antiquarian Booksellers' International, Inc.** (125 East 59th Street, Gallery 48) is a store/showroom that was founded by a group of rare-book dealers. Browsers are welcome, though, and the books, prints, autographs, maps, and manuscripts on display will provide a brief introduction to the fascinating subject of rare books and incunabula.

**B. Dalton**, the huge chain with outlets across the country, has its flagship store on Fifth Avenue (at 666). There is a vast selection of current titles here, as well as a good stock of standard titles, especially in paperback.

**Coliseum Books** (1771 Broadway at 57th Street) has an amazing number of books, mostly paperback, on all subjects. This is a great place to browse; even if you don't find what you're looking for you will certainly find something you like.

**The Complete Traveller** (199 Madison Avenue at 35th Street) specializes in travel books. It stocks most of the Nagel guides—expensive but authoritative—and also has a terrific selection of maps.

**Doubleday** (724 Fifth Avenue) has several branches, but it's best to shop in this one, at 57th Street. The selection of new fiction is excellent—occasionally, books are on sale here before the official release date. The reference section is also particularly good, and in the store's other special sections, spread out over three floors, you'll find most standard books in stock. The store is open until midnight, six days a week.

**The Gotham Book Mart** (41 West 47th Street) has a sign over the awning that says, "Wise men fish here." Indeed they do, and even the unwise may learn something here. The Gotham has made no concessions to fleeting fashion or modern marketing in its 50 or so years of existence. It remains a book-lover's bookstore, whose new and used collection of poetry, fiction, books on film and the theater, and journals reflects the taste and interests of its founder, Frances Steloff, who was an early reader and supporter of James Joyce, Ezra Pound, Henry Miller, and Dylan Thomas among many others. Give yourself an afternoon, at least, for the Gotham.

**Librairie de France** and **Libreria Hispanica** (610 Fifth Avenue and 115 Fifth Avenue) is actually one store with a downtown branch selling French and Spanish books, tapes, guides, and posters, and English books in translation. The Rockefeller Center store stocks more French books, while the 19th Street store is a bit heavier in the Spanish department.

**Mysterious Book Shop** (129 West 56th Street) is a chummy spot stocked with mysteries of every genre and populated by mystery lovers of every description. Hardcover and paperback, new and used whodunits are available.

**Rizzoli** (31 West 57th Street) is a handsome store where the oak shelves groan under the weight of the finest art, photography, and fashion books published in the United States and Europe. On hand here, too, is one of New York's finest selections of foreign periodicals. Rizzoli's store at 454 West Broadway in SoHo has a similar though smaller selection, with an emphasis on art.

**The Travellers Bookstore** (22 West 52nd Street) is a good place for both real travellers and armchair travellers. The standard guides are here, as well as a good collection of travel writing, old and new, fanciful and factual.

**Urban Center Books** (457 Madison Avenue at 51st Street) is suitably located in the historic Villard Houses, former private residences that are now part of the Helmsley Palace Hotel. The store is run in part by the Municipal Arts Society and stocks 4,000 titles on anything that has to do with cities: architecture, historic preservation, and the like.

## *Uptown: East Side*

**Books and Co.** (939 Madison Avenue at 74th Street) is a relatively new addition to New York's roster of bookstores, and it has won a wide following. This is probably because it's carefully designed to appeal to a toney crowd—classical music plays softly in the background; books about art, philosophy, and literature (with a capital L) are stressed; and there's a well-bred mein to the salespeople. Despite all this niceness, the books here are really quite good, and it's a wonderful place to browse.

**Kitchen Arts & Letters** (1435 Lexington Avenue near 93rd Street) is the right place to go when you're hungry. It stocks cookbooks of every persuasion, and the work of food writers of every kind.

**Military Bookman** (29 East 93rd Street just west of Madison Avenue, in a brownstone ground floor) carries books about military history, from the taking of Troy onward, although the emphasis is on classic battles of older wars. Some of the books are rare and quite valuable, posters and periodicals are in stock, and the salespeople here are nice as well as knowledgeable.

**Wittenborn Art Books** (1018 Madison Avenue at 78th Street) is, as its name suggests, an art bookshop. The definition of art here, however, is broad enough to include books about archaeology and fashion—and not all the books on sale are necessarily in English; they just have to be good.

## Uptown: West Side

**Applause Theatre Books** (211 West 71st Street) deals mainly in drama—British, American, and European—in anthologies, annotated versions, and single play books. Although there is an emphasis on British drama, it is not necessarily serious; it's possible to find, for instance, a collection of Monty Python skits. Applause also has a branch that specializes in the cinema at 100 West 67th Street.

**Eeyore's** (2212 Broadway near 78th Street and 25 East 83rd west of Madison) is probably the best children's bookstore in the country. The stores have a unique service: They will select and send books to kids at summer camp.

The **Gryphon Bookshop** (2246 Broadway near 80th Street, with an annex upstairs around the corner) sells used books and records. The selection is good, particularly in the children's section where all (it seems) of the Oz books are available in any edition you would care to own. Used records are also on sale; in the annex some of the books have been marked down.

**Murder Ink.** (271 West 87th Street) sells mysteries, new

and used. The books are arranged according to an impenetrable shelving system, but the salespeople can produce titles at will.

**Papyrus Books** (2915 Broadway at 114th Street) is not worth a special trip uptown, but if you are in the neighborhood, you should certainly stop by. It has a good collection of new and used fiction, particularly paperbacks, but it has a truly amazing collection of periodicals. You'll have no trouble finding *Nicaraguan Perspectives* here, for instance.

**Shakespeare and Company** (2259 Broadway at 81st Street) is an Upper West Side institution, and on sunny Sunday afternoons it gets almost as crowded as next-door Zabar's. The stock of new fiction and nonfiction here reflects the neighborhood: eclectic, offbeat, and brainy.

# OTHER SHOPPING

*By Lynn Yaeger*

It stands to reason, New York City being as it is the home base for eccentric, offbeat, oddball citizens who have emigrated here from all over the globe, that attendant unusual shops have sprung up to meet their peculiar needs. "There's a nut for every street lamp in New York," as the saying goes, and often enough there's a store shimmering under that light as well. People only visiting us will want to avail themselves of our plethora of one-of-a-kind, out-of-the-way venues in order to carry back to their peaceful homes talismans of Manhattan life.

## HOUSEWARES

Those who would rather equip their homes than themselves face an almost unlimited selection of domicile-related shops and items. Postmodernists will find matte-black metal and glass home accessories at the always mobbed **D. F. Sanders** (386 West Broadway between Spring and Broome Streets and 952 Madison Avenue at 75th Street); accompanying plain boudoir furnishings—namely the rigorously streamlined bedroll known as the futon—can be purchased at the **Futon Shop** (491 Broadway, between Spring and Broome). Parties who prefer a Georgia O'Keeffeian southwestern atmosphere in their sitting rooms can pick up a bleached animal skull from **Maxilla & Mandible** (78 West 82nd). Wicker furnishings, having recently expanded their scope beyond the exclusivity of the sagging summer porch and now bedecking rooms for all seasons, are in good supply at **Deutsch** (31 East 32nd Street). Handmade quilts to drape over the backs of these notoriously uncomfortable settees and fainting couches can be had from the **Seventeenth Street Gallery** (132 East 17th). Possessors of ill-shaped windows, who travel with or have memorized the dimensions of their unfortunate vitrines, can order custom-made lace-patterned French-style curtains from the always charming **Wolfman-Gold & Good** (116 Greene Street near Prince).

Linens are the specialty at **E. Braun** (717 Madison near 64th Street), an old-fashioned holdover from the days when Madison Avenue was just the local shopping street for rich people. **Descamps** (723 Madison) has modern, very popular sheets, towels, and pillowcases from and for upper-crust France. At **Christofle Pavillon** (680 Madison) silver-plated flatware and other more elaborate items appeal to the conservative, good-taste crowd, while across the street, **Georg Jensen** (683 Madison) flogs the Scandinavian design items that have been staples of the ritzy (but unglitzy) home for more than 40 years.

Shoppers who wish to buy into the English country-home look (of late smothering rooms all over America under oceans of chintz, mottled and faded carpeting, and hairy dogs) should head to **Evyan** (711 Fifth Avenue between 55th and 56th streets) for tabletops full of miniature English enameled porcelain boxes, and then uptown to **G. Elter** (740 Madison), where antique reproduction picture frames can be purchased. Other dust collectors can be found at the **Mediterranean Shop** (876 Madison), where hand-painted faux naïf pottery is the specialty, and the line includes some unusual items like slotted pencil cups and place-card holders. Your castle walls, albeit sagging beneath the groaning display of oil-painted Irish setters and dead relatives, should include some of mummy's needlepoint, which can be made up from kits purchased at **Erica Wilson** (717 Madison, in the same building as E. Braun). If the duke and duchess and their 15 progeny are ambling over to dinner, matching silver for incomplete sets of flatwear may be located at **Jean Silversmith** (16 West 45th). After supping, recline on Fortuny-inspired Venetian pillows from **Portantina**, the narrow velvet-encased shop at 886 Madison.

## PERSONAL EMBELLISHMENT

The number of small stores in Manhattan catering to the whims and fancies of the eccentric shopper is practically uncountable. Tiny variations in personal embellishment and style assume enormous proportions in this town, and new visitors will no doubt be taken aback by the seriousness of the pursuit.

A whole shop, **Tender Buttons** (143 East 62nd), splendid as an art gallery, is devoted to these humble items—antique, vintage, and new—sometimes made up into cuff links or earrings, but most often left in their natural state to adorn your most prosaic garments. (Those eschewing this high-class enclave and yearning for wholesale ribbons, laces, and trimmings are directed to the area of Sixth Avenue in the high 30s, where cardboard boxes showcase the wares, and trading, though brisk, will tolerate the retail customer.) Persons who wish to purchase leather skins straight off the animal's back should go to **Grosz Leather** (70 Spring Street in SoHo), a shop selling ordinary to obscure hides.

To distinguish yourself with a swaggering gait, pick up a walking stick or cane, as well as all manner of umbrellas, at **Uncle Sam** (161 West 57th). Or go even further: Purchase a leather riding crop at **M. J. Knoud** (716 Madison) or **Kauffmans** (139 East 24th) or **Millers** (123 East 24th), all of which are equestrian stores selling boots, bits, feed bags, jodhpurs, and fashionable riding habits.

Shoppers in search of the lost world of bohemian Greenwich Village may be inspired, after an interval of watching the perennial chess players at the southwest corner of Washington Square Park, to purchase a chess set of their own, available in an impressive range of styles and prices from **The Chess Shop** (230 Thompson Street). The **Glori Bead Shoppe** (172 West 4th Street) will supply appropriate strands for the neck, wrist, and ears of a surviving Joan Baez look-alike. Sinister sunglasses can be selected from an array at **Shades of the Village** (167 Seventh Avenue South).

The studious traveller, desiring neither riding crop nor rawhide, may still be able to do some satisfying shopping in New York. Exquisitely marbleized Venetian papers, in the form of stationery but also made up to cover a wide range of desk accessories, are for sale at **Il Papiro** (1021

Lexington and in Herald Center across 34th Street from Macy's). The correct pen and/or pencil for the scholarly-journal underliner is at **Arthur Brown** (2 West 46th); the right cigar for late-night musing at **Nat Sherman** (711 Fifth Avenue). Horn-rimmed or tortoiseshell-framed spectacles (as well as some other examples of the most stylish eyeglasses in the city) are at **Joel Name** (65 West Houston and 353 Bleecker) and **Robert Marc** (190 Columbus Avenue and 1046 Madison).

## ETHNIC SHOPPING

Despite varying tendencies among New Yorkers to alternately embrace and deny their immigrant origins, shops catering to merchandise from the old country abound. In addition, disparate nationalities continue to arrive and, once here, open specialty shops importing goods associated with the life left behind.

Although in no way comparable to their numbers 50 or even 30 years ago, there are still plenty of Irish in Manhattan whose ancestral longings can be assuaged by a visit to **Shamrock Imports** (205 East 75th), where, among a selection of emerald-green ephemera, hand-knit fisherman sweaters, wide caps, and *claddagh* rings are available. Fiercely nationalist remnants of the Ukrainian community, still hanging on in the rapidly gentrifying East Village, go to **Surma** (11 East 7th Street) for traditional painted Easter eggs and embroidered linens. Though burgeoning Chinese immigration is pushing northward beyond Canal Street and spilling into the Little Italy area, the Mulberry Street corridor continues, for the time being, to sell ornate Italian pottery, posters of Sophia Loren, and cappuccino machines. Chinatown's endurance as a tourist attraction, meanwhile, supports the type of (souvenir-laden) stores you would anticipate.

The needs of those recently arrived from India are met by a variety of stores located in the area of Park Avenue South in the 20s. Sari fabric off the bolt and sticks of incense are always available, and there are numerous other products less immediately accessible to the North American consumer. Those other Indians—the ones Americans like to watch on TV westerns—are an almost strictly imaginary community in New York City. Their indigenous merchandise, however, is available at a number of venues, among them the Village's **Common Ground** (50 Greenwich Avenue), handling baskets, weavings, and silver and turquoise jewelry.

Antique and modern Japanese kimonos are available in the East Village at **Yuzen** (318 East 6th Street) and due west at **Shinbi** (55 Greenwich Avenue). Tibetan textiles, mirrored caps, silver charm bracelets, and other accessories from Tibet's far-flung outposts have found a peaceful home in the heart of the West Village at **Tibet West** (19 Christopher Street). Visitors whose taste remains deeply entrenched south of the equator will like **Craft Caravan** (63 Greene Street), which sells African handcrafted tin toys among other artifacts. From this hemisphere, Mexican folkloric furniture, pottery, and glass are sold at **Amigo Country** (19 Greenwich Avenue).

## TOYS AND GADGETS

Although there remain in Manhattan a number of toy stores dedicated exclusively to a clientele composed of the under-12 set, many places that specialize in these types of things (games, kits, tricks, gadgets, miniatures) also cater to an adult audience that can't seem to get enough of this merchandise. **Mythology** (370 Columbus on the Upper West Side) is full of faddish robots, inflated dinosaurs, and the like, and is always packed with young prodigies and their proud parents. **Sweet Asylum** (416 Amsterdam), around the corner, has much lower-brow merchandise—shrunken heads, naughty alarm clocks—which nevertheless has been known to produce unsuppressible gurgles of amusement. **The Last Wound-Up** (290 Columbus at 73rd Street, 889 Broadway at 19th Street, and at the South Street Seaport) got famous selling mechanical toys, and the range of sizes and prices remains exhaustive. At **B. Shackman** (85 Fifth Avenue) the specialty is reproduction Victoriana manifested in bisque-headed dolls, paper ephemera, and miniatures, including dollhouse furniture. Prices are always inviting. Those readers obsessed with the diminutive (and this includes the growing number of adults who like to play with dollhouses) should visit **Gulliver's** (50 Grove Street in the West Village) for a full line of stunted furniture and accessories.

Children who enjoy annoying others by performing tedious magic tricks (and who among us does not know at least one of these small persons) will benefit from a trip to **Hornmann Magic Co.**, located upstairs in the office building at 45 West 34th Street. Youngsters (as well as certain older persons) whose idea of a brilliant practical joke rests at the level of the whoopie cushion should head for **Jimsons** (30 East 18th Street), where kindred items crowd the chaotic shelves.

The young science and science-fiction fanatic should visit **Forbidden Planet** (821 Broadway at 12th Street), where comic books and merchandise pack two stories in an atmosphere that can only be described as scholarly. Dungeons and Dragons partisans will enjoy the **Compleat Strategist** (11 East 33rd), a place filled with stimulating boxed mind-games and patronized by a passionate group of any-age devotees. Visitors seeking to take a break from mental activity can indulge themselves at **Go Fly A Kite** (1201 Lexington Avenue between 81st and 82nd streets), where the merchandise, once properly constructed, will (assumably) soar.

Of course, try as you may, some things remain deeply embedded in one's childish years, and must inevitably be put away as one grows older. At the famous **F.A.O. Schwartz** (767 Fifth Avenue at 59th Street) the merchandise is insufferably young, and, assuming you can abide the giant singing clock at the entrance ("Welcome to our world, welcome to our world of toys"), you'll find the scope and selection to be more than impressive. Tiny infants (are there any other kind?) can be mollified with a cozy, affectionate stuffed toy, the kind that grandma used to make, still handmade by anonymous grandmas at the charitable **New York Exchange for Woman's Work** (660 Madison). **The Lighthouse** (111 East 59th), which sells items handcrafted by the visually impaired, has extremely inexpensive crocheted farm and barn animals, of which the pastel kangaroo-en-famille is especially engaging.

## UNCLASSIFIABLE ODDITIES

Defying every attempt to codify, classify, or otherwise order Manhattan shopping venues, certain stores stand proudly outside the law of rational organization. These places sell what would be considered unsalable outside a great metropolis, and are often the chief reason people fall in love with New York City.

Prototypical of this breed of store is **Rita Ford's Music Boxes** (19 East 65th), a 19th-century sort of place featuring obviously tuneful, if not inexpensive, merchandise. At the other end of town, **It's Only Rock N Roll** (49 West 8th Street) serves a far different clientele with vintage record albums, back issues of fanzines, and assorted pop memorabilia. Old radios and phonographs (Edison wind-ups through the Art Deco years) are for sale at **Waves** (32 East 13th Street). Contemporaneous movie posters, lobby cards, and other motion picture ephemera are available at Jerry Ohlinger's **Movie Material Store** (242 West 14th Street between Seventh and Eighth avenues). A few blocks farther south is **Mouse N' Around** (197 Bleecker between Sixth Avenue and MacDougal), a mercantile homage to Disney, featuring Mickey-embellished items in a silly, slap-happy atmosphere. Likewise, **Little Rickie** (49½ First Avenue at 3rd Street), with its 1960s ephemera, Barbie-related accessories, and one of the last extant black-and-white photo booth machines in town, appeals to the laugh-riot crowd. The inveterate collector of baseball cards can visit **Jeff's** (150 Second Avenue between 9th and 10th streets). Those preoccupied with the pursuit of mummified butterflies will not want to miss the very pleasant **Mariposa** (128 Thompson Street in SoHo).

Unusual telephones (in the shape of, say, juicy puckered lips, Snoopy dogs, or cheeseburgers) are for sale at the **Phone Booth** (12 East 53rd). Set this next to a raw gemstone from **Astro Mineral** (155 East 34th) for stolen moments of contemplation. Utilitarian restaurant china and glass, not usually sold on a per-piece basis, can be found at **Wooden Indian** (60 West 15th). The vintage red, blue, and white ocean-liner tableware is especially desirable.

Travellers who desire high-quality gadgetry should visit **Hammacher Schlemmer** (147 East 57th), famous for upper-class items on the order of bun-warming frankfurter steamers and solar-charged garden sprayers. Less rarefied, though still amusing, items can be examined at **The Sharper Image** (4 West 57th), and younger visitors will undoubtedly enjoy the thought-provoking widgets (microscopes, fossils, and the like) sold by **The Nature Company** (8 Fulton Street in the Financial District).

Readers who have long since acknowledged that a gadget won't solve their problems and are still searching for answers can investigate **The Magickal Childe** (35 East 19th) or **Enchantments** (341 East 9th Street), both of which serve New York's active witch and warlock community.

Lastly, visitors desperately thrashing in the throes of wretched homesickness should pull themselves together long enough to visit **Hotalings**, the gigantic news dealer smack in the middle of Manhattan at 142 West 42nd Street. If there's anyplace in town that carries a copy of your hometown paper, this is it.

# FOOD

*By Dean J. Seal*

*Dean J. Seal was formerly associate editor of the* U.S. Food Journal, *a trend monitor of the American food industry. He is now the associate publisher of the* Manhattan Catalog *and a frequent contributor to food-related magazines.*

This international city on the go, trying to cram as much living as it can into the smallest amount of time possible, is geared to the traveller who wants to do the same. So the current trend of fresh, already prepared take-out foods for people with taste and money—but no time—directly benefits those visitors who wish to eat on the run, in the park, or back at the hotel.

## *COMING TO MARKET*

Meat comes into New York on the west side of Greenwich Village, by the Hudson River. Whole loins of choice beef can be had at a steep discount, if you know what you want, and a visit to **Florent**, a 24-hour neighborhood restaurant at 69 Gansevoort Street in the area, is alone worth the trip.

Fishing boats have unloaded at the **Fulton Fish Market** at the South Street Seaport (east end of Fulton Street next to the Financial District downtown) for more than a hundred years. Tours can be arranged, but be aware that the market opens at 3:00 A.M. The Fulton retail shop, though it may be less picturesque, keeps more reasonable hours and is geared to serving the public.

The Hunts Point Terminal Produce Market in the Bronx calls itself the world's largest single produce market, supplying the needs of both grocers and restaurants. However, many prefer one of the "greenmarkets" the city sponsors around town. Three—Union Square, West 77th Street at Columbus Avenue (Sundays only), and Federal Plaza—are year-round, and another dozen locations host seasonal markets. The produce, wine, flowers, and honey from four states get top ratings for freshness and quality.

## SPECIAL EVENTS

Some neighborhoods sponsor street fairs and festivals, which usually include food specialties of the area. The **Feast of San Gennaro**, held for two weeks at the end of September in Little Italy, for example, is an orgy of sausage-and-pepper sandwiches; and the **Ninth Avenue International Festival** (south from around 42nd Street) in May draws a million eaters to sample diverse ethnic fare. More than 60 fairs take place annually in the five boroughs.

As a convention city, New York also hosts special events for the food industry. Among them is the megashow at the Jacob K. Javits Convention Center, which combines the New York Food and Beverage, Gourmet Products, Entirely Tabletop, and Glass and China shows all at once every fall. Consult the New York Convention & Visitors Bureau at 2 Columbus Circle (58th Street and Eighth Avenue; Tel: 212-397-8222) for specifics on fairs, festivals, and conventions.

## SEASONAL FOODS

Given the variety of foods imported to New York, a diner here is almost totally free of seasonal restrictions. If there is something you want to eat, you can get it here. Everything is coming in all the time. As Douglas Levy of gourmet caterers Fisher and Levy says, "When it's winter here, it's summer somewhere else. In this day and age of cargo planes, you can find anything you want for a price." But there are seasonal highlights. Fall and spring are best for deep-water halibut; summer visitors can look forward to shad roe (a mass of shad eggs, best done gently, steamed or poached) and soft-shell crab (blue crabs recently molted, that can be crunched down shell and all, cooked on a fast, high heat by broiling or sautéing in butter and capers). Abalone oysters are here in spring, summer, and fall. Fruits and vegetables to watch for include broccoli, apples, and pears in the winter and fall, as well as a variety of squash; and fiddlehead ferns in fall. Spring is the time for spring cherries and blackberries in welcome abundance. And New York is one of the few places where Long Island duck can be had fresh, not frozen. And if you really want to indulge in indigenous food from the city itself, Steve "Wildman" Brill will give you a free tour of Central Park, pointing out edible foods that can be harvested there, like mushrooms, carrots, nectarines, mustard greens, and various berries. You can't get any fresher. (Call Steve at 718-291-6825.)

# *EATING ON THE RUN*

Manhattan's neighborhoods differ in age, makeup, and traditions, but they all share accessible food sellers that cater to America's toughest, most mobile clientele.

## Upper West Side

The food mecca of this newly gentrified neighborhood is the **Silver Palate** (Columbus between 72nd and 73rd). This tiny room gave birth to a nationally distributed packaged-goods business and two best-selling cookbooks; a gastronomically historic spot. For fresh produce, Broadway offers **Fairway** (between 74th and 75th), with heaps of fruits and vegetables, a great cheese department, and some of the most outrageous signs ever (Fresh Figs, Raw Sex, Same Thing).

Nonetheless, the hot spot is **Zabar's**, 2245 Broadway (between 80th and 81st), arguably the best food (and kitchen equipment) store in the world. It's famous for top-quality smoked fish, sausages, caviar, coffee, and cheeses; a cookware selection that is complete and competitive; and a take-out deli that cannot be beat. When it's open, it's busy, and when it's busy, it's a nuthouse. It is the only mandatory stop on this tour.

## Upper East Side

This is reputedly the richest neighborhood in the world, and this wealth is apparent in the food available. Mango curried chicken salad, fresh mozzarella with tomatoes and basil, exotic ham sandwiches on freshly baked bread abound at notables like Neuman & Bogdonoff (1385 Third Avenue between 78th and 79th streets), Fraser-Morris (931 Madison at 74th), William Poll (1051 Lexington between 74th and 75th), and the multiple locations of August and Co.

Yorkville, in the northeast, is the home of an old German neighborhood, featuring **Bremen House** at 218 East 86th Street near Third Avenue. Hungarians and Czechs maintain cooking traditions at shops like **Paprikas Weiss**, 1546 Second Avenue between 80th and 81st, the best source for Middle European spices. For Western European spices try **Saint Remy**, at 818 Lexington off 62nd Street, which specializes in French herbs and spices. **Ottomanelli Brothers**, at 1549 York (82nd Street), is known for game. Two of the most modern gourmet places are on Third Avenue: **Sweet Victory**, near 67th Street (pizza, ice cream, and restaurant serving low-calorie, high-flavor foods), and **Gourmet Gazelle**, between 69th and 70th (superb lo-cal deli).

Great bakeries flourish, notably two on East 78th Street between First and Second avenues: **Orwasher's** for bread and neighboring **Rigo** for "Hungarian Viennese" pastries. And the country's leading food bookstore is here, **Kitchen Arts & Letters**, at 1435 Lexington, between 93rd and 94th. Finally, **Grace Balducci's Marketplace** (from the famed Balducci family), at 1237 Third Avenue between 71st and 72nd, is a great grocery, where the superb produce, meats and cheeses, and deli are imbued with a warm Italian flavor.

# Midtown

This heart of corporate headquarters is a great place for lunch, except from noon to 1:00 P.M. Before or after this rush try **Piatti Pronti** for sandwiches (34 West 56th Street), or **Savories**, downstairs next to the skating rink/café in the 30 Rockefeller Center concourse, for take-out food of all types. Specialty stores attest to the proximity of the United Nations and the presence of international businessmen: **Caviarteria** (caviar and vodka), 29 East 60th between Madison and Park; **Petrossian** (caviar and smoked fish), 182 West 58th at Seventh Avenue; **Old Denmark** (smorgasbord and café), 133 East 65th between Lexington and Park; **Maison Glass** (European spices), 52 East 58th between Park and Madison; **Nyborg and Nelson** (Swedish and Scandinavian foods), 153 East 53rd at Lexington; and **Katagiri** (Japanese), 224 East 59th between Second and Third avenues. For one-stop shopping, try **Macy's Cellar**. It's a selection of "boutique" outlets of small Manhattan specialists like Ottomanelli and Gourmet Gazelle, plus Macy's own departments to fill out the line. You might find a few bargains, but mostly they offer quality and convenience with acceptable service.

## Ninth Avenue

Host to the biggest street food fair in the city (late May), Ninth Avenue in the 30s and 40s offers a cornucopia of international foods. In close proximity to one another is a clutch of some of the best. Greek pastries with mouthwatering phyllo are at **Poseidon Bakery**, number 629 between 44th and 45th. Bargain fish, served fresh by a smart staff, is at **Central Fish Co.**, number 527 between 39th and 40th. Next door is **International Grocery Store**, famous for spices and baby lamb and kid, at number 529. For Italian sausage and suckling pig, go down to **Esposito & Sons Pork Store**, number 500 at 38th Street. And top it off with a visit to java headquarters at **Empire Coffee and Tea**, number 486 between 37th and 38th, for 75 different kinds of coffee beans and a similar selection of herbs, teas, and spices.

## Greenwich Village

The West Village is New York's single best spot for buying food. Specialists proliferate: pasta (Raffetto's, 144 West Houston between Sullivan and MacDougal); pork (Faicco's, 260 Bleecker at Sixth Avenue); spices (Aphrodisia, 282 Bleecker Street, between Sixth and Seventh avenues, for a wide selection of culinary and medicinal herbs; Casa Moneo, 210 West 14th Street, between Seventh and Eighth avenues, for Latino spices); bread (Zito's Bakery, the best Italian baker in town, 259 Bleecker Street between Sixth and Seventh avenues); and coffee (Schapira, which roasts their own, at 117 West 10th Street between Greenwich and Sixth avenues; McNulty's Tea & Coffee, 109 Christopher Street between Bleecker and Hudson; and Longo's, also called Porto Rico Importing, at 201 Bleecker Street between Sixth Avenue and MacDougal Street).

**Jefferson Market**, on Sixth Avenue between 10th and 11th, is long on service and expertise for their meats and fishes, superb choices, and reasonable pricing, plus a selection of gourmet goodies. But **Balducci's**, a block south at 424 Sixth, is the real Italian treat. They have what may be the best produce selection in town, a dynamite deli, cheeses and charcuterie for the ages, and an extensive mail-order system. Balducci's is more authentic than anything in Little Italy; you will sense a real love of food here, springing from three generations of tradition. Crowds can be competitive for all this good stuff, so try to come off-peak.

## Little India

In this neighborhood (Lexington Avenue in the 20s) that offers incredibly cheap Indian restaurants are also a few places to dig up staples and exotic spices of that national cuisine. **Spice and Sweet Mahal**, at 135 Lexington Avenue at 29th Street, is the place for Indian sweets. **Tashjian Kalustiyan** is herb and spice headquarters for Indian and Middle Eastern groceries and spices; find them at 123 Lexington Avenue between 28th and 29th streets. **Annapurna Indian Groceries**, at 126 East 28th Street between Park and Lexington, is a great place not only for hot spices but also is an information vortex about all things of India. **Foods of India**, at 120 Lexington Avenue at 28th Street, is the most extensive, including cooking utensils, spices, and an energetic staff.

## Lower East Side

After perusing the latest schmattas in the punked-out East Village, a visit to the old Jewish areas of the Lower East Side can be a soothing return to reality. Russians, Ukrainians, and Poles mingle on East Houston Street, awaiting the kosher delights of **Yonah Schimmel**'s knishes (number 137); **Ben's Cheese Shop**'s cream cheese and farmer cheese (number 181); or **Russ and Daughters** for Nova, lox, smoked fish, and caviar (number 179). (Calvin Trillin singled out Russ's and Ben's as Best in Class for the perfect cream cheese and lox combo.) Bialys can be had fresh at **Kossar's** (367 Grand Street), and Ukrainian meat specialties are available at **Kurowycky Meat Products** (124 First Avenue). **Bernstein-on-Essex** (between Stanton and Rivington) calls itself the first-ever kosher Chinese restaurant, and they also have a *glatt* (strictly) kosher deli for, among other things, kosher won tons (Chinese kreplach) or Romanian pastrami fried rice. Finally, hit the **Second Avenue Deli** (at 10th Street) for traditional Yiddish K rations: kasha, kugel, kishke, and knaidel. (The *Journal of Gastronomy* quotes an exchange that could have been heard anywhere around here. Customer: "I don't like the looks of this whitefish." Waiter: "You want looks, you shoulda ordered goldfish!") Finally, one of the great unheralded spice emporiums is **Angelica's Herb and Spice Company**, 137 First Avenue between 8th and 9th, featuring over 2,500 varieties of herbs and spices.

## SoHo and TriBeCa

Aside from modern-design stores and renowned art galleries, SoHo also offers a place to find artistically prepared food. **Dean & DeLuca** (560 Broadway at Prince Street) has been a pioneer of better eating in America, deserving of the moniker "the Rolls Royce of food shops." Food to go, great breads, cheeses, oils, coffees, and esoterica make this place second only to Zabar's, and then just barely. The store also has cookware and cookbook departments and does a strong mail-order business. Worth a special trip; expensive only compared to places that offer less.

TriBeCa is an emerging neighborhood for artists and stockbrokers, but it has two established food specialists too. **Cheese of All Nations** (153 Chambers Street between Greenwich Avenue and West Broadway) is not kidding—they have everything. They allow sampling, they ship, and they put together gift packages. There is also **Commodities Natural Foods** (117 Hudson at North Moore Street), for a huge selection of organic whole foods.

## Little Italy and Chinatown

Aside from the pastry that can be had almost anywhere in Little Italy, the **Italian Food Center** at 186 Grand Street and the **Alleva Dairy**, next door, are the only two spots for special Italian materials. The first is a complete source for all things Italian, the second specializes in ricotta and mozzarella.

Chinatown offers a much more vibrant street scene, especially in the fish markets. A department store of all things Chinese, including foods and cookware, is **Kam Man** (Golden Gate) at 200 Canal. But nose around the neighborhood for little stands, especially the one that sells what can only be called Chinese doughnut holes, made for a dollar a dozen right in front of you.

## The Other Four Boroughs

Brooklyn has a Middle Eastern contingent on Atlantic Avenue, a big Russian community at Brighton Beach, West Indians in Flatbush, a thriving community of Poles in Greenpoint, and three distinct Jewish communities: Hasids in Williamsburg, Lubavitchers in Crown Heights, and Sephardics on Kings Highway and in the Borough Park area. Queens is home to many Greeks, in Astoria; Chinese, Japanese, Indians, and Koreans, in Flushing; and, in Jackson Heights, an old-fashioned immigrant neighborhood with a new-fashioned selection of immigrant foodstuffs: Argentine, Colombian, Cuban, Peruvian, Filipino, Salvadoran, Thai, Indian, and Irish populations all offer up at least a restaurant or two of home-style cooking, and most also have a store that stocks the essentials of their culinary heritage. To get to Jackson Heights, take the number 7 subway from Times Square or Grand Central to the 69th Street/Fisk stop for the Filipino area, or get off at any of the next four stops (74th, 82nd, or 90th streets or Junction Boulevard) for the Latin areas. There are Italian enclaves in all five boroughs.

*The Food Lover's Guide to the Real New York* is an excellent source for finding these areas, though the coverage for Manhattan is curiously spotty.

### SHOPPING FOR GOURMET ITEMS

Restaurateur Alice Waters once said, "I think transportation, in general, is a bad thing." This is true for many foods, but not all. Prepared foods like smoked fish, packaged goods like caviar or wine, most chocolates, and baked items like bagels can travel well, especially if they are bought the day of your departure.

Many delis put their prepared foods in containers so durable that they could conceivably be used to bring things all the way back home. When in doubt, ask the people who are selling it to you if the item is something that travels well and if it needs to have more than the usual protective wrapping. Many places also have selections of gift baskets of their most popular, and most portable, foods. Just ask. Any of the big five—Zabar's, Dean & DeLuca, Balducci's, Grace's, or Macy's Cellar—can help you with this. Other specialty shops named here and elsewhere can do this too; again, don't be shy.

For wine, four stores stand out. **Garnet Liquors** (929 Lexington, between 68th and 69th) offers the best prices for those who know what they want. **D. Sokolin**, on Madison between 33rd and 34th, offers the best learning experience for those who want to know more, with reasonable prices. **Morrell & Company**, 535 Madison (between 54th and 55th), offers the best selection, especially of exotic, rare, and expensive wines, and has an excellent staff. And **Sherry-Lehmann**, 679 Madison, has probably the best selection of New York State wines.

This town loves chocolate and has a selection of Belgian (Godiva, Le Chocolatier Manon), Swiss (Neuchatel, Teuscher), and Italian (Perugina). But the hometown entries—**Li-Lac** in the West Village (120 Christopher) and **Mondel**, 2913 Broadway at West 114th Street, by Columbia—have their own fans. Mondel has a great diet chocolate (How do they do it?), and Li-Lac has a wicked fudge they've been making since 1923. Li-Lac also has an endearing habit of closing when they've sold enough for the day, so go early.

## SHOPPING FOR GOURMET COOKWARE

For regular home cookware, try **Conran's** first, not only because they have a number of locations (at the Citicorp building in Midtown, on Astor Place in the Village, and at Broadway and 82nd Street on the Upper West Side), but also because their quality gets very high marks, and they use their international buying clout to get great stuff worldwide for cheap. **Cook World**, operated by Lamstons at 205 East 42nd Street, Sixth Avenue at 56th, and also at the World Trade Center, has an excellent selection. For the more adventurous, **Bridge Kitchenware** at 214 East 52nd Street, between Second and Third avenues, has the best selection and top quality, but they discourage retail customers, preferring the pros. So go only if you know what you want, because service is scarce.

**Robin Importers**, 510 Madison Avenue at 46th, has a decent selection of knives and tablewear, and they offer good prices too. **Zabar's** has a great selection of equipment and is relatively competitive in general cookware but is very good in discounting kitchen appliances, like CuisinArts. You can also get occasional loss leaders here. **Macy's** has a pretty good selection, but high prices to match.

There is a street of suppliers where the pros go for kitchen equipment, and if you want the very best deals, you should go there, too: the Bowery, between Houston

Street and Cooper Square. The neighborhood is a bit gamey and should not be visited alone, but **King Glassware**, at 112 Bowery at Grand Street, can be worth it. From major appliances to small gadgets, everything is at hand here, and most of it for just 10 percent above wholesale. Top chefs call it the best source, period.

# AFTER HOURS

## DINING

*By Andy Birsh*

*Since 1978 Andy Birsh has edited New York's* The Restaurant Reporter. *He is also a contributing editor to* Gourmet *magazine, for which he writes a monthly column on New York dining.*

The standard estimate of the number of restaurants in the city of New York is 15,000. Even by limiting the word "restaurant" to mean just those places where gracious and potentially enjoyable full meals are served, the number is still in the low four figures. In other words, there are years and years of interesting lunches and dinners to be had in New York—and one of the amazing things about longtime New Yorkers is the number, and the variety, of these meals that they have consumed. New Yorkers virtually live in restaurants, and restaurants easily outstrip any other sort of public place when it comes to where New Yorkers spend their often hard-won free time.

What follows is a selective survey of places to eat in Manhattan (with some forays to other boroughs). These are restaurants that please New Yorkers and convey the flavor of the city as well as the flavors of the many culinary styles that have made a home for themselves here. Missing are establishments whose tables are mostly filled with weary tourists, and missing, too, are many fine places that could easily have been included had space permitted.

Exact prices are not quoted, but general levels of expense may be gauged from the descriptions of the restaurants. Bear in mind that eating out in New York is more expensive than eating out nearly anywhere else. An ample meal that is inexpensive in relative terms will probably cost $25 to $30 per person, once drinks, sales tax, and an expected gratuity of at least 15 percent are factored in. Dinners in the middle of the local range are liable to run $40 to $60 per person (on the bottom line), and dinners at the topflight places can easily top $100 per person without anyone's ordering caviar and Champagne.

But while New York's restaurants can reveal the city at its most extravagant they can also show it at its wisest and simplest; they preserve its oldest ways and make some daring stabs at the future; some exemplify the city's competitive, fame-seeking edge, while others offer blessed relief from it. They can also provide travellers from anywhere on earth with what may be the most delightful mealtimes they will ever know.

All restaurants listed are in Manhattan or the Bronx (area code 212) unless stated otherwise.

## *ITALIAN*

In the late 1980s the Italian strain of restaurant propagates faster than any other. Indeed, a successful Italian restaurant worthy of its fresh, light tomato sauce must necessarily spawn other successful Italian restaurants within a couple of years, or people might begin to suspect that the original joint wasn't really so good. New York's Italian cooking, with roots in every corner of Italy, is what New Yorkers prefer to eat most often when they go out, and travellers to the city are usually amazed by the quantum leap in quality that Italian cooking here makes over that in most of the rest of America.

The portion of the Lower East Side that is still called **Little Italy** (in spite of the near-total relocation of Italian-Americans to the suburbs) teems with Sicilian and Neapolitan restaurants, many of which, unfortunately, serve dreary food. There are exceptions. **Villa Pensa**, at 198 Grand Street near Mulberry, which has been discreetly in business since 1898 and has been owned by only two families, makes its own excellent ravioli and manicotti, one of which will do very nicely halfway between an antipasto and some veal or chicken. The same specials have been offered on the same days of the week for generations. Caruso and Valentino ate here. Tel: 226-8830.

Far newer is **Taormina**, a spacious, bright, immaculately maintained establishment nearby at 147 Mulberry Street that is somewhat more expensive than Villa Pensa. Big tables convey a sense that families of 12 are always welcome, and the circulating antipasto cart is a nicely dated touch. The very exacting chef-proprietor is descended from cooks in the noble houses of Naples. Tel: 219-1007.

People, well . . . mostly guys, who have been waiting all week, or all their lives, to behave disgracefully in public head unerringly for **Puglia**, at 189 Hester Street near Mulberry. The kitchen does nothing to distract them from the rowdiness at hand, and the management has the decency to charge very little for what it sends out. Tel: 226-8912.

Greenwich Village, particularly on the blocks around certain churches, is also a longtime Italian enclave; and here some restaurants have also had their doors open for decades, such as the readily affordable **Grand Ticino**, at 228 Thompson Street near West 3rd, or **Villa Mosconi**, at 69 MacDougal Street. Others are part of a Florentine tide of eateries that has brought real trattoria fare to an area that ought to have a few real trattorias. **Cent'Anni**, at 50 Carmine Street (between Bleecker and Bedford just west of Sixth Avenue), has simple decor and a tiny kitchen, but is justly renowned for its cooking. Garlic, wild mushrooms, handfuls of fresh herbs, and rich fruity olive oils find their way into a remarkable range of dishes, which includes perhaps the best bowl of soup in New York. Add some rare Tuscan wines and the check will start to climb, but most of the customers are in raptures over their meals and don't care. Tel: 989-9494.

**Da Silvano**, an older Florentine standout, at 260 Sixth Avenue between Bleecker and Houston, is priced higher than Cent'Anni but has a more worldly, fashionable air and some sidewalk tables for the good weather. The place gets quite busy in the evening, but when the midday customers (some of whom are SoHo art dealers) carefully work on their artichokes, a sophisticated leisureliness prevails. The printed menu provides only a portion of the news on what's available. Tel: 982-2343.

Some newcomers seem to be here to remind New Yorkers that Italy stands for sleek design and that pasta is an art form and not just a chore for *mamma*. **Rosolio**, at

11 Barrow Street (off Seventh Avenue near Sheridan Square), doesn't require customers to appear in Milanese tailoring, but they do anyway. Low-slung black leather chairs allow for lingering conversations after the consumption of superb hand-cut pasta. Tel: 645-9224.

It may well be true that there is a good Italian restaurant out there for everyone. The well-heeled downtown art crowd takes its calamari and *tiramisù* at **Arqua** and **Barocco**, 281 and 301 Church Street (a few blocks below Canal Street). Both are modishly stark and very noisy, and both belie their black-clad patrons' apparent disenchantment with life. Cooking as good as this can put a song in the heart of the most studied nihilist. Tel: 334-1888 for Arqua; 431-1445 for Barocco.

The Florentines have set down in Chelsea, too. **Chelsea Trattoria,** at 108 Eighth Avenue south of 16th Street, is snug and small and friendly, and serves food that is far better (and a little costlier) than its unassuming façade suggests. Tel: 924-7786. **Da Umberto,** at 107 West 17th Street west of Sixth Avenue, is more expensive and more of a show, especially the mouth-watering layout of antipasti, the floor-to-ceiling bins of Italian wine, and the dizzying array of off-the-menu special dishes. This is a wonderful place to order an unlikely Florentine favorite: a juicy grilled T-bone steak served with nothing but big wedges of lemon. Tel: 989-0303. **Onini,** at 217 Eighth Avenue (corner of 21st Street), is a husband-and-wife operation that has grown from a hole-in-the-wall into a commodious and rather tranquil neighborhood place with unconventional dishes, such as salads that creatively incorporate Italian ingredients in ways not seen in Italy. Onini is also one of the rare Italian places that makes fine desserts—one of which is *prugne farcite,* surprisingly delightful stuffed prunes that must be tasted to be believed. Tel: 243-6446.

For the most part, the American public recognizes a distinction between Northern and Southern Italian cooking. Southern is synonymous with "tomatoey," and Northern means "kind of expensive." In its deep fascination with Italian cooking, New York has pushed beyond this simple formula. The cooking of Southern Italy is not only preserved (to some extent) in Little Italy, but also celebrated in stylish new places that have introduced something of a second wave of *Southern Italian* cuisine.

**Siracusa,** at 65 Fourth Avenue between 9th and 10th streets, has bare floors, nearly bare walls, and a short menu (in Sicilian) of antipasti, salads, and pasta. Quite a festive little repast can be made from a big communal plate of marinated vegetables, hard salami, cheese, and other nibbles, followed by pasta in the best Sicilian manner, such as with fresh sardines and buttery bread crumbs. For dessert: probably the best *gelato* in Manhattan, of which the hazelnut is the best of the best. Tel: 254-1940.

Bright, airy, and multi-tiered, **Positano**, at 250 Park Avenue South at 20th Street, perches its tables at various elevations, like the hotels and houses on the Amalfi coast. As befits its namesake town, the kitchen emphasizes fish and shellfish (although not at the expense of pasta), and offers a genuine *torta di mandorle,* the mild Amalfian chocolate almond cake, for dessert. During the cold and gray months in New York, the sunniness of Positano is a tonic. Tel: 777-6211.

*Northern Italian* comes in many different shapes and sizes. Apart from the Florentines, there are Venetians, Milanese, Piedmontese, and some culinary free agents who have built styles of their own. While not necessarily cooking by the old rules, these innovators would make centuries of traditional Italian cooks proud. Some of these places also have the questionable distinction of being the most expensive Italian restaurants on earth; no meal in Italy could possibly cost as much.

**Primavera** brings Old World comfort to an otherwise characterless corner of Yorkville, at 1578 First Avenue (82nd Street). Park Avenue's denizens have no trouble negotiating the distance east from their co-ops when the late autumn brings white truffles from Alba to Primavera and the waiters are shaving the precious fungi onto steaming bowls of fettucine. When the season ends, the gang gets by with meltingly tender *capretto* (baby goat), sweetly delectable veal, and game birds. An expensive outing, but a great one. Tel: 861-8608.

**Palio**, at 151 West 51st Street, not only has a major kitchen—which is run by Andreas Hellrigl, an Italian from the Alpine region who also owns the Villa Mozart in Merano, Italy—but is also a design tour de force. The downstairs bar is dominated by a four-sided depiction of *il Palio,* the reckless annual horse race run through the streets of Siena, painted by the Italian Neo-Expressionist Sandro Chia. The upstairs has an almost Japanese orderliness, and tables are set with the sort of fine wafer-thin crystal that can't possibly go into dishwashers. Risottos are to be adored here, and so is venison. Pre-theater menus are offered daily, although it's a toss-up whether or not Palio is the better show. Tel: 245-4850.

Palio has a somewhat less awe-inspiring cousin in **San Domenico**, at 240 Central Park South (equivalent to 59th Street, between Seventh Avenue and Broadway). It is named for a great restaurant in Imola, near Bologna, whose chef may sometimes be found in the New York kitchen. It faces the park across the street, which means that plenty of light comes through the gauzy curtains, but even if it did not, the delicious food would brighten the place. Look for any version of homemade spaghetti and for dishes that utilize baby artichokes or lobster. A generous bowl of crudités is served before dessert in lieu of salad. The wine list goes on forever, an array of hundreds of Italian names that perhaps 90 people in the world can sort through with any authority. It helps prove the point about Italy's bounty and sophistication, however. Tel: 265-5959.

**Bellini by Cipriani**, at 777 Seventh Avenue (51st Street), caters to worldly sophisticates who have seen everything and now would like a nice plate of creamy baked noodles. It belongs to the Cipriani family of Harry's Bar on the calle Vallaresso in Venice; a Bellini is their signature peach-nectar and Champagne cocktail. It is a frighteningly expensive joint that in its New York incarnation appeals to the folks who are made of hair, nails, luxe fabric, and stone. The simple food is often excellent, but the price is wrong. Tel: 265-7770.

Instead, you might partake of simple joys at a place like **Café Trevi**, at 1570 First Avenue between 81st and 82nd streets, where you needn't pay dearly to have the froufrou held back. This is a place with many good dishes (including plenty of fried zucchini to share over drinks), easygoing waiters, and an owner who loves a nice bowl of pasta with a bottle of red wine every bit as much as you do. The blue-checked tablecloths are authentically ordinary. Tel: 249-0040.

The cooking of the old Jewish quarter in Rome is re-created nightly at **Lattanzi Ristorante**, 361 West 46th Street, on the Theater District's generally unstimulating Restaurant Row. The dishes offered pay tribute to the people who introduced eggplants and artichokes to the Italian diet, for which they are owed a big round of thanks. Another signature of the cuisine is a delicious plate of tomatoey pasta with tuna. The meal is not kosher, however, just an homage. Tel: 315-0980.

## ITALIAN IN BROOKLYN

For those willing to travel, an expedition to Coney Island, where Brooklyn meets the Atlantic Ocean, can be an experience to treasure. Either take the B or F subways all the way to the end (about an hour), or drive along the Belt Parkway, passing under the Verrazano Narrows Bridge, until the skeleton of the old parachute-jump tower appears on the horizon. At 2911 West 15th Street (between Surf and Mermaid) is **Gargiulo's**, a monument to generations of having a really big dinner. In case Coney Island doesn't whet your appetite for seafood (Coney Island was prettier 80 years ago), the giant plaster octopus stretched across Gargiulo's ceiling should bring seafood to mind. Share a Pasta Royale (plenty of seafood, plenty of pasta), lotsa wine, and pray that you pick the lucky number from 10 to 100 that means dinner is on the house. It happens at least once a night. Tel: (718) 266-0906. Then hit Surf Avenue and its clackety, terrifying, ancient roller coaster, The Cyclone. Your car should be quite safe behind the high brick walls (topped with jagged glass) in Gargiulo's lot.


## ITALIAN IN THE BRONX

The Bronx has an interesting Italian neighborhood centered on Arthur Avenue, not far from the New York Zoological Society (the Bronx Zoo). From Manhattan take the Metro-North train on the Harlem Line from Grand Central Station to Fordham Road; walk four blocks east to Arthur Avenue. By car, cross the Willis Avenue Bridge to the Bruckner Expressway; take that to the Bronx River Parkway, and then take the Bronx River to Fordham Road, which meets Arthur Avenue at a gas station.

There are shops here that make traditional sausages, salamis, cheeses, and pastries, and several restaurants that whip it all up into finished dishes. One is **Dominick's**, at 2335 Arthur Avenue between 186th and 187th streets, which is so informal that customers all sit packed together at long communal tables and waiters heft platters of food over heads. They never prepare nearly enough divinely good stuffed peppers. No reservations, no credit cards; Tel: 733-2807. Across the street is **Mario's**, at 2342 Arthur Avenue, which has tablecloths, printed menus, and waiters with note pads. If the food is a little short of Dominick's gusto, at least no one's windbreaker is in your linguine. Tel: 584-1188.

# FRENCH

## BISTROS

Another sort of restaurant that has come to charm normally skeptical New Yorkers is the rather carefully replicated French bistro. It may well be because bistros have the reputation for bringing a certain gladdening vigor to everyday eating. Whatever the cause, they're all over town, and new ones crop up constantly. Never has so much *cassoulet, choucroute garni,* and *rillettes* of pork been dished out in Manhattan.

In its own way, the West Village has the charm of a Parisian arrondissement. It seems natural, then, to find some of the city's best bistros wedged in among the shaded, crooked streets of this neighborhood. **Quatorze**, at 240 West 14th Street near Eighth Avenue, is a classic: a quaint and handsome setting with relaxed atmosphere and lusty, authentic bistro food. It is also fairly inexpensive (a big salad with *lardons* is easily enough for two as a first course), and therefore crowded. Reservations are essential; Tel: 206-7006.

A wooden girl in traditional French country dress announces the entrance to **Chez Jacqueline**, at 72 MacDougal Street. She holds the menu card for the day, which may list such delights as quail stuffed with chicken mousse or roast pork with Dijon mustard. Other house specialties are solidly Niçoise (as are the owners), so look for *pissaladiere* and *brandade de morue.* The restaurant inside is handsome and comfortable, the service and wine list exemplary. Tel: 505-0727.

**Au Troquet** sits at 328 West 12th Street at the corner of Greenwich Street. The quiet street and richly scented small room mask the hurried jumble of the city; this is a place to pass a leisurely evening in the company of fine food and helpful service. Tel: 924-3413.

James Beard used to catch lunch at **La Gauloise**, 502 Sixth Avenue near 13th Street. Mirrored panels reflect the amber light from handsome wall sconces and the pleased faces as they dig into such traditional bistro fare as *choucroute garni* and steak au poivre. The manner is determinedly old-fashioned. Service, though, can sometimes lack warmth. Tel: 691-1363.

**Florent**, 69 Gansevoort Street, was once a meat-packing-district diner. Still open 24 hours a day, downtown types now sit elbow-to-elbow with Wall Streeters here, and they all seem to enjoy the flow of wine and the rough country cooking. Tel: 989-5779.

**Eze**, at 254 West 23rd Street near Seventh Avenue, is a bit of the South of France. The restaurant is starkly beautiful, but the food is luscious with the strong flavors of the Mediterranean. A dish such as red snapper stuffed with saffron-perfumed couscous leaves little to be desired. Eze asks a fairly steep fixed price for dinner, but its consistent high quality justifies the cost. Tel: 691-1140.

Farther uptown is **La Colombe d'Or**, 134 East 26th Street off Lexington Avenue. Its rooms have the feeling of a country inn. Large parties can sit at a big round table in the back of the room. The cooking has recently improved in a big way, so it's worth a visit for more than the pots of *tapenade*—olive and anchovy paste—to spread on the delicious yeasty bread. Tel: 689-0666.

**Chez Napoleon**, 365 West 50th Street between Eighth and Ninth avenues, is a popular place to come before or after the theater. After decades of service, the decor is a little frazzled but nevertheless comfortable, and the food is always dependably good and affordable. Tel: 265-6980.

Another popular theater restaurant is **René Pujol**, at 321 West 51st Street between Eighth and Ninth avenues. There is nothing chic about this place, but the food is reliable, the service friendly, and you'll be in your theater seat on time. It is a bit more cushy than a bistro, but the food still has gusto. Tel: 246-3023.

**Chez Josephine**, at 414 West 42nd Street, is named after Josephine Baker, and it's hard to think that she wouldn't be honored by the restaurant. Theater people and French folk feel right at home here, and the cooking, though eclectic, is fine indeed. Tel: 594-1925.

**Bistro Bamboche**, at 1582 York Avenue between 83rd and 84th streets, takes up barely a storefront, but the narrowness of the room is quickly forgotten with the skillful cooking of the young chef. Old standbys are vibrant, and the desserts, especially a piping hot soufflé small enough for one person, are memorable. Only wine is served. Tel: 249-4002.

## FRENCH RESTAURANTS

French restaurants, as in the phrase "fancy French restaurant," have a shorter history in New York than you might suspect. A hundred years ago, in the city's first heyday of grand public eating, the action was controlled by Germans and Italians. There were traditional French influences on the highest priced meals, and an evocation of Paris was always good for a few extra pennies on the right-hand column of the menu, but proud, authoritative French cooking was little known here until after World War II.

Even then there was not much of the real thing. Good little bistros that specialized in the cuisines of rigorous French frugality (plenty of tongue, kidneys, and mussels on the menu; beef and birds fit for stewing in the pots) dotted Manhattan, but *haute cuisine* meant some mushrooms and a little wine in the sauce for the Chateaubriand and, for a big occasion, lobster Thermidor—the cooking, in fact, not of the restaurants of France but of the first-class dining rooms on ocean liners.

The lighter, fresher, more delicate manner of cooking that emanated from the kitchen of Fernand Point of La Pyramide in Vienne only took hold later, at the legendary Le Pavillon (which was a holdover from the French pavilion at the 1939 World's Fair). For more than 30 years Le Pavillon was considered the best restaurant in New York, and even now, nearly two decades after the place's extinction, former employees still work many of the best dining rooms and kitchens in the city. Le Pavillon was one of a kind for many years, until other equally ambitious restaurant owners began to open places that played variations on Pavillon's theme of restrained richness of decor, exacting, laborious cooking, waiters trained in Europe, daily attention to costly flower arrangements, and prices that were unapologetically stiff. For many Americans, Le Pavillon was the only place they had ever been where their dinner gave them a thrill.

The pattern set by Le Pavillon was picked up by the newcomers La Caravelle, Lutèce, Le Cygne, and La Côte Basque (the less formal offshoot of Le Pavillon, installed in the original site when Le Pavillon moved).

All of these restaurants were, and still are, anointed with praise from newspapers, magazines, and a steady flow of testimonials from the business community (whose presence gave these restaurants their air of stodginess—a trait that is not natural to restaurant people themselves). By the late 1970s French restaurants in New York found themselves no longer setting tastes but instead reacting in a haughty, grumpy manner to changes in life around them. There were the fusses over whether women would be allowed through the door in pants, and whether a woman ought ever to see the menu with the prices on it if she was out with a grown man. But the greatest flap was over the food. A new generation in France sought to make fine cooking lighter still, more spontaneous (although spontaneity was to be granted only to those who had served grueling unspontaneous apprenticeships), and more worldly; it was no longer possible to treat Asian cooking as less than an equal of the best European.

The top French restaurants in New York reacted badly, for had not the art of cooking reached near perfection in Vienna in the 1930s? Pantsuits were pushing through the front door, and nouvelle cuisine was trying to break into the kitchen. How these places have survived is interesting.

**Lutèce** has simply stood above it all. This fixedly old-fashioned restaurant had its firmly committed regular clientele in place before the changes took place, and it only changed when the traffic would allow it. Today, Lutèce is a cozy place, an out-of-the-way restaurant that is essentially a mom-and-pop operation (Mr. and Mrs. André Soltner) in which Pop, who could be overseeing legions of cooks in some huge, frightfully posh hotel, would rather just cook (or oversee the cooking) for a few people a day and keep things cheery, personal, and actually on a higher standard than you can hit in one of those hotels with so many people coming and going.

In fulfillment of all this, Lutèce is set in a relatively unassuming town house at 249 East 50th Street, near unfancy Second Avenue. Even after a recent redecoration, the rooms still feel like those in a town house and the meal like a well-catered party. The food has gotten lighter, but only in ways that are hard to detect (sauces haven't been thinned out to broths, although they are no longer so rich as to constitute a food in their own right). Should you go to Lutèce when you have only a relatively short time to spend in New York (assuming a reservation can be obtained)? Only if some very pampered time-travel is in order, or if you know you'd like an escape from hard-driving New York while you're still in the city. Tel: 752-2225.

**La Côte Basque**, 5 East 55th Street, actually fizzled out at one point, but the sprightly, very French murals of waterfront life in Basque country were an asset worth saving. So a French chef named Jean-Jacques Rachou took over, cleaned the paintings, and brought in a cooking style that is peculiarly his own: an eye for decorating a plate that shows an affinity for nouvelle cuisine combined with a tendency to heap on the food and give things a punch of flavor that suggests an Iowa farm supper attended by Diamond Jim Brady. People who see dinner as an excuse to eat dessert are especially happy here. The frontmost tables at lunch are still occupied by the present-day equivalents of the ladies who ate here in Truman Capote's venomous unfinished novel *Answered Prayers*. They have the Dover sole and skip dessert. Tel: 688-6525.

**La Caravelle** also nearly turned into a ghost town. This had been a stylish place of the 1960s but lost its sense of fun along the way. Only a fierce commitment on the part of one of its owners (now retired) to resist the new trends, for resistance's sake, kept this pretty and conventionally deluxe spot at 33 West 55th Street alive. It survived to see the day when its good old-fashioned standards of wealthy people's cooking would be upheld with an American chef in the kitchen. This is one of the last bastions of extensive tableside carving of meats and arranging of plates. In fact, it feels like the last bastion of everything, and is valuable for that alone. Tel: 586-4252.

**Le Cygne** broke and ran from the pack. It moved into a new and very attractive Postmodern building (always filled with flowers) at 55 East 54th Street between Madison and Park before there really *were* any Postmodern buildings built. The gamble paid off, for this is the prettiest of the lot, even though it isn't roomy and the cooking tends not to thrill anyone, although most meals are safely over the line into delicious. People still come here for the soufflés, and the soufflés are still fun to eat. As at the other three grand restaurants described above, the meals at Le Cygne are at a fixed (high) price. Special goodies generally add a few dollars to the bill, and a useful rule of thumb is to estimate that each person's meal, with drinks, tax, and tips factored in, will come to about twice the fixed price. Tel: 759-5941.

The creative resurgence in cooking in France that started in the 1970s and shows no sign of slowing down has influenced New York in many ways (right down to goat cheese on salads in bars). But it is most keenly felt at some of the city's French outposts.

**Le Cirque**, at 58 East 65th Street between Madison and Park, is actually a fairly old restaurant, but it has kept up with the times by hiring highly trained Frenchmen to lead the kitchen. The current bearer of the torch is Daniel Boulud, who was something of a prize pupil of the

French titans Michel Guérard and Roger Vergé. He draws influences from traditional French haute cuisine and from French regional styles. A piece of paper pasted into each day's menu gives the latest of his discoveries (which, for example, recently included a stack of thin slices of beef layered with fine bits of Niçoise olives). He cooks fish with unerring accuracy and has one of the best pastry chefs in the city working under him. It is the sort of meal worth setting time and resources aside to enjoy.

Food at Le Cirque is only half the story, however. Under the direction of Sirio Maccioni, a veteran of many decades of restaurant life, the dining room is one of the most frenetic scenes in a frenetic town. Tables are packed together, which the regulars mind not at all. Waiters are constantly on the go, and famous people are making no effort to be unnoticed. Le Cirque is no respite from city living; it *is* city living. Tel: 794-9292.

**Le Bernardin**, at 155 West 51st Street (between Sixth and Seventh avenues), was at first intended to be the New York branch of a very successful seafood restaurant in Paris owned by a brother and sister, Gilbert and Maguy Le Coze. But given an instant blast of acclaim in New York (and a kitchen that is a professional chef's most glorious dream come true), the Paris operation seemed like old hat and was sold. Now the Le Cozes' unusual cult of fish and shellfish (meat is served grudgingly and only on special request) is centered in Manhattan, and has easily as many adherents as it had across the Atlantic. Descended from Breton fishermen, the siblings sell sparkling fresh aquatic fare that has the cold brightness of sashimi and the oceanic goodness of a dockside grill. The food is a study in minimalism, but the dining room is plush and formal, and wonderful genre paintings (heroic fishermen, still lifes of crustaceans) hang on the walls. Desserts are state-of-the-art lovely and yummy. Some people find the seafood regimen more to their liking at midday than in the evening. Very expensive. Tel: 489-1515.

**Lafayette**, in the Drake Swissôtel, at 65 East 56th Street at Park Avenue, is under the absentee supervision of the semiretired French master Louis Outhier. This smallest of the topflight French restaurants is quiet and removed, and quite forthright in its fixation with great food: There's a picture window onto the kitchen that keeps the calm, methodical chefs on view throughout the meal. The menu is revamped twice a year, and it is a safe bet that many of the dishes will never have appeared anywhere else before. Waiters are unobtrusively helpful, and if the management ever plays favorites with customers, it isn't done to a degree that could catch notice. This would be first choice for a luxurious dinner where privacy was a high priority. Tel: 832-1565.

Of similar distinction, although bigger and more bustling, is **Restaurant Maurice**, in the Parker Meridien Hotel at 118 West 57th Street near Sixth Avenue. The hotel is managed by Air France, and the pleasing modernity of the restaurant is a reminder that France itself has pushed far beyond the boiserie and chandeliers of the past (not something that could be deduced from most of the rest of the interiors in New York). The high walls have murals of fruit and musical instruments that look like fragments from a tapestry, and the furniture is low and plush. Like most of the nouvelle-influenced restaurants, plates of food are scrupulously arranged in the kitchen and then sent out under silver domes that the waiters remove with an appropriate, unspoken "Voilà!" Tel: 245-7788.

# *AMERICAN*

For the purposes of dining out, "American food" has come to mean cooking prepared by chefs with classical training that uses ingredients that most (or at least some) Americans are familar with, but that would force a normally parochial European to do a bit of head scratching.

This outlook has been raised to a highly individual art by American chef Larry Forgione at his eatery **An American Place**, at 2 Park Avenue (32nd Street). He gained attention initially by vowing not to use imported European ingredients (not something New York chefs rely on heavily in the first place), but his talent has been for taking such American vernacular items as corn relish, beef jerky, and apple brown Betty and turning them into dishes that lift the senses as vigorously as French cooking will with its own best ingredients on hand. Naturally the wine list is entirely American, too. The best thing about An American Place is that years after proving his point about American food sources, Mr. Forgione keeps using them with love and gusto. Tel: 517-7660.

Looking approvingly, one imagines, over Mr. Forgione's shoulder is Leon Lianides (both men were championed by the cooking authority James Beard), whose **Coach House**, at 110 Waverly Place (a block south of 8th

Street between Sixth Avenue and Washington Square), has been serving gracious American meals (with overtones of the South, although Mr. Lianides is a Greek) for 40 years. Rather than spin out new dishes, Mr. Lianides has spent his career perfecting a set of American basics that includes paradigmatic crab cakes, corn sticks, black bean soup, roast rack of Kentucky lamb, steak au poivre, chef's custard, and, for a few special autumn weeks, quince pie. The staff is all in the near-retirement years, and so a meal is not rapid-fire. Tel: 777-0303.

The fires of youth burn elsewhere, most strongly at Bouley and Rakel, two gracious downtown dining outposts that are firmly under the control of young American chefs. **Bouley** is the last name of chef David Bouley, and he has fashioned in a southern TriBeCa warehouse zone, at 165 Duane Street between Greenwich and Hudson, a nearly perfect re-creation of the sort of provincial French restaurant where a lovely hedge border protects a parking lot full of large Mercedes-Benzes. Bouley's ceilings are gracefully vaulted, and a dignified calm reigns. The cooking, much of which is very exciting, is French-derived, but with an increasing reliance on local producers of fine ingredients. The chef's geographic center has been moving westward, and the tastes of his customers have been driving him further into seafood. He makes a proud display of his French souvenirs (including an 18th-century walnut front door), but his style is his own. Tel: 608-3852.

**Rakel**'s chef Thomas Keller is also a French interpreter. He likes to use truffles, foie gras, and caviar in his dishes, for the éclat that they add—and it is surprising to learn here that such things as truffles really do have flavor and not just price. Mr. Keller works in a barn of a place at 231 Varick Street (actually the ground floor of a printing plant) near Houston Street. His is among the few restaurants with fine and expensive cooking that allows women to work on the dining room floor (the Four Seasons happens to be another), and this adds a friendliness to the dining ritual that a room worked only by men can lack. The style of the place is Postmodern grandiose, but it has a welcoming aspect that starts in the kitchen and is enhanced by the staff members, who can get very excited about helping you choose just the right wine. Tel: 929-1630.

Other American chefs have worked their way up to splashy addresses after making their initial marks in settings that offered good brunches and other less-formal meals. For years Patrick Clark oversaw the kitchens at both the archetypal downtown hangout **The Odeon** (for discovered and undiscovered artists, loft dwellers, people with defiantly original wardrobes, and people who happened to like a very good, fairly priced meal), at 145 West Broadway in TriBeCa (Tel: 233-0507), and its Upper West Side sequel, **Café Luxembourg**, at 200 West 70th Street west of Broadway (Tel: 873-7411). He left both in very capable hands, and both have stayed very busy (places that are well run do tend to outlive the ones that trade only on flash). Mr. Clark now has his own setup at **Metro**, in the very definitely uptown Volney Residence, at 23 East 74th Street. As he did at his earlier workplaces, Mr. Clark makes his kitchen keep long hours, which means that a fine light meal can be had long after the other serious places have stacked the chairs. Deceptively simple, lustrous salads are one of his specialties, and so are dishes based around squab and other game birds. Tel: 249-3030.

For nearly a decade **Chanterelle**, at 6 Harrison Street in TriBeCa (at the corner of Hudson Street), kept a nightly vigil on a lonely corner of SoHo that somehow remained untouched by the neighborhood's art and apparel boom. In new, slightly enlarged quarters, David and Karen Waltuck continue to turn out long, exquisite meals that seem to get better with time. They also have a following among leading artists, many of whom have designed menu covers. These friends of the house include Merce Cunningham, John Cage, Eric Fischl, and Virgil Thomson (who scored an original number for the Waltucks called "Intensely Two"). David Waltuck's own art has to do with such fine things as seafood sausage in beurre blanc and some surprisingly glamorous approaches to pork and to venison. Chanterelle also offers one of the most extensive cheese boards in the known world—a staggering variety, mostly farm-made, all in peak condition. The evening costs about as much as a minor work of art, but it might hold your affection for longer. Tel: 966-6960.

Anne Rosenzweig gained notice at **Vanessa**, which remains a good standby in Greenwich Village, at 289 Bleecker Street just east of Seventh Avenue, especially for Sunday brunch; Tel: 243-4225. Along with a business partner, she opened **Arcadia**, at 21 East 62nd Street, one of the smartest small restaurants in the city (it sports a charming panorama of the seasons by Paul Davis), where she has achieved success with such inventions as a lobster club sandwich (lunch) and "chimney-smoked" lobster (for dinner). She and her partner have also won executive positions at the refurbished "21," the big, durable Establishment hangout at 21 West 52nd Street. Her talents have for some reason proven unavailing at turning "21" into a great restaurant (it is notably dismal that the $24 hamburger at "21" can somehow come without that everyday quality that holds an ordinary hamburger together). While "21" still needs more tuning, Arcadia hasn't noticeably slipped despite the demands on Ms. Rosenzweig's time. Tel: 223-2900 for Arcadia; 582-7200 for "21."

Another often-photographed and quoted chef is Brendan Walsh, who is best known as the original chef of **Arizona 206**, at 206 East 60th Street near Third Avenue, a roaringly busy, bare-floored joint that serves his and new chef Marilyn Frobucinno's imaginative versions of Southwestern cuisine (from an imaginary Southwest where the cowboys look up at the stars as they eat rabbit *cassoulet* with white beans and *chorizo*). Tel: 838-0440.

Walsh has also devised menus for three restaurants that are bordering on Arizona 206 and conveniently close to a brace of first-run cinemas. One is a café (attached to Arizona) where a rotation of dishes emerges and is sold off in the course of the evening. The other is the longtime gathering place **Yellowfingers**, at the corner of Third Avenue and 60th Street, whose let's-grab-lunch menu has achieved new respectability. Upstairs from this is **Contrapunto**, a pasta center with good vegetables, too. Tel: 751-8615 for Yellowfingers; 751-8616 for Contrapunto.

Unpublicized but worthy of acclaim is Andrew D'Amico, who has moved the very well known **Sign of the Dove**, at 1110 Third Avenue at 65th Street, into the spotlight for its cooking as well as for its blithe atmosphere and smooth service. Lunches and dinners are rather expensive fixed-price arrays of interesting tastes, and the house-made sourdough bread may be the best loaf in New York. Tel: 861-8080.

## *LOCAL PHENOMENA*

There are some restaurants that could only happen in New York, because anything more modest than the ambitions of this city could probably not have propelled them into existence.

At the figurative epicenter stands **The Four Seasons**. Philip Johnson designed it 30 years ago under the eye of

Ludwig Mies van der Rohe, as a part of Mies's Seagram Building on Park Avenue (the restaurant's entrance is at 99 East 52nd Street). In its looks and manners The Four Seasons may be the purest statement of wealthy, confident Modernism anywhere; it pioneered sans-serif flatware and stemless brandy snifters and elevated basic American foodstuffs to international recognition. Grandly spacious and luxurious in spite of its rigorous geometry, The Four Seasons is something of a law unto itself. Menus and greenery still change on the first day of every season. Hordes of well-attired customers troop past the huge Picasso in the corridor linking the dining rooms or sip drinks beneath Richard Lippold's sculpture comprising thousands of suspended brass rods. Given the size of the place, the kitchen is staggeringly good. The Pool Room, which is named for the square, burbling fountain in its center, offers more elaborate meals than the Grill Room, which is well known for its high-profile clientele at midday (who tend to order the same simple things every time) and its chic and expensive suppers at night. The Pool Room has a long menu (which always includes a superb roast duckling), and its waiters perform the carving and plate arranging at tableside. Luscious desserts are wheeled from table to table on a cart that someone, someday, is going to hijack. As with any New York City restaurant of note, reservations should be made as far in advance as plans allow. Tel: 754-9494.

Recessed into the lower level of Grand Central Terminal is **The Grand Central Oyster Bar & Restaurant**, since 1913 a mecca for seafood lovers, commuters, business folk, and the last few travellers who expect a celebratory send-off before a journey by rail. About 2,000 people a day are served under its vast vaulted ceilings, at tables, along counters, and at the granite-topped oyster bar itself, where imperturbable chefs prepare the likes of oyster "pan roasts" or Ipswich clam stews, one portion at a time, wearing what looks like lab gear. Briny fresh oysters (bluepoints, Chincoteagues, Wellfleets, Malpeques, and so on) are pried open all day long to be savored raw, and the kitchen carefully prepares an almost confounding array of the freshest fish, such as yellow perch, Montauk bluefish, smelts, and wolffish, in addition to Atlantic salmon, lemon or gray sole, tuna, and halibut. The Oyster Bar also offers a similarly all-inclusive list of American white wines. Tel: 490-6650; closed on weekends.

Rockefeller Center, between Fifth and Sixth avenues off

50th Street, the visionary office complex in the heart of Midtown, has dramatic eateries at its pinnacle and at its base. At the very top of the RCA Building is the legendary **Rainbow Room**, a triumph of Style Moderne, recently restored to its 1930s ebullience, with a revolving inlaid dance floor, big-band music, cigarette girls, and fancy, authentically mediocre nightclub food. Many of the dancers on the floor really know their moves; they can fox-trot as gracefully as some of the ice skaters, 65 stories below, can glide. Black tie is never out of step. Tel: 632-5000. (By day the Rainbow Room is a private club.)

Adjacent to Rockefeller Center's sunken rink is the handsomely appointed, spacious **SeaGrill**, another place aiming for aquatic excellence. It lists far fewer fish than the Oyster Bar but prepares them more elaborately. In the months when there is no skating some of the Lower Plaza is given over to umbrellaed outdoor tables (sharing the territory with the less-expensive and less-wonderful American Festival Café). Very properly suited types inhabit it by day, and their very properly dressed families come in at night. Tel: 246-9201.

The magnificent view from **The River Café**, moored in the shadow of the Brooklyn Bridge on the Brooklyn side (at 1 Water Street), takes in Wall Street's towers and the bay and river that almost lap at their edges. The restaurant is a pair of barges in the East River and is also rightly famous for its sophisticated American cooking. To reach it by car or cab from Manhattan, take the first exit off the Brooklyn Bridge and follow the road that curves back down to the water. The restaurant will summon a cab or notify a car service, on request, for the return trip. Tel: (718) 522-5200.

The River Café and countless other specks on the cityscape can be pointed to from the restaurant complex **Windows on the World**, which is on the 107th floor of 1 World Trade Center (the north tower). Dinners served in "The Restaurant"—enough table linen here for a tent city—are passably good, but dinners served in the tiny room called **Cellar in the Sky**, which only offers a lengthy, imaginatively orchestrated wine-and-food blowout (it commences nightly at 7:30), are marvelous. The catch is that you are cut off from the view. Windows' bar and self-explanatory **Hors d'Oeuvrerie** permit a look at, for example, the hills of Staten Island and the familiar figure of *Liberty Enlightening the World* without obliging you to stay all evening. Tel: 938-1111.

**Tavern on the Green**, in Central Park at West 67th Street, does more business than any other restaurant in New York, so "tavern" is somewhat misleading. Tabernacle on the Green might come closer. In any case, it is also the city's leading producer of hoopla (tens of thousands of firefly-size lights in the trees, chandeliers galore, an unashamed leaning toward desserts). Birthdays are to Tavern on the Green as Christmas is to Macy's. People who think hard about their food go elsewhere, but the spectacle is unrivaled. Tel: 873-3200.

Another local spectacle is the fabled **Russian Tea Room**, best known perhaps for its slogan, "Slightly to the Left of Carnegie Hall," which translates into 150 West 57th Street near Seventh Avenue. It is home to the czars and czarinas of show business, who assemble here at lunchtime to do business. This must give the nonindustry people who watch them a delicious thrill—they could not possibly be here for the food, which is quite expensive and is doled out with very un-Slavic stinginess. The decoration is indeed cheery, and the caviar and blini are a delectable splurge after a concert, but if the crummy little pastries that pass for dessert were shown to a real czar he'd call the executioner. Tel: 265-0947.

It has long been pointed out that no all-American city is complete without something called a New York–style deli in which certain facets of traditional Jewish-Romanian party food are sold at varying stages of deep frost. But are there New York–style delis in New York?

"In name only" are the words that might come to the lips of most longtime New Yorkers, for deli food has fallen on hard times, at least as far as eating out is concerned (stunningly fine fare is still available from many sources to carry back to your lair—it's the deli-as-public-accommodation that has suffered lately). The death of Leo Steiner, a voluble, fanatical, corned beef–apotheosizing promoter was a deep blow to the noshing community. Within weeks of Steiner's passing the word was out that his headquarters, **The Carnegie Delicatessen and Restaurant**, at 854 Seventh Avenue between 54th and 55th streets (Tel: 757-2245), had taken advantage of his unavoidable absence and "changed the coleslaw." It was deemed sweeter, more luncheonette-like, and missing its more difficult sinus-clearing edge. If they could let the slaw slide, might not Steiner's whole legacy be trashed?

The next realization was that aside from the Carnegie,

most delis hadn't been very good anyway. They let their meats dry out; the yellow in their chicken broth looked suspiciously industrial; and the chopped chicken liver was clearly made by people who had no idea what it was supposed to taste like. The Carnegie Deli, The Second Avenue Kosher Deli (at 156 Second Avenue at 10th Street), and a bunch of others remain busy and popular, but the boasts about their cooking ring very hollow now. Steiner, who had an awesome temper, must be truly beside himself somewhere.

## *CHINESE*

The golden age of going out for Chinese food lasted from about the time that President Nixon stood on the Great Wall of China until approximately the time of the bicentennial of United States trade with China, a little more than ten years later. These were the years when hot, spicy, colorful, tangy dishes from Szechwan and Hunan provinces appeared in the city, and many dedicated diners had simply never in their lives eaten so well (and for so little money).

The golden age ended as the Grand Openings of Chinese restaurants started to outnumber, by an enormous factor, the number of chefs with even the most modest talent (Chinese restaurants even appeared to outnumber dry cleaners on the avenues of Manhattan). Five thousand years of culinary greatness declined rapidly into the stuff that New Yorkers sat in front of the TV eating on rainy nights.

Visits to the city's Chinatowns (or to the few relatively expensive places outside the Chinatowns that can afford a real chef) are now the only ways to relive the heyday. Nearly any New Yorker who swears that the take-out place on the corner is very good is really talking about how well the place maintains its delivery bikes and not how well it maintains its cuisine.

But out in the city's "second" Chinatown, in the Flushing section of Queens, things are starting to shake again. **Fortune Chao-Chow Seafood Restaurant**, at 135-16 Roosevelt Avenue (from Times Square, Fifth Avenue and 42nd Street, or Grand Central Station, take the number 7 IRT subway beyond Shea Stadium to the end of the line), is the first restaurant in the city to devote itself solely to the excellent subcategory of Cantonese cooking called Chao-

Chow (pronounced "jow-joe"). The spicing is restrained, sauces are thin and delicate (with a minimum of cornstarch and salt), and the natural flavors of ingredients come singing through (as in a meaty duck stewed nearly to disintegration in an anise-spiked sauce with barely cooked spinach, or warm slices of roast goose breast with lightly pickled vegetables). It is too early to say if Chao-Chow cooking will spark a rejuvenation citywide. Tel: (718) 359-4384.

Not too far away, at 137-40 Northern Boulevard, is **Stony Wok**, a Taiwanese place in a Taiwanese neighborhood that is set up with gas burners at the tables to allow customers to make elaborate meals of more or less their own devising by choosing from a list of ingredients (all priced separately) and using the provided wok to slip them into. Compared with Manhattan's far older and more complex Chinatown, the Taiwanese community in Flushing has an upbeat, spanking-clean atmosphere, and Stony Wok is a cheery sort of place (the teenagers appear to belong to after-school clubs and not to gangs). Tel: (718) 445-8535.

Manhattan's **Chinatown**, however, can still provide some magnificent eating. As the neighborhood has grown—it has essentially swallowed up Little Italy and the old Jewish Lower East Side—it has changed from a tourist attraction into a Chinese city (the eventual transfer of Hong Kong from Britain to the People's Republic has sparked a financial boom here that makes Chinatown seem like wall-to-wall banks). With many, many Chinese people to feed, the newest, biggest restaurants no longer promote such Western concerns as "our Cocktail Lounge" and don't care that their English-language menus hopelessly misrepresent what their kitchens really produce.

The way around this is simply to eat the way Chinese people eat. Gather a group of anywhere from eight to a hundred people, walk into a big, busy Chinatown restaurant at the very busiest time, and order a fixed-price banquet, which might cost $120 but will handily feed ten people. It's still $120 whether you are eight people or twelve people; the quantity of food is not adjusted until your group becomes *two* tables. Even if every dish doesn't meet with universal acceptance, there is still more than enough food to send the gang rolling home.

**Grand Palace**, at 94 Mott Street, is the sort of place to go for a huge evening banquet (no prior arrangement necessary), and so are **The Silver Palace**, at 50 Bowery, and **The Nice Restaurant** (which has a particularly adept kitchen), at 35 East Broadway. You need the names of at least three of these places because one or more are liable to be booked solid with big parties. The meal generally begins with savory hors d'oeuvres, moves through a velvety soup (often made from winter melon), and usually pushes on through shellfish, duck, chicken, beef, bean curd, and, last but not least, a glorious whole fresh fish. Coke, Sprite, Tsing-Tao beer, and tea are the beverages of choice.

From early morning until about 4:00 P.M. all of these restaurants offer *dim sum,* the small plates of dumplings, fritters, meat morsels, and sweets that are meant to accompany tea, gossip, and newspaper reading (ask for the *better* tea; it's worth the $1.50). Women circulate through the restaurants pushing carts, each laden with several different dishes. The Nice Restaurant has an outstandingly broad and well-prepared selection. H.S.F. (for Hee Seung Fung), at 46 Bowery, offers its daytime *dim sum* along with explanations for the inexperienced, and consequently a long line can form at peak times on weekends. You pay in cash based on a tally of your empty plates (the range is from one to three dollars per plate).

Diners unable to summon legions of companions have their Chinatown options, too. Excellent Cantonese food is offered at **The Phoenix Garden**, a tiny place in an arcade off 46 Bowery, where the specialty is crabs and salt-and-pepper shrimp. **Siu Lam Kung**, at 18 Elizabeth Street, is another seafood haven; the house has a knack for introducing genuine Cantonese dishes to Westerners whose notions of Cantonese cooking were ruined in childhood by bad takeout. **Great Shanghai**, at 27 Division Street, has playful Postmodern decor and offers do-it-yourself hot-pot meals with a marvelous sauce you blend to your liking from 12 ingredients. Whole fish are prepared particularly well here, and the best dessert in Chinatown, a hot "eight-treasure" rice gateau (*ba bo fan*), is on hand, too; place the order for it at the beginning of the meal. Tel: 966-7663.

Away from Chinatown are the myriad Hunans (Lake, Park, House, Tower, Cottage, Balcony, and so on) and Szechwans, but few serve food worth stopping for. The hot-and-spicy spirit does live on, however, aboard **Tang's Chariot**, at 236 East 53rd Street between Second and Third avenues, which is run by the family of one of the first

Hunan master chefs in New York. It has a moderately formal air and tuxedoed waiters, but the peppers are in the right places. Tel: 355-5096. The heat is also on at **China Gardens**, at 936 Second Avenue between 49th and 50th streets, one of the last of the uptown places that still takes pride in its kitchen (without charging too terribly much). Tel: 308-4777.

Good food, matched with handsome surroundings, is to be found in **Chin Chin**, at 216 East 49th Street between Second and Third avenues, which is run by two brothers named Chin. Elegantly framed studio photos of their Taiwan boyhood line the walls, and the back room is one of the most austerely elegant eating salons in the city. Just the place to gnaw delicately tea-smoked duck. Tel: 888-4555.

Exactingly executed Cantonese cooking is the reason to visit **Fu's**, at 1395 Second Avenue between 72nd and 73rd streets. The decor is hard-edged glitz, and the staff is less than chummy, but there is no argument with the kitchen and its way with glistening fresh seafood. Tel: 517-9670.

# *JAPANESE*

Real Japanese food came to the city not to provide Americans with something new to eat but to supply much-needed tastes of home to the growing numbers of Japanese businessmen dispatched to the New York office. For their sake, Japanese restaurants (down to the actual building materials) were shipped (stamped "Midtown Manhattan," it seemed) across the Pacific. The surprise was that curiosity about a sushi bar or a warren of tatami rooms or buckets of noodles would pull New Yorkers in off the streets as well, and that they would come back for more.

Sushi and sashimi were the Japanese specialties that attracted the most attention, and eating raw fish, like jostling for lox at Zabar's, became a rite of passage for newcomers to the city. The ability to order individual portions of sushi or sashimi in passable Japanese was a badge of worldly sophistication. This fashion for raw fish has waned among the non-Japanese, which must come as a relief to homesick Japanese businessmen who now can peacefully soak up some of the raffish conviviality that characterizes sushi bars in the old country. To this end, the Japanese flock to **Sushiden**, at 19 East 49th Street, an architecturally pleasing spot with two long counters made of traditional

Japanese cypress as well as some regular tables. It's best to order "piece by piece" at the counters. Tilefish, ark shell, yellowtail, and *toro* (the richest cut of tuna) all have their seasons, and the chefs behind the counters will gladly point out what is best at the moment. At the tables it is customary to order a large assortment of sushi or sashimi for communal delectation. There are also some hot dishes on the menu. The waitresses are as adept and polite as their counterparts in Japan. Tel: 758-2700.

Of longer standing and in perpetual struggle for the number one spot in the "Best Of" lists are **Hatsuhana** (with branches at 17 East 48th Street just east of Madison and 237 Park Avenue in an arcade between 45th and 46th streets) and **Takesushi** (with only one venue, at 71 Vanderbilt Avenue, which is the street bordering Grand Central Station to the west). Both cater to an interestingly international clientele and have a busy, no-nonsense air that makes you feel you are in the right place. (Tel: 355-3345 and 661-3400 respectively for Hatsuhana; 867-5120 for Takesushi.)

It isn't clear yet what effect New York City's recently enacted ordinance calling for segregation of smokers and nonsmokers will have on sushi bars. Cigarettes (and beer) are as integral to the experience as fish and shellfish, especially at night when the Japanese businessmen come around to blow off some steam.

Noodle joints are everywhere in Japan but have not caught on as they ought to in New York (beware of branches of the Larmen Dosanko chain that dot the city!). An exception is **Taro Japanese Noodle Restaurant**, at 20 East 47th Street, where noodles are made fresh every day and boiled up in hearty broths with a variety of garnishes: a perfect lunch or a quick inexpensive supper before a show. For those not ready to face a steaming soup, the noodles also find their way into tasty salads. Tel: 986-7170.

In New York (as opposed to Tokyo), other Japanese specialties such as sukiyaki, tempura, yakitori, and so forth are usually served under one roof. An example of this is **Nakagawa**, a large and fairly formal establishment at 7 West 44th Street, which has a bustling sushi scene on the first floor but also provides as much culinary variety as perhaps ten restaurants in Japan. It has a short menu of savory little bar treats meant to go well with liquor or sake, and tables where people come to eat sukiyaki (the sweet, oniony stew) and *shabu-shabu* (the Mongolian-inspired boiled dinner of beef, many vegetables, and sloppy, slippery noodles). There are also tatami rooms (with wells under the tables to prevent leg cramps in the unpracticed), where long, multicourse banquets can be served in dignified privacy. Tel: 869-8077.

More lavishly lovely is **Seryna**, at 11 East 53rd Street, which, in the spirit of the grandest restaurants in Japan, has very good art, demure, overqualified waitresses, and tiny portions of luxurious food, some of which is cooked at the table on a heated rock. Tel: 980-9393.

Then there are restaurants that have shown what might be considered unseemly Western leanings back in Japan (Kentucky Fried Chicken is fine, but not on the same menu with an airy, subtle bean-curd creation). **Nishi NoHo** (380 Lafayette Street near Great Jones Street) is the lofty, gigantic downtown branch of **Nishi**, a very tiny place at 325 Amsterdam Avenue (between 75th and 76th Streets), whose creators realized that a decorous evening of sushi could come to a rousing good finale with an ice-cream sundae (called a Hot Fuji). Some Nishi dishes are dainty, others are in-jokes (a flaming conch shell is a nod to the naïve spectacle of "Polynesian" restaurants), and some, such as various pastas, are in the East-meets-West middle ground that is probably the food of the 1990s. Nishi NoHo is so huge that full-size ceremonial kimonos hang on the wall almost unobtrusively, looking like something some aristocratic ghosts left behind when they fled the Hot Fujis in terror. Tel: 677-8401 for Nishi NoHo; 799-0117 for Nishi on Amsterdam.

Diners looking for the serene, beautiful side of Japanese life (free of commerce, kitsch, and that Japanese specialty, commerce *in* kitsch) tend to find **Omen**, at 113 Thompson Street in SoHo. The cooking is delicious and the pottery is also worthy of contemplation. The crowd is young, poised, and wears its basic black attire in a way that is somehow not glum. Tel: 925-8923.

At various locations in Midtown and elsewhere around town are mid-priced Japanese restaurants called **East— The Town of Taste**, a name doubtlessly selected by one of those writers who also decides what faddish Japanese clothes should have written on them ("Key Staff," "New York Sick—I'll Never Forget You," and so on). An optimistic attempt to make dining sans shoes a part of ordinary Manhattan life, the various Easts have a mission to civilize; they also have good sushi and tasty little beef-and-scallion *negimaki*.

# SPANISH AND LATIN AMERICAN

Spanish cooking has a long history in New York, and many denizens of the city fondly remember the Spanish restaurants of their youth, places where brimming pots of paella or *mariscado* fed them amply for very little money on their first big dates. The encouraging thing is that the Spanish restaurants of almost everyone's youth are still in business and still feed all comers heartily.

Most typical of the venerable spots is **Sevilla** in Greenwich Village, at 62 Charles Street near West 4th Street (west of Seventh Avenue). The room is dark and filled with music, the Spanish wine flows freely, and waiters practically buckle under the weight of the pots of food they carry to the tables. The big decisions are whether to have seafood or land food in the paella and whether to try to go it alone or split the main course two ways. Whichever, the prices are an act of mercy. Tel: 929-3189.

Another sure Village bet is **El Rincon de España**, at 226 Thompson Street near West 3rd Street, south of Washington Square. The savory octopus here is outstanding, and so are the soups and the flan. If you can somehow pass on the paella, there are other excellent main courses, too. The setting is small, cozy, and a little dim; a Spanish guitarist strums through the night. The cost is slightly higher than at Sevilla. Tel: 260-4950.

**Café San Martin**, at 1458 First Avenue near 76th Street, is blessedly un-dim. In fact, it has a big skylight, which it hardly needs because its charming host, Ramon San Martin, could easily brighten the place himself. While still an excellent value, dinner here is more elaborate than at the previous places mentioned, and the roast meats and splendid desserts are actually to be preferred to filling up on a big rice dish. Some house specialties include *chorizo* sausage braised in red wine, and a genuine delicacy: baby eels from Spain flash-cooked with garlic and hot pepper flakes. Tel: 288-0470.

Adventuresome diners may want to try **Rio Mar**, a little splinter of Bilbao among the trucks of the meat-purveying district at 7 Ninth Avenue, near Little West 12th Street. The specialty here is phenomenally low-priced juicy steaks with huge fried potatoes, but the bar serves up real *tapas*, the little tidbits meant to foster drink sales, and was doing so long before *tapas* became chic. You are more than welcome to toss your peanut shells on the floor. Tel: 243-9015.

The reason *tapas* became so chic in the first place is that they were offered in glorious profusion by Chef Felipe Rojas-Lombardi at the bar in **The Ballroom**, 253 West 28th Street, near Eighth Avenue. The chef is Peruvian by birth, but he has mastered the Spanish idiom and was a protégé of James Beard. The Ballroom itself is best known for its classy cabaret performers, but Rojas-Lombardi is one of the best cooks in America, and he lends a rich, suave touch to everything on his menu. A dinner can be rather expensive, but the buffet lunch offered here from autumn through spring is a chance to sample some of his best for a ridiculously low price. Tel: 244-3005.

Brazilian cooking can be found in generous supply and close concentration along two blocks west of Fifth Avenue in Midtown. A pleasant introduction can be made at **The Brazilian Coffee Restaurant**, at 45 West 46th Street. Spit-roasted chicken and the Brazilian "national dish," a dark, starchy ham and sausage stew called *feijoada,* are the usual things to order, after hearts of palm and shrimps cooked a variety of ways. To finish: guava jelly with cream cheese and, of course, a cup of Brazilian coffee. The management, which seems far more concerned with soccer than money, asks surprisingly little for such a big meal. Tel: 719-2105.

Not far away, at 123 West 45th Street, is **Cabaña Carioca**, a joint where music reigns instead of soccer and the menu includes a few Portuguese dishes, as well as the Brazilian standbys. The portions of food are gargantuan, which you might not notice after a few shots of *cachaça,* the Brazilian white-lightning sugar-cane liquor (which is also used in the "Brazilian margarita," the *caipirinha*). People come here to make noise, and the place is built to take it. Tel: 581-8088.

Hearty Cuban cooking is best represented at a long-running establishment called **Victor's Cuban Café**, 240 Columbus Avenue, at the corner of 71st Street, which was thriving long before Columbus Avenue became an elongated shopping mall. This is the place for roast suckling pig, for the stewed beef called *ropas viejas,* and for plenty of rum. Tel: 595-8599.

The IRT number 7 subway train can whisk you from Times Square or Grand Central in Midtown Manhattan out to Jackson Heights in Queens, where at the intersection of Roosevelt Avenue and Junction Boulevard (which is the name of the stop at which you detrain) there is a concentration of Argentine enterprises that includes several good restaurants. One of them is **La Cabaña Argentina**, at 95-91 Roosevelt Avenue. A gigantic wood-stoked grill in the front window should give it away that platters of juicy meats and sausages, the traditional *parillada*, are the house specialty, which is meant to be washed down with robust Argentine wine—all an excellent value to boot. Dinner only. Tel: (718) 429-4388.

# *STEAKS*

You could always get a good steak in New York, from the time when slaughterhouses lined the piers of the East River and the best cattle in the West were sent to New York, where they could command a higher price than anywhere else in the country. The slaughterhouses have been replaced by the United Nations and the leafy tranquillity of Beekman Place, but New Yorkers are still willing to pay exorbitant prices for a good cut of meat.

There are, essentially, two types of restaurants in New York that serve steak. There is the old-fashioned steak house where, if there is anything besides beef on the menu, it will most likely be a lamb chop or, perhaps, a lobster. At the other type of restaurant, steak shares the menu with more ornately prepared dishes, and the beef itself may come topped with a fancy sauce. The old-style steak house tends to have a rough edge, with bare wood or simply draped tables, boisterous crowds, no-nonsense service. All the amenities of a high-priced restaurant are installed in the new steak house: beautiful rooms, fine linen, and service without gruffness, plus wonderful wines. People may quarrel over who serves the best, but it really comes down to how you like to eat your steak. No matter where you go you'll pay dearly, but the steak will be of the very highest quality.

What **Christ Cella** (pronounced Cri-SEL-la), 160 East 46th Street near Third Avenue, lacks in decor, it makes up tenfold in service and the quality of its cooking. Attention is paid to the simple requirements of meat and potatoes as well as to shellfish. There are no menus, so listen carefully to the waiter's catalog of appetizers and entrées—it's not long, but you don't want to miss a single thing. Tel: 697-2479.

**Peter Luger** is worth a trip to Williamsburg in Brooklyn (where it is located at 178 Broadway). Left behind in what was once a prosperous commercial neighborhood, the restaurant is surrounded by the massive Romanesque hulks of great banks that now serve as social-service centers. But stepping into the restaurant transports you back to a more prosperous time. The waiters, one and all, are good-natured characters, and the steaks—for one, two, or three large appetites—are perfect. Reservations are required for dinner; at least a week's notice for weekends. Lunch is less hectic and full of businessmen who have cabbed over from Wall Street. To find Peter Luger look for the big signs at the end of the Williamsburg Bridge. Tel: (718) 387-7400.

**Sammy's Famous Rumanian Restaurant**, at 157 Chrystie Street, a few blocks south of Houston Street, is in yet another desolate part of the city, this time the Lower East Side. But the luxury cars are still parked, unmolested, outside, and on winter nights fur coats drape across the backs of chairs and lap into the aisle. It's an experience just to squeeze into this tiny basement room. There are seatings at 7:00 and 9:00 every night, and you are expertly hustled in and out. Cuts of beef stick out over the edges of plates, but no one seems to need a doggy bag. Jars of U-Bet chocolate syrup, seltzer, pickles, and chicken fat threaten you from the center of every table. Tel: 673-0330.

Perhaps the best example of the new-style steak house is **Sparks Steakhouse**, 210 East 46th Street just east of Third Avenue. The dining rooms are plush in a manly way, and the wine list is staggeringly vast. Steaks are cooked exactly to order, and the lobsters are so huge that diners are draped, from neck to waist, in a protective cloth. Tel: 687-4855.

Despite Italian origins, **Palm** and **Palm Too** (between 44th and 45th streets at 837 Second Avenue and 840 Second Avenue respectively) are noted for their steaks. There is sawdust on the floor and there are cartoons on the walls, but the loud and at times raucous crowds have been coming here for a good part of this century mostly for the delicious chops and T-bones. But the Italian specials—linguine in clam sauce, for one—are not to be forgotten, either. Tel: 687-2953 (837 Second Avenue); 697-5198 (840 Second Avenue).

**The Post House**, at 28 East 63rd Street, is a very handsome place with a ritzy clientele that comes for the genteel atmosphere and the excellent wine list. Nothing is a bargain here, but the cooking is carefully done and the restaurant is quiet enough to allow you to actually get some work done or hold a conversation that requires concentration. Tel: 935-2888.

# *SEAFOOD*

Every place serves fish and shellfish these days; it's what New Yorkers like to eat. Thus the old boundary between restaurants that do best by meat and restaurants that do best by fish has blurred. An institution such as Spark's Steakhouse sells virtually as much seafood as it does beef (although the bias here is toward steaklike hunks of swordfish and Norwegian salmon). But there is still a special allure to a place that conjures up sea imagery, and even if the cuisine is no better than it is in less specialized establishments, there is still something joyful in a communal gathering over the bounty of the oceans.

For some of the very best: Refer to the French Restaurants section for Le Bernardin; to Local Phenomena for The Grand Central Oyster Bar & Restaurant and The SeaGrill; to Japanese for a number of sushi bars; and to For All Ages for The Ocean Reef Grille. Here are other aquatic-oriented places.

**Le Laurier** recently opened its doors on the Upper East Side, at 1155 Third Avenue near 67th Street. It is a slightly less expensive version of Le Bernardin, but has the same devotion to an all-seafood menu (followed by luscious desserts). The stately French touch does not dim the essential goodness of the fresh catch that Le Laurier offers. The price is a notch or two below some other grand meals. Tel: 879-1199.

There are two branches of **Dock's Oyster Bar**, one on the Upper West Side at 2427 Broadway near 89th Street, and the other in Midtown on Third Avenue at 40th Street. Both cater to a lively youngish crowd that doesn't mind a fairly long wait for some fairly ordinary seafood. But the prices aren't bad, the white-tiled floors are correct, and the white wine is tossed back merrily. Tel: 724-5588 (Upper West Side) or 986-8080 (Midtown).

Similarly lively, and stronger in the stove department, is **Claire**, at 156 Seventh Avenue, near 20th Street in Chelsea. Claire has a sister restaurant in Key West, and so the mood is subtropical. The Bahaman conch chowder is zesty with pepper, the fish list changes daily, and the Key lime pie wraps it all up nicely. This is also the only place in town where the menu credits the designer of the waiters' shirts. Tel: 255-1955.

For a big, messy crab feast, you may tie on your bib and wield your mallet at **Sidewalkers'**, on the Upper West Side at 12 West 72nd Street, across the way from the Dakota Apartments. The crabs are heaped on your brown-paper-covered table with the Old Bay spices still clinging to them. After a while your fingers may be scratched and weary, but the feeling in your belly is a happy one. An array of other, very decent seafood is available, too. Tel: 799-6070.

If going for seafood also means going to the sea, then head for one of the city's little fishing ports: City Island in the Bronx or Brooklyn's Sheepshead Bay. There are plenty of restaurants on City Island, but the cooking is uniformly and inexplicably poor. Not so in Sheepshead Bay, and especially not so at **The Captain's Quarters**, at 2990 Avenue U near Batchelder Street. The Captain's Quarters buys all its fish whole and does its own filleting daily. Many of the preparations are vaguely Italian, but keep an eye out for "specials" that use some delicious fish caught locally: black sea bass, tautog (also known as blackfish), bluefish, and flounder. By car from Manhattan, take the Battery Tunnel to the Belt Parkway and get off at Knapp Street (Exit 9); follow Knapp Street and make a left on Avenue U. Or take the letter D or Q subway train to the Avenue U stop and then change to the Avenue U bus going east to Batchelder Street. The restaurant can summon a cab, on request, for the return trip. Tel: (718) 934-6800.

## *SPICY FOOD*

There are a slew of places around town that cater to the need for spicy food. Some are straightforward, serving the cuisine of countries such as Mexico and Indonesia, where spices are an intrinsic part of cooking. Others are a hodgepodge of styles—Tex-Mex, Southern, Soul Food, Cajun—where the food is often great, but the atmosphere and action are even better.

**Cinco de Mayo** has two restaurants, the original at 349 West Broadway in SoHo, and another uptown at 45 Tudor City (on an overpass near First Avenue and 42nd Street). Both serve authentic Mexican dishes—robust, lusty fare. The SoHo restaurant is a bit more casual and relaxed; the uptown branch is elegant and has a long list of regional Mexican beers. Tel: 226-5255 (SoHo); 661-5070 (uptown).

**Rosa Mexicana**, at 1063 First Avenue on the corner of 58th Street, is very stylish. The menu is unusual and often intriguing, but the cooking tends to be uneven. Guacamole, made fresh at tableside in a large, handsome stone mortar, is tops. Tel: 753-7407.

Nothing beats **Zarela**, a duplex joint at 953 Second Avenue near 51st Street. Zarela Martinez is considered by some to be the best Mexican chef in town, and her exquisite, innovative dishes go a long way to prove it. Her side plates of *arroz con crema* and *torta de arroz* are required eating. Surprisingly inexpensive. Tel: 644-6740.

**Nusantara**, at 219 East 44th Street between Second and Third avenues, is a startlingly beautiful restaurant, filled with art treasures from Indonesia. The food is intriguing, subtly spiced, and deeply flavorful, and the place is convenient to the United Nations for the Indonesian diplomatic corps who entertain here. Tel: 983-1919.

**Tommy Tang's**, 323 Greenwich Street between Duane and Reade streets (not far from the river), is both naturally and stylistically hot Thai food provides the spice and TriBeCa patrons bring the funk. The food is good, though expensive, but portions are shared so a little goes a long way. Tel: 334-9190.

**Acme Bar & Grill**, 9 Great Jones Street, near Lafayette Street and the big NoHo emporiums, proclaims its theme with hot-sauce bottles—all makes and origins—lined up on shelves around the room. You can even grab one and douse the already spicy Cajun–Gulf Coast food with a little more fire. This is a place to kick back and down a few beers. Tel: 420-1934.

The surprise at **Gulf Coast**, 489 West Street (the corner of West 12th Street and the West Side Highway), is that the restaurant manages to serve some very good Cajun food in the midst of all the drinking going on around the room, the loud music from the jukebox, and its quasi-waterfront seediness. The jambalaya and gumbos are worth the detour around the roistering patrons and their huge margaritas. Tel: 206-8790.

The best chili in town is served at the booths and counter of **Exterminator Chili**, at 305 Church Street, at White Street, south of Canal. The restaurant is tacky—some would even say intentionally so—with its Elvisiana and chile-pepper light bulbs, but prices are ridiculously low for a big bowl of the stuff. There are many varieties, graded Residential, Commercial, Industrial, or Agricultural (vegetarian); all are exceptional. Tel: 219-3070.

**Sylvia's Restaurant**, at 328 Lenox Avenue between 126th and 127th streets in central Harlem (take the 1, 2, or 3 IRT subway to 125th Street), is unequaled in the city for its Southern cooking. Black-eyed peas, collard greens, and fried chicken are served in great heaps in a casual, homey atmosphere. Pies here are pretty darn good, too, and the breakfasts are life enhancing. Tel: 534-9414.

You can also get some fine soul food at **Jezebel**, 630 Ninth Avenue, at 45th Street. The room is decorated with lace, funky antiques, and lavish flowers. Smothered pork chops and spare ribs are excellent. Tel: 582-1045.

## *CROWD SCENES*

With the exception of a few hushed gastronomic laboratories, all of New York's restaurants are sociable places, but some go a step beyond and are dominated by people who have turned socializing into a craft, or possibly a cause, one that they pursue with more ardor than they do their daytime activities. In some, the clubbishness of Wall Street, the media, or sports devotion transforms the jammed-in conditions of a subway at rush hour into many people's idea of a good time.

Almost every night of the week, a very hip, aggressively dressed crowd packs **Indochine**, at 430 Lafayette Street, just south of Astor Place and 8th Street, across the street from the Public Theater. Eccentric eyeglasses appear to serve as talismans that unleash kooky, insistent behavior among the young things crushed together along the banquettes. Along with the finely prepared Cambodian cooking, you'll get valuable pointers on hair styles, clothing extremes, and conversation stoppers. Tel: 505-5111.

After wandering around NoHo (around Broadway north of Houston Street) for a while or flipping through the racks at Tower Records on Broadway and East 4th Street, check out **Bayamo**, at 704 Broadway. The place is huge and often filled to the rafters with New York University students pledging allegiance to their first well-made cocktails and talking up a storm. The rafters themselves are hung with examples of huge, wacky East Village sculpture. The cooking is based on the Cuban-Chinese style of the barrios and happens to be delicious. Tel: 475-5151.

The far smaller **Great Jones Café**, 54 Great Jones Street, east of Lafayette Street in NoHo, is open very late, and the later it gets the wilder the crowd seems to be. Many of the people pushing through the door haven't seen one another since yesterday, and the sight of these friends being reunited is touching. And if that's not enough, the rib-sticking, down-home food is very good, and the Cajun martinis are narcotic. Tel: 674-9304.

Very serious Cajun-Southern food is dished up at **Memphis**, 329 Columbus Avenue near 76th Street. Remember the address, because the restaurant is unmarked. The activity at the bar, when viewed from a dinner table on the balcony, might recall a big market day in Memphis, Egypt, while the music is a big night in Memphis, Tennessee. Very high voltage and very high decibels, but the food is even more potent. The mystery is how so many great-looking people can eat this way and still look as though they never have. Tel: 496-1840.

**107 West**, at 2787 Broadway (near West 107th Street), is an offshoot of Memphis. Columbia students and young people spending the big money they're earning from their first jobs fill the place. From the way they take to the surroundings, you can easily see that many nights in their future will be spent in restaurants. It's more casual and less expensive than Memphis, but just as crowded and hopping. Tel: 864-1555.

A newcomer to the scene is **Delta 88**, 332 Eighth Avenue near 27th Street. Funky, low-life decor meant to seem (somewhat patronizingly) like a Mississippi sharecropper's social seems to heighten the flavors of the Southern cooking. Proximity to the Fashion Institute of Technology means extraordinary clothes on young customers who are very unlikely to ever reel in a catfish on their own hook. Frosted bottles of Dixie beers are the thing to drink. Very reasonably priced. Tel: 924-3499.

The hangar-size hangout of the moment is **Café Iguana**, which tries to dominate the corner of Park Avenue South and 19th Street but has competition from a similarly gigantic bar-restaurant across the way. At nightfall you can see a throng of business-suited Romeos and their Juliets, fresh from work or a workout, hastening down the avenue to take places on the line to get into the Iguana for big drinks and some incidental Mexican food. Places like this don't last long (their formerly devoted customers abandon them without a thought), but their short lives are a blast. Tel: 529-4770.

**B. Smith's** is a beacon of civility at the fairly grimy

intersection of Eighth Avenue and 47th Street, near the Theater District. It is not only a good place to eat, with a wide-ranging menu, but is also a gathering place for members of New York's soigné black elite, who have coalesced around the gracious and quite beautiful Barbara Smith, a former actress and fashion model, who lends her presence to the place most nights. Many of the impeccably dressed customers have perfected the art of occupying a table with such relaxed, almost Parisian confidence that the act of conversing seems pointless. Tel: 247-2222.

The Upper East Side is dotted with places that have their almost religious adherents among the very-well-to-do who live nearby. **Mortimer's** (at the corner of Lexington Avenue and 75th Street), **J. G. Melon** (at the corner of Third Avenue and 74th Street), **Jim McMullen** (on Third Avenue near 76th Street), **Sam's Café** (on Third Avenue near 80th Street), and many others might strike the uninitiated as overcrowded, uncomfortable, and charmless, but to many of the locals they are kitchen, pantry, dining room, and clubhouse rolled into one. All serve a reliable hamburger and respectable salads, but their social cachet stems more from what they lack (the obvious trappings of luxury) than what they provide (which is a hearty welcome to the regulars). None is terribly pricey. Tel: Mortimer's, 517-6400; Melon, 744-0585; McMullen, 861-4700; Sam's, 988-5300.

Younger East Siders and young Europeans love to shoehorn themselves into places that specialize in pastas and dressy little pizzas. **Mezzaluna** and nearby **Ciao Bella**, both on Third Avenue near 75th Street, are always hopping, even though tables are so close together you might mistake the neighbors' conversation and food for your own. The style has spread to SoHo, in the form of **Mezzogiorno** at the corner of Spring and Sullivan streets, and to Greenwich Village in **Mosaica** at 24 Fifth Avenue, on the corner of 9th Street. The meals in all of them are usually simple and delicious, but service is often infuriatingly muddled, and no one speaks with a soft voice. Tel: Mezzaluna, 535-9600; Ciao Bella, 288-2555; Mezzogiorno, 334-2112; Mosaica, 529-5757.

# *INDIAN*

The string of Indian restaurants on East 6th Street, between First and Second avenues, has benefited from the redevelopment of the East Village. The street, once dark and grungy, is now well lighted, with fashionable clothing stores and galleries open late into the evening. The restaurants themselves, as befitting the neighborhood's new prosperity, have been spruced up and are very welcoming indeed.

The best restaurant on the strip is **Mitali**, at 334 East 6th Street. Except for very large groups, reservations are not taken—hence the long line outside the door on weekends. Arrive before 7:00 or after 9:00 and the wait won't be as long. Once you are inside the low-ceilinged room, which is hung with tapestries and billowing cloth, such dishes as quail stuffed with almonds and ground meat, or coriander-infused *dansak* curry take precedence. Beer is the drink that helps with the spices. Tel: 533-2508.

The attraction at both **Romna**, at 322 East 6th Street, and **Bombay**, at 330 East 6th Street, is the live music. Sitar and drums heighten the authentic taste of the curries and tandoori specialties. Tel: 475-9394 for Romna and 260-8229 for Bombay.

Around the corner, on First Avenue, a lavish banquet for a crowd can be had for very little money in **Royal India** at 93 First Avenue. The two long, narrow rooms are pretty and fill quickly on most nights. The food is a blend of Northern and Western styles; the first includes cream-based specialties such as *tikka* chicken *mahani* sweetened with pineapple, and the second means fiery hot ones, as evidenced by the Madras Special's combination of chiles and aromatic spices that have been rubbed deeply into pieces of tender lamb. Tel: 533-2508.

Another pocket of Indian cooking is on and near Lexington Avenue between East 27th and 29th streets. The sharp, almost sweet scent of heady seasonings fills the air from the many spice shops in the neighborhood.

**Annapurna**, at 108 Lexington Avenue, is a little fancier than other restaurants on the block. The room is very attractive, and delicious regional specialties are served in a friendly manner. Tel: 679-1284.

**Madras Palace**, 104 Lexington Avenue, serves only vegetarian dishes from the south of India. Rich sauces and earthy combinations of beans and vegetables, such as cauliflower with ginger and coriander, or potato patties stuffed with lentils and chiles, make up for the lack of meat. The kitchen declares itself "kosher" because it is so rigorously vegetarian. Tel: 532-3314.

**Tabaq**, at 101 Lexington Avenue at 27th Street, has a

tandoor oven in the window. The dining rooms are down a flight of stairs, brightly lighted and very plain. The cooking is rough with spices, so there is a slow, steady burn to the food, but everything is prepared to order and, if you can handle it, decidedly delicious. Tel: 683-1030.

As you head uptown, Indian restaurants become more lavish and seem to compete with one another for beautiful decor and genial service. **Darbar**, 44 West 56th Street, has long been considered the most elegant, with its intricately carved screens and luxurious velvet covering the walls. The food is also exquisite. A buffet of wonderful dishes is provided at lunch in the upstairs portion of the restaurant, and it is a real bargain. Tel: 432-7227.

One of the most unusual restaurants in the city is **Bukhara**, at 148 East 48th Street between Lexington and Third. When the restaurant first opened, patrons were provided with eating utensils only on request. The tandoori cooking was so luscious—the meat came smeared with a combination of spices mellowed with yogurt or lemon—that eating with your hands seemed natural. Now forks and spoons are at every place, but the cooking is still wonderful. The restaurant is also a treat for its beautiful display of rugs and copperware. Tel: 838-1811.

**Dawat**, 210 East 58th Street, is a very spacious and pretty newcomer to the scene. Madhur Jaffrey, star of films by Ismail Merchant and James Ivory and a renowned cooking teacher and cookbook author in her own right, developed the dishes on the menu. Here you'll find *bhel poori,* a plate laden with crisp wafers, puffed wheat, and sweet chutneys that is a re-creation of the legendary street snacks of Delhi; and *rogan josh,* here, goat simmered in a cardamom-infused sauce until it falls deliciously off the bone. These are classic, authentic dishes, beautifully rendered. Tel: 355-7555.

## *KOREAN*

West 32nd Street off Fifth Avenue is the hub of Korean cooking in the city. Surrounded by businesses connected with the Korean community, the restaurants on these streets fill with businessmen on the weekdays and families out on the town on the weekends.

**New York Kom Tang House**, at 32 West 32nd Street (off Broadway), is noted for its beef barbecue. The diner sits at a table with a metal well in the middle, where a hibachi is placed. The waitress brings a pile of marinated short ribs of beef and spreads it onto the grill. Once the meat is cooked, the diner rolls the meat in a lettuce leaf along with a garlic clove and hot pepper, and dabs it with *miso* sauce. Bowls of *kim chi*—pickled vegetables—and soup precede the meat; fruit and a stick of gum follow, along with the very reasonable check. Tel: 947-8482.

Nearby is **Kang Suh** at 1250 Broadway (32nd Street). Downstairs is a Japanese-style sushi bar; upstairs are the tables with wells. Barbecued pork is the specialty—be sure to let the edges burn to a savory crispness. Tel: 564-6845.

**Seoul House**, at 9 West 32nd Street, is the fancy spot on the block for celebrations. Downstairs is rather plain, but upstairs is luxurious and, on most nights, there is a lot of toast making and clinking of glasses. Prices are slightly higher here than elsewhere, but the cooking is very good. Tel: 279-9400.

**Woo Lae Oak of Seoul**, at 77 West 46th Street, is ideal for pre-theater dining, but make a reservation, especially on the weekends. The large room fills up quickly with families and, later, with big groups of young people, all having a boisterous time as the room fills with smoke from the table grills and the air becomes scented with warm, delicious aromas. Tel: 869-9958.

# *MEDITERRANEAN AND MIDDLE EASTERN*

Many purveyors of Middle Eastern food have come to feel uncomfortable with that designation lately. Somehow the heading "Mediterranean" fits more agreeably, and the justification comes from the interrelatedness of cuisines from Morocco to Turkey to Greece. Fortunately the change hasn't compromised their spice-loving, vibrant style of cooking.

One of the embodiments of it is Andree Abramoff, who, along with her husband, Charlie, runs the charming little **Café Crocodile**, at 354 East 74th Street, near First Avenue. The crocodile motif stems from Andree and Charlie's youth among the cosmopolitan Jews of Egypt (she occasionally offers a selection of appetizers that she calls an "Alexandria Quartet"). Her family was of French nationality, and so she claims Pan-Mediterranean rights as a cook. Her style is earthy but subtle, and Charlie stocks very good, very affordable wines (several bottles can go down for the price of one bottle elsewhere). Tel: 249-6619.

**Anatolia** is a bright and airy Turkish restaurant at 1422 Third Avenue, near 81st Street. Homesick Turks really do come here for the classic eggplant dish *iman bayaldi* (literally, "the iman swooned") as well as for an ungodly succulent quail grilled in grape leaves. The Turkish desserts are light and delectable (including an authentic pudding made from pounded chicken), and the Turkish coffee is as dark, sludgy, and revivifying as expected. Costs are reasonable. Tel: 517-6262.

Greek food is not the ready-to-hand specialty here that it is in a number of American cities, despite the huge Greek community in Astoria, Queens. But one bright spot is **Periyali** at 35 West 20th Street. It has an uncluttered Aegean atmosphere and lovingly prepared food, some of which is set out on a display table for all to admire. Tangy, garlicky flavors predominate, and dishes such as moussaka are rescued from heaviness by a deft kitchen. Tel: 463-7890.

A strip of little Israeli and Lebanese spots along MacDougal Street in Greenwich Village caters to those in search of vegetarian nourishment and those in search of an inexpensive piquant meal. The street might well be renamed Pita Place someday. Most of the restaurants here are undecorated storefronts where falafel and gyros and salads are ready in a jiffy. You can sit down and spend a little more time in the **Olive Tree Café**, 117 MacDougal Street, a short stroll south from Washington Square, and still enjoy the same restorative, easily affordable cooking. A comedy club beckons from downstairs. Tel: 254-3630.

## BROOKLYN MIDDLE EASTERN

Along Atlantic Avenue, between Court and Henry streets, and a few blocks from Brooklyn's Borough Hall (and easily reached from Manhattan via the 2, 3, 4, 5, N, and R subway lines), there is a high concentration of Middle Eastern shops and restaurants. Jars of spices, nuts, and grains line the shelves of the shops, and from the bakeries comes the smell of honey and ground pistachios and the warm fragrance of baked phyllo dough.

It's impossible to walk down the avenue and not become incredibly hungry. Head for **Dar Lebnan**, at 151 Atlantic Avenue, for some *babaganouj* (smoked eggplant with tahini, garlic, and lemon juice) or hummus (mashed and spiced chick peas) and lamb kebabs. The restaurant is clean and sparsely decorated and, at night, liable to be crowded. It's also very inexpensive. Tel: (718) 596-9215.

Another good restaurant on the strip is **Almontaser**, at 218 Court Street. *Tabouli*—cracked wheat salad—and *glabas*—spiced lamb with green peppers—are very good here. Tel: (718) 624-9267.

**Sido Restaurant**, 151 Atlantic Avenue, is new and rather luxurious, with fine wood paneling and beautiful paintings of the major Muslim capitals, but the prices are still low. The "Sido dinner" includes soup, appetizers (hummus, stuffed grape leaves, and *babaganouj*), and kebabs for a main course, all for $14. A good deal by any standard. Tel: (718) 237-4019.

A long and beautiful wooden boat is moored inside the **Tripoli**, at 156 Atlantic Avenue. At night when the lights are low the room seems magically out to sea. The lamb dishes are very good here, and the service is excellent. Tel: (718) 596-5800.

## *MIDDLE AND EASTERN EUROPEAN*

Like many groups before and after them, the German and Slavic immigrants who came in the great wave that hit American shores in the latter half of the 19th century settled on the **Lower East Side**. What remains today of their early efforts in this new land are a few good restaurants that serve honest home cooking at a very reasonable price.

Chief among these places is the **Ukrainian Restaurant**, at 140 Second Avenue near 9th Street. You enter through a long, drab hallway into a spartan dining room, where the tables are filled with Ukrainian families and the new, more prosperous (or artistically bent) residents of the neighborhood. Try to sit in the front room—it's more pleasant and the service is better—and bring a healthy appetite. Portions are large and the food—pickled herring, borscht, stuffed cabbage, and *bigoš*, to name a few specialties—is hearty. To wash this all down try one of the rich dark beers. No credit cards are accepted. Tel: 533-6765.

The **Veselka Coffee Shop**, at 144 Second Avenue between 9th Street and St. Mark's Place, is a neighborhood landmark. The swirling murals inside and outside the restaurant depict shop owners and old residents of the area. The pirogi here are excellent, as are the blintzes—with plenty of sour cream. Veselka is open late and becomes very lively with a good cross section of the East Village population. Tel: 228-9682.

**Leshko Coffee Shop**, on the corner of Avenue A (number 111), across from Tompkins Square Park, has very good borscht and stews. People tend to linger long in the comfortable booths and watch the action in the park through the large windows. Tel: 473-9208.

**Jolanta**, 119 First Avenue between 7th and 8th streets, is little more than a counter, but it is also one of the finest Polish restaurants in the city. The hunter's stew, a rich, glimmering concoction of meat and cabbage, is delicious, as are the various kinds of pirogi. To feel like one of the locals, just grab a stool and point to whatever you want. Tel: 473-9936.

When the *General Slocum,* an excursion steamer, capsized on June 15, 1904, more than a thousand people from the Lower East Side lost their lives. The victims were mostly of German descent, and the disaster forced the surviving grief-stricken families to move to other parts of the city. One of the areas they settled in was **Yorkville** on the Upper East Side. There they joined Czechs, Slovaks, Hungarians, and a smattering of Irish.

**Csarda**, at 1477 Second Avenue between 77th and 78th streets, is a reminder of what this neighborhood was like in the old days. A bright and trim room, decorated with colorful Hungarian rugs and glazed earthenware, the restaurant serves big platters of hearty, delicious food. The smell of paprika, sweet onions, and garlic from such dishes as stuffed peppers, roasted chicken, and veal *flecken* fill the air. Tel: 472-2892.

**Café Geiger**, at 206 East 86th Street near Third Avenue, looks like a pastry café, but it also serves such traditional German fare as *eisbein* (steamed pigs' feet), Wiener schnitzel, and sweet-and-sour red cabbage. The desserts are elaborate whipped-cream affairs, and all are delicious. Tel: 734-4428.

**The Red Tulip**, 439 East 75th Street between York and First avenues, is a very lively and pretty Hungarian restaurant. This is no place to go if you're in a quiet mood; the dining room becomes very crowded and gay, with strolling musicians dressed as gypsies. Stuffed cabbage, grilled Hungarian sausage, and crackling duck here are exceptional. Tel: 734-4893.

**Brighton Beach** has come to be known as "Odessa by the

Sea" because of the thousands of Russians who emigrated in the 1970s and settled here. The restaurants in the area not only serve terrific Russian food but offer a crash course in a very lively culture.

The D train stops right in the heart of Brighton Beach, which is also the name of the stop, and the **Odessa** (at 1113 Brighton Beach Avenue between 13th and 14th streets) is close by. Don't come any earlier than 9:30 on a weekend night or you are liable to have the whole garishy decorated room to yourself. And don't order from the menu; have the buffet at about $26 (it goes up, but only slightly, with the quality of the evening's musicians). The price includes a bottle of vodka for a party of four, two trays worth of cold and hot appetizers (anything from homemade ham to smoked fish to ribs with potatoes), main courses (lamb kebab, roast chicken), and dessert. The music is lively, and everyone dances. It makes for a memorable night. Tel: (718) 332-3223.

The action at **The National**, at 273 Brighton Beach Avenue, begins even later, but, like the Odessa, it goes on and on. The National holds 200 people, and on a good weekend it seems to hold more. Tel: (718) 646-1225.

**Gastronom Moscow**, on the Brighton Beach boardwalk near 6th Street, is a dimly lit boardwalk café that serves tea and vodka, a place to linger and watch the ocean, especially when the beach crowds are gone. Tel: (718) 934-7418.

For lunch there is **Café Armenia**, on Brighton 4 Street, just off Brighton Beach Avenue. It's a homey, comfortable little restaurant that serves stews and soups, coffee and tea. Tel: (718) 743-2444.

## A PROPER TEA

Not everyone stops for high tea in New York, but those who do don't mind being different. It leaves more room for them. At four o'clock these days it's not just maiden aunts and their visiting relatives who settle down with their cups and plates, but business people, too, who find the calm and elegant surroundings of the best tearooms to be conducive to the closing of a deal. Tea is the relaxed and perfect setting for catching up with friends, cooling your heels after a day's shopping, or simply recharging for the evening ahead.

**The Mayfair Regent**, at 65th Street and Park Avenue,

provides a perfect tea. At four the ivory-colored velvet settees and armchairs slowly fill with an elegant clientele. Potted palms and silk lampshades reflecting soft lights give the room an intimate feeling. There are seven kinds of teas to choose from, such as Lapsang Souchong, Russian, and jasmine. Finger sandwiches are delicious, especially the smoked salmon and chicken, and the scones... well, it's hard not to eat a stack of them. Tel: 288-0800.

The problem with **The Rotunda**, where tea is served at the Pierre Hotel, at Fifth Avenue and 61st Street, is that there are only eight tables nestled in this lavishly decorated room. Trompe l'oeil arches filled with romantic vistas of the Italian countryside and balconies, with handsome men and women of another age leaning over to see the real people below, give the room a playful air. But once you are seated upon a coveted sofa or in the arms of an overstuffed chair, the focus is on the table spread. A three-tiered silver dumbwaiter is brought to the table, laden with savory sandwiches, Dundee fruitcake, scones, and tarts. The wide choice of teas almost seems to be an afterthought. Reserve a table. Tel: 838-8000.

**The Gold Room** at the Helmsley Palace, at 455 Madison Avenue at 50th Street, is as beautiful as the Pierre. The room was designed by Stanford White as part of the 19th-century Neo-Renaissance Villard Houses and modeled after the Palazzo della Cancelleria in Rome. The tables are set with gold-trimmed china and, on an overhead balcony, a harpist plays. Eighteen teas are offered with the three-course menu. First there are the properly thin finger sandwiches. Next come warm scones with Devonshire cream and fruit preserves. Last is a tray of fruitcakes, tarts, and pastries. Tel: 888-7000.

For a bit more fun during tea repair to **The Gallery** at the Carlyle Hotel, 35 East 76th Street. Nestled to the side of the lobby, the comfortable arrangement of velvet love seats and upholstered armchairs gives a bird's-eye view of the interesting comings and goings in the lobby. The offerings are not as lavish here as at the three places above, with only a few types of teas available, but everything is quite good. Slipping into the cocktail hour with a sherry is encouraged. Tel: 744-1600.

Downtown at Barney's New York clothing store there is **Le Café**, at 106 Seventh Avenue at 17th Street. On the lower level, in a charming garden setting—complete with a rustic fountain of frogs and hand-painted palm frond mirrors—Le Café offers a buffet of cold seafood, smoked fish, egg salad, and Polish ham. There are also luscious cheeses and many, many cakes and sweets, such as poppy seed, flourless chocolate cake, and profiteroles. And not everyone is sipping tea: A nice wine list is available, too. Tel: 929-9000.

## *FOR ALL AGES*

"In America, there are two classes of travel," Robert Benchley wrote. "First class, and with children." The same could be said for dining out. Given enough money and a few years of vigorous training, it's possible that a parent could walk into the finest restaurant in the city with his or her children in tow and have a pleasant meal. But the evening would do little to promote how much fun eating out should be, and it would do less to improve the quality of family relations.

Better to take the kids to a place where everyone can truly enjoy themselves, like **The Hard Rock Café**, at 221 West 57th Street between Seventh Avenue and Broadway. Everything is here: the constant beat of music, personable, good-looking young help, big hamburgers, and gooey desserts. There is often a long line outside the door to endure before you're allowed in to wait still longer for a table, but once inside you can get a drink at the bar and stare at the memorabilia: Joan Jett's black high-top sneakers, Prince's purple cape, Elvis's guitar, and stacks of gold records. Tel: 489-6565.

Across town there is **Serendipity**, at 225 East 60th Street. Young "society" girls who didn't want to go to the Village in the 1960s used to hold court amid the exuberantly funky decor of this toy shop–restaurant. You'll still catch them here, but now they bring their children and discreetly chow down on bowls of chili, hamburgers, and foot-long hot dogs. No one passes on dessert, especially "F-f-f-frozen hot chocolate." Tel: 838-3531.

Outside **Two Boots** at 37 Avenue A on the Lower East Side there's a brightly painted seal balancing a ball on the tip of his nose. A ride on him will cost a quarter. The very good Cajun-Italian food served inside is only slightly more expensive. A hip, East Village crowd fills the place on most nights. Tel: 505-5450.

The second floor of the main market building in the **South Street Seaport** is filled with stalls that offer food of every description. Long curls of french fries, oysters and clams on the half shell, barbecue, deli, pastries—it's a glutton's (or growing child's) delight.

For a more relaxed (and perhaps more balanced) meal, the seaport has a few good restaurants. At the top of the main market building there is the **Ocean Reef Grille**. Tables outside on pleasant days afford a wonderful view of the ships and bridges on the river, and the bustle below of the seaport square. The menu has an Oriental touch, so it's best to keep it simple. Tel: 608-7400.

Across the square, at the corner of Fulton and South streets, is the **Northstar Tavern**. Housed in one of the oldest buildings in the city (where slave runners used to congregate), the tavern offers a large selection of domestic and imported beers for adults, and simple, English pub–type food for the young people. Tel: 509-6757.

For dessert, or to hold you over until the next meal, stop in at **Die Fledermaus**, across the square from the main market building at Front Street. There are salads and tiny sandwiches, but they're incidental compared to such Viennese pastry delights as chocolate mousse cake, lemon swirl, and raspberry tarts. Tel: 269-5890.

Across Front Street at Pier 17 there is **Pedro O'Hara's**. The swirling blue murals inside give the restaurant a sort of fun-house look, and the Tex-Mex food is not to be taken too seriously, but you can sit outside and enjoy the sailing boats. (Best for children at lunch; evening brings the Wall Street singles horde.) Tel: 267-7634.

What the **Boathouse Café** on Central Park's Lake, on the East Drive north of 72nd Street, sorely lacks in culinary delights it makes up for in charm. Selections from the Northern Italian menu should be kept simple. Better yet, come for drinks and dessert, then a row across the lake. Tel: 517-2233.

If you've been wandering around the city and you need a respite, give the children a bellyful of good things to eat at **Sarabeth's Kitchen** at 423 Amsterdam Avenue at 80th Street (not far from the Museum of Natural History) and 1295 Madison between 92nd and 93rd. Prices are moderate, and the room is homey and relaxed. Brunch is particularly good and, for munching later, stock up on the brownies and cookies from the case up front. Tel: 496-6280.

**Hamburger Harry's** has two locations: 145 West 45th Street, and 157 Chambers Street south of Canal. A battalion of cooks man charcoal grills on a raised station in the back of the room and flip big, juicy meat patties at an astonishing rate. To go with the burgers there are interesting toppings as well as great french fries. Kids will like to drink the lime Rickies. Tel: 840-2756 (West 45th); 267-4446 (Chambers Street).

On the edge of SoHo, the **Moondance Diner**, at 80 Sixth Avenue (Grand Street), serves standard American road food at a decent price. The diner is open 24 hours; it gets busy at lunch, then again after midnight when the clubs let out. Tel: 226-1191.

A lot of food for a little money is the main attraction at a number of other diners around town. **The Horn & Hardart Dine-O-Mat**, at 942 Third Avenue at 57th Street, is the queen of the pack. Meat loaf and open-faced turkey sandwiches are terrific here, as are the retro decor and rock 'n' roll. Tel: 755-3755.

**Ellen's Stardust**, at 56th Street and Sixth Avenue, accepts only cash, but the prices seem to be the same as they would have been during the Eisenhower administration. Not to be missed here are Brown Cows and hamburgers. Tel: 307-7575.

Another good buy are pasta restaurants. **Pasta Bella**, at 754 Ninth Avenue at 51st Street, serves big bowls of noodles, generously sauced. For children who clean their plates, the restaurant has been known to add an extra dollop of whipped cream to their desserts. Tel: 307-5484.

**Spaghetti Western**, 59 Reade Street between Church and Broadway in the southern part of TriBeCa, is often crowded and noisy, but the pasta is delicious. Complicated, filling sauces and very good crunchy bread will be enough to make even the most voracious appetite sleepy. Tel: 513-1333.

## *OUT LATE*

If you're up past midnight there are many places around town where you can still get a good feed. Some are scenes unto themselves, and just getting admitted to them may take until the wee hours of the morning.

**Nell's**, 246 West 14th Street, **M.K.**, at Fifth Avenue and 25th Street, and **Au Bar**, 48 East 58th Street, are just such places. Nell's began the trend in this category—mock gentlemen's clubs, decorated in English style—but the differences between them can sometimes be detected only by the chosen few who attend regularly. In all you'll find good dance music, a very stylish crowd, a lot of posing, and, surprisingly (especially at Nell's), some darn good food. Reservations for dinner allegedly help, and there is of course a cover charge if you're fortunate enough to be chosen by the nice men at the doors. Tel: 675-1567 for Nell's; 779-1340 for M.K.; 308-9455 for Au Bar.

**The Canal Bar**, 511 Greenwich Street (corner of Spring Street, west of SoHo), is another club that masquerades as a restaurant. It's very trendy, hip, and packed on most nights. The food is uneven but no one in the room seems to care. The good thing here is you can reserve a spot (mandatory past 10:00 P.M.) and avoid humiliation at the hands of the doormen. Tel: 334-5150.

**Trixie's**, 307 West 47th Street between Eighth and Ninth avenues, is loud and fun, and the dancing in the aisles just goes on and on. Although diners are crowded into small tables, the simply prepared food is pretty good. Entertainment is provided, on occasion, by the illustrious Mr. Spoons and, more often, the audience at large. Tel: 840-9537.

**Acme Bar & Grill**, 9 Great Jones Street, is a good restaurant that serves fiery Southern cooking (see Spicy Food, above). But past midnight the crowds come more to drink and mingle than to eat. Tel: 420-1934. This is also true at the **Great Jones Café**, 54 Great Jones Street. Cajun martinis and the very good jukebox fuel the frenzy. The cooking is tasty, too. Tel: 674-9304.

**Le Zinc**, 139 Duane Street in TriBeCa, is a Paris-style bistro, a long red room with azure clouds painted on the ceiling. It helps to be dressed beautifully, or just to *be* beautiful, to get a good seat. The food is incidental to the scene after 10:00 P.M. Tel: 732-1226.

For just a good hamburger and beer in a convivial setting there is **The Broome Street Bar**, at 363 West Broadway in SoHo. There's a long bar in front and a pleasant, dimly lighted back room. Tel: 925-2086.

Another good hamburger joint is the **Moondance Diner**, 80 Sixth Avenue at Grand Street (see For All Ages, above). The menu is pretty standard, but the fare is revitalizing, especially after a night of dancing. Tel: 226-1191.

Breakfast begins at 1:00 A.M. at **The Empire Diner**, 210 Tenth Avenue at 22nd Street. An assorted clientele from all parts of the city congregates for scrambled eggs and hash browns or a very rich and satisfying sundae. Tel: 243-2736.

For a little more substance try **The Ballroom**, at 253 West

28th Street near Eighth Avenue (see Spanish, above). Chef Felipe Rojas-Lombardi cooks like no one else in New York the luscious and aromatic dishes of Spain. The cabaret offers top talent, and the relaxed bar area is crowded with little plates of lusty *tapas*. (The Ballroom also offers a luncheon buffet that is one of the city's least known culinary treasures.) Tel: 244-3005.

What's bad about going late to the **Hard Rock Café**, 221 West 57th Street between Seventh Avenue and Broadway, is the line out front. It can get longer and longer as the night progresses. Once inside, and once you're seated (another wait; see For All Ages, above), it's like being at a good loud party, provided you're young and you like your music strong and uninterrupted. Good hefty hamburgers, chicken club sandwiches, and desserts. Tel: 489-6565.

If you're in the East Village try the **Tompkins Park Restaurant**, at 141 Avenue A at the corner of 9th Street. The food and service are casual and good, though prices have inched up a bit with the changing neighborhood. Tel: 260-4798.

## *RESTAURANTS BY NEIGHBORHOOD*

The following is a list of New York restaurants organized by neighborhood; for descriptions, addresses, and telephone numbers, consult the preceding listings, organized by type of food and special interest.

### *Lower Manhattan*
Acme Bar & Grill (Cajun) (see Spicy Food)
Bouley (American)
Chanterelle (American)
Die Fledermaus (dessert) (see For All Ages)
Exterminator Chili (American) (see Spicy Food)
Grand Palace (Chinese)
Great Shanghai (Chinese)
H.S.F. (Chinese)
Hamburger Harry's (For All Ages)
The Nice Restaurant (Chinese)
Northstar Tavern (pub food) (see For All Ages)
Ocean Reef Grille (seafood) (see For All Ages)
The Odeon (American)
Pedro O'Hara's (Tex-Mex) (see For All Ages)
The Phoenix Garden (Chinese)
Rakel (American)

Sammy's Famous Rumanian Restaurant (Steaks)
The Silver Palace (Chinese)
Siu Lam Kung (Chinese)
South Street Seaport (see For All Ages)
Spaghetti Western (Italian) (see For All Ages)
Windows on the World (Multinational) (see Local Phenomena)
Le Zinc (Out Late)

## Downtown above Canal Street

Annapurna (Indian)
Arqua (Italian)
The Ballroom (Spanish and Latin American)
Barocco (Italian)
Bayamo (Cuban-Chinese) (see Crowd Scenes)
Bombay (Indian)
Broome Street Bar (Out Late)
Le Café (Tea)
Café Iguana (Mexican) (see Crowd Scenes)
The Canal Bar (Out Late)
Cent'Anni (Italian)
Chelsea Trattoria (Italian)
Chez Jacqueline (French)
Cinco de Mayo (Mexican) (see Spicy Food)
Claire (Seafood)
Coach House (American)
La Colombe d'Or (French)
Delta 88 (Southern) (see Crowd Scenes)
Empire Diner (Out Late)
Eze (French)
Florent (French)
La Gauloise (French)
Grand Ticino (Italian)
Great Jones Café (Cajun) (see Crowd Scenes)
Gulf Coast (Cajun) (see Spicy Food)
Indochine (Cambodian) (see Crowd Scenes)
Jolanta (see Middle and Eastern European)
Leshko Coffee Shop (see Middle and Eastern European)
M.K. (Out Late)
Madras Palace (Indian)
Mezzogiorno (Italian) (see Crowd Scenes)
Mitali (Indian)
Moondance Diner (American) (see For All Ages)
Mosaica (Italian) (see Crowd Scenes)
Nell's (Out Late)
Nishi NoHo (Japanese)

Olive Tree Café (Middle Eastern) (see Mediterranean and Middle Eastern)
Omen (Japanese)
Onini (Italian)
Periyali (Greek) (see Mediterranean and Middle Eastern)
Positano (Italian)
Puglia (Italian)
Quatorze (French)
El Rincon de España (Spanish and Latin American)
Rio Mar (Spanish and Latin American)
Romna (Indian)
Rosolio (Italian)
Royal India (Indian)
Second Avenue Kosher Deli (delicatessen) (see Local Phenomena)
Sevilla (Spanish)
Da Silvano (Italian)
Siracusa (Italian)
Tabaq (Indian)
Taormina (Italian)
Tommy Tang's (Thai) (see Spicy Food)
Tompkins Park Restaurant (Out Late)
Au Troquet (French)
Two Boots (Cajun/Italian) (see For All Ages)
Ukrainian Restaurant (see Middle and Eastern European)
Da Umberto (Italian)
Vanessa (American)
Veselka Coffee Shop (see Middle and Eastern European)
Villa Mosconi (Italian)
Villa Pensa (Italian)

## *Midtown*

An American Place (American)
Au Bar (Out Late)
B. Smith's (American) (see Crowd Scenes)
Bellini by Cipriani (Italian)
Le Bernardin (French)
The Brazilian Coffee Restaurant (see Spanish and Latin American)
Bukhara (Indian)
Cabaña Carioca (Brazilian Portuguese) (see Spanish and Latin American)
La Caravelle (French)
The Carnegie Delicatessen and Restaurant (delicatessen) (see Local Phenomena)
Chez Josephine (French)

Chez Napoleon (French)
China Gardens (Chinese)
Chin Chin (Chinese)
Christ Cella (Steaks)
Cinco de Mayo (Mexican) (see Spicy Food)
La Côte Basque (French)
Le Cygne (French)
Darbar (Indian)
Dawat (Indian)
Dock's Oyster Bar (Seafood)
East—The Town of Taste (Japanese)
Ellen's Stardust (American) (see For All Ages)
Four Seasons (American) (see Local Phenomena)
The Gold Room (Tea)
Grand Central Oyster Bar and Restaurant (seafood) (see Local Phenomena)
Hamburger Harry's (see For All Ages)
Hard Rock Café (burgers) (see For All Ages)
Hatsuhana (Japanese)
The Horn & Hardart Dine-O-Mat (see For All Ages)
Jezebel (Southern) (see Spicy Food)
Kang Suh (Korean)
Lafayette (French)
Lattanzi (Italian)
Lutèce (French)
Restaurant Maurice (French)
Nakagawa (Japanese)
New York Kom Tang House (Korean)
Nusantara (Indonesian) (see Spicy Food)
Palio (Italian)
Palm and Palm Too (Steaks)
Pasta Bella (Italian) (see For All Ages)
Rainbow Room (American) (see Local Phenomena)
René Pujol (French)
The Rotunda (Tea)
Russian Tea Room (Russian) (see Local Phenomena)
San Domenico (Italian)
SeaGrill (seafood) (see Local Phenomena)
Seoul House (Korean)
Seryna (Japanese)
Spark Steakhouse (Steaks)
Sushiden (Japanese)
Takesushi (Japanese)
Tang's Chariot (Chinese)
Taro Japanese Noodle Restaurant (Japanese)
Trixie's (Out Late)

"21" Club (American)
Woo Lae Oak of Seoul (Korean)
Zarela (Mexican) (see Spicy Food)

*Upper East Side*
Anatolia (Turkish) (see Mediterranean and Middle Eastern)
Arcadia (American)
Arizona 206 (American)
Bistro Bamboche (French)
Boathouse Café (Italian) (see For All Ages)
Café Crocodile (Mediterranean) (see Mediterranean and Middle Eastern)
Café Geiger (German) (see Middle and Eastern European)
Café San Martin (Spanish)
Café Trevi (Italian)
Ciao Bella (Italian) (see Crowd Scenes)
Le Cirque (French)
Contrapunto (Italian) (see American)
Csarda (Hungarian) (see Middle and Eastern European)
Fu's (Chinese)
The Gallery (Tea)
J. G. Melon (bar food) (see Crowd Scenes)
Jim McMullen (bar food) (see Crowd Scenes)
Le Laurier (Seafood)
The Mayfair Regent (Tea)
Metro (American)
Mezzaluna (Italian) (see Crowd Scenes)
Mortimer's (bar food) (see Crowd Scenes)
The Post House (Steaks)
Primavera (Italian)
The Red Tulip (Hungarian) (see Middle and Eastern European)
Rosa Mexicana (Mexican) (see Spicy Food)
Royal India (Indian)
Sam's Café (bar food) (see Crowd Scenes)
Sarabeth's Kitchen (see For All Ages)
Serendipity (burgers and sweets) (see For All Ages)
Sign of the Dove (American)
Yellowfingers (American)

*Upper West Side*
Café Luxembourg (American)
Dock's (Seafood)
Memphis (Cajun) (see Crowd Scenes)
Nishi (Japanese)

107 West (Cajun) (see Crowd Scenes)
Sarabeth's Kitchen (see For All Ages)
Sidewalkers' (Seafood)
Tavern on the Green (American) (see Local Phenomena)
Victor's Cuban Café (see Spanish and Latin American)

*Harlem*
Sylvia's (Southern) (see Spicy Food)

## OTHER BOROUGHS

*The Bronx*
Dominick's (Italian)
Mario's (Italian)

*Brooklyn*
Almontaser (Middle Eastern)
Café Armenia (Armenian) (see Middle and Eastern European)
The Captain's Quarters (Seafood)
Dar Lebnan (Middle Eastern)
Gargiulo's (Italian)
Gastronom Moscow (Russian) (see Middle and Eastern European)
The National (Russian) (see Middle and Eastern European)
Odessa (Russian) (see Middle and Eastern European)
Peter Luger (Steaks)
River Café (American) (see Local Phenomena)
Sido Restaurant (Middle Eastern)
Tripoli (Middle Eastern)

*Queens*
La Cabaña (Argentine) (see Spanish and Latin American)
Fortune Chao-Chow Seafood Restaurant (Chinese)
Stony Wok (Taiwanese) (see Chinese)

# BARS AND CAFES

*By Heidi L. Kriz*

*Heidi Kriz, a resident of the Upper West Side, is a graduate of Columbia University—as well as its famous bartending course. She has written about the people, places, and bars of New York City for such publications as the* Village Voice *and* 7 Days.

Manhattan, a city of countless choices, must be sampled in a discriminating fashion. We have attempted to reduce the hundreds of bars that might interest a visitor to a select handful, keeping in mind the broad range required to represent the bar bounty of this island accurately. (There are nice bars in the other boroughs, too, but you'll have your hands full without having to transit a bridge or a tunnel.)

New York City has the good fortune to possess some of the finest restaurants and clubs in the world. They are also some of the loftiest and most exclusive places, seemingly not very accessible to most visitors. But never say die, for the bars of this city are often an entrance into places otherwise unapproachable.

In many ways this survey mirrors the motivations and desires of the people of the city—quirky, quixotic, sleazy, or sophisticated. It also holds, for the careful observer, an insight into the differing characters of the neighborhoods.

## THE WALL STREET AREA

The thousands of people who work and live in this area used to have a problem. To have a good meal and drink in a nice place often required a tedious trek uptown. But lo and behold, the real-estate gods heard their prayers, and in what seemed like six days the **South Street Seaport** was born.

If you have made no plans to visit the Seaport, at the east end of Fulton Street, then make them, for it really does have something for everyone. Wander around until you are parched, and then choose from the myriad bars and night spots available.

At the end of the pier are two versions of **Flutie's**, a heavy-duty singles scene so vigorous it would make mama blush. Other places to ask after are **Roeblings**, the **Fulton Street Café**, **McDuffy's Irish Coffee House**, the **Liberty Café**, **Pedro O'Hara's**, and **Caroline's Comedy Club**. Each differs slightly in mood from the others. The **Paris Café** on South Street right in the Fulton Fish Market complex (which is contiguous to the Seaport attractions) and **Jeremy's Ale House** nearby on Front Street are two other busy after-work retreats. **The Ocean Reef Grille** stands apart from the others with its spectacular boats, 13 of them, that hang from the rafters on steel cables and look glorious against the midnight sky. On Fridays, a veritable tidal wave of young bankers and stockbrokers washes over the Seaport.

Outside the Seaport area is **Harry's at Hanover Square**, between Pearl and Stone streets, one block from Water Street. Harry's, like every other place in this part of town, has a mostly financial and banking clientele, but a bit older here than at the Seaport.

## TRIBECA

Even the name of the area known as "TriBeCa" is illustrative of New Yorkers' desire to be distinctive. A chunk of the Lower West Side was annexed, Texas-style, and identified with a name derived from its location: the *Tri*angle *Be*low *Ca*nal Street. The neighborhood's shopkeepers, barkeepers, and restaurateurs have accordingly striven to be unique—resulting in a variety of funky shops and eateries.

Currently at the top of the heap of de rigueur restaurants is **The Canal Bar** (actually just north of Canal, at the corner of Greenwich and Spring streets). The decor is pointedly eclectic, with some details recognizable as requisite Postmodern and other items completely incomprehensible. The bar and restaurant region are perpetually filled, but the people eating are predominantly Armani-garbed businessmen with leggy dates, while those carousing at the bar are younger and firmer—but poorer. There seems to be a tacit, ongoing beauty contest between the staff and the bar folk. *Très cher,* but not *trop cher* to preclude at least one plunge.

**The Odeon** (145 West Broadway at Thomas Street) began as, and remains, the triumph of TriBeCa. Once a 1950s cafeteria, it kept its clean, streamlined Art-Deco feel and spacious, uncluttered interior when it became a restaurant. Having been a pioneer in the now completely transformed TriBeCa, the Odeon has passed, well preserved, into its golden years. Food, drink, and company here are of the highest order, and the Odeon remains one of the few good restaurants in town offering late-night dinner. The crowd has toned down a bit, but there is still a staple of glamorous types: models, celebrities, artists, and the usual associated sycophants. The bar itself is wonderfully large and well stocked, the sign of a quality rare in popular restaurants: encouragement to remain at the bar all night should you so desire. The menu is a little pricey, but worth it. Wear something retro, or black, or better yet, both.

## SOHO

SoHo (*So*uth of *Ho*uston Street) went through the gentrification shakedown a long time ago, and as a result the area has settled into the Middle Ages of its time span. Everything is comfy and prosperous, but there are few vanguard establishments left. SoHo's original character has been obliterated by bourgeois desires.

Speaking of bourgeois, "oenophobia," or an aversion to drinking overpriced wine in pretentious surroundings, has long been the unintended effect of many a wine-tasting place. Put out of mind whatever mediocre glasses of wine in mediocre bars you have already reluctantly swallowed: **I Tre Merli** on West Broadway near Prince Street is authentic, and it's good. The menu is heavy with 28 choices of wine, demonstrated by two oversize wine racks, obviously not made just for show. The interior is accented with black and brick, and has an exciting cavelike air. The matching black bar downstairs seats about 25; single glasses of wine run about $3.50. The crowd is SoHo, which means wear black again. Anticipate a lively learning experience.

Keep that black outfit on, get a trendy haircut, then enter **Raoul's** (180 Prince Street between West Broadway and Sixth Avenue) with your head held high, nose raised to the ceiling. Actually, for all its hipness, the place manages to be toney without being elite. The decor recalls the look of an early Truffaut film: very French, with brown tin ceilings and warm cream walls. The crowd could be effortlessly transplanted to the Odeon, and vice versa. The bar is always interesting, and sitting next to the likes of Richard Gere is not unusual. Expensive, of course.

## LOWER EAST SIDE/EAST VILLAGE

For a long time, the Lower East Side of Manhattan had the air of a freshly bombed war zone. At least this was true of the very, very East Side, otherwise known as Alphabet City (Avenue A, Avenue B, etc.). This area was even once the focus of a film by the same name, a B movie about gangs that lived in a desolate neighborhood. Alphabet City and much else of the Lower East Side fit that description—that is, until danger became hip and condemned buildings cool. Like flies to honey, entrepreneurs zoomed in at the first sign of a real-estate gold mine. Overnight, slumlords became landlords and rich kids appalled daddy by insisting on paying an uptown price for a downtown hovel. Consequently, this state-of-the-art scene demanded state-of-the-art clubs, which (along with still relatively low rent) is why most of the city's cutting-edge clubs can be found on the Lower East Side. What are less predominant are solid, made-for-drinking hangouts, places with more gin and less din. Hence, the following selection will be brief, and will include bars that actually encourage the art of drinking—along with a few other things.

**The Bar** (Second Avenue and 4th Street) is completely representative of the East Village gay scene. The tattered awnings and darkened windows make the place look sleazy—and it is. But it's also filled with a very colorful local crowd that makes drinking here (if you're straight and uninformed, that is) a very educational experience. Dress is strictly casual: boots, sweaters, and jeans—the tighter the better. The place is throbbing by 1:00 A.M.

Often a bar's reputation is self-perpetuating, even though yesterday's praises far surpass today's reality. Good for the bar owner, not so good for the potential customer. **McSorley's Old Ale House** (15 East 7th Street) is a prime example. Lines extend outside on the weekends with people willing to cram themselves into the bar for two mugs of beer for $2.00. Its resemblance to a frat party is no accident; the bar did not accept women until 1970. Go on a weeknight, when you'll be able to raise your elbow to drink, and the pub itself is rather nice.

It has been around for 50 years and is twice as old as most of its clientele on the weekends, but **Vazac's** (108 Avenue B at 7th Street) will undoubtedly continue to have a long and prosperous life. The scene is simple and mellow most nights, and the massive dark horseshoe bar always offers a place to sit. Proudly calling itself a neighborhood place, it has all the accoutrements, from ceiling fans to pinball and a well-stocked jukebox. The weekends get very collegiate, but Vazac's is commodious and there's nary a class clash to speak of. If the bar looks familiar, it could be because it was the site of Paul Newman's dipsomania early in the movie *The Verdict*.

## GREENWICH VILLAGE

The Village area appeals to the gamut of society—much of it tri-state (New York, New Jersey, and Connecticut) and adolescent on the weekends. Its density of shops and sights reflects this range, and a scrutinizing eye is necessary to catch that gem of a jazz bar, one-of-a-kind clothing store, or art-film house. The attention required in the hunt for quality is part of this area's immense charm, and far outweighs the unpleasantness of being jostled on Saturday nights by teenagers from New Jersey.

Tiny **Arthur's Tavern** (57 Grove Street west of Seventh Avenue across from Sheridan Square), squeezed in between some cheesy "Broadway tune" bars, is worth squinting for. It's dark, steamy, and very sexy, and serves up some of the best jazz in town for the price of a drink—which will run about three dollars but is easily nursed through a set or two. The crowd is mixed: lots of mid-20s one-timers "getting down and dirty," and a few fond regulars who know good jazz when they hear it. This place is a fabulous late-night stop-off, and a good way to impress your companion.

Equally low-key from the outside but very hip indoors is the recently arisen **Automatic Slims** (733 Washington Street at Bank Street). Not only is the crowd eye-pleasing—arty, attractive, interesting—but the conversation here reflects more than the depth of the latest issue of *National Enquirer* or *The Sun*. Generally in their 30s, and with friends, the customers make the place lively and fun. The bar is always crowded, but standing won't prove unpleasant; you can always turn and talk to that model on the latest cover of *Vogue*.

Cerebral celebrities whose names are more familiar than their faces can be found at **Bradley's** (70 University Place), a polished restaurant usually populated by very dedicated jazz aficionados. With no cover charge and an accommodating bar, an evening of solid jazz is very affordable here. If you are travelling en masse, get there before 10:00 P.M., grab a table, and pay the pittance of a five-dollar cover charge. Dress is tweedy or upscale post-bohemian.

When the crowd from Bradley's is "slumming it" they

might be found at **Chumley's** (86 Bedford Street at Barrow Street—no sign). Homely but cozy, the pub has long served as a wateringhole for neighborhood journalists and the poor but ponderous. A burger and a beer are very reasonable, and the fireplace will help ease a hangover from the night before. (Dylan Thomas used to drink at the nearby **White Horse Tavern**, Hudson at 11th street, and it's still pretty much of a saloon-goer's saloon.)

After you've recovered, you might well venture forth to a Brazilian bar that puts Ricky Ricardo to shame. **S.O.B.'s**—Sounds of Brazil—(204 Varick Street near West Houston) is a hot, loose club with a knockout mixture of Latin, African, and Caribbean sounds. Brazilians and Haitians mingle comfortably with Wall Street yuppies—all willing to pay the $15 cover charge. The bar is spacious and amply stocked with alcoholic exotica. For bar seating, get there by 11:00 P.M., and expect to dance later.

**The Gotham Bar and Grill** (12 East 12th Street, off Fifth Avenue near University Place) is a three-star restaurant first, but its bar runs a close second to the kitchen. Columned, marbled, and Postmodern, the place resembles many an upscale restaurant conceived in the past six months, but despite its lack of design inspiration, Gotham stands out for one good reason—people still go there. Gotham, and especially its bar, survived the attack of the "beautiful people," and when the dust cleared and the limousines retreated, a very snazzy, solid group of regulars remained. (No longer young, but no longer living on a shoestring either, many of them travel from the Upper East Side to drink and eat here.) Now the bar itself is less frantic, and is a fine place to have an elegant drink in lovely surroundings.

After the workday, professionals are often seen relaxing in a much heralded Village "spot"—the **Union Square Café** (21 East 16th Street off Union Square West, north of the Village proper in the Flatiron District). This restaurant is casual but well bred, and there's a lengthy, gleaming wooden bar holding a variety of bar snacks and relishes. Early evening, women in business suits and Reeboks often sit at the white-linen-covered window tables, looking very relaxed and watching the world go by.

## CHELSEA TO GRAMERCY PARK

The neighborhood known as Chelsea has absolutely blossomed in the past few years with quality shops, sights, and places to eat and drink. A relatively small area, it is thick with attractions for natives and out-of-towners alike. In spite of being flanked by other, trendier neighborhoods in lower Manhattan, Chelsea holds its own with a kind of discount funkiness, and continues to grow in popularity and consideration.

**The Ballroom** (253 West 28th Street) exemplifies the eclecticism of Chelsea. A bar, restaurant, and cabaret all in one, The Ballroom is clean, breezy, and elegant, and the waiters in their stiff black-and-white uniforms convey a formal but unimposing air. The bar area is always bustling, but its popularity rests less on alcohol than a spectacular buffet of *tapas,* Spanish hors d'oeuvres. Two drinks and a plate of hors d'oeuvres will run about $15. Men wear business suits, women wear furs, and both genders tend to be divorced. If appetizers and drinks don't fulfill, there's more to The Ballroom: the cabaret. Amid typical high-tech club decor, performers like Karen Akers and Marthe Raye sing magnificently, catering to a dressy, enthusiastic crowd. A set costs about $15 with a two-drink minimum. Reservations are required; Tel: (212) 244-3005.

New York restaurant regulars are a contingent with almost impossible aesthetic standards and, in their efforts to please the unpleaseable, restaurant owners often overextend themselves financially or decoratively. The result is often a dark, empty building that a year before was bright and busy. However, the most dour of critics, social and gastronomical, have difficulty finding fault with one relatively recent hot spot near Chelsea, **Lola** (30 West 22nd Street). Even Humbert Humbert, a character of scrupulous taste and European airs, might conceivably have brought his precious charge here in an attempt to find a restaurant that matched her fresh beauty. Highlights include a tiled foyer, fresh flowers, and soft lighting (everywhere the eyes rest they find unique lighting fixtures, lovely artwork, and special details). You encounter the bar in the entranceway to the restaurant. Cocktail tables with upholstered chairs elegantly extend the drinking area. Weekends at Lola are enhanced by jazz combos in the front room. The crowd is youngish but urbane. A two-drink tab runs about nine dollars. Experience this study in New York haute hangouts. You might even catch a glimpse of Lola herself, whose own beauty is unsurpassed by her club.

Chelsea, like every other New York neighborhood on the rise, is subject to rapid real-estate turnover, and an example of that is found in the **Man Ray Bistro** (169 Eighth Avenue at 19th Street), which occupies the former sight of L'Express. As the name might indicate, the defunct L'Express had a French railroad theme, as is illustrated by the imported original Art Deco details and marble parts from vintage French trains that remain. The bar area itself is usually well populated but poses a problem many popular bar-restaurant combos share: Intimacy is impossible, in this case because of both the diners' din and the strange acoustics shaped by the marble cocktail tables. So come with a group. The crowd is filled with neighborhood regulars, a sure sign of quality, but also with tri-staters (New York State, New Jersey, and Connecticut) who want to be "in."

Those women who frequent **Café Society** (915 Broadway at 21st Street) need to be able to afford not only the prices but also the weekly shopping spree to Saks or Betsey Johnson that will protect them from the humiliation of wearing the same overpriced ensemble more than once. Furniture and attitude are both overstuffed, but if the clientele is sometimes annoying, the grace and beauty of the restaurant itself is soothing. The place is constructed with lofty ceilings and a soaring staircase to the cloakroom, complemented by columns of the currently requisite pink and black Art Deco hues. Imagine Bette Davis descending the staircase, step by step, pausing with a portentous "Fasten your seat belts: it's gonna be a bumpy night," and then slinking down the rest of the way.

Near Café Society, on the south side of 23rd Street between Fifth Avenue and Park Avenue South, is **Live Bait**, a supposedly Cajun restaurant whose cheek-to-jowl crowd starts changing at around 9:00 P.M. from young insurance executives (Metropolitan Life and other insurers are nearby) to young inhabitants of the hip demimonde. Crowded and noisy, but the food is pretty good.

Just south of Gramercy Park, on Irving Place at 18th Street, is **Pete's Tavern**, once a drinking place of O. Henry's. The bar itself is most evocative of old New York, with its wood carving, beveled glass and grime. A slightly younger, more boisterous clientele prefers the likewise ancient **Old Town** on 18th Street between Park Avenue South and Broadway.

**The 23rd Street Bar and Grill** (just west of Third Avenue on the south side of the street) attracts freshly showered young middle-management people, hair in place. There's nothing stiff about the well-stocked bar itself, however, which is made of gleaming dark wood and has plenty of seats. Which it needs, because the cocktail, dinner, and going-out hours Wednesday to Saturday are extremely busy here, and the bar glows then with a warm, chatty atmosphere. Because of its convincing turn-of-the-century decor, this site of casual prosperity has served as a set for some major film releases—including *The Cotton Club* and *Rage of Angels*.

## MIDTOWN

Midtown Manhattan is dense with the diversity you find only in New York City. Moving west from the epicenter, you encounter both the glitzy and the grotesque. The glamorous Theater District of Midtown West is only an X-rated movie house or two away from West 42nd Street, an area rife with street crime, prostitution, and pornography. Midtown East is hushed and refined, and far less visually dramatic. A common denominator of the two areas is the presence of some of the finest drinking establishments in New York City.

### *Midtown East*

Hotels made to appeal to the rich, famous, and successful house bars that cater to the same clientele. The beauty of barhopping, however, is that you need not be Donald or Ivana Trump to be able to afford to drink in the most elegant of locations.

**The Four Seasons**, located in the Seagram Building on 52nd Street east of Park Avenue, is a perpetual hangout for political and publishing heavyweights—the names change but the status level remains the same. The bar is located in the Grill Room, which was probably the site of the first power lunch. If you go (which you must, at least once), dress to impress, and try not to stare when a famous politician enters with a leggy blonde on his arm—and she's not his wife.

For relaxing among more cerebral inebriants, saunter over to the **Algonquin Hotel** (44th Street between Fifth and Sixth avenues). Here sat the Round Table, a 1920s ensemble of writers, artists, and celebrated tipplers, caustic wits of the likes of Dorothy Parker, Ring Lardner, and Robert Benchley. (The offices of *The New Yorker* are, not coincidentally, nearby.) The large bar—actually a sitting room—is plush without being prim, and the clientele, literary to international, and always well bred, may remind you of a set of extras for a BBC production. Off the lobby to the right of the entrance is the snug **Blue Bar**.

Though Leona Helmsley was not around to play ultimate hostess to the Round Table, you can safely bet that the Helmsley Palace at Madison Avenue and 50th Street, home of the Helmsley bars, would have been the target of satire more likely than satiation for those literati. Nonetheless, the glittering grandness of the Helmsley bars is to be experienced at least once, like Saks Fifth Avenue the week before Christmas. **Harry's New York Bar** is the hotel's one bar that doesn't overtly bear the telltale stamp of Leona's rampant femininity. The room is dark and pubby, with a professional crowd of both locals and out-of-towners. Look in, then move on to the real lookers: first, **The Gold Room**—really an understated name for what must be a replica of one of Leona's living rooms. Men in jackets and women with fresh hairdos drape themselves around the 100-year-old Roman Renaissance-style room. With its gold-leaf walls, garlands of foliage, and stained-glass windows, it is regal and spectacular.

**The Hunt Room**'s name and decor are evocative of those turn-of-the-century English hunt scenes with noblemen and squires relaxing with pipes. Understated and elegant, it's a perfect place to sip fine Scotch and pretend you're landed gentry. Gentlemen, get out your jackets and gray slacks; ladies, look refined and self-possessed.

But wait, the gold-leaf paint runneth over, all the way to the **Madison Room**. Looking a bit like a certain Andrew Lloyd Weber set, or a revamped Limelight club, this is high camp at its finest. With its green marble fireplaces, marble columns capped with bronze mountings, and tinkling pianist, this room could have served as Liberace's mausoleum. Actually the room is fun and splashy, and a drink or two is recommended by the window overlooking Madison Avenue.

Nestled in the block of luxury hotels that line Central Park South, the Ritz Carlton Hotel's **Jockey Club** is why expense accounts exist. Elegant and traditional, the wonderful bar also serves as a place where the upper classes and high-level executives meet and greet, relaxing in the genteel atmosphere. One or two martinis should smooth any nervousness about the horsey atmosphere. Just remember to play dress-up, for this is a place for the "properly attired." Relax in comfort at the bar or at a table in the foyer. Women should check out the w.c.—Laura

Ashley would have been green with envy. And bring a wallet fat with cards or cash—such gentility costs.

Finally, in this luxury hotel genre there is the Plaza Hotel's esteemed **Oak Bar**. Suffice it to say it's still everything your father said it was: a venerated New York drinking establishment filled with the very rich and very powerful—or just wealthy women tired from shopping on Fifth Avenue all day. All designer accessories worn here are the real thing, and there are understated signs of money everywhere in this dark, clubby room. While the bar is small, most of the drinking is done at the tables anyway, where you can get a magnificent view of the park.

In the Midtown East area the hotels seem to have a monopoly on good places to drink, but there *are* some standard bars that deserve more than a pass. Reflective of this area's cultural sophistication, there exists a place that is less a bar than a showplace for some of the finest musicians in town. **Michael's Pub** (211 East 55th Street) is a cabaret restaurant where the well-heeled come to catch performers like Julie Wilson. Monday nights Woody Allen sometimes leaves his urban angst at home with Mia and plays a damn good clarinet. The trick is to be early to the no-cover, no-minimum bar space and nurse a drink all the way through a show. The menu is solid, however, and the show is always one of the best deals in town.

A horse of a dramatically different color (probably red, white, and blue) is **P. J. Clarke's** (915 Third Avenue at 55th Street), a grown-up frat boy's dream. With an abundant selection of beer, and a big, beautiful carved bar at which to chug it, this drinking haunt accommodates a mass of aging preppies and after-work yuppies. Woody and masculine, P. J. Clarke's exemplifies the best of New York pubbing—and the chili and hamburgers are great. If you go, be prepared to rave about your alma mater.

## *Midtown West*

Over on the west side of town a few new restaurants have cropped up that stand out, either in quality or gimmick. A longtime pioneer in establishing regal restaurants in Gotham City, Harry Cipriani bounced back from the closing of the restaurant that bore his name, and did so beautifully. His new place, **Bellini** (777 Seventh Avenue at 51st Street), is the offspring of a stylistic marriage between Harry's first restaurant and the famous Hemingway haunt, Harry's Bar and Grill in Venice. The low ceilings, pale peach fabrics, and Art Deco decor provide a wonderfully elegant atmosphere for sophisticated drinks and drinkers. The patrons, as in the bar that was Bellini's inspiration, often represent the best and the brightest of the local society of the arts and fashion.

The "beautiful people" have short attention spans when it comes to night spots, but for the moment they can be found at **Trixie's** (307 West 47th Street, west of Eighth Avenue), a newcomer "alternative" club on the western edge of the Theater District. Trixie herself presides over her trendy diners, dances the samba three or four times a night, and generally stirs up trouble (which is good for business). The bar is petite and always crowded, but worth the discomfort on a busy Saturday night, offering a prime view of a stream of people rivaled only by the Halloween parade in Greenwich Village. Only beer is served; no matter—the general atmosphere is wacky enough to preclude the need to be gin-soaked in order to be amused.

Another West Side hot spot is **Un Deux Trois** (123 West 44th Street), obviously French and very much the perpetual scene: another "beautiful people" place, only with patrons a bit older than at Trixie's. If you have a contract with Ford's, or at least good bone structure, you'll feel right at home. The bar itself is small but noisy and fun, and you might need the intimacy to decipher everyone's heavy European accent anyway.

## THE UPPER WEST SIDE

While no area of New York is truly homogeneous, there are some neighborhoods that seem to be filled with people either from the same year at Princeton or the same jail cell. However, the people and places on the Upper West Side make this neighborhood one of the most varied in all of New York City. In many ways, gentrification has a lot to do with the area's broad range. Visually dramatic, and currently predominant in this neighborhood, gentrification reflects the almost schizophrenic quality of the Upper West Side. One day a bodega coexists next to a gleaming new Tex-Mex eatery; a week later, the Tex-Mex eatery is competing with a new sushi place. This kind of rapid commercial turnover helps explain why the neighborhood consists of genteel older men and women who have lived in the same magnificent prewar buildings for 50 years, and the young middle-class men and women who have lived in their brand new condos for six months—and will probably move within a year. Reflective of this dual consumerism are the many bars and restaurants of the Upper West Side.

### Lincoln Center

The bars near this epicenter of the arts in Manhattan are of course designed for, and filled with, the pre- and post-theater or concert crowd. But just because they are soliciting the same consumer source doesn't mean the bars look the same. They range from the pedestrian to the posh, and one restaurant that practically defines the latter is **Café Des Artistes** (1 West 67th Street off Central Park West). The fact that this glorious restaurant is praised to the heavens for its food results in its bar being overlooked. This is good, for the bar, though small, is very cozy, and while a meal at Des Artistes would wipe out the wallet, the intimate, romantic bar serves as the perfect alternative. Dress here is stylishly conservative; clothes worn for the theater are probably just fine. Middle-aged men and women discuss the performance they just saw in refined, hushed tones, and the service people glide by so as not to disturb the avid conversation.

Equally stylish, but in a very different manner, is the **Café Luxembourg** (200 West 70th Street, between Amsterdam and West End avenues). It looks like the Odeon (see the TriBeCa section), and its clientele is much the same: attractive and model-like. The decor is very clean lined, done in pink, black, and white Art Deco details, replete with columns and a terrazzo floor. The effect is very 1920s and Parisian; *The Sun Also Rises* comes to mind. The scene, however, is right now, and film and TV stars, young and not-so-young, are often tucked away in the anonymous corners of the restaurant. The bar is relatively small and always crowded, but if you are lucky enough to grab a stool, stay. The atmosphere is lively and good fun, and when you get tired of looking for celebrities, turn to the staff: They all have the bodies of dancers and the cheekbones of Paulina.

A bar that is more representative of the old guard of the Upper West Side is the **Ginger Man** (51 West 64th Street east of Broadway). The bar itself is very tasteful, with dark wood and Tiffany lamps that create the perfect atmosphere for a post-matinee drink, and especially a late nightcap after a concert or performance. The men and women who frequent the bar are older, well heeled, and established. However, there is none of the stuffiness that often goes with such a crowd, and the tone here is usually hale. The bar is, however, compact, thus usually close, so consider the level of intimacy you desire for a setting. The ABC television studios are very close by, and the boys from the newsroom often fill the place with smoke and hearty gossip at lunchtime. TV newsman Peter Jennings is also a regular, though he tends to sit at a table in the restaurant late at night, after the taping of his final broadcast. Often there is live entertainment, usually a pianist. The dress is clubby and the prices are right up there, but it's worth it.

So far, every place mentioned in this category has been a little on the staid side. This is perhaps due to the often subdued and reflective audiences that emerge from Lincoln Center. But theater or no theater, that doesn't press upon the wild bunch at **The Saloon** (1920 Broadway at 64th Street). The restaurant's bar is large and commodious, and even offers those displaced from the bar itself an area to stand in. The Saloon obviously caters to a different type of crowd from Café des Artistes, but the diversity exists because of the nature of the Upper West Side, not in spite of it. The drinkers at the Saloon are young, rowdy, and often single; you might leave with a date for your next theater event. When the weather is warm the staff breaks out the sidewalk tables, creating one of the finest people-gazing spots in the city.

During warm weather, out-of-towners and natives alike can be found sipping aperitifs on the brick patio café of **Tavern on the Green** (in Central Park at 67th Street). Ignore the touristy types and the creepy feeling of being in a coffee commercial: The establishment is indeed an Establishment in the restaurant circles of New York, and Tavern on the Green is a place to have experienced.

## *Columbus Avenue*

A special section has to be allotted for the area known as Columbus Avenue. Once an area filled with bodegas and run-down shops, the upper portion of this broad street has become overrun with designer places peddling designer food, shoes, clothes, cookies, and ice cream. There are even designer pet stores, so your greyhound won't feel gauche. The problem is, the modern definition of "designer" doesn't mean singular or special, it means expensive. And, in the case of Columbus Avenue, redundant. Which is why, despite the plethora of bars and restaurants in this area (and that of the nearby portion of

Amsterdam Avenue, which is well on its way to parity with Columbus Avenue), there are only a few bars that distinguish themselves in one way or another.

One such bar is, appropriately, **Columbus** (201 Columbus Avenue at 69th Street). Here you can drink, gawk, and be merry, for the trendy restaurant is frequented by celebrities (recently, Tom Selleck, for example) who call the Upper West Side home. The look indoors is plush, velvety, and Victorian—reminiscent of a fading but once-luxurious hotel lobby—and the clientele look and dress like the latest Barbie doll issue. Pricey, but very, very popular, Columbus is the moment's place to see and be seen.

The next stop is **Lucy's Restaurant** (503 Columbus Avenue near 84th Street). The girls wear pink, the boys are neophyte investment bankers, and the bar is almost larger than the eating area. With everyone's hormones popping, Lucy's practically oozes sly thoughts. Everybody is having a smashing time, drinking colorful outfit-matching concoctions topped off with a plastic fish. Later in the evening the toy sea creatures often provide conversational access to that hot babe or super stud at the end of the bar. Goofy but fun, this place helps lighten the load of making an entry-level living in New York City.

More contemplative moods are well served by a restaurant a few blocks down the street. **The Museum Café** (366 Columbus Avenue at 77th Street) is sophisticated and serene, with a sidewalk enclosure that allows sitting indoors with an outdoors sensation. The woody interior is dark and polished, and the inside bar is rarely overcrowded. Customers, usually established West Siders, often come alone, read a novel, or just sit and think. The place seems to be very therapeutic, and speeds recovery from the night before.

## *Jazz and the Upper Upper West Side*
The one-time countenance of the Upper Upper West Side, rough-hewn but full of character, has developed some unsightly blemishes in the form of pasta pits, sushi bars, and salsa scenes. Even the world-renowned West End Café, site of the sodden scribbling of young Kerouac and Ginsberg and venue for jazz greats like Louis Armstrong, has resoundingly closed its heavy wooden doors. But the owners of the downtown Village Gate (see Popular Music and Nightlife) plan to open the West End's doors again in

early 1989—as the **West End Gate** (on Broadway between 113th and 114th streets)—pledging to maintain a dedication to pub atmosphere and jazz performance.

For uptown jazz in a more upscale atmosphere, the newish **Birdland** (corner of Broadway and 105th Street) is having a go with a streamlined bar, menu, and jazz. The people and the music are handsome and polished—and so are the bartenders, who are invariably on hiatus from a soap opera.

The final point in the triangular combo is **J's** (on Broadway between 97th and 98th streets), a piano/jazz bar, smallish and cozy, perched a story above Broadway. Red velvet and schmoozy waiters are minor drawbacks; the music and atmosphere are elegant and lively. The well-dressed patrons are either single or in groups, but all look lean and hungry.

## THE UPPER EAST SIDE

Maligners of the Upper East Side often claim it is elitist, Waspy, frigid, and unfriendly. Well, it's not exactly untrue. But New York would not be New York without rich people (and would-be rich people) and a place to put them, and the side of town where furs are a familiar sight can also be classy, cultured, and traditional. Rich people like to have fun too, and a nice feature of the Upper East Side is that almost anyone can do as the rich do, by sipping at their wateringholes.

**The Beach Café** (1326 Second Avenue at 70th Street) does its best to soothe the tender nerves of executives who just couldn't get away to the Hamptons in time. The walls are covered with seascapes that can be purchased for anywhere from $200 to $1,000 (no black velvet, paint-by-number art here). The decor is like a lofty beach house, with pretty tile and brick walls and a lovely mahogany bar that is a delight to drink at. If you close your eyes and sip your Scotch slowly, you can almost imagine being in George Plimpton's country home, chatting about safaris until the Kennedys arrive for dinner. There's even a courtesy Rolls-Royce sponsored by J & B Scotch—ask the maître d' and you can get a lift home.

If it's seclusion you want—and the real thing when it comes to the music—one of the best shows in town still takes place in the **Café Carlyle** (Carlyle Hotel, Madison Avenue and 76th Street). Go on a weekday, sit at the bar in elegant surroundings, and hear brilliant Bobby Short play and sing for only ten dollars—fifteen dollars less than the cost of sitting at a table. Otherwise, the general atmosphere is stuffy, and the place is filled with self-preoccupied businessmen and their much younger dates.

The infamous **Elaine's** (1703 Second Avenue near 88th Street) is a tad tired but still something of a spectacle. Woody is sometimes here eating dinner quietly in a corner with Mia. Powerful publishers and literary giants often dine here too. Elaine's bosom may be generous, but *she* is not, at least to "outsiders." Don't be daunted; the large bar has a very good view of the restaurant, and, late at night, you might catch snatches of conversation and Hollywood shop talk, if you like that sort of thing. Dress here is chic but understated.

An elitism of a different sort permeates the air at **Mortimer's** (1057 Lexington Avenue at 75th Street). Fame (though it never hurts) is not a key to the entrance here, but what might be persuasive is if you and some of Mortimer's regulars had wintered together in Gstaad. Add an Ivy League education (preferably at one of the less "bohemian" ones), no chin if you're a man, and flat chest and bony ankles if you're a woman. Now you not only fit in, you look as if you're related to everyone else in the place. The crowd at the bar is young and boisterous, while those dining tend to be more sedate. The decor is pretty, the waiters are pretty, and Mortimer's itself is a great spot to ogle the rich and feel somehow superior to them.

Specialty bars often lean toward the gauche, especially sports bars, which makes **Rusty's** (1271 Third Avenue at 73rd Street) earthy and genuine, a super exception. Mets paraphernalia abounds, which makes a lot of sense, because Rusty, the owner, is the former Mets right fielder and pinch hitter Rusty Staub, now an announcer and special assistant to the Mets general manager. The bar is always filled with team members—not just of the Mets but of every professional New York sports team, including the Giants, the Knicks, and the Jets. When out-of-town teams come in to play, they can usually be found at Rusty's, and where the pros go, so goes a mob of related professionals—announcers, producers, and reporters—who converge upon the place to interview the players and fans, arranged so nicely under one roof. A great view of the big-screen TV can be had from every cleverly placed table in the main room, but the best seats in the house are at the bar, which actually has indentations for resting your elbow. The walls of Rusty's are packed with photos of sports greats and sure beat yet another curling photo of Brooke Shields in a Chinese restaurant. Rusty's is most busy after work, at dinnertime, and for brunch on weekends during a game. Because Rusty tips his cap to all major athletic events, his bar remains one of the best year-round sports bars anywhere.

Her name, or nickname at least, appropriately up in lights, Mariel "Sam" Hemingway has managed to defy the stuffiness of the bars surrounding her on the Third Avenue strip and create a sincere, light, and airy restaurant dubbed **Sam's Cafe** (1406 Third Avenue at 80th Street). The decor is reminiscent of one of her favorite spots, Ketchum, Idaho, also a one-time haunt of Papa Hemingway. The genuine country feel of the place is a surprise: The tone is low-key and pleasant, and the bar, which runs the length of the place, is filled after work with couples, mostly in their late 20s to late 30s, and usually on dates. Dress is casual.

Down Third Avenue between 78th and 79th streets is **The Ravelled Sleave**, a rather clubby singles bar for workers in the financial industry who were educated at good southern colleges. If you're able to pass for one of them—or *are* one of them—you'll have a good time here.

## BARS WITH COUCHES

There is a new style manifested in a handful of very popular, very chichi bars about town. One descriptive phrase might be the "parlor phenomenon." It refers to the timely embrace of certain social and political themes by designers of new restaurants: clubs made to look like homes. Not just any homes, but the homes—and specifically the living rooms—of the very rich. The decor of such places usually includes many plush couches, settees, and any type of furniture that indulges. There are often fireplaces, and always low, warm lighting. The fixtures tend to be brass. This return to luxury and wealth, combined with the concept of the Great American Home, was practically George Bush's political platform. In any case, the following clubs are something to see, and they *do* serve as relaxing alternatives to the stiffer, stand-up type bars.

A Roman bath may have been one of the first practical temples built in honor of the wealthy (today of course Donald Trump takes care of such things), but the reputation of bathhouses has declined. Nevertheless, **Cave Cannum** (24 First Avenue near 2nd Street) attempts to resurrect the Roman Empire and all of its sensual recreations. There are richly upholstered settees that Caesar would have liked, and the marble interior and elaborate fixtures of this former bathhouse are essentially intact. The rooms are dark and smoky and seem ripe for sexual drama—which they might be if the clientele wasn't basically the same tired bunch wearing black that has driven miles (i.e., from the suburbs) to get there. Drinks are, as for all clubs of this order, overpriced, but the setting can be amusing if you come with friends; you could all lurk in the magnificent, empty old marble "Jacuzzi" left untouched in the middle of the floor.

There once was a time when only the very best friends of Jay McInerney could get into this place, but if you haven't had the good fortune to cultivate a relationship with him you're in luck: **Nell's** (246 West 14th Street) has relaxed its entry criteria a bit. In other words, it has become a bit passé. The premises are still lovely, though, and very grand, with a number of huge rooms to wander through, all done up in various fin-de-siècle detail. Witty, bubbly conversation is a must, and the owners (the same people who own the Odeon) have thoughtfully provided conversation pits that tend to determine the action of the rooms they are in. Everyone used to be young and gorgeous; now some are a little bit older, but all very gracious and well dressed. The younger set can usually be found on the dance floor (which has an excellent sound system) dancing to the likes of old Madonna. The "madame" of Nell's may look familiar: She is Little Nell from *The Rocky Horror Picture Show*.

**M.K.** (204 Fifth Avenue at 25th Street) is the inheritor of the Nell's snob crowd, and its previous door policy. Stories of irate celebrities and power-broker types being turned away with the same gesture as a carload from New Jersey has shaken the city's In crowd to the core. But of course, instead of graciously accepting the rejection, their ardor to get in is increased exponentially. Since getting in is damn near impossible, here is a description so that you can fake having been there. There are three levels to M.K.: The first is a restaurant with mediocre food served practically all night long. In the basement, where the frenetic dancing takes place, the people visible are either models and their dates or someone's bratty teenage son with a group of bratty friends, the son having coerced someone with daddy's money or connections. All is flashing, silvery lights that tend to make people look attractively purple.

People drink at the bar—but don't stand there, or they would be crushed—and then wander upstairs to the hunting lodge and princess bedroom. Exactly as it sounds, the denlike trophy room is filled with exotic stuffed animal heads on the walls, staring down glassy-eyed at the people playing at the pool table. The princess bedroom has an enormous four-poster bed and various pieces of accommodating furniture. Those in this area tend to be very young, masterful at draping themselves over select upholstered chairs. Food and drink prices are hefty, but you'll actually save a lot of money the night you go to M.K., because you won't get in.

**Sofi** (102 Fifth Avenue at 15th Street) takes its name from the new acronym of the district—*S*outh of *F*lat*i*ron—but is original in every other way. The breathtaking textile-showroom space that houses Sofi's is utilized in a very space-efficient but beautiful manner. The foyer is dotted with richly upholstered chairs and couches that invite patrons to sip aperitifs or cocktails before dinner. The dining room is built on the lower split level, the room itself long and cavernous, and very impressive looking. The dark wooden bar is handsome, with green glass reading lamps that cast a flattering light on each of the 13 places at the bar. The clientele is well dressed and sophisticated, and the atmosphere is perfect for intimacy and even romance.

## BARS WITH A VIEW

One of the most fantastic sights in New York City is the city itself—seen from on high. A bird's-eye view of the island of Manhattan is a wonder, and is fortunately possible to obtain in comfort and style from many restaurants around town that might be called simply "view bars."

**The Boathouse Café** (Central Park at the Fifth Avenue and 72nd Street entrance) is not on high, but it has a view of skyline and lake that lies somewhere in between the fish and the fowl. With a rear cocktail area that overlooks the lake, the romantic scene is marred only by the plastic cups that hold the cocktails. Bring a sweetie at dusk and hold hands till the sky lights up.

**Il Mondo**'s glass-walled atrium has an incredible frontal view of the Chrysler Building. As if that weren't enough, the position of the restaurant results in a wondrous view of the United Nations building. The atmosphere of the restaurant is tasteful and dignified, and the patrons, 30 and over, are also. The bar itself is small but plush, and there is a prim, elderly lady, a tiara perched on her head, who trills traditional songs and plays the piano beautifully. At the eastern end of 43rd Street off Second Avenue.

**The Rainbow Room**, high atop the RCA Building, is a 1930s dream come true, or, in light of recent renovation, déjà vu. Luckily, the media ballyhoo over the revamping was not for naught: The place is a wonderland; from the staff to the silverware, all looks authentic. There's an air of expectation, as if Fred and Ginger were going to whirl around the corner at any moment. At lunch the two dining rooms are open only to those who are members. The bar itself—called the Grill—is as luxurious and well appointed as the other rooms. Details include a long, gleaming mahogany bar, inviting leather furniture, and deep red carpeting. Then there is the view: Ceiling-to-floor windows reveal a magnificent view of Midtown in all its illuminated glory. This is the spot for a special evening—and special dress. The bar has a light menu; cocktails are $6.50—a pittance for paradise.

When announcing a trip to this next "view bar," ignore the shouting and vehement protests that leaving Manhattan requires a bilingual guide book and a shotgun. This next place is as thrilling as any location in Manhattan, shotgun or no. Besides by taxi, a one-stop subway ride from Wall Street or a pleasant walk over the Brooklyn Bridge are two easy ways to get to Brooklyn, home of the renowned **River Café** (1 Water Street, Brooklyn); the management will help arrange for you to get back. This gourmet bar-restaurant is built on a barge that sits at the foot of the Brooklyn Bridge. The food is so widely lauded that dinner reservations must be made weeks in advance. Here's where the beauty of the bar comes in. No elaborate plan is needed to drop in for a cocktail, and the extraordinary view of Manhattan costs drinkers a fraction of the cost to diners. This place is so special, Woody Allen would probably film here—*if* it were in Manhattan.

**The Terrace** (400 West 119th Street near Columbia University) is the place where professors take visiting scholars to dine at their department's expense, and father takes graduate and family to dine at his business's expense. Though the Terrace is known as the gourmet restaurant of the area, its food is actually rather ordinary. The bar is large and has a great view of the downtown skyline, but the decor is hotel-like; after catching the view plan on going elsewhere.

**The Top of the Sixes** (666 Fifth Avenue between 52nd and 53rd streets) has a memorable address and view, but that's about it. The decor is stale and reminiscent of a family restaurant, and the patrons are not particularly chic or elegant. The view offered is from atop 39 stories, and includes Central Park and Fifth Avenue. This otherwise prime location may one day be given the makeover it deserves.

Imagine Frank Sinatra crooning his trademark about you-know-what city. The camera pans to the Empire State Building, the Citicorp Building, and the 59th Street Bridge—all from the top of the Beekman Tower, 26 floors high. At the **Top of the Tower** (3 Mitchell Place off First Avenue at 49th Street) there's a two-drink minimum from 9:00 P.M. to 1:00 A.M. that will cost close to the price of three elsewhere, but the romance here is well worth it.

Logically, the higher the building, the better the view, right? Well, how does 107 stories sound? The view from the top of the World Trade Center *is* great. The twin buildings are the tallest on the East Coast, and the north tower (number 1) serves as the home of a restaurant with a peerless view of New York City, Windows on the World. Adjacent to the dining room is the bar itself, named the **Hors d'Oeuvrerie**. It should not be missed. There's a $2.95 cover charge for the jazz combo after 7:30 P.M.; drinks for two run $15. Men must wear coat and tie, women, no denim. Windows on the World is an appropriate place to end a visit to New York, and an equally appropriate place to end our bar section.

# POPULAR MUSIC AND NIGHTLIFE

*By David Frankel*

David Frankel, *formerly an editor of* New York *magazine, has written on music for* New York *and for* Rolling Stone *magazine. He is an editor of* Artforum *magazine.*

Generations in New York nightlife come and go, but having gone they don't necessarily disappear—they just move out of the consciousness of the public, or at least of the particular public that decides what clubs and practices are hot and of the moment. For some, New York club life died in 1973 with the closing of the old Copacabana. For others it was 1980, when Steve Rubell and Ian Schrager, the owners of the seminal late 1970s discotheque Studio 54, faced the tax-evasion charges that eventually sent them to jail; or perhaps it was 1982 and the loss, after similar tax charges, of Steve Mass's Mudd Club, a rudimentary below-Canal establishment that began as a kind of artists' and downtowners' bar. Yet not only are people still going out in the evenings, they're going to rooms that are basically similar to those older haunts—or at least to Studio and the Mudd. It's just that they're also going to, and talking about, what came after—or whatever may have come after that by the time you read this book.

The Copacabana is a different story. From the 1940s through the 1960s, the club defined the image of the New York night spot as many imagined it: big-name entertainers, a floor show, glamour. It had its own chorus line, the Copa Girls (a tall dancer was called a show girl; a short one, unimaginably today, a "pony"), and its ever-so-vaguely Brazilian decor—the palm trees are concrete—was for countless Americans the instantly evocative epitome of show biz. In its billing, the Copa found ways to cope with the times, moving from Brazilian Bombshell Carmen Miranda in designer fruit-salad hats to a twisting Chubby Checker to Tom Jones, creating lines, the story goes, four times around the block. But the club did not survive Las Vegas. The big casino hotels that went up there in the 1960s hired singers like Jones as part of the bait to lure players in to the tables, and could pay extraordinary fees out of their gambling income. Relatively small rooms couldn't compete. The Copa is now a discotheque, and the only regular chorus line left in town is Radio City Music Hall's Rockettes.

For many, of course, chorus-line-type entertainment isn't such a great loss. Still, New Yorkers who remember the Copa kind of club sometimes malign the contemporary scene: It's all geared for teenagers and the rock 'n' roll crowd; there's nowhere left to eat a good supper in a sophisticated surround and see a big star; and so forth. It's certainly true that rock, disco, and their variants are the popular music of the day, that their audiences tend to be young (though aging all the time), and that their settings take rough wear. It's also true that the economics of nightlife have changed; Frank Sinatra doesn't play supper clubs anymore.

As for the rest of us, New York is a very big town with a long and thrilling tradition in every branch of the performing arts. It attracts singers and dancers, pianists and horn players, cabaret acts and comedians, and rock 'n' rollers from all over the country as well as rearing its own, and these people expend a great deal of energy, both competitive and collegial, on figuring out how to put themselves in front of a crowd that will listen while they do what they do. If New Yorkers like to appear jaded to the city's nightlife, that may be because there's more of it here than they can possibly see; and if you have to miss a good cabaret act or club date or jazz gig, why not pretend you did it on purpose.

The different modes of night spots from the different eras cohabit, whether or not they're in the spotlight. Fifty-second Street—Swing Street, the Jazz Capital of the World—once a night owl's delight of side-by-side jazz clubs from speakeasy days in the 1920s on, no longer exists. A row of high-rises has replaced the clubs, but that only means that jazz spots are diffused around town, from a concentration in the Village to a scattering on the residential Upper West Side.

Cabarets and piano rooms are sprinkled throughout Midtown, in the still raffish neighborhoods around Times Square and Broadway, sifting out strollers from the theater crowd; their performers too are sometimes spun out of Broadway, as when singers and musicians from the stage moonlight, or just drop in to some loosely organized bar that welcomes anyone with a voice (and some without). Places like these coexist with well-run cabarets such as Jan Wallman's, a room that's a firm retort to the nowhere-to-go-for-a-civilized-evening-out complaint. The Village still bears traces of its 1960s folk scene, rock 'n' roll is pretty much everywhere, and the discotheques that dominated nightlife in the late 1970s are still laying down their old beat (though maybe lightening it some through the more jittery rhythms of hip-hop and house music). And in addition, of course, there's whatever superseded these spots—whatever's of the moment at the moment.

Right now, supposedly, is the moment of what's been christened the Dim Age. This phase was ushered in late in 1986 with the opening of a club called Nell's, far west on 14th Street. Whereas the preceding era of clubs had gone for glitz and light shows and fabulous technology on the one hand, or for hole-in-the-wall funk on the other, Nell's tried to conjure a softly lit sitting-room mood. It may seem paradoxical to line up and pay for something like home, but people do, in a hip, downtown version of 1980s American conservatism. Several clubs that have opened since play variations on Nell's (M.K., and Au Bar on East 58th Street), and preexisting spots have nudged corners of their spaces in Nell's direction. But this doesn't mean that the older disco palaces are empty. Abandoned by the scene setters, they're simply made available for everyone else.

All this activity doesn't mean that New York makes life easy for aspiring club owners. An urgent issue is the city's high rent scale, which to people who live here sometimes appears a threat to all civilized life as we know it. New Yorkers pay for this all around—in their own living expenses of course and (as concerns nightlife) in ever-higher admission fees and cover charges—but also in terms of the community of performing artists here, who need space to rehearse in, experiment in, and, of course, to live in—space that is less and less available. New York State's residential rent-control laws tend to make apartments cheaper in relation to the market the longer a tenant has occupied them (the rent increases less when a lease is renewed than when it changes hands), which is fortunate for the town's longer-standing citizens but unhelpful to its newcomers. And because New York's cultural life depends on its centripetal power to attract to itself the newcomers who will contribute to it and constitute it, some worry is attached to the question of whether those people will find a room of their own here.

The early 1980s saw a revealing confrontation with these issues in the East Village, traditionally a part of Manhattan that was low rent to the extent that large sections of it were derelict (fewer but still numerous blocks remain so). The relative cheapness of life there made the area attractive to artists and other low-budget young people, and some of them opened night spots of a kind, in the lineage of the Mudd Club, with names like 8 BC (on 8th Street between Avenues B and C), Darinka, the Limbo Lounge, and King Tut's Wah-Wah Hut. As these logos may suggest, East Village cabarets catered to a crowd that was youthful at least in heart and usually also in actuality. They were small establishments, storefronts and tenements converted to their new use at minimal expense and often rudely and imperfectly—a 1980s version of the "Hey kids, let's put on a show" movies of the 1930s, and infinitely tackier though just as enthusiastic. The entertainment was of a kind with its location: raw, or at least unafraid to be so. Some East Village performers now have movie careers (Ann Magnuson) or have seen the inner meaning of their work discussed in art magazines and the *Village Voice* (Karen Finley). The unpretentiousness of their environment, which was cultivated, and their own Dada familiarity with the shock tactic as stage business have not obscured their inventiveness.

Today, however, most of these cut-rate nightclubs are gone. As Cornelius Conboy, the former co-owner of 8 BC, told *The New York Times* in 1985 when the club closed, the city government hit them with wall-to-wall paperwork: "license fees, certificate of occupancy, cabaret license, lease or bill of sale, nonflammability of drapes, public assembly permit, fire inspection, electric and gas inspection, health permit, liquor license, consumer affairs...." Few of the Lower East Side cabarets were operating on that bureaucratic level. Though some, such as the Pyramid, have survived, an arrest or two for selling alcohol without a license, or the prospect of having to scrape up lawyers' fees to stay open, was enough to fold the rest.

Now, any visitor to a nightclub has of course a justifiable interest in whether the ceiling will collapse and the sprinkler system will work (or whether there *is* a sprinkler system). Still, given the number of basement social clubs operating illegally in New York—unlicensed rooms offering liquor, some of them staying open for years without police action (a while ago there was a fatal fire in one of these bars)—the city's attention to the East Village scene seemed out of scale. And it played a part in the escalation of rents. The unsafe and empty streets of the Lower East Side had discouraged landlords from repairing the area's derelict buildings. With clubs and art galleries attracting crowds to those streets again, developers began to rebuild the neighborhood, and the shoestring operations that had touched off the cycle were pressured to leave—in some cases, conveniently, by the city—so that more lucrative businesses could replace them. The effect was a contribution to the conservative drift defined by Nell's, a reclaiming of the night by establishments with relatively abundant capital. (And after the East Village, everyone wanted a little comfort.) But clubs like 8 BC did set a vital example, and though the odds against them seem higher with every storefront Lost Our Lease sign, it's worth noting the arrival of Trixie's, a loose and funny restaurant in Midtown with a lot of the old spirit. It and places like it may mark a brightening of the Dim Age.

In one respect the bureaucratic load night spots bear has lightened lately, with the demise, in early 1988, of a cabaret law that had been a consistent source of complaint. Originally passed in 1926 as a tool for crackdowns on speakeasies, the law forbade certain instruments, and restricted to three the number of musicians who could perform simultaneously in clubs without a cabaret license. These licenses demanded annual fees and the fulfillment of certain zoning and safety requirements, and many rooms functioned quite well, and quite safely, without one—but they couldn't legally book four or more pieces, or horn players, or even drummers. Bands got around the law by organizing wrestling-type tag teams—you would see players waiting to step onstage as soon as one of the three already there stepped off. The practice was sometimes diverting but more often distracting. It ended on January 28, 1988, when a New York State Supreme Court judge found the law an unconstitutional violation of performers' freedom of expression. That evening bandstands all over town were packed as musicians asked their friends to step up and jam with them. It was a happy night—and, clearing the way for larger bands, it offered more musicians the chance of employment. Now the city is trying to write a new law, one that will restore some of its lost control. "To some people on the city council," said one cabaret owner a while ago, "all music is noise."

Another legal change in the last few years that directly

affected nightlife was the 1985 raising of the state drinking age from 19 to 21—a particularly important development for rock clubs and discos, which have a large teenage clientele. Theoretically, everyone 16 or over can go to a club that serves liquor, though they now have to be 21 to be served a drink. In practice, it's easier to keep under-21s out of a club than to let them in and then try to identify them at the bar. (Though some clubs have begun to do this, rubber-stamping adults' wrists or giving them a rubber bracelet once they've proved their age. They have to show the stamp to buy a drink.) The under-21 crowd is important enough to discotheques that some have to set aside rooms for them where no liquor is served. Others are open only to teenagers on selected nights of the week. This last wrinkle puts the newly 21-year-old in a novel position: Having spent the last several years trying to persuade a club's bartenders that he's old enough to drink there, he now has to persuade the club's doorman he's young enough to be let in at all.

Doormen have a very up-and-down reputation in New York—doted on by some, loathed by others. The doorman has absolute say as to whether or not you're admitted. And the fashionable clubs use the door as a tool: Creating a crowd outside is the approved way of letting the city know the place is hot. Stories are told of waiting outside the velvet ropes in front of some new venue only to enter at last and find the place half empty. And those who are allowed in, at least when a club is of the moment, are carefully chosen: If the crowd outside is a draw because it creates an impression of the club's exclusivity and of the lengths people will go to to be there, the crowd inside is the main attraction and has to look exciting to be with. Most Manhattan clubs have regulars, a set that goes there all the time and never worries about admission. People outside those cliques tend to show up looking their best, or at least dressed for maximum self-confidence. They arrive early rather than late—late being after midnight, when the clubs fill up, early varying from place to place but probably not after 11:00. They may go on a weekday rather than a weekend. They may try calling in advance to make a reservation, which some establishments accept depending on the positions of the planets. And they try not to take things personally.

The buzz about a nightclub lasts for a while, then moves to somewhere else. The set that once loved the place now complains that it's full of "bridge-and-tunnelers"—off-islanders who, like virtually everyone who wasn't born here, have come to Manhattan by one of those two types of entry. Bridge-and-tunnelers, of course, and every other visitor from outside the club's set, both out-of-towners and New Yorkers as well, are paying guests, and the clubs are in the business of earning money. After making themselves visible by whatever means they can, including invidious door policies, club managements settle down to turnover and emptying the till. Watching outside the Limelight (opened 1984) and the Palladium (opened 1985) in the fall of 1988, we saw no one forced to wait to get in. Watching outside Nell's (opened 1986) we saw a few people waiting; outside M.K. (opened 1988), a crowd. If you have trouble (and you may have none), remember it's only a business ploy, and go instead to S.O.B.'s, which runs a great live-music program with dancing for a strictly first-come-first-served crowd. Or call the Vanguard, or Bradley's, and see if they can seat you for jazz. It's a big town.

In the descriptions that follow, we haven't tried to provide specific times or prices for the various night spots, since they may change at the drop of a hat. Jazz clubs and cabarets tend to start their programs at 9:00 to 10:00-ish, and run till after midnight. They may open earlier, particularly if they serve food. Dance clubs may not open till 10:00, and close at 3:00 or 4:00 in the morning; or they may move their hours forward on weekdays. A lot of jazz clubs close on Mondays, which may also be a cheap night at places that stay open. Many charge a cover plus a drink minimum at your table; it's often worth checking whether the cover is dropped if you sit at the bar. Some discotheques bump up their prices during the course of the night—it's cheaper or even free (try the Copa) early on. (The management's bet is that you'll spend money in the club while you're waiting for everyone else to arrive.) A lot of residents here use *New York* magazine, *The New Yorker,* and the *Village Voice* for listings, ads, and reviews that will tell them what's going on—those, and plentiful use of the telephone.

We don't talk about a lot of places, just the best or most interesting in a reasonable range of types with various types of clientele. Once you're in one that sounds good to you you'll have no trouble finding out from fellow revelers about other places to your taste, if you're the restless type.

## JAZZ AND PIANO

The **Village Vanguard** is the oldest jazz room in the city—it opened in 1935—and a much-beloved local institution. The music that's been played here over the years seems to have seeped into the walls and furniture to give the place its particular jazz-nirvana feel. It's a basement, down a steep flight of stairs from the street; dark walls laden with photographs and posters, red banquettes underneath them (more comfortable than the tables crowded together out on the floor), an informal crowd with high standards in what it expects to hear. 178 Seventh Avenue South, just south of 11th Street; Tel: 255-4037.

A few blocks south of the Vanguard is **Sweet Basil**, a club and restaurant that bills equally classic jazz, if perhaps slightly more eclectically. There's an outer room, a kind of porch, which generally substitutes a view of the street for a view of the stage, though the music is still perfectly clear. Inside, a wood-paneled room under a nice tin ceiling squeezes in a half dozen tight rows of tables full of well-heeled West Villagers on a civilized evening out. 88 Seventh Avenue South, between Bleecker and Grove streets; Tel: 242-1785.

**The Blue Note**'s glass and mirrors, its darkness, and its bluish decor give it an underwater feel. Upstairs there's a gift shop selling Blue Note pens, tee-shirts, spoons, and watches; out in the bar, which you have to pass through to get to the main room, there's a hard stone floor to take the busy milling about that the place seems to attract. Still, the club books good bills, ranging from the R & B side of jazz to (on one occasion recently) Sarah Vaughan, who can fill halls many times this size: 131 West 3rd Street, just east of Sixth Avenue; Tel: 475-8592.

The French *mardi gras* literally means "fat Tuesday," and refers to Shrove Tuesday, the spring day before Ash Wednesday and the beginning of the Christian calendar's 40 days of fasting over Lent. So *mardi gras* was the last chance for a blowout, and in New Orleans and other tropical cultures it became a carnival. In New York, **Fat Tuesday** is a basement jazz club with a pretty good rep for its bookings. 190 Third Avenue, at 17th Street; Tel: 533-7902.

**Zinno** takes up the ground floor of a nice old brownstone on a tree-lined street in the Village. Inside, it's an elegant but warm contemporary space, and between the bar and the larger main room is an alcove with enough room for a jazz duo or trio to accompany diners through a refined Italian supper. The bar also takes listeners, for the price of two or three drinks, and the music is choice. 126 West 13th Street, west of Sixth Avenue; Tel: 924-5182.

On a good night, **Bradley's** may be as close as a bar comes to a concert hall: Jazz pianists and bass players get a beautiful sound here, and the usual restaurant noises of cutlery, talk, and general coming and going seem voluntarily muted so people can listen. The dark wood paneling and low black-painted tin ceiling somehow help, framing the light in the room the same way a deep double bass frames the clarity of a piano. This is a popular place for serious jazz fans, who stand packed in the bar, or who book a table for an unfancy meal. 70 University Place, a block east of Fifth Avenue and just south of 11th Street; Tel: 473-9700.

**Greene Street** is *on* Greene Street in SoHo, the former light-industry and warehouse neighborhood whose sweeping lofts have mostly been converted into equally sweeping galleries, restaurants, and boutiques. This particular place has a 30-foot ceiling so that you dine here in subtle light topped by volumes of dim air. Pianists usually play during the week, trios on weekends. Up the gantrylike stairs by the bar is a cabaret room. 101 Greene Street, south of Prince Street; Tel: 925-2415.

The **Fortune Garden Pavilion** is a Chinese restaurant of the Upper East Side variety rather than the Chinatown variety—a plush-carpeted, jacket-and-tie kind of place. The olde stone façade on the street is deceptive, as the establishment backs onto a contemporary atrium-type building on Third Avenue, which seems to have determined its interior—a glass ceiling, for example, looking out on the tops of the local architecture and, when visible, the moon. The room also has expensive-looking chinoiserie dotted about, and a Steinway for the use of the distinguished jazz pianists who pass through. 209 East 49th Street, just east of Third Avenue; Tel: 753-0101.

**Mikell's** lives in a one-story postwar building in a neighborhood of modern high-rises on the Upper West Side—a rather aseptic environment, especially in relation to the older tenements it replaced, blocks of which stretch to the north. Inside, however, is a bright wood-beamed space with ferns scattered about, and also crayons, so you can draw pictures on the paper tablecloths. The main room is long and narrow—a bar, a single row of tables, and standing space crammed between; an outer room gives a view through an elongated window. Most often the music is young people's jazz—electric rather than acoustic, and flavored with rock and soul. The juke runs all the way from Dave Brubeck to Michael Jackson. 760 Columbus Avenue at 97th Street; Tel: 864-8832.

**The Knitting Factory**, a bare-bones but friendly walk-up on the western edge of the East Village, is a pleasant reminder of the city's old jazz-loft days and, at the same time, a workshop for the present Lower East Side artist community. The music here may be rock-based, may be jazz-based, may be the guy drinking beer at the bar (which trembles when you lean on it) getting up to play guitar by himself; generally, it's experimental and personal. On the ground floor there's a small restaurant with speakers hooked into the sound system above, and the prices throughout are low enough that people from the neighborhood can easily drop in. The neighborhood is young and *avant*. 47 East Houston Street, between Mott and Mulberry streets north of Chinatown and Little Italy; Tel: 219-3055.

## CABARET AND SUCH

When Jan Wallman closed her cabaret in the Village for a move to Midtown, old friends—Dick Cavett, Joan Rivers, Margaret Whiting, and others—performed in a benefit at Carnegie Hall to help her fund it. The result, **Jan Wallman's**, which opened in 1987, is a welcoming room that avoids both the slight pomposity of the hoity-toitier cabarets and the raffishness of its relatives to the west, the Times Square–area piano places. Wallman is a veteran of the business, and a lot of her patrons come to dine and be entertained without knowing the act booked for the evening, relying instead on her knowledge and taste. 49 West 44th Street, west of Fifth Avenue; Tel: 764-8930.

**The Carlyle**, one of New York's most elegant hotels, runs two music rooms outfitted accordingly. The **Bemelmans Bar** is a tenebrous room, full of dark leather upholstery. (The management has sometimes considered redesigning and brightening up the bar, but neighbors have always written enough letters of protest to forestall them, in the Upper East Side version of social activism.) On the walls are the brownish-toned murals of Ludwig Bemelmans, well known as the illustrator of the "Madeleine" children's books. These paintings, which date from 1947, are whimsical and playful, with balloon sellers and bulldogs and snowy skating scenes and kangaroos. In the middle of the room is a piano; the program changes somewhat with the seasons, but the regular here is Barbara Carroll. Next to the bar is the **Café Carlyle**, with more original murals, these from 1955 by the French artist Vertès—a kind of post-Fauvist idyll of harlequins and horses, musicians and birds. Many of the tables here have cushioned love seats instead of chairs. This rather luxurious space is the supper club in which the supremely accomplished pianist and singer Bobby Short has played, again depending on the season, for over 20 years. Madison Avenue at 76th Street; Tel: 570-7189.

On a rather unprepossessing block in north Chelsea is a classy, elaborately Continental restaurant and cabaret called **The Ballroom**. Attended by black-bow-tied-and-waistcoated waiters, patrons snack on *tapas* and martinis at the bar, which is decorated with ornamental foodstuffs—smoked hams, plaits of garlic bulbs, dried peppers—and then take their drinks through a mirrored double door to a dark, simply designed room supplied with a sizable stage and a piano. The tables are on gently descending terraces, so everyone gets a good view of the singers and accompanists and good-taste comedy acts the place books. Some of The Ballroom's performances are in the early evening, right after work, which is unusual for the city. 253 West 28th Street, east of Eighth Avenue; Tel: 244-3005.

The bar of **Michael's Pub** is all dolled up with oak and old mirrors to look like what a visitor from Ireland might—might!—expect to find in some Victorian remnant back home. This is incongruous, given the building's steel-and-glass exterior, but it makes for a pleasant environment in which to hear music. That last comes from an inner room, a supper club, which takes acts ranging from cabaret and stand-up comedy to serious jazz, and regularly bills big names. The Dixieland band that plays here every Monday is known for featuring Woody Allen on clarinet, though he doesn't invariably show up. If you're not in the mood to sit down (the service here, incidentally, is sometimes brusque), all this can be heard, though not seen, relatively inexpensively from the bar. 211 East 55th Street, east of Third Avenue; Tel: 758-2272.

**Nickels** is a civilized Upper East Side restaurant that sets a classic piano bar up front, the kind with sitting space built close around the piano so you can get sentimental without fear of intervention. 227 East 67th Street, west of Second Avenue; Tel: 794-2331.

Broadway attracts actors, dancers, and singers to New York, then doesn't hire them all, so the balance have to keep their hand in however they can. **Eighty-Eights**—the name, of course, refers to the number of keys on a piano—is the kind of place where the pianist sings and the waiters sing and people dropping in sing, some of them very well. It's a contemporary room full of blond wood and black glass and dove gray carpeting; there's a cabaret upstairs. The club has a Midtown cousin, **Don't Tell Mama** (same management), which is much closer to Broadway, and much more rowdy and casual.

Eighty-Eights, 228 West 10th Street, west of Bleecker Street; Tel: 924-0088. Don't Tell Mama, 343 West 46th Street, west of Eighth Avenue; Tel: 757-0788.

## BLEECKER STREET

The string of clubs along Bleecker Street between Sullivan and La Guardia Place is the gradually mutating corpus of the Village's old folk-and-rock scene, now catering to a rowdy mix of tourists, young bridge-and-tunnelers in for the evening, college students from nearby New York University, and neighborhood folk preserving their own corner of the 1960s. With a few exceptions, there's not much to tell between these places. However, the **Village Gate**'s cavernous basement room is large enough to bill significant, mainly jazz, names, with some of the rootsier rock mixed in; every Monday evening it runs a terrific series of salsa concerts that set a jazz soloist in the context of a Latin orchestra and watch what happens.

Along the street is the **Village Corner**, a dark and ancient bar (here in one form or another since 1904) with a grand piano. Since 1975, a regular player here has been Lance Hayward, who is worth travelling to hear. And around the corner on MacDougal is **The Speak Easy**, a traditional folk club that books quiet singers who sound like the Joni Mitchell of 20 years ago, as well as robust old-timers such as Dave Van Ronk.

The Village Gate is at Bleecker and Thompson streets; Tel: 475-5120. The Village Corner, at Bleecker Street and La Guardia Place; Tel: 473-9762. The Speak Easy, 107 MacDougal Street, north of Bleecker Street; Tel: 598-9670.

## ROCK AND OTHER LIVE PERFORMANCES

It seems symbolic that Bleecker Street, the main drag of New York's 1960s folk scene, should end abruptly on the Bowery at **CBGB**. In the late 1970s this club was the heart of the city's punk-rock movement, which set out to replace everything sensitive and singer-songwriterly in popular music with the abrasive, the aggressive, the loud. Some of the groups that played here back then (the Talking Heads, for example) have ended up as arty as rock comes, but CBGB hasn't changed: it's the archetypal dive, dark, worn, graffitied, and odorous of beer. Generally speaking, the bands haven't changed either, so the place can be tough on the ears. But CBGB is historic in its way. Old habitués feel affectionate about it, and sometimes musicians now quite elevated in the world come back to play. The letters of the name, incidentally, are not, as is sometimes thought (given the club's aura and skid-row location), a riff on "heebie-jeebies"; they stand for country, bluegrass, and blues, none of which has been booked here in years. 315 Bowery, at Bleecker Street; Tel: 677-0455.

**The Bottom Line** is a basic rock 'n' roll club, considerably less raunchy than CBGB, where record companies like to see breaking acts showcased for the influential New York media searchers. It also features long-established people who have sizable followings but may not fill a big hall; recently, for example, Donovan and Laura Nyro passed through. The club is near New York University, so it gets a student audience, and when jazz players like Sun Ra and his Arkestra play here they pull out all the stops to grab the young crowd. 15 West 4th Street, west of Broadway at Mercer Street; Tel: 228-6300.

**S.O.B.'s**—Sounds of Brazil—grew out of a season owner Larry Gold spent going to Brazilian bars in Paris and wondering why there was no equivalent in New York. Since his club opened, in 1982, the city's enthusiastic dance and music crowd has proven he asked the right question. S.O.B.'s specializes in the rhythms of Brazil, tapping both the country's local expatriate community for acts and bringing them up here from Rio and Bahia and beyond. It also explores the music of Africa and the Caribbean, and the purview is gradually expanding. This is a supper club, and a lot of patrons have dinner here—a Brazilian menu—before settling in to samba. The place is noisy and energetic, the music both ambitious and wildly danceable. 204 Varick Street, near Houston Street; Tel: 243-4940.

There used to be a wide banner hung across the façade of the **Lone Star Café** proclaiming "Too Much Is Not Enough." On the roof, and visible from the street, is a giant iguana, the length of the building or so. The Lone Star works hard at an image of excess. It calls itself "the official Texas embassy in New York," and to get the message across it's full of cow skulls and steer horns, neon signs for Texian or Mexican beers, Texas flags, and cowboy boots (one on every leg of the airborne dragonfly above the stage, about as outsize as the iguana). The curving staircase and balcony suggest that this must once have been an elegant room, but unless you sit right at the edge of that balcony you won't be able to see, and this isn't the kind of place you go to for conversation along with your music: The acts are roadhouse rock 'n' roll, R & B, blues, western swing, anything that sounds like a party. 61 Fifth Avenue, at 13th Street; Tel: 242-1664. The club has an uptown twin at 240 West 54th Street, west of Broadway, which takes the roadhouse label seriously by making its front wall out of a tour bus.

**The Ritz** was once Webster Hall, a gorgeous Art Deco–style institution where the likes of Benny Goodman made people dance. It's still billing the popular music of the day, which these days is all kinds of rock 'n' roll. Much of the old interior survives: the marble stairs, the gold-and-rust striped patterns on the walls, the ornate caissoned ceiling with its gigantic central boss tapering down to a mirrored globe. And the main space is all open floor. (There's quite limited seating on the balcony upstairs.) Often, buying your ticket in advance here is a little cheaper than buying it on the night of the show. 119 East 11th Street, west of Third Avenue; Tel: 254-2800.

**The Big Kahuna** is the theme club taken to the extreme. The motif is Hawaiian, which means the tables are fragments of surfboards, you scuff through sand in the aisles, and a breaking wave, in painted fiberglass, looms high over the bar. In every other respect this is your basic rock 'n' roll dance hall. There is a bar scene, though, before the music starts at 10:00 or 11:00-ish. 622 Broadway, south of Bleecker Street; Tel: 460-9633.

The **Eagle Tavern** is an Irish bar, a basic kind of place, much more like most of the pubs we remember in Ireland than the more deliberately "Gaelic" drinking spots in which the city abounds. There's a back room decorated, inexplicably, with a maritime motif (eagles swim?), and here, on Saturday nights, visiting fiddlers and tin-whistlers and button accordionists spin out jigs and reels. Some of the musicians are Irish-American, some are from the Old Country, and the crowd seems similarly mixed. On Mondays there is another Irish evening, with the stage open to all comers; Friday nights are for this music's American cousin, bluegrass. 355 West 14th Street, at Ninth Avenue; Tel: 924-0275.

New York is not the obvious place to go for country music, but it's the city with everything, so **O'Lunney's** bills the stuff seven nights a week. This is basically a simple Irish bar, but it makes a few bows to the West in its decor, has a small dance floor, and if the bands sometimes have accents that seem local, they play pedal steel just like they're supposed to. 915 Second Avenue, south of 49th Street; Tel: 751-5470.

## *Performance Art*

**The Pyramid** is an unlikely storefront nightclub on the Lower East Side, a home for the unpredictable, no-rules kind of entertainment known as performance art. In the early to mid-1980s the East Village held a sizable nightclub and gallery scene of young entrepreneurs evading the high rents of the established art districts by operating here instead, in pocket-size spaces where they showed the emerging local talent. Today a few remain, but most have either closed or, in the case of many of the galleries, moved to upgraded spaces in and around SoHo. The Pyramid is a reminder of the old days. Outside is an ornately but funkily decorated façade standing out from the grayish tenement fronts around it on Avenue A; inside is a pair of rooms in every shade of phosphorescent, one a bar painted in purple and orange paisley, the second the black-lit performance space. What plays here varies wildly: On quiet evenings it's a loud discotheque (if for a young Loisaida—Lower East Sider—crowd that might be called adventuresome); often it's a rock club for bands unheard of outside a ten-block radius; then there's performance, which is virtually anything the artist in question decides it is, from the humdrum to the hilarious to the cover-your-eyes-and-pretend-you-didn't-see-that. 101 Avenue A, south of 7th Street; Tel: 420-1590.

Performance art also plays in spaces a little more sedate. **P.S. 122**, a former schoolhouse become neighborhood art center, is a few blocks away from The Pyramid, and the auditorium here takes some of the same performers and some of the same crowd, but the mood is more theatrical than clubbish—though with bleacher seating and no air conditioning in summer. Many New Yorkers uncomfortable with the close-packed standing-room-only let's-all-throw-things-at-the-stage exigencies of club life may come here to see a performance artist stretch to engage a larger and calmer audience, or they may go to **The Kitchen**, which also runs an ambitious contemporary-music program. These places, some of whose income comes from public grant money, are less free-for-all than the private performance houses; hey, this stuff is supposed to be art. So a performer may debut with an ambitious project here and then go back to the clubs.

P.S. 122, 150 First Avenue, at 9th Street; Tel: 477-5288. The Kitchen, 512 West 19th Street, west of Tenth Avenue; Tel: 255-5793.

## COMEDY CLUBS

In the late 1970s, when the satiric TV show "Saturday Night Live" was at the height of its cult popularity, standup comedy took on a whole new glamor in New York. Young comics achieved for themselves the kind of media stardom that had once been linked mainly with rock 'n' roll—which for many culture consumers had begun to seem either overly well established and safe, or, in the hands of the punksters who were trying to make the music risky again, a little too confrontational for comfort. Part of rock's role has been to offer an identity, a feeling of group community, to whatever generation is growing up at the time, and as music slackened its hold (not that it isn't still popular) comics were the perfect substitute, especially if their humor was of that nervy kind that kids weren't sure was funny, suspected was shocking, but at least knew that their parents weren't laughing at. That moment has to some extent passed, but its legacy is today's comedy clubs in the city, which are full of young comedians looking for their break. Their models are less Henny Youngman and Rich Little than John Belushi and Steve Martin; some of their jokes you can go to hell just for hearing told. On good nights these places are full of fresh energy.

In comedy clubs, however, good nights are unpredictable. These rooms are where comics learn as well as practice their craft. Sometimes they fly and sometimes they flop, and the best can flop in front of an audience that just isn't amused. A crowd that goes to see Richard Pryor at Radio City Music Hall goes ready to laugh, wanting to laugh, knowing the night will be funny. A comedy-club crowd expects the quality to vary, and can be ungenerous. Two clubs on the Upper East Side sometimes demonstrate this clearly. The Comic Strip and Catch a Rising Star are within walking distance of each other, and people who aren't enjoying the one can easily stroll over to the other to see what's going on. If they do, they may find that a comic they saw earlier in the evening has taken the same walk, and though they just watched him bomb, now he's rolling. The act itself is probably identical.

Given the proviso of variable evenings, **Catch a Rising Star** is a good bet for hilarity. It's a popular club (the bigger the crowd, the better the probability of laughter, which is infectious), and it's a comfortable and friendly spot. **The Comic Strip** is a barer and less-polished room, but not necessarily the less funny for that, and it's nice to sit at the bar here and listen to the comics hanging out and telling stories about horrible audiences they have known.

Downtown is **Caroline's** at the South Street Seaport, which is a kind of urban theme park designed for picturesqueness; yet Caroline's is a modern room, and a little antiseptic. It is, however, well sited to attract good crowds.

A lot of the same performers circulate from one to the other of these clubs—and we've only mentioned a few; check the nightlife ads in the *Village Voice* or the entertainment listings in *New York* magazine for more—which means that the chances for enjoyment are spread around. An evening in any of these places may see a dozen young aspirants chewed up or coming off smiling. And although the clubs may have open evenings when anyone can stand up to take his or her knocks, these are not amateur outfits. Many of the comics who play them are very polished indeed, with a lot of pro experience, and well-known names sometimes pass through.

Catch a Rising Star, 1487 First Avenue, south of 78th Street; Tel: 794-1906. The Comic Strip, 1568 Second Avenue, south of 82nd Street; Tel: 861-9386. Caroline's, South Street Seaport, Pier 17, at Fulton Street and the East River; Tel: 233-4900.

## DANCE HALLS, SOIREES, AND DISCOS

**Roseland** is New York's classic Broadway ballroom. It has been where it now stands since 1956, but it opened around the corner on 51st Street in 1919. A renovation in the mid-1980s didn't do too much harm. The decor looks pretty much as always, though the red-rose-studded green carpet is actually new; the dance floor, ringed by a sinuous wrought-iron balustrade punctuated by low lampposts, is still half a block long, and there are clubs in the city smaller than its bandstand. The versatility of the lighting system, however, is entirely modern. From Thursday to Sunday people can dance here for up to nine and a half hours a day—disco late nights on Friday and Saturday, ballroom and Latin on the other days, beginning in midafternoon. These events can be fascinating, allowing a glimpse of an older Broadway culture. A "wall of fame" on the way in is a display case of the shoes of famous dancers, from Ruby Keeler to Ann Reinking, from George Raft to Gregory Hines. Pop acts in need of a hall with a floor sometimes stop in, but the air still breathes Stan Kenton and the Dorsey Brothers. 239 West 52nd Street, west of Broadway; Tel: 247-0200.

**The Rainbow Room** is in Rockefeller Center, and you can reach it from Sixth Avenue and 50th Street, but don't. Take the processional walk in from Fifth Avenue, with your destination, 30 Rockefeller Plaza, brilliantly spotlit in front of you at night above the golden statue of Prometheus. The gentle descent of the pavement pulls you on, and the architecture tells you you're going somewhere big. Inside, the floor continues its easy slope, and you reach the private burl-paneled elevators that will whisk you express to the 65th floor; step out, turn around, and there's a sudden view of the Empire State Building with all of southern Manhattan laid out around it.

The Rainbow Room first opened in 1934, an Art Deco palace in the sky. It reopened at the end of 1987, after a two-year, $20 million renovation, in all its former stylishness, with contemporary design and *objets* artfully complementing the old. The band plays Glenn Miller; the dance floor revolves; the floor-to-ceiling windows frame . . . practically everything. Fred Astaire and Ginger Rogers do not go swinging by, but in the general flurry of evening gowns and tuxedos it's easy to pretend. Dinner and dancing here may run $100 or so a person; from the neighboring bar you can enjoy the same views for the price of a drink, though the music is now remote, and gentlemen still must wear a jacket there. 30 Rockefeller Plaza near 50th Street off Fifth Avenue; Tel: 632-5000/5100.

The **Red Blazer Too** is a relaxed dinner and dancing place that specializes in the jazz of the 1920s and 1930s: Dixieland, swing, and the chunkily swinging stuff in between. Some of the bands that run here feature players from those times. There aren't many rooms around anymore in which this music can be heard from a dance floor instead of from a chair, so the people who come to the Red Blazer seem both to know their jazz history and to get up and enjoy it in the best, nonacademic way—in their dancing shoes. 349 West 46th Street, west of Eighth Avenue; Tel: 262-3112.

The **Cat Club** on ordinary days is a standard rock 'n' roll place, but most Sundays since 1985 it has belonged to the New York Swing Dance Society, who use it to do the lindy and other steps of that family to the music of big orchestras (including, one night a while ago, the Basie band). These Sundays are like club nights—a lot of people are regulars, and there's that sociable feeling of a not necessarily fashionable common interest. Some of the dancers remember the Savoy Ballroom (of Chick Webb's "Stompin' at the Savoy," a famous Harlem hall torn down in the 1950s); others barely remember the Beatles. All are welcome. From a framed photograph on the wall, David Bowie looks on, impassive as ever. 76 East 13th Street, west of Fourth Avenue (a southern incarnation of Park Avenue); Tel: 505-0090.

For over 30 years, from its opening in 1940, the **Copacabana**, almost always called the Copa, was a hegemonic presence in New York nightlife. Everybody played there, from Frank Sinatra to Chubby Checker to the Supremes and on. A booking there marked a performer as a star, like a stamp he needed in his passport. There are volumes of Copa lore—how co-owner Jules Podell was an associate of underworld crime boss Frank Costello; how Desi Arnaz and Lucille Ball first met in the club, when she was in its chorus line; how Dean Martin and Jerry Lewis both began and ended their career as a comedy team there. After Podell's death in 1973 the club closed its doors. It reopened in 1976, and is now a regular discotheque, open Tuesdays, Fridays, and Saturdays and booking live, mainly Latin bands. But the downstairs room has been restored rather than renovated, and has the same Carmen Miranda-headgear-painted mirrors, the same concrete support columns made over into white-enameled palm trees, the same frond-pattern carpeting that made the rat pack feel at home. 10 East 60th Street, east of Fifth Avenue; Tel: 755-6010.

In a heavily Hispanic Upper West Side neighborhood, above a jeans outlet and beside a McDonald's, is the blue-velvet-interiored **Club Broadway**, an unpretentious but capacious and comfortable ballroom open on Wednesdays and late weekend nights for dancing to Latin big bands. 2551 Broadway, south of 96th Street; Tel: 864-7600.

**The Palladium** is housed in a big and battered old theater, from 1926, that used to be called the Academy of Music. This discotheque's designer, the Japanese architect Arata Isozaki (creator of the new Museum of Contemporary Art in Los Angeles, among other buildings), has kept large chunks of the original decor. The parts of the interior that were decaying he preserved or even encouraged in their decay, but he mixed them with decisively modern elements. The dance floor, for example, is encased in a high-tech open-sided cube, with built-in lights and video banks, and paintings and designs by significant current artists are scattered about the walls. This is a spectacular space, full of dramatic lighting effects and vistas, jumbling the antiqued with the contemporary, that make you feel as if you were living out the transition from one kind of world into another. As architecture it's as worthy of a visit, as indicative of its time, as, say, Grace Church or the lobby of the Woolworth Building. As a dance club, it's been on the scene a little too long to be called state of the art—it opened in 1985, a long time ago in some circles—but, at least in its visual style, few of the hot clubs of the present day really advance on it, and many of them are in its debt. Run by Steve Rubell and Ian Schrager, whose Studio 54 was the big daddy of New York's late-1970s disco scene, the Palladium is almost a necessary stop for nightclubbers. 126 East 14th Street, west of Third Avenue; Tel: 473-7171.

**The Tunnel** is a discotheque built over one of the old railway lines that hauled freight up and down the west side of Manhattan in the now-vanished days of working docks and warehouses there. As you'd expect, then, it's a narrow, elongated space (well, it's a tunnel), with the old train tracks still visible at one end, though subject to a light show novel in their history. Sitting rooms off the main dance floor are done up in a variety of decors—Aubrey Beardsley, Neoclassical, all-mirrored—and big old-fashioned glass chandeliers above the dance floor sit oddly within the bare-brick walls. This glamor-in-the-ruins effect seems a cop from the Palladium, however. 220 12th Avenue, though the door is actually around the corner on 27th Street; Tel: 244-6444.

Those who see New York as Sin City, a destroyer of all Christian values, might surely support their argument by citing the **Limelight**. For most of the years since the 1840s this building was the Church of the Holy Communion; now it's a discotheque. When the Limelight opened, in 1984, the regional Episcopal bishop pronounced himself "horrified," but the church had already been sold into secular use. Now light towers and catwalks scrape the gothic arches, and dancers pump to disco in the nave. A marble tablet in the vestibule advises them that "this house was created to the honor of God and for the good of His children"; maybe, in their own way, they agree. 47 West 20th Street, at Sixth Avenue; Tel: 807-7850.

When it opened in 1986, **Nell's** was something new under the sun, or at least in the New York club life of the preceding decade. Where discos from Studio 54 on had emphasized a high-tech glamor that reached its peak in the Palladium, Nell's decided to be an Edwardian salon. On the ground floor is a rather beautiful room, all softly lit red-velvet sofas and low coffee tables on faded carpets, with dark wood paneling on the walls and gilt-framed mirrors stretching back under a dim but lustrous chandelier. In the far section of the space you can dine, or you can converse on a couch as if in a more luxurious version of your sitting room, but with a bar. For dancers there's a floor in the basement, so they don't have to go somewhere else. Nell's is one of those clubs that likes to keep people standing outside; but it's not a huge space, and a chunk of its nightly clientele will be the in-crowd "registrants," the regulars who get precedence at the door. You can try to assure entry by calling ahead, early, to make a reservation. 246 West 14th Street, east of Eighth Avenue; Tel: 675-1567.

**M.K.** takes the premises of what used to be a bank, and, like the Palladium, it keeps some of the old interior decor (for example, the marble-paneled walls) and adds some of its own (the balcony restaurant space and the stuffed Dobermans). The art on the walls also recalls the Palladium (at this writing a Basquiat, some Schnabels, etc.), the chandeliers recall Nell's and the Tunnel, and the sitting-room mood of the ground-floor bar is definitely out of Nell's. Still, at this writing M.K. is a hot club. In the basement, which used to be the vault, is a late-night discotheque; the coat check is in what was once the safe, with the massive, rather beautiful steel doors standing polished and open. Upstairs there's a nice little balconied window where patrons can stand and watch the bouncer outside turning people away. Those who do get in tend to be young and affluent and very chic. If you must visit here, try calling in advance to make a reservation for dinner. 204 Fifth Avenue, north of 25th Street; Tel: 779-1340.

**The World**, like the Ritz and the Palladium, is an old auditorium made over to new use, but where the Ritz preserves its original fittings and the Palladium makes decay look dressy, here the dilapidation is a value in itself. Downstairs is a smallish, moderne, relatively soigné space; upstairs is a cavernous hall of peeling plaster and ratty brick, supplied, of course, with high-tech lights and sound. Some evenings this is a regular rock 'n' roll concert space, but the time to go is from midnight or one-ish until around 4:00 A.M., say, Tuesday through Sunday, when it turns into a dance club for an eclectic cross section of the city's most knowledgeable nightlife crowd, and a very hot place to be. 254 East 2nd Street, just west of Avenue C; Tel: 477-8677.

**Trixie's** is a wonderful anomaly: a hot spot that's actually hot instead of cool. Kids seem to come here to have fun rather than to see and be seen and to demonstrate their hipness. A former Greek diner, Trixie's is actually a restaurant rather than a nightclub—to get in here, you call and make a reservation for dinner—but it's a restaurant that fancies itself a nightclub, though circumstances suggest otherwise. There's no room; lounge-lizard crooners stride up and down the crowded aisles between the tables, singing to backing tapes because there's nowhere to put a band. Or an all-women samba drum outfit in sarongs squeezes itself in next to the bar and ends up snaking through the place in a conga line, followed by half the diners. Between acts, the PA plays loud rock 'n' roll and everyone sings along. 307 West 47th Street, west of Eighth Avenue; Tel: 840-9537.

# INDEX

ABC Antiques, 219
Academy Book Store, 283, 304
Aca-Joe, 264
Acme Bar & Grill, 357, 372
Actors Heritage, 296
Admiral George Dewey Promenade, 55
Adnan, 169
Adorama, 272
Agnès B, 254
AIN Plastics, 216
Alain Mañoukian, 251
Alan Moss Studios, 219
A La Vieille Russie, 220
The Algonquin Hotel, 39, 126, 387
Alice in Wonderland statue, 151
Alice Kwartler, 221
Alice's Antiques, 219
Alice Tully Hall, 277
Alice Underground, 263
Alleva Dairy, 321
Almontaser, 365
Alternative Museum, 79
B. Altman & Co., 118, 235, 255
Alvin Ailey Company, 285
*Amagansett,* 200
America, 107
American Academy of Arts and Letters, 147
American Ballet Theatre, 285
American Craft Museum, 128
American Geographical Society, 147
American Museum of Immigration, 54
American Museum of Natural History, 140, 236
American Numismatic Society, 147
An American Place, 338
Amigo Country, 312
Amsterdam Avenue, 218
André Emmerich Gallery, 209
Andy's Chee-Pees, 263
Angelica's Herb and Spice Company, 321
Annapurna (restaurant), 112, 361
Annapurna Indian Groceries, 320
Ann Taylor, 250
The Ansonia, 138, 232
Antiquarian Booksellers' International, Inc., 305
Antiquarium Fine Ancient Arts, 221
Antique District, 218
Antique Doll Hospital of New York, 224
Antique Supermarket, 224
Applause Cinema Books, 270
Applause Theatre Book Publishers, 295, 307
The Apthorp, 232
Arcadia, 157, 340
Ares Rare, 221
Ariba Ariba!, 143
Arizona 206, 157, 341
Army & Navy Stores, 264
Army's Italian Cuisine, 185
Arnold Constable, 235
Arqua, 328
Arthur Brown, 216, 311
Arthur's Tavern, 383
Artist Pianos, 282
Artists Space, 79, 213
Artwear, 262
Asia Society, 156
*Astoria,* 182
Astor Place, 104
Astro Mineral, 314
Atlantic Avenue, Brooklyn, 169
Atlantic Avenue Beach, Amagansett, 200
A. T. Stewart's, 234
AT & T Building, 244
Au Bar, 371
Audubon Terrace, 146
Aunt Sonia's, 171
Aunt Suzie's, 171
Automatic Slims, 383
Au Troquet, 332
Avery Fisher Hall, 136, 277

La Bagagerie, 258
Baldi's Italian Pastry Shop, 186
Balducci's, 319
The Ballet Shop, 288
The Ballroom, 352, 372, 385, 411
B. Altman & Co., 118, 235, 255
Bamonte's, 173
The Bar, 382

423

# INDEX

Barbara Gee Danskin Center, 288
The Barbizon, 36
Barnard Book Forum, 145
Barnes & Noble, 126, 271, 304
Barney Greengrass the Sturgeon King, 143
Barney's, 115, 251
Barocco, 328
Barrymore's, 295
Barry of Chelsea, 223
The Battery, 52
Battery Park City, 244
Bayamo, 358
*Bayside,* 178
B. Dalton, 305
The Beach Café, 394
Bebe Thompson, 265
Bed & Breakfast (& Books), 47
Beekman Arms, 195
Beekman Tower Hotel, 44, 124
Beinecke Library, 198
The Belleclaire, 232
Bellini by Cipriani, 37, 330, 389
Belvedere Castle, 151
Bemelmans Bar, 34, 410
Ben's Cheese Shop, 320
The Beresford, 233
Bergdorf Goodman, 130, 235, 255, 264
Le Bernardin, 337
Bernard Krieger & Son, 259
Bernstein-on-Essex Street, 88, 320
Bertha Black, 219
Bessie Schönberg Theater, 115, 286
Bethesda Fountain, 151
Betsey, Bunky, Nini, 248
Betsey Johnson, 254
Better Times Antiques, 219
Beverly, 41
C. O. Bigelow Chemists, 100
The Big Kahuna, 414
Birdland, 394
Bistro Bamboche, 333
Bistro du Nord, 162
Bleecker Street, 97

Bloomingdale's, 157, 255
Blue Bar, 388
The Blue Note, 408
Boathouse Café, 370, 398
Bogie's, 263
Bok Lei Tat Trading Co., 266
Bomba de Clercq, 254
Bombay, 361
Bonwit Teller, 255
Books and Co., 306
Bottega Veneta, 257
The Bottom Line, 413
Bouley, 339
*The Bowery,* 88
Bowling Green, 59
Boyd Chemists, 259
Bradley's, 383, 409
Brasserie, 125
The Brazilian Coffee Restaurant, 352
Breakaway, 256
Bremen House, 318
*Bridgehampton,* 200
Bridge Kitchenware, 323
*Brighton Beach,* 172, 366
Brighton Beach Avenue, 172
*The Bronx,* 187
The Bronx Zoo, 187
*Brooklyn,* 164
Brooklyn Academy of Music, 169, 280, 286, 293
Brooklyn Botanic Garden, 171
Brooklyn Bridge, 69, 165
*Brooklyn Heights,* 168
Brooklyn Museum, 171
Brooks Brothers, 263
Broome Street Bar, 95, 372
Bryant Park Ticket Booth, 281
B. Shackman, 312
B. Smith's, 359
Buccellati, 261
Bukhara, 362
Burberry's Ltd., 250, 264

La Cabaña Argentina, 353
Cabaña Carioca, 352

Le Café, 368
Café Armenia, 367
Café Borgia, 103
Café Borgia II, 95
Café Carlyle, 34, 394, 411
Café Crocodile, 363
Café des Artistes, 137, 391
Café Europa, 172
Café Geiger, 366
Café Iguana, 359
Café La Fortuna, 141
Café Luxembourg, 340, 391
Café Madeleine, 294
Café San Martin, 351
Café Society, 386
Café Trevi, 330
Café Zodiac, 172
Caffè Biondo, 83
Caffè Dante, 103
Caffè Reggio, 103
Caffè Roma, 83
Caffè Strada, 155
Camera Mart, Inc., 273
Canal Bar, 95, 372, 380
Canal Jean Co., 256
Canal Street, 79
Capezio, 252, 287
The Captain's Quarters, 356
La Caravelle, 336
La Caridad, 143
Carl Schurz Park, 158
The Carlyle Hotel, 34, 156, 410
Carlyle Restaurant, 156
Carmel Middle Eastern Grocery, 184
Carnegie Delicatessen and Restaurant, 131, 344
Carnegie Hall, 131, 278
*Carnegie Hill,* 160
Caroline's Comedy Club, 68, 380, 417
Caroll, 251
Cartier, 260
Cary Building, 78
Cashmere/Cashmere, 249
Castle Clinton National Monument, 53
Caswell-Massey, 259

# INDEX 425

Catch a Rising Star, 160, 417
Cat Club, 419
Cathedral Church of St. John the Divine, 146
Cave Cannum, 396
Caviarteria, 318
CBGB, 412
Cellar in the Sky, 343
Cent'Anni, 327
Central Carpet, 222
Central Fish Co., 319
*Central Park,* 148, 280
Central Park Zoo, 148
The Century, 233
Cerutti, 265
Chanel, 250
Chanin Building, 241
Channel Gardens, 127
Chanterelle, 340
Charivari 5, 250
Charivari 72, 251
Charivari Workshop, 251
Charles' Place, 262
Charlie's Restaurant, 295
Charrette, 216
Cheap Jacks, 263
Cheese of All Nations, 321
*Chelsea,* 115
Chelsea Commons, 116
Chelsea Hotel, 46, 115
Chelsea Trattoria, 115, 328
The Chess Shop, 310
Chez Aby, 256
Chez Jacqueline, 332
Chez Josephine, 333
Chez Napoleon, 333
China Gardens, 348
*Chinatown,* 79, 321, 346
Chinatown Books, 81
Chinatown Fair Amusement Arcade and Chinese Museum, 81
Chin Chin, 348
Chipp, 263
Chiuzac Gallery, 220
Cho Sun Ok, 183
Christ Cella, 353
Christie's, 156, 212, 226, 275
Christie's East, 156

Christofle Pavillon, 309
Christopher Street, 98
Chrysler Building, 122, 241
Chumley's, 98, 384
Church of the Heavenly Rest, 163
Church of the Holy Trinity, 159
Church of the Transfiguration, 114
Ciao Bella, 360
Cinco de Mayo, 123, 356
Circle Repertory Theater, 294
Le Cirque, 35, 157, 336
Citarella's, 143
Citicorp Center, 244
City Center, 285
City Hall, 69, 228
City Hall Park, 69
City Lights Bar, 63
City Lights Bed & Breakfast Ltd., 47
Civic Center, 68
CK & L Surplus Store, 216
Claire, 355
The Clocktower, 213
The Cloister (restaurant), 105
The Cloisters, 147, 279
Club Broadway, 419
Coach House, 99, 338
Coach Leather, 257
C. O. Bigelow Chemists, 100
Cobweb, 218
Coisa Nossa, 126
Coliseum Books, 131, 305
La Colombe d'Or, 333
Colony Records Center, 282, 296
Columbia University, 145
Columbus Avenue, 140, 218
Columbus Circle, 134
Columbus Restaurant, 393
The Comic Strip, 160, 417
Comme des Garçons, 254, 264
Commodities Natural Foods, 321

Common Ground, 311
The Compleat Strategist, 313
The Complete Traveller, 305
Congregation K'Hal Adath Jeshurun, 84
Conran's, 323
Conservatory Café, 38
Conservatory Garden, 152
Contrapunto, 157, 341
Conway, 257
Cook World, 323
Cooper-Hewitt Museum, 163, 231, 245
Cooper Union for the Advancement of Science and Art, 104
Copacabana, 419
Cora Ginsburg, 222
Corona Park Salumeria, 185
La Côte Basque, 335
Courtyard Café, 43
Cousin John's Café, 171
Craft Caravan, 312
Crawdaddy Restaurant, 42
Crisci, 173
Crouch & Fitzgerald, 257
Crown Building, 235
Crystal Garden, 183
Csarda, 366
Culinary Institute of America, 195
Cupping Room, 90
Custom Shirt Shop, 264
Le Cygne, 336
Cynthia Beneduce, 220


Daily News Building, 123
The Dakota, 139, 232
Dalva Bros., 219
Damages, 257
Damrosch Park, 277
Dance Theater of Harlem, 285
Dance Theater Workshop, 286
Danielle Like Mother Like Daughter, 266
Darbar, 362
Dar Lebnan, 364

## 426   INDEX

Darrow's Fun Antiques, 224
Da Silvano, 327
Da Umberto, 328
David Davis, 215
Dawat, 362
Dean & DeLuca, 91, 321
Debris, 263
Delacorte Theatre, 151
Delta 88, 359
Depression Modern, 219
Descamps, 309
Detail, 261
Deutsch, 309
D. F. Sanders, 308
Dia Art Foundation, 214
Diamond District, 126, 261
Didier Aaron, Inc., 219
Die Fledermaus, 370
Dinosaur Hill, 265
Dock's Oyster Bar, 355
Dominick's, 331
Donnell Library, 269
Don't Tell Mama, 412
Doral Court, 43
Doral Inn, 41
Doral Park Avenue, 42
Doris Leslie Blau, 222
The Dorset, 38
Doubleday, 305
*Douglaston,* 178
Doyle Galleries, 226
The Drama Bookshop, 270, 296
The Drawing Center, 246
D. Sokolin, 323
Duggal Color Projects, 272
Dumont Plaza, 45

Eagle Tavern, 414
Ear Inn, 95
Eastgate Tower, 45
*East Hampton,* 200
East—The Town of Taste, 350
*East Village,* 103
East West Books, 304
E. Braun, 309
Eclair, 139
Eclectiques, 223
Eeyore's, 307

Eighty-Eights, 411
Einstein's, 262
Elaine's, 159, 395
Eliot Feld, 286
Ellen O'Neill's Supply Store, 223
Ellen's Café, 71
Ellen's Stardust, 371
*Ellis Island,* 54
Elysée Hotel, 41
Emanuel Ungaro, 249
Empire Coffee and Tea, 319
Empire Diner, 116, 372
Empire Hotel, 45
Empire State Building, 118, 241
Enchantments, 314
Endicott Bookseller, 142
Enz, 253
Erica Wilson, 309
Esposito & Sons Pork Store, 319
Essex Street Market, 88
Europa Delicacies, 182
Evyan, 309
The Excelsior, 142
Exterminator Chili, 79, 357
Eze, 333

Fairway, 142, 317
Fanelli, 91, 211
Fanelli Antique Timepieces, Ltd, 221
F.A.O. Schwartz, 313
Fashion Institute of Technology, 117
Fat Tuesday, 408
Fausto Santini, 248
FDR Drive, 254
FDR Drive Men, 264
Feast of San Gennaro, 82, 316
Federal Hall National Memorial, 66
Federal Reserve Bank of New York, 64
Feld, Eliot, 286
Ferragamo, 250
Ferrara Café, 83
Fifth Avenue, 125
Fifty-50, 219
57th Street, 130, 209, 217
Le Figaro Café, 103
Film Forum, 95

*Financial District,* 59
Fine & Klein, 256
First 1/2, 219
Flatiron Building, 114, 240
Die Fledermaus, 370
Fleur de Lis Antiques, 219
Florent, 315, 332
*Flushing,* 183
Flushing Yuet Tung, 183
Flutie's, 379
Flying Cranes Antiques, 223
Foffe's, 169
Folklorica, 251
Food (restaurant), 94
Foods of India, 320
Footlight Records, 283
Forbes Magazine Galleries, 101
Forbidden Planet, 304, 313
*Forest Hills,* 183
*Forest Hills Gardens,* 179
Fortune Chao-Chow Seafood Restaurant, 345
Fortune Garden Pavilion, 409
42nd Street, 119
47th Street Photo, 126
Foto-Care, 273
Four Seasons, 124, 341, 387
Franklin D. Roosevelt National Historic Site, 194
Franklin Furnace, 79
Fraunces Tavern, 67
Fred F. French Building, 242
Fred Joaillier, 260
Fred Leighton, 220
Freed of London, 288
French Connection, 251
*Fresh Meadows,* 180
Frick Collection, 156, 279
F. R. Tripler, 263
Fulton Fish Market, 68, 315
Fulton Street Café, 380
Furla, 258
Fu's, 348

## INDEX 427

La Fusta, 182
Futon Shop, 308

Gage & Tollner, 169, 287
The Gallery, 368
G & A Rare Records Ltd., 283
Gargiulo's, 331
Garment District, 117, 248
Garnet Liquors, 322
Gastronom Moscow, 367
La Gauloise, 332
Gaylord's, 105
G. Elter, 309
Gem Pawnbrokers, 262
Gem Spa, 105
Georgette Klinger, 259
Georg Jensen, 309
Gianni Versace, 249
Gil Ghitelman Cameras, 272
Ginger Man, 391
Giorgio Armani, 249, 264
Glori Bead Shoppe, 310
Goethe House New York, 163
Go Fly A Kite, 313
Golden and LeBlang, 292
The Gold Room, 368, 388
The Good, The Bad and The Ugly, 220
Gordon's, 201
Gorham, 46
Gosman's Dock, 201
The Gotham Bar and Grill, 384
Gotham Book Mart, 126, 270, 305
Gould Trading, 272
Gourmet Gazelle, 318
Grace Balducci's Marketplace, 318
Grace Rainey Rogers Auditorium, 279
Gracie Mansion, 158
Gracie Mansion Gallery, 209
*Gramercy Park,* 110
Grand Army Plaza, 130, Manhattan; 170, Brooklyn
The Grand Bay, 37

Grand Central Oyster Bar & Restaurant, 122, 342
Grand Central Terminal, 122, 238
Grand Dairy Restaurant, 85
The Grand Hyatt, 45
Grand Palace, 346
Grand Shanghai, 347
Grand Ticino, 327
Grant's Tomb, 146
Gray's Papaya, 138
Great American Salvage Co., 223
Great Jones Café, 358, 372
Great Lawn, 152
Great Shanghai, 347
Greene Street, 409
*Greenpoint,* 172
Green Tree, 146
*Greenwich Village,* 96, 217
Grey Art Gallery, 101
Grosz Leather, 310
Gryphon Bookshop, 143, 307
Gryphon Records, 283
Gucci, 258
Guggenheim Museum, 163
Guinness World Records Exhibit Hall, 119
Gulf Coast, 357
Gulliver's, 312
Gwenda G., 262

Hacker Art Books, 131
Halina's, 259
Hamburger Harry's, 370
Hammacher Schlemmer, 314
*The Hamptons,* 200
Hard Rock Café, 131, 369, 373
Harriet Love, 262
Harry Kirshner, 260
Harry's at Hanover Square, 66, 380
Harry's New York Bar, 388
Harry Winston, 261
Hatsuhana, 349
Haughwout Store, 234
The Hedges, 201

Helmsley Palace Hotel, 39, 127
Henderson Place Historic District, 158
Henri Bendel, 131, 255, 260
Henry's End, 169
Hermès, 258
H & H Bagels, 143
Hickey's, 292
Hilton, New York, 45
Hirschl & Adler, 210
Hirschl & Adler Folk, 210, 221
Hirschl & Adler Modern, 210
Hispanic Society of America, 147
Holly Solomon Gallery, 210
Hong Kong Bookstore, 81
Horn & Hardart Dine-O-Mat, 371
Hornmann Magic Co., 312
Hors d'Oeuvrerie, 343, 400
Hosts & Guests, Inc., 47
Hotalings, 314
Hotel Wales, 46, 162
H.S.F., 347
H. Stern, 260
Hudson Guild Theatre, 115
*Hudson Valley,* 192
Hungarian Pastry Shop, 146
The Hunt Room, 388
Huntting Inn, 201
Hwa Yuan, 183
Hyde Park, 194

Ibiza, 252
IBM Building, 130, 244
IBM Gallery of Science and Art, 130, 244
If, 253
Independent Feature Project Market, 269
Indochine, 104, 358
Industrial Plastic, 216
Institute for Advanced Studies, 203
Inter-Continental New York, 40

# INDEX

International Center of Photography, 126, 163, 231, 268, 271
International Grocery Store, 319
Irving Trust Co., 242
Isaac Mendoza Book Company, 68
Isamu Noguchi Museum, 184
Island, 162
Israel Sack, 219
Italian Food Center, 321
Itokin Plaza, 248
It's Only Rock N Roll, 313

Jaap Rietman, 95
*Jackson Heights,* 180, 182
Jacob K. Javits Convention Center, 118, 239
Jacques Français, 282
Jaeger, 250
Jamaica Arts Center, 178
Jam Envelope and Paper, 216
James Robinson, 220
James Watson House, 58, 228
Jams, 159
Jana Starr/Jean Hoffman Antiques, 263
Janet Sartin, 259
Jan Wallman's, 410
Jay Gorney Modern Art, 208
Jean Cocteau Repertory, 294
Jean Silversmith, 309
Jefferson Market, 100
Jefferson Market Inc., 319
Jeff's, 314
Jeremy's Ale House, 380
Jerry's Restaurant, 91
La Jeunesse, 258
Jewish Museum, 163, 231
Jezebel, 358
J. G. Melon, 360
Jim McMullen, 160, 360
Jimsons, 313
Jindo Furs, 260
Jockey Club, 37, 388

Joe Allen, 120
Joel Name, 311
Joffrey Ballet, 285
John Weber Gallery, 209
Jolanta, 366
Jolie Gabor, 261
Joseph Tricot, 248
Joyce Leslie, 256
Joyce Theater, 115, 286
J. Press, 263
J & R Classical Outlet, 283
J's, 394
Juilliard School, 137, 276
Junction Diner, 179
Junior's, 287

Kam Man, 79, 321
Kang Suh, 363
Karyatis Restaurant, 182
Katagiri, 318
Katz's, 88
Kauffmans, 310
Kaufman/Astoria Movie Studios, 181
Kelter-Malce, 220
Ken Hansen Photographic, 272, 273
Ken Leiberman, 272
Kent Fine Art Gallery, 210
Kenzo, 248
*Kew Gardens,* 179
Kiehl's, 259
Kiev, 104
The Kimberly, 44
King Glassware, 324
Kitano, 43
The Kitchen, 416
Kitchen Arts & Letters, 307, 318
K & L, 272
Klein's of Monticello, 265
Knitting Factory, 410
Kossar's, 320
Kurowycky Meat Products, 320

Lace-Up Shoe Shop, 256
Ladies' Mile, 116, 234
Lafayette, 337
Lahiere's, 203
Lasker Rink, 152

Last Wound-Up, 142, 312
Lattanzi Ristorante, 330
Launch Café, 160
Laura Ashley, 250
Laura Fisher, 220
Laurent, 44
Le Laurier, 355
Ledel, 274
Lederer, 257
Lefkos Pirgos Bakery, 182
Lemon Ice King of Corona, 185
Lens & Repro Equipment Corporation, 272, 273
Leo Castelli, 208
Leo Kaplan, 222
Leshko Coffee Shop, 366
Lever House, 125, 243
Liberty Café, 380
Liberty of London, 265
Librairie de France, 306
Library and Museum of Performing Arts, 137, 269, 296
Libreria Hispanica, 306
Lieberman & Saul, 274
The Lighthouse, 313
Li-Lac, 323
Lilla Lova, 253
Limelight discotheque, 117, 421
Lincoln Center for the Performing Arts, 135, 277, 284
Lindy's, 290
La Lingerie, 258
Lionel Madison Trains, 224
Lion's Head, 99, 303
*Litchfield, Connecticut,* 198
Little Europe, 173
Little India, 112, 320
*Little Italy,* 82, 321, 326
Little Rickie, 314
Live Bait, 386
Liza's Place, 263
Loeb Boathouse, 151
Lola, 385
Lombardy, 44

# INDEX 429

Lone Star Café, 413
Lo: New York, 252
Long Wharf Theater, 198
Lord & Taylor, 235, 255
Lost City Arts, 223
Louis, Boston, 263
Louise Nevelson Plaza, 64
Louis Mattia, 223
Love Saves The Day, 263
The Lowell, 43
Lower Broadway, 64
*Lower East Side,* 84, 320, 365
Lower East Side Tenement Museum, 85
*Lower Manhattan,* 52
Loxtown, 184
Lucille Lortel, 98
Lucy's Restaurant, 393
Lusardi's, 159
Lutèce, 335
The Lyceum, 121
Lyden Gardens, 45
Lyden House, 45

Mabou Mines, 294
MacDougal Alley, 101
MacDougal Street, 103
McDuffy's Irish Coffee House, 380
McFeely's, 170
Macklowe Gallery and Modernism, 220
McSorley's Old Ale House, 105, 382
Macy's, 118, 254, 323
Macy's Cellar, 318
Madison Avenue, 156, 208, 217
The Madison Room, 388
Madison Square, 113
Madison Square Garden, 118
Madras Palace, 361
Magickal Childe, 314
Main Beach, East Hampton, 200
Maison Gerard, 219
Maison Glass, 318
The Majestic Apartments, 233
Majestic Theater, 170
La MaMa Experimental Theater Company, 105, 293
Manhattan Brewing Company, 90
Manhattan Viscount, 41
Man Ray Bistro, 115, 386
Marcuse Pfeifer, 274
Margo Feiden Galleries, 297
Marian Goodman Gallery, 210
Marie's Crisis Café, 98
Mario's, 331
Mario Valentino, 249
Mariposa, 314
The Mark, 36
Marlborough Gallery, 274
Marriott Marquis, 45
Mary Boone, 208
Matsuda, 250, 264
Maud Frizon, 250
Maurice, 38, 338
Maxilla and Mandible, 142, 309
Max Protetch, 209, 246
Mayfair Regent, 35, 367
The Mayflower, 38
Mediterranean Shop, 309
Meisel-Primavera, 222
Mel's, 201
Memphis, 359
Merce Cunningham, 286
Metro, 340
Metro Pictures, 209
Metropolitan Life Tower, 240
Metropolitan Museum of Art, 162, 236, 245, 268, 279
Metropolitan Opera House, 136, 277
Mezzaluna, 360
Mezzogiorno, 360
Michael B. Weisbrod, 223
Michael's Pub, 389, 411
Michelle Nicole Wesley, 258
Midnight Records, 283
*Midtown,* 106, 234
M & I International Foods, 172

Mikell's, 409
Mikimoto, 261
Milan D'Or, 249
Military Bookman, 307
Millers, 310
Mill Garth, 201
Millionaires' Row, 160
Minna Rosenblatt, 222
Misha & Monya's, 184
Missoni, 249
Mitali, 361
M. J. Knoud, 310
M.K., 371, 397, 421
M. Knoedler & Co., 210
Model Boat Basin, 151
Modern Girls, 252
Moe Ginsburg, 256
Mondel, 323
Monde Magique, 224
Il Mondo, 398
Monkey Bar, 41
Montague Street Saloon, 169
Montenapoleone, 258
Mood Indigo, 222
Moondance Diner, 371, 372
Morgans, 42
Morrell & Company, 323
Mortimer's, 360, 395
Mosaica, 360
Mott Street, 81
Mouse N' Around, 314
Movie Material Store, 314
Mulberry Street, 82
Municipal Building, 71
Murder Ink, 307
El Museo del Barrio, 164
Museum Café, 393
Museum Mile, 162
Museum of Broadcasting, 128
Museum of Holography, 95
Museum of Modern Art, 128, 245, 268, 269, 280
Museum of the American Indian, 146
Museum of the City of New York, 164
Museum of the Moving Image, 181, 185, 270

# INDEX

My Kitchen, 180
Mysterious Book Shop, 306
Mythology, 142, 312

Nakagawa, 349
Nassau Hall, 202
Nassau Inn, 203
National Academy of Design, 163
The National Restaurant, 172, 367
National Tennis Center, 185
Nat Sherman, 311
The Nature Company, 314
Nea Hellas Restaurant, 182
Near East, 169
Neil Isman Gallery, 262
Nell's, 371, 397, 421
New Era Building, 241
New Museum of Contemporary Art, 91, 215
New School for Social Research, 100
New World Bed and Breakfast Ltd., 47
New York Botanical Garden, 190
New York Center for Art and Antiques, 219, 225
New York Central Art Supply, 215
New York City Ballet, 284
New York City Courthouse, 70
New York City Fire Museum, 95
New York Convention and Visitors Bureau, 135
New York Exchange for Woman's Work, 313
New York Film Festival, 269
New York Hall of Science, 185
New York Hilton, 45
New-York Historical Society, 140
New York Kom Tang House, 362
New York Panorama, 185
New York Public Library (main branch), 121, 237
New York Shakespeare Festival, 293
New York State Theater, 136, 277
New York Stock Exchange, 16, 66
New York University, 102
New York University Bookstore, 270
New York University School of Fine Arts, 231
Next Wave Festival, 280
The Nice Restaurant, 347
Nickels, 411
Nicole Farhid, 253
998 Fifth Avenue, 233
92nd Street Y, 279
Ninth Avenue, 319
Ninth Avenue International Festival, 316
Nishi, 350
Nishi NoHo, 350
Norman Crider Antiques, 220
Northstar Tavern, 370
Nusantara, 357
Nyborg and Nelson, 318
N.Y. Leather Co., 264

Oak Bar, 37, 130, 389
Oak Room, Algonquin, 126
Ocean Reef Grille, 370, 380
The Odeon, 78, 340, 380
Odessa, 367
Old Denmark, 318
Olden Camera, 272
Old Merchant's House, 231
Old St. Patrick's Cathedral, 84
Old Town Bar, 117, 268, 386
Olive Tree Café, 364
Omen, 350
O'Mistress Mine, 262
O'Neal's Balloon, 45
One Fifth, 101
109 St. Mark's Place, 253
107 West, 359
One If By Land, 99
One Shubert Alley, 296
Onini, 328
Opium, 256
Orchard Street, 85, 256
Orso, 294
Orwasher's, 318
Oscar Wilde Memorial Bookshop, 98
Ottomanelli Brothers, 318
The Outback, 160
Oyster Bar, 122, 342

Pace/MacGill Gallery, 274
Paley Park, 129
Palio, 329
Palladium, 110, 420
Palm, 201, East Hampton; 354, Manhattan
Palm Court, 37, 130
Palm Too, 354
Panache, 262
Pan Am Building, 124
Paolucci's Restaurant, 83
Il Papiro, 310
Paprikas Weiss, 318
Papyrus Books, 308
Parachute, 254
Paragon Sporting Goods, 288
Paris Café, 380
Parisi Bakery, 84
Park Avenue, 124, 161
Le Parker Meridien, 38
Parkside Restaurant, 185
*Park Slope*, 170
Pasta Bella, 371
Patchin Place, 99
Patelson, 282
Patricia Field, 252
Paul Smith, 264
Paul Stuart, 263
Paul Taylor, 286
Peanut Butter & Jane, 265
Pearl Paint, 215
Pearl River, 83
Pedro O'Hara's, 370, 380
Peninsula, 36
Penn Station, 118
The Penta, 45
Pepe's, 198

# INDEX 431

La Pequeña Columbia, 182
Performing Arts Library at Lincoln Center, 137, 269, 296
Performing Arts Shop, 289
Performing Garage, 95, 294
Periyali, 364
Peter Fox, 254
Peter Hilary's Bar and Grill, 169
Peter Luger, 173, 354
Peter Roberts Antiques, 219
Pete's Tavern, 110, 386
La Petite Marmite, 44
Petrossian, 318
Philipsburg Manor, 192
Phillips, 212, 226, 275
Phoenix Garden Restaurant, 81, 347
Phone Booth, 314
Photocollect Gallery, 274
Photo District, 267
Photofind, 274
A Photographers Place, 270
Photographics Unlimited, 273
Photo Marketplace, 273
Phyllis Kind Gallery, 209
Piatti Pronti, 318
Pierpont Morgan Library, 118
The Pierre, 34
Pierre Balmain, 249
Pierre Deux, 258
Pink Teacup, 99
P. J. Clark's, 389
Place des Antiquaires, 220, 225
Plaza Athénée, 35
Plaza Fifty, 45
The Plaza Hotel, 37, 130
Le Plumet Royal, 203
Plymouth Church, 168
Police Academy Museum, 110
Polk's Model Crafts, 216
Polo Lounge, 35

Polo/Ralph Lauren, 249
Pomander Walk, 144
Ponica, 253
Pony Circus Antiques, 219
Portantina, 310
Portfolio Restaurant and Gallery, 268
Poseidon Bakery, 319
Positano, 112, 329
Post House, 354
Primavera (restaurant), 329
Primavera (shop), 220
Primorski, 172
Princeton University, 202
Princeton University Art Museum, 202
Printed Matter Bookshop, 79
Professional Camera Repair Service, 273
Profoto, 273
Promenade, 165
Prospect Park, 171
Provence, 96
Provincetown Playhouse, 103
P.S. 1, 184, 213
P.S. 122, 415
Public Theater, 104, 293
Puck Building, 89
Puglia, 327
Puss N Boots, 265
The Pyramid, 415


Quatorze, 332
*Queens,* 174
Queens Museum, 185


Radio City Music Hall, 128
Rainbow Room, 128, 343, 399, 418
Raintree's, 171
Rakel, 339
Ralph M. Chait, 222
Raoul's, 96, 381
Raoul's Butcher Shop, 96
Ratner's, 85
The Ravelled Sleave, 396
Red Blazer Too, 418
The Red Tulip, 366
Le Refuge, 159

La Regence, 35
The Regency, 35
Le Relais, 156
Remi, 159
Reminiscence, 252, 262
René Pujol, 333
Restaurant Maurice, 38, 338
Retro-Modern, 219
Rex, 170
Richard Stoddard Performing Arts Books, 296
*Richmond Hill,* 179
Rigo, 318
Rincon Criollo, 182
El Rincon de España, 351
Rio Mar, 351
Rita Ford's Music Boxes, 313
The Ritz, 414
The Ritz Carlton, 37
River Café, 168, 343, 399
Riverside Drive, 144
Riverside Park, 145
Rizzoli Bookstore, 94, 245, 270, 306
R. Jabbour & Sons, 258
Robert Henry, 198
Robert Marc, 311
Robin Importers, 323
Rockefeller Center, 127, 242
Roeblings, 71, 380
Rogers and Barbero, 115
Romna, 361
Ronald Feldman Gallery, 209
The Roosevelt, 42
Rosa Mexicana, 357
Roseland, 417
Rose Room, 39
Rosolio, 327
The Rotunda, 34, 368
Roumely Taverna, 182
Roundabout Theatre Company, 294
The Row, 228
Royal Athena Galleries, 221
Royal India, 361
Royal Silk, 251
The Royalton, 37
Rug Warehouse, 222
Russ and Daughters, 320

Russian Tea Room, 131, 344
Rusty's, 395

Sacha London, 251
Safani Gallery, 221
*Sag Harbor,* 200
St. Ann's and the Holy Trinity, 168
St. Mark's Bookshop, 105
St. Mark's-in-the-Bowery, 105, 286
St. Mark's Place, 103
St. Patrick's Cathedral, 127
St. Paul's Chapel, 69
Saint Remy, 318
Saks Fifth Avenue, 235, 249, 255
Sal Anthony's, 110
Salisbury, 45
Sally's Pizza, 198
The Saloon, 392
Salvage Barn, 219
Sammy's Famous Rumanian Restaurant, 88, 354
Sam's Café, 360, 396
Samuel French, 295
San Domenico, 330
The San Remo, 233
Sapore di Mare, 201
Sarabeth's Kitchen, 162, 370
Sardi's, 120, 290
Savage, 261
Savories, 318
Schermerhorn Row, 68
Schomburg Center for Research in Black Culture, 146
Seagram Building, 124, 243
SeaGrill, 343
Seaport Gallery, 68
Second Avenue Deli, 320
Second Childhood, 224
Second Hand Rose, 223
Seoul House, 363
Serendipity, 369
Seryna, 350
The Set Shop, 273
1770 House, 201
Seventeenth Street Gallery, 309

79th Street Boat Basin, 145
72nd Street, 138
Sevilla, 351
S. Gould, 261
Shades of the Village, 310
Shakespeare and Company, 143, 308
Shamrock Imports, 311
The Sharper Image, 314
Shea Stadium, 185
Sheep Meadow, 150
Shelburne–Murray Hill, 44
Sheraton Centre, 45
Sheraton Park Avenue, 42
Sherry-Lehmann, 323
Shinbi, 312
Shrimpton & Gilligan, 253
Sidewalkers', 356
Sidney Janis Gallery, 209
Sido Restaurant, 365
Sign of the Dove, 157, 341
Silver Palace, 347
Silver Palate, 317
Singer Building, 240
Siracusa, 328
Siu Lam Kung, 347
Slade's, 169
S.O.B.'s, 384, 413
Socrates Sculpture Park, 184
Sofi, 114, 398
*SoHo,* 89, 208, 217, 321
SoHo Kitchen, 94
SoHo Wine Bar, 90
Soldier Shop, 224
Solomon R. Guggenheim Museum, 163
Sonia Rykiel, 249
Son of Sheik, 169
Sotheby's, 159, 212, 226, 275
*Southampton,* 200
Southgate Tower, 45
South Street Seaport, 67, 228, 369, 379
Space Kiddets, 265
Spaghetti Western, 371
Sparks Steakhouse, 354

The Speak Easy, 412
Spice and Sweet Mahal, 320
Spring Street Bar and Restaurant, 95, 211
Spring Street Books, 95
Squadron A Armory, 161
Stair & Co., 219
The Stanhope, 34
Staten Island Ferry, 16, 55
Statue of Liberty, 54
Steinway & Sons, 282
Steven Corn Furs, 260
Stewart Ross, 248
Stony Wok, 346
Storefront for Art & Architecture, 246
Strand Book Store, 107, 271, 304
kiosks, 155
Strawberry, 256
Strawberry Fields, 139, 151
Street Life, 251
Striver's Row, 230
Sulka, 263
Sunnyside (Tarrytown), 192
*Sunnyside Gardens,* 180
Surma, 311
The Surrey, 45
Susan Parrish, 220
Sushiden, 348
Sutton Place Mews, 221
Suzanne Daché, 259
Swann Galleries, 275
Swantje-Elke, 265
Sweet Asylum, 312
Sweet Basil, 408
Sweet Victory, 318
S. Wyler Inc., 221
Sylvia's Restaurant, 358

Tabaq, 361
Takesushi, 349
Tang's Chariot, 347
Taormina, 327
Tappan Hill, 193
Taro Japanese Noodle Restaurant, 349
Tashjian Kalustyian, 320
Tavern on the Green, 137, 344, 392

# INDEX 433

Temple Emanu-El, 156
Tender Buttons, 310
The Terrace, 163, The Stanhope; 399, Columbia University
Thayer Hotel, 196
*Theater District,* 121, 290
Theater Row, 293
Theatre Arts Bookshop, 270, 296
Theatrebooks, 296
Theodore Roosevelt Birthplace, 112, 231
Thomas Street Inn, 78
Tibet West, 312
Tierras Colombianas, 182
Tiffany's, 130, 234, 235, 260
Times Square, 119
Time Will Tell, 220
T & K French Antiques, 219
TKTS, 63, 121, 291
Toll Gate Hill Inn, 199
The Tombs, 72
Tommy Tang's, 357
Tompkins Park Restaurant, 373
Tony's Ristorante, 182
Tootsie Plohound, 254
Top of the Sixes, 129, 400
Top of the Tower, 44, 400
Tourneau Corner, 261
Tower Records, 283
Trash and Vaudeville, 264
The Travellers Bookstore, 306
I Tre Merli, 94, 381
Triangle Hofbrau, 179
*TriBeCa,* 76, 321
Trinity Church, 65
Tripoli, 169, 365
Triton Gallery, 297
Trixie's, 372, 390, 422
Trump Tower, 130, 244
Tudor Hotel, 46
Tudor Rose, 221
The Tunnel, 420
Tweed Courthouse, 70
"21" Club, 129, 341

23rd Street Bar and Grill, 386
22 Steps, 257
Two Boots, 369
2 Park Avenue, 242

Ukrainian Restaurant, 365
Uncle Peter's, 182
Uncle Sam, 310
Un Deux Trois, 390
Union Church of Pocantico Hills, 193
Union Square, 107
Union Square Café, 107, 303, 384
Union Square Gallery, 274
Unique Clothing Warehouse, 256
United Nations, 16, 123
United Nations Delegates Dining Room, 123
United Nations Plaza Hotel, 40
United States Custom House (former), 58, 236
United States Military Academy, 195
University Press Books, 305
Untitled (clothing), 252
Untitled II (books), 271
*Upper East Side,* 153
*Upper West Side,* 131
Urban Archaeology, 89, 223
The Urban Center, 245
Urban Center Books, 127, 245, 306
Urban Ventures, Inc., 47
Utrecht, 216

Van Cortlandt Manor, 192
Vanessa, 340
Vasata, 159
Vazac's, 382
Veselka Coffee Shop, 365
Via Brazil, 126
Victoria Dinardo, 259
Victoria Falls, 253

Victoria's Secret, 258
Victor's Cuban Café, 142, 352
A La Vieille Russie, 220
The View, 120
Village Corner, 412
Village Gate, 412
Village Vanguard, 408
Villa Mosconi, 327
Villa Pensa, 326
Villard Houses, 231
Visitor Information Center, 120
Vista International, 45
Vivian Beaumont Theater, 137
V & T Pizzeria, 146


The Waldorf-Astoria, 40, 124
Waldorf Towers, 40
Wales (hotel), 46, 162
Wall Street, 65
The Warwick, 39
Washington Arch, 101
Washington Mews, 101
Washington Square, 101
Water Mill, 200
Wave Hill, 191
Ye Waverly Inn, 99
Waves, 314
Weill Recital Hall, 278
Weiss and Mahoney, 264
The Westbury, 35
West End Gate, 394
*West Point,* 195
*West Village,* 97
White Columns, 95
White Eagle Bakery, 173
White Horse Tavern, 99, 303, 384
Whitney Museum of American Art, 64, 122, 128, 156
Willie Wear, 251
Windows on the World, 63, 343, 400
Winter Garden, 244
Witkin Gallery, 274
Wittenborn Art Books, 307
Wolfman-Gold & Good, 309
Wollman Rink, 150

Wooden Indian, 314
Woo Lae Oak of Seoul, 363
Woolworth Building, 69, 241
The World, 422
World Financial Center, 63, 244
World Trade Center, 62
WPA Theatre, 115
Wyndham Hotel, 39

Yale Center for British Art, 197
Yale Repertory Company, 198
Yale University, 197
Yale University Art Gallery, 198
Yamaha, 282
Yellowfingers, 341
Ye Waverly Inn, 99
Yivo Institute for Jewish Research, 163
Ylang Ylang, 262

Yohji Yamamoto, 254, 264
Yonah Schimmel, 320
*Yorkville,* 157, 366
Yuzen, 312
Yves St. Laurent, 249


Zabar's, 143, 317, 323
Zarela, 357
Le Zinc, 372
Zinno, 408
Zoe Coste, 262
Zoo, 251

# FOR THE BEST IN PAPERBACKS, LOOK FOR THE

In every corner of the world, on every subject under the sun, Penguin represents quality and variety—the very best in publishing today.

For complete information about books available from Penguin—including Pelicans, Puffins, Peregrines, and Penguin Classics—and how to order them, write to us at the appropriate address below. Please note that for copyright reasons the selection of books varies from country to country.

**In the United Kingdom:** For a complete list of books available from Penguin in the U.K., please write to *Dept E.P., Penguin Books Ltd, Harmondsworth, Middlesex, UB7 0DA*.

**In the United States:** For a complete list of books available from Penguin in the U.S., please write to *Dept BA, Penguin, Box 999, Bergenfield, New Jersey 07621-0999*.

**In Canada:** For a complete list of books available from Penguin in Canada, please write to *Penguin Books Canada Ltd, 2801 John Street, Markham, Ontario L3R 1B4*.

**In Australia:** For a complete list of books available from Penguin in Australia, please write to the *Marketing Department, Penguin Books Australia Ltd, P.O. Box 257, Ringwood, Victoria 3134*.

**In New Zealand:** For a complete list of books available from Penguin in New Zealand, please write to the *Marketing Department, Penguin Books (NZ) Ltd, Private Bag, Takapuna, Auckland 9*.

**In India:** For a complete list of books available from Penguin, please write to *Penguin Overseas Ltd, 706 Eros Apartments, 56 Nehru Place, New Delhi, 110019*.

**In Holland:** For a complete list of books available from Penguin in Holland, please write to *Penguin Books Nederland B.V., Postbus 195, NL-1380AD Weesp, Netherlands*.

**In Germany:** For a complete list of books available from Penguin in Germany, please write to *Penguin Books Ltd, Friedrichstrasse 10–12, D-6000 Frankfurt Main 1, Federal Republic of Germany*.

**In Spain:** For a complete list of books available from Penguin in Spain, please write to *Longman Penguin España, Calle San Nicolas 15, E–28013 Madrid, Spain*.

**In Japan:** For a complete list of books available from Penguin in Japan, please write to *Longman Penguin Japan Co Ltd, Yamaguchi Building, 2-12-9 Kanda Jimbocho, Chiyoda-Ku, Tokyo 101, Japan*.

# WHEN TRAVELLING, PACK

All the Penguin Travel Guides offer you the selective and up-to-date information you need to plan and enjoy your vacations. Written by travel writers who really know the areas they cover, The Penguin Travel Guides are lively, reliable, and easy to use. So remember, when travelling, pack a Penguin.

☐ *The Penguin Guide to Australia 1989*
 0-14-019905-5 $11.95

☐ *The Penguin Guide to Canada 1989*
 0-14-019906-3 $12.95

☐ *The Penguin Guide to the Caribbean 1989*
 0-14-019900-4 $9.95

☐ *The Penguin Guide to England and Wales 1989*
 0-14-019901-2 $12.95

☐ *The Penguin Guide to France 1989*
 0-14-019902-0 $14.95

☐ *The Penguin Guide to Ireland 1989*
 0-14-019904-7 $10.95

☐ *The Penguin Guide to Italy 1989*
 0-14-019903-9 $14.95

☐ *The Penguin Guide to New York City 1989*
 0-14-019907-1 $12.95
 (available March 1989)

---

You can find all these books at your local bookstore, or use this handy coupon for ordering:

**Penguin Books By Mail**
Dept. BA  Box 999
Bergenfield, NJ 07621-0999

Please send me the above title(s). I am enclosing _____
(please add sales tax if appropriate and **$1.50** to cover postage and handling). Send check or money order—no CODs. Please allow four weeks for shipping. We cannot ship to post office boxes or addresses outside the USA. *Prices subject to change without notice.*

Ms./Mrs./Mr. _____

Address _____

City/State _____ Zip _____

**Sales tax:**   CA: 6.5%   NY: 8.25%   NJ: 6%   PA: 6%   TN: 5.5%